Language
Sense and Non...

Language,
Sense and Nonsense

*A Critical Investigation
into Modern Theories of Language*

G. P. Baker & P. M. S. Hacker

Fellows of St John's College · Oxford

Basil Blackwell

© G. P. Baker and P. M. S. Hacker 1984

First published 1984
First published in paperback 1985
Reprinted 1985, 1986

Basil Blackwell Ltd
108 Cowley Road, Oxford OX4 1JF, UK

Basil Blackwell Inc.
432 Park Avenue South
Suite 1503, New York
NY 10016, USA

British Library Cataloguing in Publication Data

Baker, G. P.
Language, sense and nonsense.
1. Linguistics   2. Languages–Philosophy
   I. Title   II. Hacker, P. M. S.
         401   P121

ISBN 0–631–13519–7
0–631–14657–1 Pbk

Library of Congress Cataloging in Publication Data

Baker, Gordon P.
Language, sense and nonsense.
Includes index.
1. Languages–Philosophy.   I. Hacker, P. M. S.
(Peter Michael Stephan)   II. Title.
P106.B335   1984   401   84–14653

ISBN 0–631–13519–7
0–631–14657–1 (pbk.)

Typeset by Oxford Verbatim Limited
Printed in Great Britain by
T.J. Press Ltd, Padstow

For
Alan and Jonathan

*La direction de notre esprit
est plus importante que son progrès*

The emperor walked in the procession under his crimson canopy. And all the people of the town, who had lined the streets or were looking down from the windows, said that the emperor's clothes were beautiful. 'What a magnificent robe! And the train! How well the emperor's clothes suit him!'

None of them were willing to admit that they hadn't seen a thing; for if anyone did, then he was either stupid or unfit for the job he held. Never before had the emperor's clothes been such a success.

'But he doesn't have anything on!' cried a little child.

Hans Christian Andersen

Preface

Between 1978 and 1981 we busied ourselves investigating the origins of modern logical theory and the inspiration for much contemporary philosophical logic in the works of Gottlob Frege. The results of our historical investigations were startling, for the picture of Frege's thought that emerged from our labours diverged in many fundamental respects from what might be called the standard average conception of his philosophy. The roots of modern logic did not lie in semantic investigations into the structure of natural languages, but in his application of sophisticated mathematical techniques to the traditional subject-matter of logic, viz. the nature of concepts, judgments and valid inference. What Frege had done was to invent a new and powerful method of representation for presenting the forms of judgment and valid inference which are recognized and expressed in natural languages and in mathematics. What his successors did was to project this novel form of representation back on to natural languages, the mind or the world in the guise of theories about the 'depth structure' of any possible language, the 'logical form' of thoughts, or the logical structure of the states of affairs described.

The fruits of our labours we presented in *Frege: Logical Excavations*, in which we analysed the function-theoretic mainspring of his logical theory and subjected its philosophical foundations to thorough criticism. This exercise in philosophical archaeology left much important unfinished business. First, establishing the formal and ultimately mathematical inspiration of his reflections had the effect of divorcing much of the criticism of his main ideas from a critical analysis of the major conceptions informing modern philosophy of language (many of which are wrongly attributed to Frege by most authors). Secondly, making out a case for a predominantly negative verdict on the coherence, intelligibility, and interest of his work for modern philosophical and logical investigations might falsely suggest that we were picking a quarrel with a past genius for not matching present-day standards of sophistication. In fact we do consider that the guidelines of modern philosophical logic or philosophy of language are worth careful analysis in their own right, and we think ourselves to have batteries of arguments available to demonstrate that modern wisdom is in many fundamental respects not at all superior to Frege's (different) conception. We had a double motive to investigate modern theories of language. To that task the present book is dedicated.

Contemporary philosophers, competing in the market-place of ideas, have produced a wide range of different theories about the nature of a language, of mastery of a language, of thought and understanding. Modern theoretical linguists present as diverse a spectacle of wares. Passionate controversies rage between different brands of transformational generative grammarians, truth-conditional theorists, speech-act theorists, and many other doctrinaires. To confront each *seriatim* would be both lengthy and unprofitable. Amidst the roar and hubbub of conflicting voices we have tried to discern not the differences between the competing theories, but the agreed presuppositions, the common Idols of the Market-place and the accompanying Idols of the Theatre[1] set up in the colourful adjoining booths.

That there is wide agreement (not, of course, universal, or uniform) can hardly be doubted. Most theorists view the fact that a speaker of a language can understand sentences he has never heard before as a deep observation calling out for explanation. Many theorists concur in the conception of a language as a calculus of rules for the use of symbols. These hitherto unknown rules determine the grammaticality of combinations of words, as well as the senses they convey. Speaking and under-

---

[1] Cf. F. Bacon: 'There are also idols formed by the intercourse and association of men with each other, which I call Idols of the Market-place, on account of the commerce and consort of men there. For it is by discourse that men associate; . . . And therefore the ill and unfit choice of words wonderfully obstructs the understanding. Nor do the definitions or explanations wherewith in some things learned men are wont to guard and defend themselves, by any means set the matter right. But words plainly force and overrule the understanding, and throw all into confusion, and lead men awry into numberless empty controversies and idle fancies.

'Lastly, there are idols which have immigrated into men's minds from the various dogmas of philosophies . . . These I call Idols of the Theatre; because in my judgment all the received systems are but so many stage plays, representing worlds of their own creation after an unreal and scenic fashion. Nor is it only of the systems now in vogue, or only of the ancient sects and philosophies, that I speak: for many more plays of the same kind may yet be composed and in like artificial manner set forth; seeing that errors the most widely different have nevertheless causes for the most part alike. Neither again do I mean this only of entire systems, but also of many principles and axioms in science, which by tradition, credulity and negligence have come to be received.' (*Novum Organum*, xliii–xliv)

standing a language is commonly conceived as a matter of operating this complex calculus of precise rules, even though speakers have no conscious knowledge of them. Only thus can one explain and predict the limits of grammaticality and the bounds of sense, as well as render intelligible the mysterious processes of understanding. It is precisely because a language is a calculus of rules that it is possible to understand *new* sentences. The task of the theorist of language is to discover the forms of these rules, and thus to lay bare for the first time the hidden structures of languages. The task of the logical theorist is to demonstrate that the validity of the inferences we correctly take to be valid is explained and guaranteed by the underlying rules of a language.

This modern conception of a language is the work, not of one pair of hands, but of many. It lies at the confluence of numerous different streams of thought. The invention of modern mathematical logic at the hands of Frege and his successors gave philosophers a particular vision of the underlying logical structure of language, thought and reasoning. The development of post-Saussurean synchronic linguistics has tended to move along parallel tracks, thus reinforcing that vision. The development of computers, the operation and programming of which rests on logico-mathematical principles, gave further impetus to the idea that the human mind works on the same principles as its recent favoured brain-child. Advances in neurophysiology have taken inspiration from the much over-worked analogy between the functioning of the brain and the operations of a computer. And these in turn served to reinforce a variety of trends in modern philosophy of mind as well as empirical psychology towards mind-brain identity theories or computational functionalism. If some version of the predicate calculus is not, as Russell and the young Wittgenstein thought it was, a mirror of the logical structure of reality, at least it seems that it (or at any rate the depth-grammar of a natural language) must be a mirror of the logical structure of the mind and of the functional structure of the cognitive capacities of the brain.

If the favoured pictures of language are, as we argue in this book, misconceived, the misconceptions are deep and numerous. They are held firm not by one fallacy but by many mutually reinforcing fallacies. And given the multiplicity of their sources, they are not refutable by frontal assault. But where the curtain walls and bastions of a fortress are impregnable, the foundations may yield to undermining. We have chosen four related points from which to tunnel, four fundamental themes commanding widespread consensus. These are, first, the doctrine of the separation of the sense of a sentence from its force; secondly, the conception of the truth-conditions of a sentence as the key to a comprehensive theory of meaning; thirdly, the notion of a hidden, 'tacitly known', system of linguistic rules underlying our thought and speech; and finally, the alleged mystery of our capacity to understand sentences we have never heard before. If our strictures on these themes are right, then most of what goes by the name of 'theories of meaning' or 'scientific study of language' needs not remedial readjustment, but wholesale abandonment.

The issues we examine are important, not only for philosophy and the philosophical understanding of the nature of thought and language, but also for empirical linguistics and psychology. The misconceptions we identify ramify widely, contributing greatly to the barren mythology of late twentieth century culture. Hence this book is written with more polemical passion than is common in the typical reserved and detached forms of academic philosophy. For this we make no apology.

It would be foolish to hope, let alone to expect, that a great structure, as attuned to the spirit of the age as modern theories of meaning in philosophy and theoretical linguistics, with their richness, diversity and complexity, will crumble as a consequence of our efforts. The most that we hope for is not the immediate collapse of the ramparts, but rather that some of those who man them, in particular prospective recruits who have not yet taken the Queen's shilling, will abandon them in the realization that for all the apparent power of the structure, the foundations rest on sand. But perhaps even this is too optimistic, in which case we can only endorse the observation that 'there is nothing so plain boring as the constant repetition of assertions that are not true, and sometimes not even faintly sensible; if we can reduce this a bit, it will be all to the good'.[2]

We are happy to record our gratitude to Dr John Dupré, Bede Rundle, Stuart Shanker and Dr Talbot Taylor, who read and commented on several draft chapters of this book. We benefited from numerous conversations with them. Our greatest debt is to Professor Roy Harris, who guided us through many of the thickets of modern linguistic theory, patiently answered our endless questions, and most helpfully criticized drafts of many chapters. His kindness, wit and encouragement sustained us in hours of gloom. Our college, St John's, generously reduced our teaching load while we wrote this book and gave us liberally of its many facilities.

G. P. B. & P. M. S. H.
1983

Note to Second Impression

On pp. 2, 43–4, 305–6 we have corrected a misleading characterization of the *Tractatus* as conventionalist. Analysis of its relation to the Vienna Circle's conventionalism is given in our forthcoming *Frege, Wittgenstein and the Vienna Circle*.

[2] J. L. Austin, *Sense and Sensibilia* (Clarendon Press, Oxford, 1962), p. 5.

Contents

Prolegomenon:
the New Philosopher's Stone

Since the dawn of their subject twenty-five centuries ago, philosophers have sought to clarify fundamental notions such as appearance and reality, substance and property, truth and falsehood, justice and virtue, notions which play a crucial role in our understanding of the world in which we live, of ourselves as fleeting inhabitants of it, and of the goals and values which we pursue and which give meaning to our lives. Throughout its long history, they have constantly deployed arguments of a broadly linguistic nature in pursuit of their aims. Socrates, in his endeavour to understand the nature of the virtues, sought for clear *definitions* which would capture the essence of courage or friendship, of justice or wisdom. And proposed definitions are examined, sometimes rejected, sometimes modified, in the light of what we would, in various circumstances, find it appropriate to say. Aristotle's subtle discussions of the voluntary and involuntary, of choice and deliberation, of responsibility and culpability, abound in arguments showing that one kind of thing cannot in general be identified with another kind of thing because what can legitimately be said of one cannot be said of the other, or because the name of the one cannot be exchanged for the name of the other in an utterance without a change in what is said. Such arguments can fairly be characterized as being, in a loose sense, linguistic.

Nor is this all. From the beginnings of philosophy, writers have sought to clarify the nature of thinking and reasoning, to codify the canons of valid argument and to demonstrate their ultimate grounds in the nature of the thinking mind or in the nature of the realities thought about. Here too philosophers have always viewed language as *a* guide to the nature of the thoughts and arguments expressed. It was, to be sure, commonly viewed as a wayward guide, pointing to a reality which underlies it, and not always accurately reflecting what it thus represents. But by cautiously and critically following its lead, the logician can learn much about concepts and judgments, valid arguments and the nature of inference.

To be thus concerned with language, to deploy such linguistic arguments and to see the grammar of language and the structure of sentences as valuable clues to the nature of thought is one thing. But to declare that language actually provides part of, perhaps indeed the main part of, the subject-matter of philosophy, is another thing altogether. For past generations the investigation of a fairly narrow range of features of language, of different kinds of words and their distinctive roles, of the grammatically licit forms of combinations of words into different kinds of sentences, was an important preliminary undertaking in preparation for larger philosophical enterprises. Linguistic and grammatical data provided tools in the philosophical workshop, tools which could be put to use, by a skilled craftsman, in pursuit of solutions to fundamental philosophical questions. But it was only relatively recently that some philosophers began to conceive of the philosophical study of language, not merely as a tool, but as a task, indeed as the primary task of philosophy.

This shift in philosophers' conception of their subject-matter was produced to a large extent through the examination of the apparent philosophical implications of the discovery, in the nineteenth and early twentieth centuries, of rich and sophisticated logical calculi. These formal inventions were the fruits of the labours of philosopher–mathematicians such as Boole, Frege, and Russell and Whitehead. The actual transformation in the conception of philosophy can be dated, with fair accuracy, to Wittgenstein's *Tractatus Logico-Philosophicus* (1921). In it he argued that the hidden structure of any possible language is akin to that of a (correct) formal, function-theoretic, logical calculus. He paved the way for a strikingly original and satisfying conventionalist explanation of the nature of logical truth, dissolving logical necessity into conventions for the employment of symbols. And he argued that the sole task of philosophy is the clarification, by logical analysis, of sentences of natural language, and the eradication of pseudo-propositions (in particular, metaphysical ones) which violate the logical syntax of language. 'All philosophy', he declared, 'is a critique of language'.[1]

These ideas caught on, particularly among the logical positivists in the 1920s and 1930s. Schlick, the leader of the Vienna Circle, declared:

---

[1] L. Wittgenstein, *Tractatus Logico-Philosophicus*, tr. D. F. Pears and B. F. McGuinness (Routledge & Kegan Paul, London, 1961), 4.0031.

I am convinced that we now find ourselves at an altogether decisive turning point in philosophy ...

Leibniz dimly saw the beginning. Bertrand Russell and Gottlob Frege have opened up important stretches in the last decades, but Ludwig Wittgenstein (in his *Tractatus Logico-Philosophicus*, . . .) is the first to have pushed forward to the decisive turning point.[2]

This sentiment was shared by members of the Circle,[3] and their conception of philosophy as the analysis of the language of science (in a broad sense) and the extirpation of metaphysics rested on what they conceived to be the central lessons of the *Tractatus*. 'All philosophical problems', Carnap boldly announced, 'are questions of the syntax of the language of science.'[4] Schlick proclaimed that 'Investigations concerning the human "capacity for knowledge" . . . are replaced by considerations regarding the nature of expression, of representation, i.e. concerning every possible "language" in the most general sense of the term.'[5] Ayer declared that the function of philosophy 'is to clarify the propositions of science, by exhibiting their logical relationships, and by defining the symbols which occur in them'[6] ... 'A complete philosophical elucidation of any language would consist, first, in enumerating the types of sentence that were significant in that language, and then displaying the relations of equivalence that held between sentences of various types.'[7]

This conception went into eclipse in the 1950s and 1960s when, paradoxically, a movement popularly (and misleadingly) known as 'linguistic philosophy' was in its heyday. That 'movement' spurned common goals or ideology in the grand manner of the Vienna Circle. If it can be generally characterized at all, it is primarily by its employment of linguistic *methods*, rather than by its avowal that the investigation of natural language was the *subject-matter* of philosophy, or that a subject called 'philosophy of language' was the foundation of the whole of philosophy. Its leading representative, J. L. Austin, explicitly declared that 'ordinary language is to be our guide', that proceeding 'from "ordinary language",

[2] M. Schlick, 'The Turning Point in Philosophy' in *Logical Positivism*, ed. A. J. Ayer (Free Press, Illinois, 1959), p. 54.

[3] Cf. their manifesto 'The Scientific Conception of the World: The Vienna Circle'.

[4] R. Carnap, 'On the Character of Philosophical Problems' (1934), in *The Linguistic Turn*, ed. R. Rorty (University of Chicago Press, Chicago, 1967), p. 61.

[5] M. Schlick, 'The Turning Point in Philosophy', p. 55.

[6] A. J. Ayer, *Language, Truth, and Logic*, 2nd edn (Pelican, Harmondsworth, 1971), p. 42.

[7] Ibid., p. 83.

that is by examining *what we should say when* . . . [is] . . . *one* philosophical method'.[8] Practitioners of this method were not given to large-scale theory-construction, nor to grandiloquent pronouncements about systematic theories of meaning. They did not conceive of philosophy as continuous with the empirical sciences, nor did they conceive of its task as the analysis, reconstruction or regimentation of the language of science. They were united only by a common belief that many philosophical problems could be resolved by linguistic methods, that many philosophical puzzlements arose out of misunderstandings concerning our use of words, and by a piecemeal rather than holistic approach to philosophical issues. Ryle's *Concept of Mind* was not conceived as an investigation into the logical syntax of the language of psychological science (as Carnap might have conceived of such a project) but as a study of 'the logical geography' of ordinary mental concepts. Austin described his essay 'A Plea for Excuses' as a branch of the philosophical study of conduct,[9] and Hart declared that his *Concept of Law* aimed 'to further our understanding of law, coercion and morality'. Though it employed analytical linguistic methods, it was, he insisted, also an essay in 'descriptive sociology'.[10] He quoted with approval Austin's remark that we may use 'a sharpened awareness of words to sharpen our perception of, though not as the final arbiter of, the phenomena'.[11]

Towards the end of the 1960s, the waves of 'ordinary language philosophy' gradually subsided. And although the central contentions of the *Tractatus* were explicitly disowned by the older Wittgenstein, the seeds sown by his younger self and fostered by the logical positivists, sprouted afresh. In the late 1960s and throughout the 1970s a second generation of philosophers flooded the market-place with ideas explicitly or tacitly harvested from the fields of the *Tractatus* and the logical positivists.[12] The first and foremost task of philosophy, it was proclaimed, is to construct a *theory of meaning for a natural language*, to elicit the underlying principles of construction of any language in virtue of which we can construct and understand the infinite array of meaningful sentences with which we can express our thoughts. M. A. E. Dummett, in Oxford, maintained that

[8] J. L. Austin, 'A Plea for Excuses', in *Philosophical Papers*, 1st edn, ed. J. O. Urmson and G. J. Warnock (Clarendon Press, Oxford, 1961), p. 129.
[9] Ibid., p. 128.
[10] H. L. A. Hart, *The Concept of Law* (Clarendon Press, Oxford, 1961), p. vii.
[11] Austin, *Philosophical Papers*, p. 130.
[12] Although by a curious misreading of history, they tended to conceive of Frege as their honorary ancestor (see pp. 32–9).

'philosophy has, as its first if not its only task, the analysis of meanings',[13] that 'the philosophy of language is the foundation of all other philosophy',[14] and that 'the most urgent task that philosophers are now called upon to carry out is to devise . . . a "systematic theory of meaning" '.[15] Indeed, 'If we had an agreed theory of meaning, then that theory could be appealed to in order to find a resolution of [the] problems [of philosophy in other localized areas, e.g. metaphysics or philosophy of mathematics].'[16] A philosophical theory of meaning is here advertised as the true Philosopher's Stone.

A similar vision captured the imagination of some American philosophers. D. Davidson declared:

I dream of a theory that makes the transition from the ordinary idiom to canonical notation purely mechanical, and a canonical notation rich enough to capture, in its dull and explicit way, every difference and connection legitimately considered the business of a theory of meaning. The point of a canonical notation so conceived is not to improve on something left vague and defective in natural language, but to help elicit in a perspicuous and general form the understanding of logical grammar we all have that constitutes (part of) our grasp of our native tongue.[17]

And he too thought that remarkable consequences would flow from the realization of this dream. For example, a correct semantic analysis of action- and event-sentences will, he suggested, constitute a *proof* that events actually exist.[18] Ontological truths can thus be proved from premises provided by a theory of meaning.

The renaissance of interest in global questions about the nature of language and the renewal of effort to construct comprehensive theories of meaning has been stimulated by a fascination with the fact that language-users are able to understand a potentially infinite array of sentences never heard before (a thought explicit in the *Tractatus*). Since what a language-user learns is surely finite, these resources must somehow suffice for the

[13] M. A. E. Dummett, *Frege: Philosophy of Language* (Duckworth, London, 1973), p. 669.
[14] M. A. E. Dummett, 'Can Analytical Philosophy be Systematic and Ought it to be?', in *Truth and Other Enigmas* (Duckworth, London, 1978), p. 442.
[15] Ibid., p. 454.
[16] Dummett, *Frege: Philosophy of Language*, p. 672, cf. p. 676.
[17] D. Davidson, 'The Logical Form of Action Sentences', in *The Logic of Decision and Action*, ed. N. Rescher (University of Pittsburgh Press, Pittsburgh, 1967), p. 115.
[18] A bizarre view, given that events neither exist nor fail to exist, but rather occur, happen or take place. It is difficult to see why one would want a *proof* that things happen.

generation of, and possibility of understanding, any of the infinite sentences of this language. This alone seems to prove that a speaker has an implicit grasp of a variety of constructional principles of language, knowledge of which will explain this capacity. And an explicit statement of these principles, which displays how to derive the meanings of sentences from the meanings of constituent words and their principles of composition into sentences, is precisely what a complete theory of meaning for a language is. Philosophers see in this reasoning a 'transcendental deduction' of the existence of a theory of meaning.

Despite many differences in the methods and products of theory construction, it is possible to give a rough sketch of typical theories of meaning (of the simple type). More elaborate accounts will be given later. The theorist distinguishes sharply between three enterprises: syntax (the science of the principles for constructing grammatical sentences), semantics (the study of the truth-conditions of sentences) and pragmatics (the investigation of all those features of sentences related to their use by speakers in particular contexts). Employing the familiar distinction between type- and token-sentences, he focuses upon the type-sentence as the primary bearer of meanings, relying on pragmatics to bridge the gap between the meaning of the type-sentence and the description of what a speaker has done in uttering one of its tokens on a given occasion. The type-sentence is conceived as having priority over words in the order of semantic analysis, its meaning being thought of as given by its truth-conditions, viz. a specification of the conditions under which instances of it can be used to propound a truth. Its constituent words are conceived as having a meaning which consists in their contribution to determining the truth-conditions of sentences in which they may occur. So the meaning of a (type-) sentence (its truth-conditions) is viewed as a function of the meanings of its constituent expressions and of its *structure*, the manner in which the words are concatenated to form a sentence. Compound sentences are then conceived as built up (systematically) by operations on simple sentences. The picture underlying this theory-construction is a two-tiered explanation of language-use. An adequate syntax for a language should, when supplemented by a lexicon specifying the meanings of its words (and idiomatic phrases), assign a definite meaning to every well-formed sentence. This semantic theory, when supplemented by a specification of the relevant context of utterance of a sentence-token, should determine exactly what a speaker has done in uttering this token sentence (*whether* he has made an assertion, issued an order, etc., and also *what* he has asserted, ordered, etc.). Since a theory of meaning aims at perfect generality, and since the notion of a truth-condition is obviously tailored for declarative sentences typically used to make assertions, it is commonly thought that a *sine qua non* of such a theory is to distinguish between *force* (e.g. assertoric, interrogative, imperative force) and meaning (or sense). Every significant sentence is held to be analysable into a force-indicating device, e.g. 'It is the case . . .' 'Is it the case . . .?' 'Make it the case . . .', and a truth-value bearing component, e.g. 'that so-and-so'. Sentences with different forces may yet have a common component, a description of a state of affairs, whose sense is given by its truth-conditions. This state of affairs may be asserted to obtain or ordered to be brought about, or one may query whether it obtains. In general, the underlying logical structures of the descriptive component of type-sentences are held to be given, *mirabile dictu*, by (some version) of the function-theoretic forms of the predicate calculus invented early in this century.

This new philosophical vision has not occurred in a cultural vacuum. A common climate of thought has fostered parallel developments in linguistics. The resultant theories in the two subjects have reinforced each other. Modern 'structuralist' linguistics originated with the work of Saussure at the turn of the century. In sharp reaction to nineteenth century historical linguistics, he distinguished between the historical or *diachronic* study of language and *synchronic* study. The latter, conceived as an instantaneous cross-cut of the former,[19] is the domain of the science of language. Language (*la langue*) he viewed as an abstract structure of relations which govern the overt manifestations of speech (*la parole*) in the activities of language-users. It is the former which concerns the linguistic theorist. Although *la langue* was conceived, in Durkheimian fashion, as a supra-individual social 'construct', it also had to be thought of, in some sense, as 'existing virtually inside everyone's head'. It was held to consist of a finite array of uniquely identifiable signs, governed by determinate rules of combination, and each sign (*signifiant*) was correlated by a (theoretical) 'lexicon' with a meaning (*signifié*). Saussure thought of the relata as acoustic images and concepts. His successors modified this in various ways, but retained the 'biplanar'[20] model of correlation, viz. of form and 'interpretation'. This conception of language involved a bold abstraction at more than one level. A language was not conceived as primarily a social practice, the existence of which is eminently visible (if not easily survey-able) in the temporal stream of the activities of language-users, employing

[19] For extensive criticisms of this very idea, see R. Harris, *The Language Myth* (Duckworth, London, 1981) and *The Language Makers* (Duckworth, London, 1980).
[20] Cf. Harris, *The Language Myth*, p. 11.

signs for a huge variety of human purposes in the context of ramifying auxiliary behaviour against the background of our familiar complex material and social realities. These mundane features of historical development, temporality, social practice, individual acts of speech, conventional and natural purposes, behaviour, context, etc. were, of course, recognized. But they were viewed as consequent upon the true nature of a language as an abstract, self-contained sign-system with a psychological reality of its own. The resultant conception of the science of language removed it from the sphere of socio-historic studies, allocating it instead to a branch of cognitive psychology. But it was successfully insulated from empirical psychology inasmuch as its subject-matter was held to be a wholly self-contained abstract structure amenable to study only by linguistic techniques. For its only observable manifestation amenable to experimental psychological methods is overt speech (*la parole*) which itself must be viewed as a consequence of the internalized structures of *la langue*. The new linguistics planted its flag on virgin territory, confident in the strength of its defences against encroachment from adjacent academic disciplines.

After a brief behaviourist interlude, led by Bloomfield in America in the 1930s and 1940s, Saussurean structuralism (like the programme of the *Tractatus*) received a new lease of life (on a much larger scale) in the 1960s and later. It was in effect revitalized, modified and extended by the development of transformational grammars at the hands of Chomsky and his followers. Like Saussure, they conceived of linguistics as essentially synchronic. Parallel to Saussure's distinction between *la langue* and *la parole*, they differentiated between a speaker's *competence* (his tacit knowledge of the system of language which the linguist studies) and his *performance* (the overt (and often faulty!) manifestations of his competence). The grammatical rules they sought to elicit, as well as the abstract lexicon assigning 'interpretations' to signs, were conceived as 'internalized' in the mind or encoded in the brain, although (conveniently) inaccessible to introspection or to current neurological investigation. Their primary innovations lay in the development of the distinction between surface and deep structures of sentences, in the construction of syntax on the basis of transformations, and in the priority assigned to the sentence over sub-sentential expressions for purposes of grammatical theory. All of these features of modern linguistics have close parallels in the reflections of modern philosophers.

The appearance of convergence between the theories of linguists and philosophers is striking. At first sight nothing seems more improbable than that ideas inspired by the *Tractatus* should have extensive parallels among those inspired by Saussure. Surely the most obvious explanation is that there is an important niche in the ecology of the intellect which earlier evolution of ideas has left empty and which is now in the process of being occupied by independently evolved organisms. This seductive picture can be somewhat weakened by noting certain superficialities in the convergence. Linguists, lacking any direct check on the deep structures of sentences, are at liberty to borrow any advanced mathematical notions for characterizing deep structures, and they are strongly inclined to draw on the very same general ideas (sets, functions, quantifiers, variables) that are built into modern formal logic. Similarly, in considering meaning as a theoretical notion, they feel free to identify sentence-meanings with truth-conditions and to treat this as the foundation of the science of semantics. Contrariwise, philosophers have drawn a blank cheque on the notion of logical form in stressing that grammatical form need not coincide with logical form, and therefore they are willing to cash this cheque in terms of the concept of depth-structure provided this manoeuvre promises to bestow some scientific cachet on their reflections. These points of convergence nicely manifest intellectual opportunism. It is no surprise at all that philosophers and even some linguists are inclined to view the deep structure of language to be an elaboration and enrichment of the logical forms embodied in the predicate calculus. There is little to wonder at in the declaration 'It is rather generally supposed that we shall arrive at a satisfactory syntactic analysis of natural language only by exhibiting its sentences as having an underlying (or deep) structure analogous to that of sentences of Frege's formalized language [viz. the predicate calculus].'[21]

What is genuinely surprising is that linguists and philosophers are now so widely in agreement about the *aims* of their theory-construction and also about the *methods* appropriate for achieving these aims.

Two prominent linguists declared that:

Empirical linguistics takes the most general problem of the study of language to be that of accounting for the fluent speaker's ability to produce freely and understand readily all utterances of his language, including wholly novel ones. To explicate this ability, linguists construct a system of description which seeks to capture the regularities of the language used by speakers to produce and interpret sentences.[22]

This precisely mirrors the philosopher's inspiration:

[21] Dummett, 'Frege's Distinction between Sense and Reference', in *Truth and Other Enigmas*, p. 118.
[22] J. Fodor and J. J. Katz, 'What's wrong with the Philosophy of Language?', in *Philosophy and Linguistics*, ed. C. Lyas (Macmillan, London, 1971), p. 281.

a satisfactory theory of meaning must give an account of how the meanings of sentences depend upon the meanings of words. Unless such an account can be supplied for a particular language, ... there would be no explaining the fact that we can learn the language: no explaining the fact that, on mastering a finite vocabulary and a finitely stated set of rules, we are prepared to produce and to understand any of a potential infinitude of sentences.[23]

The philosopher declares that a theory of meaning is a 'theoretical representation of a practical ability',[24] while the linguists announce 'The goal of a theory of a particular language must be the explication of the abilities and skills involved in the linguistic performance of a fluent native speaker.'[25] The philosopher typically *explains* linguistic performance in terms of the 'psychological reality' of the theory of meaning he constructs:

A theory of meaning will ... represent the practical ability possessed by a speaker as consisting *in his grasp* of a set of propositions; since the speaker *derives his understanding* of a sentence from the meanings of its component words, these propositions will most naturally form a deductively connected system [viz. an axiomatic theory of meaning]. The knowledge of these propositions that is attributed to a speaker ... [is] ... implicit knowledge.[26]

In parallel fashion, the transformational-generative grammarian argues that 'Grammar is a system of rules and principles that determine the formal and semantic properties of sentences. The grammar *is put to use, interacting with other mechanisms of the mind*, in speaking and understanding language.'[27] This convergence of the two enterprises is explicitly acknowledged:

Philosophers of a logical bent have tended to start where the theory was [viz. the formal semantics of logical calculi] and work out towards the complications of natural language. Contemporary linguists, with an aim that cannot easily be seen to be different, start with the ordinary and work towards a general theory. If either party is successful, there must be a meeting.[28]

If the true Philosopher's Stone is at last almost within our reach, if a theory of meaning, once properly constructed, holds within it the key to

[23] D. Davidson, 'Truth and Meaning', *Synthese* 17 (1967), p. 304.
[24] M. A. E. Dummett, 'What is a Theory of Meaning? (II)' in *Truth and Meaning*, ed. G. Evans and J. McDowell (Clarendon Press, Oxford, 1976), p. 69.
[25] Fodor and Katz, 'What's wrong with the Philosophy of Language?', p. 277.
[26] Dummett, 'What is a Theory of Meaning? (II)', p. 70 (our italics).
[27] N. Chomsky, *Reflections on Language* (Fontana, London, 1976), p. 28, our italics.
[28] D. Davidson, 'Truth and Meaning', p. 315.

the great problems of philosophy, if grammar holds the key to the structure of the human mind, then indeed this wonderful insight and advance must be hailed with fanfares. And philosophers, together with theoretical linguists, must bend their wills to a united effort to grasp this treasure. Then they may go on to explain the deep mysteries of our ability to understand new sentences, to discover what really exists (e.g. whether events are essential for our 'ontology'), to reveal what is innately known to the human mind, to uncover the true logical form of our thoughts and the essential nature of our understanding. But the Last Trumpet has been blown with tiresome regularity in the history of philosophy, and false prophets have been legion. If the promises held out by the possibility of constructing a theory of meaning are false promises, and if the very idea of such a theory of meaning as is currently envisaged is incoherent, then this too must be proclaimed, the incoherences made clear and the hopes dashed. For then, far from being at last upon the true path of a science, theorists are merely pursuing yet another monstrous chimera. Lacking a true Philosopher's Stone, they will be in dire need of a Philosopher's Egg, a panacea against diseases of the intellect.

In this book we shall subject to critical scrutiny the fundamental ideas informing current theories of language. Although the focus is on conceptual issues, and the primary target modern 'theories of meaning', we shall examine parallel manifestations of underlying conceptions (and misconceptions) in modern linguistics. In spite of passionate disagreements between the various theorists, there are important and seldom considered common presuppositions. Although we shall not disregard the arguments dividing theorists of meaning, we shall concentrate on what unites them. Our approach to this theatre of war will be indirect.

One aspect of this strategy is that we shall focus upon just those topics which are introduced in most theories of meaning with the barest of explanation, taken to be altogether perspicuous and treated with nonchalance. We shall probe the seemingly clear notion of the truth-conditions of a sentence, which is commonly taken to be the key to any cogent semantic theory. We shall place pressure upon the apparen' obvious distinction, within every sentence, between its descriptive cor (the state of affairs it describes, its *sense*) and its force (e.g. wheth asserts or orders something). We shall test the soundness of the sup tion that a language is a *system*, a calculus consisting of a networ. hidden rules tacitly employed whenever we speak or understand wha, spoken. And we shall examine whether the question of how it is possible t understand sentences never heard before really is as deep as it is commonly taken to be. In general we shall resist by argument the theorists' habit of frog-marching the neophyte straight to a ceremony of initiation into the full mysteries of the modern science of language. We shall unmask their conceptual conjuring tricks and break the mesmerizing force of their incantations by critical questioning. Our method will be the clarification of concepts, not the amassing of new evidence about phenomena.

A second, related, aspect of our strategy is to by-pass controversies about the truth or falsity of various doctrines in theories of meaning and to focus on the logically prior questions of the intelligibility and purpose of salient theses. A presupposition of the identification of the meaning of a sentence with its truth-conditions is that truth is coherently predicated of sentences and that a certain expression is properly characterized as stating a *condition* for the truth of a given sentence. If the purpose of a semantic theory is to show how words engage with the world, then it is assumed that there is a coherent notion of a connection between language and reality on the lines envisaged by the theory. Such questions about the coherence of concepts are matched by questions about the intelligibility of questions. If a sense/force distinction is offered to explain how speakers recognize how an utterance is used, then it is presupposed that the question 'How does a speaker recognize how this utterance is used?' invariably makes sense. Or if an explanation is given to resolve the mystery of understanding new sentences, it is presupposed that the questions 'How does a person under- stand a sentence?' or 'How is it possible to understand a sentence?' are intelligible questions calling for answers. It is a mistake in addressing theories of meaning to rush headlong into attempts at testing their truth or falsity. There is a fundamental disanalogy between the response appro- priate to a new theory in physics and that appropriate to the great 'dis- coveries' in theories of meaning. In the first case the primary issue is typically the *truth* of an hypothesis, whereas in the second it is usually the *intelligibility* of a thesis. The abundance of available theories of meaning is no guarantee that any comprehensible answer is being given to any intel- igible question. It has frequently happened in the history of human tellectual endeavour that much ingenuity and effort has been expended o avail because of a defective discrimination of sense from nonsense. goal is to trace the bounds of sense in a region where many are now e to be led astray by grotesque conceptual confusions.

third aspect of our strategy is to cultivate and refine an awareness of most fundamental elements of the modern conception of language and eaning through an historical sketch of its origins and evolution. The differentiation of what is taken for granted from what is questionable, or of what makes good sense from what strikes us now as nonsensical, depends to a great extent on how we have been educated and on the unquestioned framework of ideas which we have been trained to accept. The claim that some group of thinkers has laboured under certain radical misconceptions is greatly strengthened if we can demonstrate that it is intelligible that they should have thought what they did, even if what they thought now seems patently false or even incomprehensible. To this extent conceptual clarification has an essentially historical aspect and thus differs from most scientific research. Even if the history of science is generally merely of interest to antiquarians, the history of philosophy and knowledge of the evolution of concepts is vital to making sense of what now confronts us in the guise of theories of meaning, just as the full intelligibility of a painting depends on the historical investigation of a tradition to which it belongs.[29] By giving rough sketches, sometimes only a bird's-eye view, of the historical origins of certain contemporary conceptions, we shall show the relevance of the history of philosophy and linguistics to the appreciation of what is now of concern in theories of meaning, and we shall urge the importance of history for philosophical understanding, whether in formal logic or in the philosophy of language. Our aim is to illuminate the present by opening up appropriate vistas into the past.

The spirit informing this book is obviously sceptical and critical. In pursuing the clarification of concepts, we also demonstrate a readiness to demolish large parts of what pass for significant modern intellectual achievements. But our ultimate purpose is not to persuade linguists or philosophers that their theories are false, thereby encouraging them to redouble their efforts and to construct ever more sophisticated and subtle theories. It is rather to suggest that their endeavours are futile because pointless and misconceived. It will, no doubt, appear to them that we are trying to suppress the light, to deflect them from the true path of a science. In fact we are suggesting that what appears to be sunrise is merely a false dawn, that the path they are following with such enthusiasm leads to the wastelands of the intellect where there is only 'dry sterile thunder without rain'.

---

[29] For a more detailed investigation of this point, see G. P. Baker and P. M. S. Hacker *Frege: Logical Excavations* (Blackwell, Oxford, 1984), pp. 4ff.

CHAPTER 1

Historical Bearings

1 The post-Cartesian tradition

Modern philosophy, typically dated from the writings of Bacon in England or Descartes on the continent, has its roots in the scientific revolution of the sixteenth and seventeenth centuries. It is, no doubt, difficult for us to recapture the sense of excitement, illumination and depth which was associated with the advances in the physical sciences pioneered by Kepler and Galileo and culminating in Newton. Nature was, for the first time, revealed to be intelligible to human reason, subject to laws accessible to human thought. The particular form which such laws assumed was mathematical. Astronomy ceased to be merely the inexplicable 'geometry of the heavens' and became a branch of mathematical physics. Physics, no longer earthbound and confined to the investigation of terrestrial motion in the sublunary sphere, expanded into the study of the fundamental laws governing the behaviour of matter throughout the physical universe.

These conquests, however, were achieved only at the cost of a new range of pressing questions. The most dramatic advances in physics involved explanations which employed only geometric or mechanical properties of matter (extension, shape, motion, solidity, etc.). And side by side with the new mechanics there evolved a speculative but fruitful corpuscularian theory of matter, which attributed to matter, in its fine as in its gross structure, only the self-same geometric properties relevant to available hysical explanations of observable phenomena. This elementary rpuscularian theory was utilized to sketch a rudimentary scientific ory of perception in terms of the impact of invisible corpuscles, emitted bjects, upon our sensory organs, and the consequent agitation of the imal spirits' in the nervous system. Not surprisingly these forms of xplanation bred an array of metaphysical and ontological doctrines. The rue nature of reality, it seemed, was mechanical and mathematical. Consequently a yawning gulf opened between appearance and reality, between the world as it appears to us to be and the world as it is independently of our observations of it. For the world as it appears to us is multicoloured, noisy, odorous, hot or cold, replete with variegated textures and tastes. But the objective world as conceived by the physicists is only a 'silent buzzing' of invisible particles in motion – all the rest is merely the product of the impact of colourless, tasteless, soundless corpuscles upon our sensibility.

If the physicists' story were true (and who could gainsay their remarkable achievements?) then a host of new and pressing conceptual questions had to be faced. For if the world is not really at all as it appears to us to be, then can we actually come to know it as it really is? And if we can, how is this possible? Can we know anything at all about the objective world with certainty? And if we can, what are the marks whereby we may distinguish such genuine knowledge from mere appearance? Philosophers were forced to reconstruct our conception of the objective world and of our cognitive faculties in such a way as would make room for what seemed to be the indisputable advances of science.

If the dramatic gulf which the new scientific world-vision had opened up between appearance and reality was to be bridged at all, it seemed that there was little option but to begin from appearances and to construct a picture or conception of reality which was in broad agreement with the deliverances of physics. This required various principles, *a priori* or empirical, to legitimate the appropriate inferences from how things appear to us to be to how things, surprisingly and hitherto unexpectedly, really are. Hence seventeenth century philosophy displayed a profoundly egocentric, subjective character. For appearances constitute the subjectively 'given', the impact of the world as it is in itself, upon the sensory apparatus of the human perceiver. The result of such impact is the rich array of sensory data, variously called 'impressions' or 'ideas', which furnish the mind of any subject of experience. The analysis of such sensory data, the discovery of the principles of the mind which organize it into our ordinary, but apparently misleading and deceptive, conception of reality must provide the materials whereby the philosopher can simultaneously justify the ways of the mathematicizing God of physics to man, and also plot the nature, extent and limits of possible human knowledge.

The picture with which seventeenth and eighteenth century philosophers worked represented the human mind, equipped with various organizing dispositions or principles, as receiving, in experience, a wide range of *ideas*. These included ideas of colour, taste, smell, sound and texture, which, according to the mainstream of thought, misrepresented the nature of the objective reality which gave rise to them (viz. the hypothesized corpuscularian structure of matter and the corpuscularian mechanisms of perception), and also ideas of shape, motion, extension, solidity (?), which more accurately represented the nature of the objective world. Further ideas arose, it was argued, from apprehension of the workings of the mind itself, e.g. ideas of the 'passions of the soul'. This huge array of distinct ideas furnished the mind with its main (according to the empiricists, its only) materials for human thought. Philosophical reflection on the possible operations of the mind would reveal both the nature of reality, in so far as it is cognizable, the limits of possible knowledge, and the nature and limits of thought and imagination.

This picture moulded the questions which philosophers felt called upon to answer as well as the principal strategies to be used in developing such answers. The ideas with which the mind is furnished could be validated, it seemed, to the extent that they could be shown to be derived, immediately or proximately, from experience, and, if so derivable, to the extent that they could be shown accurately to represent things as they really are. Since not all ideas are so derivable, those which fail the test must be fictitious, and attributable to the workings of the imagination, or innate and so part of the native equipment of the mind, or *a priori* and structural, and hence attributable to the inherent organizing powers of the mind. The seventeenth and eighteenth century debates between rationalists and empiricists polarized around these various, seemingly exhaustive, possibilities. And the salient issues debated, e.g. the possibility of non-trivial *a priori* knowledge, the possibility and extent of *certain* knowledge, the analysis and validation of fundamental ideas or concepts such as self, substance, space and time, the relation of mind to body, were introduced and 'resolved' within this framework of thought.

Ideas (mental representations, sometimes, but not by any means always, pictorially conceived) constituted the interface between the knowing subject and objective reality.[1] By analysing ideas into their simple unanalysable components, by scrutinizing their combinations into complexes, by examining their derivation from experience and the principles whereby

---

[1] Cf. I. Hacking, *Why Does Language Matter to Philosophy?* (Cambridge University Press, Cambridge, 1975). Of course, in the hands of Berkeley the apparently mind-independent objective reality was reduced to an array of mind-dependent ideas appropriately shared out between God and other spirits. Hume went further, for in his metaphysical system both the knowing subject and the objective reality known disintegrate into no more than fictions generated by the workings of our faculty of imagination.

they may be variously organized, philosophers tried to resolve all the epistemological and metaphysical problems which confronted them.

2   The conception of language within the post-Cartesian tradition

The problem-setting context of philosophy during the seventeenth and eighteenth centuries was the picture of reality that informed the developments in the physical sciences. The materials upon which philosophers conceived themselves as required to work were the various ideas in the mind and the principles of organization whereby the mind orders them to achieve whatever knowledge it may have. Within this framework of thought, language had relatively little claim on philosophical attention. Ideas, and their forms of organization, were typically conceived to be altogether language-independent. And thought, conceived as a variety of more or less complex operations upon ideas, was held to be equally language-independent. A language was generally thought to be no more than a vehicle for the communication of ideas. Hobbes remarked that:

the most noble and profitable invention of all other, was that of *speech*, consisting of *names* or *appellations*, and their connection; whereby men register their thoughts, recall them when they are past, and also declare them one to another for mutual utility and conversation . . .

The general use of speech is to transfer our mental discourse into verbal, or the train of thoughts into a train of words . . .[2]

Thought was generally conceived as a mental transaction with ideas, private to the thinker and in general independent of language. But since ideas are not themselves transferable from one thinker to another, they can be represented by words. Each man, Locke noted, will 'use these sounds as signs of internal conceptions; and . . . make them stand as marks for the ideas within his own mind, whereby they might be made known to others, and the thoughts of men's minds be conveyed from one to another'.[3] This 'telementational'[4] conception of a language was the received wisdom of the age. The Port-Royal *Logic* (*The Art of Thinking* (1662)), the most influential logic text until the middle of the nineteenth century, proclaimed

[2] T. Hobbes, *Leviathan*, ch. IV.
[3] J. Locke, *Essay Concerning Human Understanding*, III, i, 2.
[4] Cf. R. Harris, *The Language Myth* (Duckworth, London, 1981) pp. 9f.; Harris traces this conception back to Aristotle.

that 'if the reflections which we make on our thoughts referred to ourselves alone, it would suffice to consider them in themselves, without having recourse to words or any other signs. But . . . we are not able to express our thoughts to each other, unless they are accompanied with outward signs . . .'[5]

This picture of language has dominated European thought ever since. It is noteworthy that it is incorporated into theoretical linguistics. Saussure, the founder of this modern science, accepted it without questioning. Speech he conceived as following a 'speech circuit' from the brain (mind) of one speaker to audible words emitted, to sounds received, to the brain (mind) of a hearer, and, given a reply, back again:

the opening of the circuit is in A's brain, where mental facts (concepts) are associated with representations of the linguistic sounds (sound-images) that are used for their expression. A given concept unlocks a corresponding sound-image in the brain; this purely *psychological* phenomenon is followed in turn by a *physiological* process: the brain transmits an impulse corresponding to the image to the organs used in producing sounds. Then the sound waves travel from the mouth of A to the ear of B: a purely *physical* process. Next, the circuit continues in B, but the order is reversed: from the ear to the brain . . . in the brain, the psychological association of the image with the corresponding concept.[6]

Apart from the quaint physiology, and the substitution of 'concept' for 'idea', the primitive picture is identical.

Ideas (on the classical conception) are typically given in experience. These may be complex or simple. Complex ideas decompose upon analysis into simple ones. Language encodes ideas for communicative purposes. Words typically correspond to ideas, definable words corresponding to complex ideas, indefinable words to simple unanalysable ideas. The mind, with its various innate associative propensities and its faculty of imagination, was pictured as a sort of kaleidoscope. The powers and limits of thought were conceived, by the empiricists, as determined by the possibilities of arrangement, decomposition and recomposition of ideas. The

[5] *The Art of Thinking*, Introduction; we shall refer to this famous work by its customary name – the Port-Royal *Logic*. We have used the translation of T. S. Baynes, 2nd edn (Sutherland and Knox, Edinburgh, 1851).

[6] F. de Saussure, *Course in General Linguistics*, tr. W. Baskin (Fontana, London, 1974), pp. 11f. Nor has this picture yet exhausted its mesmerizing power, e.g. 'Language enables a speaker to transform configurations of ideas into configurations of sounds, and it enables a listener within his own mind to transform these sounds back into a reasonable facsimile of the ideas with which the speaker began' (Wallace L. Chafe, *Meaning and the Structure of Language* (University of Chicago Press, Chicago, 1970)).

words of a language and their concatenation into significant sentences were thought of as mirroring the kaleidoscopic arrangement of ideas into judgments by the mind. This primitive picture, of course, required a host of modifications and epicyclical hypotheses to cope with special cases and complexities. In various more or less sophisticated forms, these were elaborated by the major philosophers of the seventeenth and eighteenth centuries. But the fundamental biplanar conception of a language as composed of words corresponding to ideas and of sentences corresponding to concatenations of ideas into judgments remained a constant guiding force shaping the reflections of thinkers throughout the period.

The primitive picture underlying the sophisticated embroideries woven by such philosophical theories as well as by their modern correlates, was later to be dubbed 'Augustine's picture of language' by Wittgenstein.[7] It consists of the notion that all words are names of entities (whether material, mental or Platonic) and that all sentences are descriptions.

Given the conception of a language as a public code in which ideas, concepts or thoughts may be encoded for communicative purposes, it may seem puzzling that our august philosophical predecessors should have had any interest in language at all. Berkeley went so far as to insist that 'so long as I confine my thoughts to my own ideas divested of words, I do not see how I can be easily mistaken. The objects I consider, I clearly and adequately know. I cannot be deceived in thinking I have an idea which I have not.'[8] Though this may appear faintly comical to a sophisticated modern philosopher of language, Berkeley was merely repeating, in empiricist garb, a conception which runs through the Cartesian method: 'We shall never take the false as the true if we only give our assent to things that we perceive [by 'intellectual vision'] clearly and distinctly . . . [M]ost men apply their attention to words rather than things, and this is the cause of their frequently giving their assent to terms which they do not understand'.[9]

Nor was this conception of the matter demolished by the repudiation of the New Way of Ideas. Frege (1848–1925), considered by some to be the fountain-head of modern analytical philosophy, was a relentless opponent of psychologism or idealism in logic, language, and metaphysics. He

---

[7] Cf. L. Wittgenstein, *Philosophical Investigations* (Blackwell, Oxford, 1953), §§1ff.; for detailed analysis of the Augustinian picture, see G. P. Baker and P. M. S. Hacker, *Wittgenstein: Understanding and Meaning*, (Blackwell, Oxford, 1980), pp. 33ff.

[8] G. Berkeley, *A Treatise Concerning the Principles of Human Knowledge*, Introduction, §22.

[9] R. Descartes, *Principles of Philosophy*, part I, Principles XLIII and LXXIV.

approached the problems of logic from the very different angle of Platonism, holding that a language encoded not ideas, conceived as mental objects, but concepts and thoughts, conceived as mind-independent Platonic entities. Yet he too argued similarly for an emancipation from language: 'if we . . . attend instead to the true nature of thinking, we shall not be able to equate it with speaking. In that case we shall not derive thinking from speaking; thinking will then emerge as that which has priority and we shall not be able to blame thinking for the logical defects . . . in language.'[10] In fact, the concern of these generations of post-Cartesian philosophers with language was largely a consequence of their conception of a language as an interpersonal code for communicating language-independent thoughts or ideas. The reasons they adduced for examining language were two, one negative and one positive.

The negative consideration was that language obscures thought, misrepresents the ideas which constitute the gold-backing of the paper-currency of words and sentences. The Port-Royal *Logic* argued that 'the necessity which we have for employing outward signs in order to make ourselves understood, causes us to attach our ideas to words, [so] that we often consider the words more than the things. Now this is one of the most common causes of the confusion of our thoughts and discourse.'[11] Consequently, a significant part of that book is concerned with words and propositions. So too Locke, who treated 'Of Words' throughout the long Book III of the *Essay*, excused this digression in the 'Epistle to the Reader':

To break in upon the sanctuary of vanity and ignorance will be, I suppose, some service to human understanding; though so few are apt to think they deceive or are deceived in the use of words; or that the language of the sect they are of has any faults in it which ought to be examined or corrected, that I hope I shall be pardoned if I have in the Third Book dwelt long on this subject, and endeavoured to make it so plain, that neither the inveterateness of the mischief, nor the prevalency of the fashion, shall be any excuse for those who will not take care about the meaning of their own words, and will not suffer the significancy of their expressions to be inquired into.[12]

Similar sentiments are expressed by most philosophers in this period. Philosophical investigations into language are undertaken by way of a prophylactic. The philosopher, in pursuit of quite a different quarry, must

[10] G. Frege, *Posthumous Writings* (Blackwell, Oxford, 1979), p. 270.
[11] Port-Royal *Logic*, part I, ch. xi.
[12] Locke, *Essay*, 'Epistle to the Reader'.

describe this Idol of the Market-place[13] in order to emancipate us from its sway. In order to penetrate to the true nature of thought, and thence to the true nature of things, we must free ourselves from the trammels of language. This is to be done by examining the workings of our language and its relation to ideas, noting everywhere how we may guard against error.

The positive motive for investigating language was superficially in diametric opposition to the negative one. Language is worthy of philosophical investigation because it is a guide to the nature and structure of the ideas or thoughts it represents, and hence, proximately to the nature and structure of what *they* represent. The Port-Royal *Logic* prefaced its remarks on language with the observation that 'it is certainly of some use to the *end* which logic contemplates – *that of thinking well* – to understand the different uses of the sounds devoted to the expression of our ideas, and which the mind is accustomed to connect so closely with them, that it scarcely ever conceives the one without the other'.[14] Locke similarly remarked that 'The ordinary words of language, and our common use of them, would have given us light into the nature of our ideas, if they had been but considered with attention.'[15]

Given the basic strategy, it may seem curious that these philosophers thought that any merit at all might attach to scrutiny of language. To the extent that the telementational conception of language viewed language as *externally* related to thought, it is *prima facie* paradoxical to contend that we can profitably extract philosophical morals about the nature of thought and its relation to reality from scrutiny of a language, when we can by-pass it altogether and attend directly to the ideas underlying it. This embarrassment is superficially covered up by claiming, as the Port-Royal *Logic* did, that we are so accustomed to use words in communication that language becomes a partial barrier to reflection upon the ideas behind it. Hence by analysis of language, we can use language itself as a guide to the forms of thought:

since this custom [of verbal expression] is so strong, that even when we think alone, things present themselves to our minds only in connection with the words to which we have been accustomed to have recourse in speaking to others; – it is necessary, in

[13] F. Bacon, *Novum Organum*, xliii, lix: 'words plainly force and overrule the understanding', they 'react on the understanding; and this it is that has rendered philosophy and the sciences sophistical and inactive'.
[14] Port-Royal *Logic*, part II, ch. i.
[15] Locke, *Essay*, III, viii, 1.

logic, to consider ideas in their connection with words, and words in their connection with ideas.[16]

A further consideration reinforced this. If our ideas, *to the extent that they are clear and distinct*,[17] contain no falsehood, but represent in their combinatorial possibilities, the combinatorial possibilities of the entities in reality of which they are ideas, then our language, *to the extent that it is clearly constructed*, must represent our ideas and hence also represent, mediately, the self-same possible realities which our ideas represent. Though words are arbitrarily annexed to ideas, though a language is an arbitrary, conventional artefact, once given the arbitrary conventions, representation of thought by language is not arbitrary. Hence the Port-Royal *Logic* argued

when we speak of the signification of words as arbitrary, there is much that is equivocal in the term *arbitrary*. It is indeed a thing quite arbitrary whether we join a given idea to a certain sound, rather than to another: but the ideas are not arbitrary things, and do not depend upon our fancy, – at all events those which are clear and distinct . . . [A man's reasoning is] not an assemblage of names according to a convention which depends entirely on the fancy of men; but a solid and effective judgment on the nature of things, through the consideration of certain ideas which he had in his mind, and which it has pleased men to represent by certain names.[18]

This doctrine of approximate correspondence between thought and language and between reality and whatever is clear and distinct in thought contained the seeds of much later, specifically nineteenth and twentieth century, philosophical reflection. It was, however, rarely explicitly thought out or exploited. An exception to the rule, however, was Leibniz.[19] In contradistinction to the prevailing tradition, he thought that 'if there were no signs, we should never think or conclude anything intelligibly'.[20] In his work a doctrine of correspondence between language and what it represents was more thoroughly and self-consciously developed:

---

[16] Port-Royal *Logic*, Introduction.
[17] According to the Cartesian conception ideas of colour, sound, smell, are *not* clear and distinct, and accordingly do not represent correctly the objective qualities which cause them.
[18] Port-Royal *Logic*, part I, ch. i.
[19] In very many ways he stood outside the prevailing tradition, being less enmeshed in the confused doctrine of ideas that bedevilled the empiricist tradition.
[20] G. W. Leibniz, 'Dialogue on the Connection between Things and Words', in *Leibniz: Selections*, ed. P. P. Wiener (Scribner's, New York, 1951), p. 10.

characters must show, when they are used in demonstrations, some kind of connection, grouping and order which are also found in the objects, and . . . this is required, if not in the single words – though it were better so – then at least in their union and connection. This order and correspondence at least must be present in all languages, though in different ways . . . [E]ven though characters are as such arbitrary, there is still in their application and connection something valid which is not arbitrary; namely, a relationship which exists between them and things, and consequently, definite relations among all the different characters used to express the same things. And this relationship, this connection is the foundation of truth.[21]

Though this relationship is obscured in natural languages, Leibniz dreamt of an ideal language, a *characteristica universalis*, in which the basic signs would represent simple and unanalysable concepts and all complex signs would be defined precisely in terms of the simple ones.

The idea of a universal character was not, as such, original.[22] Leibniz acknowledged his debt to Ramon Lull, Athanasius, Kircher, George Delgano and John Wilkins, and he was familiar with Descartes's discussion of the issue. The bare idea of a universal character was a commonplace in the seventeenth century. In its minimally ambitious form it derived from a perceived need for an international language. The programme for such a project had been formulated by Bacon. What Descartes added to this idea was the vision of an analytical language the primitive words of which would correspond to

the simple ideas in the human imagination out of which all human thoughts are compounded, and if [this] explanation were generally received, I would dare to hope for a universal language very easy to learn, to speak and to write. The greatest advantage of such a language would be the assistance it would give to men's judgment, representing matters so clearly that it would be almost impossible to go wrong.[23]

Such a language would provide an exact and structurally perspicuous system of symbolization for the precise expression of all actual and possible scientific knowledge. Numerous seventeenth century writers pursued this will-o'-the-wisp of a universal character. What Leibniz added to existing projects was the idea of a *calculus ratiocinator*, a calculus of symbols

[21] Ibid.

[22] For a detailed discussion of this fascinating episode in European letters, see L. J. Cohen, 'On the Project of a Universal Character', *Mind*, LXIII (1954), pp. 49–63.

[23] Letter to Mersenne, 20.11.1629, from *Descartes: Philosophical Letters*, ed. and tr. A. J. P. Kenny (Clarendon Press, Oxford, 1970), p. 6.

which would operate on the formulae of the universal character. Because
he had a clearer conception of a logical calculus, and a deeper respect for
formal logic, Leibniz's remarks on the correspondence between language,
thought and reality are deeper than those of his precursors. The ideal
language he envisaged would be an 'algebra of thought' in which simple
and indefinable ideas are conceived, as it were, as the alphabet of thought,
so that by their combinations all possible thoughts would be expressible.
Leibniz envisaged representing these simples by numerical values, and
imagined devising a set of combinatorial rules which would synthesize into
one system the merits of a deductive logic and those of a Cartesian logic of
discovery.

That nothing came of these seventeenth century visionary projects is
hardly surprising. They muddled up inconsistent requirements and failed
to distinguish profoundly different projects. Devising an international
language that can be easily learnt and widely used in everyday international transactions is one thing. It needs a much simplified grammar and
pared down vocabulary of a flexible, non-specialized, kind. Concocting a
taxonomic vocabulary for scientific classification, description and
generalization is a different task altogether. It must involve a specialized
vocabulary, often of a highly theory-laden kind (as in chemistry), and the
idea that there might be one unique such language suitable for all sciences
(never mind about other more important purposes) is a dream founded
upon the mythology of the unity of the sciences. So too, the vision of a
powerful deductive system in which all patterns of proof and deductive
reasoning can be represented is one thing. It may be associated with the
hope that *some* sciences can be given an axiomatic representation in the
notation of the calculus. But the notion of a formal logic of discovery, in
which 'Calculemus' might be our motto, is another thing altogether. The
amalgamation of all these into an envisioned *characteristica universalis*
was a pipe-dream bred of confusion. But the differentiation of the elements
of the project was, two centuries later, to bear fruit. The idea of a rough
correspondence between thought and language remained a muted but
persistent theme in the ensuing period. Thomas Reid, in 1774, argued that

Language, being the express image of human thought, the analysis of the one must
correspond to that of the other . . . The philosophy of grammar, and that of the
human understanding, are more nearly allied than is commonly imagined.[24]

[24] Thomas Reid, 'A Brief Account of Aristotle's Logic', *Works*, vol. II, ed. Sir William
Hamilton (Edinburgh, 1863), pp. 691f.

A century later the same picture was sketched explicitly by Boole (1854):

> though in investigating the laws of signs, *a posteriori*, the immediate subject of examination is language, with the rules which govern its use; while in making the internal processes of thought the direct object of our inquiry, we appeal in a more immediate way to our personal consciousness, – it will be found that in both cases the results obtained are formally equivalent. Nor could we easily conceive, that the unnumbered tongues and dialects of the earth should have preserved through a long succession of ages so much that is common and universal, were we not assured of the existence of some deep foundation of their agreement in the laws of the mind itself.[25]

The philosophical study of language was, on this conception, no more than a useful tool for the truly philosophical investigation into the nature, powers and limits of the human mind on the one hand, and into the essential (metaphysical) nature of reality on the other. Apart from that it provided no more than a negative instruction, a prophylactic against errors rooted in a defective use of, or understanding of, words or in the structural defects of language which only imperfectly or confusedly re-presents thoughts. The idea that language might constitute part of, let alone the whole of, the subject-matter of philosophy was unthought of. No philosophers dreamt of constructing theories of meaning for natural languages, and the contention that such a theory would constitute a new Philosopher's Stone would have appeared positively bizarre.

3   The logical tradition

We have focused primarily on the mainspring of post-Cartesian philo-sophical reflection, the attendant conception of language and its relation to thought, and the relevance which investigation into language was conceived to have. Did logicians think differently on the matter? To a modern student, educated in contemporary logic, it is a commonplace that logic is concerned with structural features of *languages*, since it is typically conceived as studying relations of derivability and entailment between *sentences*. This idea, however, is a distinctively twentieth century one. With a handful of exceptions (e.g. Whateley and De Morgan in the nineteenth century) the post-Cartesian tradition in logic did not think it

---

[25] G. Boole, *The Laws of Thought* (Dover, New York, 1958), ch. II, §1.

the business of logic to study a language and its formal structure, but rather to study concepts and judgments.

Descartes, apart from his great influence on the Port-Royal *Logic* (which, though lucid and elegant, made barely any advance), contributed greatly to the relative demise of logic in the seventeenth and eighteenth centuries. He was altogether contemptuous of formal logic (syllogistic). His reasons were fourfold. First, this traditional logic did not satisfy his requirements of a method, viz. 'certain and simple rules, such that if a man observes them accurately, he shall never assume what is false as true, and will never spend his mental powers to no purpose'.[26] Since formal logic can only guarantee the preservation of truth in valid inferences from the premises to the conclusion of an argument, but cannot guarantee the truth of the chosen premises, it does not satisfy Descartes's demand for a correct method of reasoning. Secondly, he claimed that the syllogism commits a *petitio*, for the premises must 'contain' the conclusion; hence one can learn nothing new from a syllogism inasmuch as one cannot assert the premises unless one already knows the conclusion to be true. The 'logic of the schools' therefore is only a dialectic which teaches us how to present things already known. (This idea continued to be influential right down to Mill's *System of Logic*.) Thirdly, formal logic is redundant, since if ideas are analysed according to the Cartesian method into their simplest components or 'simple natures', then any possibility of error in inference is ruled out. Inference is a matter of intuitive insight into necessary relations between simple natures. Intuition, Descartes thought, is unerring, and any mistake is attributable to a failure in analysis into clear and distinct ideas. Not only are rules of inference redundant, but they are impediments to thought, since nothing can be added to the 'natural light of reason', the capacity of 'logical intuition', without hindering it. Finally, formal logic is concerned with validity, not with truth; it is a logic of exposition, not of discovery.

These views were exceedingly influential, stifling formal logic for two centuries. Locke slavishly followed Descartes, arguing that

This way of reasoning [i.e. a syllogism] discovers no new proofs, but is the art of marshalling and arranging the ones we have already . . .
. . . A man knows first, and then he is able to prove syllogistically; so that syllogism comes after knowledge and then a man has little or no need of it.[27]

---

[26] Descartes, *Rules for the Direction of the Mind*, rule IV.
[27] Locke, *Essay*, IV, xvii, 6.

With the notable exception of Leibniz, whose influence was negligible, no major philosopher made any significant contribution to formal logic between the time of Descartes and the revival of logic in the mid-nineteenth century. Kant went so far as to declare

That logic has already . . . proceeded upon this sure path [of a science] is evidenced by the fact that since Aristotle it has not required to retrace a single step . . . It is remarkable also that to the present day this logic has not been able to advance a single step, and is thus to all appearance a closed and completed body of doctrine.[28]

It is noteworthy that when logic did revive, the originators of the logical renaissance were primarily mathematicians, not philosophers. Nevertheless, logic continued to be taught through this period of dogmatic slumber, the most influential work being the Port-Royal *Logic*.

The title of that work, *The Art of Thinking*, indicates its conception of its subject-matter. It opens with the observation that

Logic is the *art of directing reason aright, in obtaining the knowledge of things, for the instruction both of ourselves and of others*. It consists in the reflections which have been made on the four principal operations of the mind: conceiving, judging, reasoning, and disposing.[29]

Accordingly, the book is divided into four parts, each of which examines one of the fundamental operations of the mind. The examination of *conceiving* analyses the materials of thought, viz. ideas, clarifies their origins, their relations to their objects (that of which they are ideas), their division into categories, their classification into simple and complex ideas. From ideas the mind forms judgments, in which it combines ideas and affirms or denies one or the other. The *theory of judgment* is therefore the analysis of the different kinds of judgments or propositions and of their structure. A proposition is composed of two terms, a subject, of which we affirm or deny something, and a predicate which we affirm or deny of the subject. The copula represents the union of the constituent terms into a judgment. The subject of a proposition may be universal (or singular) or particular, and the proposition may be affirmative or negative; hence the authors follow tradition in reducing all propositions to four kinds, universal affirmative or negative, particular affirmative or negative. Since propositions may themselves be compounded, a large part of Book II concerns the

[28] I. Kant, *Critique of Pure Reason*, B, viii.
[29] Port-Royal *Logic*, Introduction; 'disposing' is the study of method.

various forms of complex propositions. The rules of reasoning are the
norms of valid inference from the premises to the conclusion of an argument. The exposition of syllogistic in Book III of the Port-Royal *Logic*
became the canonical source of the formal theory of logic for most writers
of textbooks of logic for almost two centuries.

Throughout this period logic was conceived, in nineteenth century
jargon, to be a normative science of judgment. It studied the normative
laws of thought, i.e. how inference should be conducted, what ought to be
concluded from given premises, etc. What validated these normative laws,
how they are related to the descriptive laws of human thinking, remained
problematic. That the laws of logic are, in some sense, necessary was
readily acknowledged. But what explains their necessity, whence its origin
and what its nature was an issue around which writers typically skirted
rather gingerly. By the mid-nineteenth century, opinions had polarized
around two unhappy alternatives, psychologism and Platonism.
Psychologism, which assumed various forms, conceived of the laws of
thought as determined subjectively, by the nature and structure of the
human mind. This in turn might be explained transcendentally, as in the
writings of Kantians, or merely empirically, as in the works of the
nineteenth century German psychological school. Sir William Hamilton, a
neo-Kantian psychologician, expressed his position in a manner that
cannot but seem curious and self-contradictory to the modern reader:

[I]nsofar as a form of thought is necessary, this form must be determined or
necessitated by the nature of the thinking subject itself; for if it were determined by
anything external to the mind, then would it not be a necessary but a merely
contingent determination. The first condition, therefore, of the necessity of a form
of thought is, that it is subjectively, not objectively determined.[30]

A less Kantian form of psychologism conceded that the laws of thought are
valid only conditionally, *sub specie humanitatis*, in virtue of *empirical*
constraints:

We cannot help admitting that all the propositions whose contradictories we
cannot envisage in thought are only necessary if we presuppose the character of our
thought, as definitely given in our experience: they are not absolutely necessary, or
necessary in all possible conditions. On this view our logical principles retain their
necessity for our thinking, but this necessity *is not seen as absolute, but as hypothetical*.
We cannot help assenting to them – such is the nature of our presentation and

[30] Sir William Hamilton, *Lectures on Metaphysics and Logic*, vol. III, ed. H. L. Mansel and
J. Veitch (Blackwood, Edinburgh & London, 1860), pp. 24f.

thinking. They are universally valid, provided our thinking remains the same. They are necessary, since to think means for us to presuppose them, as long, that is, as they express the essence of our thinking.[31]

This not only left the status of logical necessity in a curiously contingent limbo, but it also failed to explain the relation between the logician's study of the normative laws of thought and the psychologist's study of the empirical laws of thought. Indeed, it failed to explain how it was possible to reason erroneously, viz. contrary to the forms allegedly determined by the nature of the mind.

The alternative conception still viewed logic as a normative science, but adamantly denied that it studied the nature of human thinking. Rather, its subject-matter was the objective relations between mind-independent entities, not ideas, but concepts Platonistically conceived, not judgments viewed as mental objects, but contents of judgment or propositions (the *Satz-an-sich*) conceived as abstract, sempiternal, objects. The most prominent proponent of this view early in the nineteenth century was Bolzano, and its most august later supporter was Frege. Laws of logic, Frege declared, are not laws of 'takings-to-be-true', but absolute laws of truth:

If being true is . . . independent of being acknowledged by somebody or other, then the laws of truth are not psychological laws: they are boundary stones set in an eternal foundation, which our thought can overflow, but never displace. It is because of this that they have authority for our thought if it would attain to truth. They do not bear the relation to thought that the laws of grammar bear to language; they do not make explicit the nature of our human thinking and change as it changes.[32]

This strategy could readily explain the contrast between the normative laws of thought and the psychological laws of thinking, but only at the cost of Platonic mystery-mongering.

Psychologism and Platonism seemed the only viable alternatives. With very few exceptions, neither logicians nor philosophers thought that the laws of logic might be rooted in the essentially *arbitrary* conventions for the use of arbitrary linguistic signs. Nor did they think that logic was concerned, save indirectly and instrumentally, with language or grammar.

---

[31] B. Erdmann, *Logik*; quoted by E. G. A. Husserl, *Logical Investigations*, vol. I, tr. J. N. Findlay (Routledge & Kegan Paul, London, 1970), p. 162.

[32] G. Frege, *The Basic Laws of Arithmetic*, vol. 1, tr. and ed. M. Furth (University of California Press, Berkeley, 1964), Introduction, p. xvi.

4   The invention of formal calculi

From the middle of the nineteenth century formal logic underwent an unprecedented revolution. The application of generalized mathematical ideas and techniques to the formal representation of patterns of logically valid reasoning led to the development of modern logical calculi, the powers of which go far beyond anything possible in the limited forms of syllogistic.

The philosophical interest of the invention of new logical calculi lay not only in the fact that, and the ways in which, forms of reasoning hitherto beyond the sway of logic became tamed, but also in the philosophical implications of the new discoveries. Did the new logic finally uncover the fundamental forms and mechanics of the human mind? Did it inform us about the ultimate logical or metaphysical structure of reality? Could it, for the first time, reveal the true nature of that great mystery, logical necessity? And did it draw back the veil enshrouding the inner nature of a language? It would be no great exaggeration to suggest that the invention of powerful formal calculi has fulfilled a similar role with respect to mainstream twentieth century analytical philosophy as the new physics fulfilled for seventeenth and eighteenth century philosophy. Where the new physics seemed to require a fundamental re-evaluation of our conceptions of appearance and reality, of the powers of the mind and the limits of possible knowledge, the new logic seemed to demand an equally fundamental reorientation of our conceptions of language and its relation to the reality it depicts, of the forms and mechanics of understanding, and of the limits of possible thought.

The inspiration for the new logic came from the generalization of mathematical techniques. Its pioneer was George Boole (1815–64), a mathematician rather than a philosopher, who sought to clarify and generalize syllogistic reasoning in terms of algebraic operations on sets. His fundamental insight was that there could be an algebra of entities that are not numbers at all, since there are important analogies between disjunction (or conjunction) of concepts, and addition (or multiplication) of numbers. Of course, not all the laws of algebra which apply to the calculus of numbers also apply to the logical calculus of concepts. But that revolutionary idea had already been mooted by mathematicians themselves within the domain of mathematics. For with the introduction of new mathematical entities, in particular hyper-complex numbers, and the development of an algebra of these objects at the hands of Sir William Rowan

Hamilton, it became evident that not all the laws of algebra applicable to complex numbers could be retained, e.g. the commutativity of multiplication. This necessitated a new perspective upon algebra, which was a prerequisite for Boole's invention of *logical* algebra. For in his calculus of classes $x^n = x$ (since the intersection of a class with itself is the same class), and there is no satisfactory analogue of division. With great originality and ingenuity Boole gave algebraic representations of the forms of reasoning recognized in traditional logic. In effect he elaborated a theory of truth-functions, a technique for their presentation in disjunctive normal form, and a mechanical decision-procedure. His achievement provided the foundations for the invention of calculating machines, and, later, for computers.

Boole's mathematicization of logic was a decisive step in the development of the subject, and was immediately recognized as such. De Morgan, in 1858, proclaimed that 'As joint attention to logic and mathematics increases, a logic will grow up among the mathematicians . . . This *mathematical* logic . . . will commend itself to the educated world by showing an actual representation of their form of thought – a representation the truth of which they recognize – instead of a mutilated and one-sided fragment . . .'[33] Fifteen years later Jevons enthusiastically (and prematurely) declared that 'it will probably be allowed that Boole discovered the true and general form of logic, and put the science substantially into the form which it must hold for evermore. He thus effected a reform with which there is hardly anything comparable in the history of logic between his time and the remote age of Aristotle.'[34]

Boole no more thought that his new calculus was a study of sentential relations or an exploration of the 'depth-grammar' of any language than his predecessors had thought syllogistic to be an investigation of forms of language. He conceived of logic as the algebra of *thought*, and characterized his abstract algebra as a 'cross section' of rational thinking. His declared aim was 'to investigate the fundamental laws of those operations of the mind by which reasoning is performed . . . and upon this function to establish the science of Logic'.[35] His new calculus of logic, far from being an 'analysis' of the forms of any language, was meant to be a step towards a new, logically more perspicuous, language: 'A successful attempt to express logical propositions by symbols, the laws of whose combinations

[33] Augustus De Morgan, 'On the Syllogism: III', in *On the Syllogism and Other Logical Writings*, ed. P. Heath (Routledge & Kegan Paul, London, 1966), p. 78n.

[34] W. S. Jevons, *The Principles of Science*, (Dover, New York, 1958), p. 113.

[35] G. Boole, *The Laws of Thought*, (Dover, New York, 1958), ch. 1, §1.

should be founded upon the laws of the mental processes which they represent, would, so far, be a step toward a philosophical language.'[36] His mathematicization of logic remained firmly wedded to psychologism. Indeed, he thought that his discovery of a logical algebra was not merely the invention of a useful artificial device, a logically convenient (because logically perspicuous) conventional form of representation, but a revelation of the hidden nature of human thought: 'The laws of thought, in all its processes of conception and of reasoning, in all those operations of which language is the expression or instrument, are of the same kind as are the laws of the acknowledged processes of Mathematics.'[37] Ordinary languages in effect conceal, in his view, what his new notation reveals, viz. the abstract mathematical forms of human thought.

Boole's ideas were enthusiastically taken up and further developed by other logicians such as Jevons, Venn, Huntington, Peirce and Schröder. But mathematical logic came of age with Gottlob Frege (in 1879), who acted as Newton to Boole's Copernicus. Where Boole conceived of logic as part of mathematics, Frege aimed to demonstrate that the whole of arithmetic is deducible from logic. Where Boole had generalized algebraic principles and applied them to logic, Frege invoked a more avant-garde branch of mathematics, namely function theory, subsuming syllogistic within a much more general logical system which sought to display all sound patterns of reasoning as theorems derived from a few function-theoretic axioms. He explicitly referred to Leibniz's idea of a *characteristica universalis*, and viewed his function-theoretic calculus not as an analysis of natural languages, but as a logically perfect language which, for the restricted purposes of deductive sciences, would replace natural languages. Calling it 'concept-script' (*Begriffsschrift*), he conceived of it as accurately representing the structures and articulations of contents of possible judgments (propositions) and of the concepts of which they are composed. He thought of judgeable-contents and of concepts as abstract, Platonic, entities rather than as mental ones.

Frege's crucial innovation was to repudiate the traditional conception of (the content of) judgment as composed or synthesized from subject and predicate, and to replace it by a conception of judgment as decomposable or analysable into function and argument. He conceived of a mathematical function as a law of correlation of (mathematical) entities, and accepted the mathematicians' differentiation of functions according to the number

---

[36] G. Boole, *The Mathematical Analysis of Logic*, (Oxford, Blackwell, 1948), p. 5.
[37] Boole, *The Laws of Thought*, ch. XXII, §11.

of arguments taken and according to the types of the arguments. His generalization of function theory beyond the confines of mathematical entities depended upon various forms of liberalization of the concept of a function *within mathematics* which had taken place earlier in the nineteenth century, just as Boole's generalization of algebra had been dependent on the increasing abstraction of algebra within mathematics. (Mathematicians had already recognized as second-level functions those functions which take first-level functions as arguments, e.g. integration and differentiation.) He took the radical step of recognizing any entities whatever (and not just mathematical ones) as arguments and values of functions. Consequently he proposed viewing judgments (conceived as objects) as the values of concepts for arguments, and concepts as functions mapping arguments on to judgments. The apparatus of function theory enabled him to construct the first formal logic of generality. For he analysed expressions of generality ('all', 'some', 'exists') as variable-binding, variable-indexed second-level functions. These quantifiers he thus represented as second-level concepts taking first-level concepts as arguments and mapping them on to judgeable-contents. With this apparatus he was able to give the first complete formalization of the predicate calculus with identity, and so to master, for the first time in the history of formal logic, the formal presentation of inferences involving multiple generality (e.g. if every number has a successor, then there is no number such that it is larger than every other number).

Like his predecessors, Frege conceived the business of logic to be the analysis of relations between judgments. The well-formed formulae of his concept-script, in the initial formulation of his logical system in *Begriffs-schrift*, were conceived as standing for (contents of possible) judgments, just as declarative sentences used in assertion stand for what is judged. Since a precondition for the application of function/argument analysis in logic is that the value of a function for an argument be an 'object', Frege was constrained not only to view the content of a judgment as an (abstract) object, but also to view the symbol representing it as a name. Hence the formulae of concept-script, and indeed the corresponding declarative sentences of natural language, were, *ab initio*, conceived as singular referring expressions. This idea he never relinquished. But in his final formulation of his system of logic, in *The Basic Laws of Arithmetic*, he distinguished within an expression for a judgment between the sense expressed which he called 'a thought' (in a non-psychological sense) and a reference, viz. a truth-value: truth or falsehood. This distinction between sense and reference he also applied to the constituent elements of a symbol for a judgeable-content, i.e. the argument-expression and function-name (concept-word) are likewise held to express senses and refer to referents. His conception of a concept altered correspondingly, since it was now conceived as a function which takes a *truth-value* for any possible argument. The sense of a well-formed formula or declarative sentence was conceived as the object of assertion, or more generally, the sense of *any* expression was conceived as the mode of presenting a reference (viz. *as* the value of a given function for some argument). The sense of a sentence (a thought) was conceived as the manner in which a truth-value (its reference) is presented as the value of a function (denoted by its constituent concept-word) for an argument (denoted by its constituent argument-expression).

Frege's function-theoretic apparatus was the engine of his logical machinery. His most fundamental innovation was to conceive of concepts as first-level functions taking truth-values as their values for any argument, and of quantifiers as second-level functions (concepts) mapping first-level concepts on to truth-values. It was this which enabled him to construct the formal logic of generality. Once he split judgeable-content into the two strata of sense and reference, conceiving of concepts and truth-values as belonging to the domain of references, he felt constrained to apply his function-theoretic apparatus also to the level of senses. Hence he conceived of the thought, as he had earlier conceived of the judgeable-content, as the value of a function (namely the sense of a concept-word) for an argument (the sense of the argument-expression – in the simplest case, of a proper name). The functional analysis was also applied, *ab initio*, to the logical connectives. The negation-stroke and the condition-stroke were the two primitive connectives in his system, and he conceived of both as literal *function*-names. Negation was conceived as a unary function (a concept) mapping a judgeable-content on to a judgeable content. Conditionality was conceived as a binary function (a relation) mapping a pair of judgeable-contents on to a judgeable-content. Although his explanations of these logical operators are isomorphic with modern truth-tabular explanations, they are not identical. In his early system these logical constants are not *truth*-functions, i.e. functions taking truth-values as arguments, but rather functions taking *judgeable-contents* as arguments (and values). In his mature system, he construed them as functions taking truth-values as their *values*, but since he then thought that every function had to be defined for *any object* as argument (and not just truth-values), he had to offer complex explanations stipulating values when objects other than truth or falsehood are their arguments. They were simply two out of a myriad of concepts and relations, with no more right to be deemed truth-functions than any other concept or relation.[38]

This difference between Frege's conception and that of a modern logician is not a mere slip of the pen, but rather reflects his conception of logic and its laws. His explanations of the logical constants are not conceived as formal definitions, and the axioms of his logical system are not presented as *consequences* of these explanations, but as indemonstrable self-evident truths. The axioms of logic are no more analytic consequences of definitions than are the axioms of geometry (on his view); they are rather an unfolding of the essences of primitive concepts and relations. Just as our faculty of spatial intuition delivers the axioms of geometry, so too the axioms of logic are directly certified by a 'logical source of knowledge'. It is these axioms which secure the certainty of all the validly derived theorems of logic, but they are ultimate intuitive truths, not verbal trivialities. They can no more be justified than the ultimate truths of geometry: 'The question why and with what right we acknowledge a law of logic to be true, logic can answer only by reducing it to another law of logic. Where that is not possible, logic can give no answer.'[39] This conception is a reaffirmation of the venerable idea that all knowledge ultimately rests on self-evident truths. It leaves the normative status of logical truths (as canons of correct reasoning) shrouded in clouds of Platonic mysteries.

In the course of his exposition of his logical system, Frege introduced numerous novel ideas which provided grist for philosophical and logical mills for subsequent decades. Apart from those already mentioned we shall select three more which proved seminal.

First, he propounded as a salient principle of his analysis that a word has a meaning or content (signifies something) only in the context of a sentence. This principle is evidently associated with his insistence upon the priority of judgments over concepts for purposes of logical analysis, viz. that we view concepts as derived by functional decomposition of judgments, rather than viewing judgments as synthesized from antecedently given concepts (subject and predicate). That principle in turn can be seen as a straightforward consequence of his function-theoretic analysis. For although functions are, in his view, abstract, language-independent entities, the logical type of a function is determined by the categories of its arguments and values. Since, in his initial system, the judgment *is* the value of a function (concept) for an argument, the function (concept) is viewed as

---

[38] For a more detailed and precise statement of this claim, see G. P. Baker and P. M. S. Hacker, *Frege: Logical Excavations*, (Blackwell, Oxford, 1984), pp. 117f.

[39] Frege, *The Basic Laws of Arithmetic*, vol. 1, xvi.

abstracted from the judgment by considering how arguments (in the simplest case, objects) are correlated with values (viz. judgments). Frege employed the principle for a variety of purposes. In particular, he insisted that in *concept-script* the sense of an expression that is a constituent of a well-formed formula consists in its contribution to determining the truth-value which is the reference of the formula.[40] His successors seized on his 'contextual principle' and enshrined it as the foundation stone of modern philosophical semantics, viewing the sentence as taking priority over its subsentential constituents in the semantic analysis of language.

Secondly, although Frege agreed with the venerable tradition that all valid inferences are from judgments (assertions) to judgments (assertions), he emphatically distinguished (as did many of his predecessors) between the judgment or assertion and what is judged or asserted. That which is asserted (the *content* of judgment, or 'thought') can occur unasserted, e.g. in the antecedent of a conditional. This is the basis of the claim that he distinguished between *force* and *sense*. A sentence or formula may be uttered with assertoric force, but the sense it expresses (viz. that such-and-such) remains constant even if it is not asserted but occurs as the antecedent of a conditional. He did not generalize this distinction to imperatives, optatives and other syntactical forms. But it has become a major inspiration of modern philosophical semantics.

Thirdly, Frege carried further the old idea of a form of correspondence between language, thought and reality. His concept-script, conceived as a *characteristica universalis*[41] as well as a *calculus ratiocinator*, and designed according to the canons of function theory, displayed perspicuously the logical articulations of the thoughts it expressed and the metaphysical

[40] Cf. Frege, *The Basic Laws of Arithmetic*, vol. 1, §32. It is on the strength of this passage that Frege is generally held to be propounding a truth-conditional theory of meaning. This is, however, highly misleading. What he claimed was that by stipulating references for constituent names of his formulae, he also thereby assigned a sense to a well-formed formula, namely that given such-and-such references of constituent names, the conditions under which the formula (sentence) refers to the truth-value True are fixed. The thought expressed by such a formula is therefore the thought that these conditions are fulfilled, viz. that the True is the value of the denoted function for the denoted argument. Since we do not conceive of sentences as names of truth-values, nor of truth-values as objects that are the values of functions for arguments, this conception of sense (the mode of presentation of a truth-value as the value of a given function for a specified argument) cannot coherently be said to encapsulate the modern idea that the sense of a sentence is given by specification of its truth-conditions.

[41] Though rid of all the seventeenth century associations between a universal character and an international language useful for commerce and easily learnable by all, as well as the idea of a single unified taxonomic language for the whole of science.

articulations of the objects and concepts it denoted. Natural language only corresponds in a rough and ready fashion with the forms of thought and the metaphysical structure of reality. Language is not constructed from a logical blueprint, Frege insisted, and one can no more learn logic from studying grammar than one can learn how to think from a child. Natural language, he thought, is rife with vagueness, ambiguity, lack of logical perspicuity, and, indeed, logical incoherence. To a large degree he identified as 'logical defects' in a language those features of it which fail to correspond with the articulations of his concept-script. The logical powers of concept-script in the presentation of arguments so far outstripped anything hitherto available that Frege unwittingly employed his invention as a yardstick against which to measure natural language. The old idea of isomorphism between a form of representation and thought or reality was, however, resuscitated by the invention of a much improved logical calculus. This idea too was to bear fruit in the next stage in this history.

It is noteworthy that the invention of powerful formal calculi gave impetus to the 'biplanar' or Augustinian conception of language. It is a distinctive feature of Frege's calculus, conceived as an improvement over natural language for special scientific purposes, that in it all the constituent symbols (with the exception of variables and the assertion-sign) *stand for* extra-notational entities. To be sure, he distinguished entities into different logical types (objects, functions, first-level concepts, second-level concepts, etc.) and differentiated kinds of names according to the different kinds of entities they stood for (proper names, first-level concept-words, second-level concept-words, etc.). He also correlated each name not with one entity, but with two, viz. a sense and a reference, the former being an abstract entity which determined the latter as correlated with the name. But it was precisely the sophisticated function-theoretic apparatus informing these complex innovations which also preserved the fundamental Augustinian picture, since the core idea of a function is that of a law of correlation of *entities*. It took only one step from Frege to conceive of a formal calculus as a perfected syntax of a language merely awaiting an *interpretation*, which would be given by assigning entities in reality to the uninterpreted signs of the calculus.

This became even clearer in the reflections of Russell, who pursued further Frege's vision of reducing arithmetic to logic, and who developed further the formal apparatus of a rich function-theoretic calculus:[42]

[42] The following illustrative quotation postdates Russell's association with Wittgenstein, and bears the mark of the latter's influence. Russell's conception in *Principia* was very different.

In a logically perfect language the words in a proposition would correspond one by one with the components of the corresponding fact, with the exception of such words as 'or', 'not', 'if', 'then', which have a different function. In a logically perfect language, there will be one word and no more for every simple object, and everything that is not simple will be expressed by a combination of words, by a combination derived, of course, from the words for the simple things that enter in, one word for each simple component. A language of that sort will be completely analytic, and will show at a glance the logical structure of the facts asserted or denied. The language which is set forth in *Principia Mathematica* is intended to be a language of that sort. It is a language which has only syntax and no vocabulary whatsoever. Barring the omission of a vocabulary I maintain that it is quite a nice language. It aims at being that sort of language that, if you add a vocabulary, would be a logically perfect language.[43]

Russell's famous Theory of Descriptions, which showed how to paraphrase sentences containing singular referring expressions of the form 'The so-and-so' into sentences which do not, was designed to demonstrate that the appearance in ordinary language of significant phrases lacking a reference, like 'the present King of France' or 'the golden mountain', only deceptively suggested that there could be meaningful expressions which nevertheless did not stand for something. The true logical form of a sentence of the form 'The φer ψs' is 'There exists one and only one object such that it both φs and ψs', and here each significant expression, *in the forms of the language of Principia*, actually stands for something. Thus the Theory of Descriptions was designed to preserve intact the putative insights of the model of correlation enshrined in the Augustinian picture.

The conception of a logical calculus as an ideal, and ideally perspicuous, syntax to which semantics adds an interpretation by assigning entities to the constituent designating symbols was to dominate subsequent philosophical reflections.

Unlike Russell, Frege had little interest in drawing any extensive general philosophical morals from his logical investigations save in the area of philosophy of mathematics. Indeed, it was here (and not in formal or indeed philosophical logic) that the *raison d'être* of his endeavours lay. For the whole point and purpose of his labours in inventing a concept-script lay in devising a proof of the reducibility of arithmetic to logic. Apart from this, which proved a failure, he had no interest in exploring in anything but minimal detail any implications within philosophy of the possibility of representing the forms of thought and inference in the notation of a formal

---

[43] B. Russell, 'The Philosophy of Logical Atomism', in *Bertrand Russell: Logic and Knowledge, essays 1901–50*, ed. R. C. Marsh (Allen & Unwin, London, 1956), pp. 197f.

function-theoretic calculus. This task was left to his successors, in particular the young Wittgenstein.

5 The watershed

Wittgenstein differed from his predecessors above all in conceiving of logic neither as the study of language-independent relations between abstract entities nor as the study of the laws of thinking, but rather as the investigation of the fundamental forms of any system of symbolic representation whatever. One great question dominated his first book, the *Tractatus Logico-Philosophicus*: what are the most general conditions for the possibility of representation? The abstract logical structure of a correct conceptual notation would reveal, he thought, the essential nature of any possible sign-system which can represent reality. Hence, unlike his predecessors, he thought that ordinary language was in good logical order.[44] For to constitute a system of representation at all, it must have that essential structure which makes representation possible, viz. logical structure. However, that structure is not perspicuously revealed in the surface forms of a natural language, but is only uncovered by philosophical analysis. Hence investigations into an ideal logical notation are not a project of devising an 'improvement' relative to any natural language (as Russell, Frege, and their predecessors had thought) but rather a matter of bringing to light what is hidden in the symbolism of a language itself.

The essence of representation, Wittgenstein thought, lies in description, in the representation of a state of affairs by means of a proposition. Whether such a description is used to assert that that is actually how things are in reality, or whether it is used to query whether things are thus, or to order that things be made thus, is a further matter which is of no concern to logic. All that interests logic is the unasserted proposition.

Since we describe how things are in reality by means of propositions (conceived neither as abstract entities nor as mental ones but rather as sentences with a sense), the simplest possible proposition must contain whatever essential features are required for description (representation). Hence the beginning of wisdom must lie in clarification of the logical nature of the 'elementary proposition', viz. a sensible sentence which is

---

[44] This is not to say that it is without defects. Nor is it to say that it contains no pseudo-propositions. It is rather that what it does say, it says clearly. There is no halfway house between expressing a sense, and being a nonsensical pseudo-proposition. The genuine propositions of ordinary language are in good order.

logically independent of every other such sentence, i.e. which has no
(non-trivial) entailments, but merely describes the existence of an
elementary state of affairs. Investigating the essence of the elementary
proposition (which is the first part of Wittgenstein's renowned 'picture
theory of the proposition') will give the essence of all description, and that
in turn will capture the essence of the world. For what is essential for a
description is whatever makes possible the representation of states of
affairs in reality, and whatever structural features states of affairs possess
in virtue of which they can be described at all are themselves the essence
(the essential form) of reality. Wittgenstein's logical investigations were,
therefore, elaborated on a vast backcloth of the most general philosophical
import. For, in his view, the investigation into the essence of the proposition will reveal the essential nature and limits of language, the range of all
possible worlds and the limits of thought, since thought too is representation. 'My work', he wrote, 'has extended from the laws of logic to the
essence of the world'.[45]

Wittgenstein had welcomed the demise of traditional subject/predicate
logic, and greeted function-theoretic logic with enthusiasm, although also
with fundamental disagreement. Frege and Russell had pioneered the
route to the Promised Land, but had not arrived there. Like Frege and
Russell, he conceived of a proposition as a function of its constituent
expressions,[46] i.e. as decomposing into function and argument. He accepted a version of Frege's sense/reference distinction, but quarrelled with
Frege's employment of it. He conceived of sentences as having senses, but
denied that they had references. Fully analysed names had references, but
no senses. An elementary proposition, he argued, is composed of simple
indefinable names. These denote simple sempiternal objects in reality,
which were conceived as the metaphysical substance of the world (such as
spatio-temporal points; simple, unanalysable qualities). The connection of
these names with their referents is arbitrary and conventional. We combine
these names to form elementary propositions according to conventional
logico-syntactical rules which specify possible (significant) combinatorial
possibilities. These conventions determine the logical forms of the names.
To assign a given object to an arbitrary name as its referent, the logical

[45] L. Wittgenstein, *Notebooks 1914–16*, 1st edn, ed. G. H. von Wright and G. E. M.
Anscombe (Blackwell, Oxford, 1961), p. 79.
[46] Wittgenstein, *Tractatus*, 3.318; Frege had conceived of a *judgeable-content* as the value
of its constituent concept, Russell of the proposition as the value of its constituent propositional function.

syntax of the name must mirror the combinatorial possibilities of the object in reality, viz. its ability to combine with other such objects to constitute a state of affairs (e.g. a given spatio-temporal point's having such-and-such a quality). Though the names of objects are arbitrary, and though logical syntax is conventional, once these conventions are fixed by us, the relation between an elementary proposition and the state of affairs it depicts is essential and internal. The proposition must be isomorphic with the state of affairs it depicts, it must have the same logical multiplicity and identical logical form. These theses enshrined a form of the Augustinian picture at the heart of the *Tractatus*, as a picture, not of the surface forms of language, but of its underlying structure.

It is of the essence of an elementary proposition to be bi-polar, i.e. to fix a 'logical space' which reality either does or does not fill. Contrary to Frege, truth and falsity are not accidental features of a sentence with a sense, but rather to have a meaning or sense *is* to be either-true-or-false, i.e. to restrict reality to a 'Yes/No possibility'. The combination of names according to the rules of logical syntax represents, is a logical picture of, a state of affairs. Once we know the meanings of the unanalysable names, and grasp their mode of combination, we know what states of affairs are represented by their configurations in elementary sentences. To understand a proposition all that is necessary is to understand its constituents (names and form); what we then know is what is the case *if* it is true (although not necessarily whether it is true). It is this, Wittgenstein thought, that explains the fact that we can understand sentences we have never heard before. The rules of the logical calculus of language determine in advance all possible significant sentences, and mirror all possible elementary states of affairs in reality.

This doctrine of *strict* isomorphism between fully analysed sentences and reality, of an *internal, necessary,* relation between the sentence and what it depicts which is a consequence of arbitrary conventions, was indeed novel. But the depth of the gulf separating Wittgenstein's philosophy from that of his predecessors only emerges clearly in his account of molecular propositions, of the nature of their mode of combination, and of his consequent radical conception of logic, logical truth and necessity.

The *Grundgedanke* (fundamental thought) of the *Tractatus*, he announced, was that the logical constants (logical connectives, quantifiers, identity sign) are not representatives. Frege had conceived of these crucial syncategorematic expressions as denoting actual concepts and relations (unary and binary functions), mapping (*inter alia*) truth-values on to truth-values. Wittgenstein thought this was quite wrong:[47] these expressions are not names at all, and there are no such 'logical objects'. Rather, they signify 'operations' whereby we generate compound propositions from elementary ones. Any atomic proposition may be true and may be false. We can draw up truth-tables correlating any number of propositions with all possible distributions amongst them of truth-possibilities. Coordination of propositions with 'logical constants' simply indicates a select distribution of truth-possibilities amongst the constituent propositions. Thus 'p & q' is true if and only if both p and q are true; '$p \lor q$' is true if either 'p' or 'q' is true or both are true, etc. And Wittgenstein showed how the different combinations thus selected can be generated by the operation of joint negation upon sets of propositions. The logical constants are thus defined by appropriate truth-tables. The truth-grounds, or truth-conditions, of a molecular proposition consist of those distributions of truth-possibilities of its constituent propositions that make it true.

The sense of a molecular proposition is thus given by its truth-conditions, which reality may or may not satisfy. Thus 'p & q' allow reality only the conjoint realization of the states of affairs p and q, whereas '$p \lor q$' allows the realization of p alone, of q alone or of both. It is a cardinal thesis of the *Tractatus* that all significant propositions are analysable into truth-functional combinations of atomic propositions; quantified propositions are conceived to be infinite conjunctions or disjunctions of propositions, and apparently non-extensional contexts (such as 'It is necessarily true that p' and 'A believes p') are shown by analysis either to be pseudo-propositions or to be, in fact, extensional.

---

[47] He gave various reasons, e.g. (i) the so-called 'primitive signs' of logic '$\sim$', '$\lor$', '$\supset$', '&', are interdefinable, hence not genuine primitive signs, nor names of relations; (ii) a function cannot be its own argument (one cannot substitute the function 'ξ is a fish' in the argument place of 'ξ is a fish', but one can take the result of an operation, e.g. '$\sim p$' and use it as the base for that very operation to produce '$\sim\sim p$'; (iii) operations can 'vanish', e.g. $\sim\sim p = p$, $\sim(\exists x)\sim fx = (x)fx$, $(\exists x)fx. (x = a) = fa$; (iv) If '$\sim$' were a function name, then '$\sim\sim p$' would be a different proposition from 'p'; (v) If '$\sim$' were a genuine function, infinitely many propositions would follow from every elementary proposition, viz. '$\sim\sim p$', '$\sim\sim\sim\sim p$', etc., which is absurd. He also pointed out that Frege's explanation of negation as a function which takes the true as its value for the false as argument (and the false as value for any other object as argument) leaves the *sense* of this function absolutely undetermined, despite these stipulations. For on this account, provided 'p' and 'q' have the same truth-value, e.g., false, then '$\sim p$' and '$\sim q$' would have the same sense, viz. that the false falls under the concept of negation, which is absurd.

His reasoning was extended, with additional arguments, to encompass identity and quantification.

Typically the truth-value of a molecular proposition will depend on how truth-values are distributed among its constituents. But there are two limiting cases, viz. a tautology, which is true however truth-values are assigned to its constituents, and a contradiction, which is false however such as assignment is made. Tautologies and contradictions are the *propositions of logic*, e.g. $\sim(p \;\&\; \sim p)$, $((p \supset q) \;\&\; p) \supset q$. They are limiting cases of propositions, for they are not bi-polar: tautologies leave open, as it were, the whole of logical space, since they are true however things are in the world, and contradictions close off the whole of logical space, since they are false no matter what. The propositions of logic have no sense, for they have no truth-conditions, tautologies being unconditionally true, contradictions unconditionally false.

All true propositions of logic, Wittgenstein thought, are tautologies. And all, uniformly, have no content. They do not, as Frege thought, describe fundamental timeless relations between abstract entities, nor are they, as Russell believed, a description of the most general features of the universe. They are simply (senseless) consequences of the essence of any symbolism for combining propositions:

some things are arbitrary in the symbols that we use and . . . some things are not. In logic it is only the latter that express: but that means that logic is not a field in which *we* express what we wish with the help of signs, but rather one in which the nature of the natural and inevitable signs speaks for itself . . .

One can calculate whether a proposition belongs to logic, by calculating the logical properties of the *symbol*.

And this is what we do when we 'prove' a logical proposition. For, without bothering about sense or meaning, we construct the logical proposition out of others by using only *rules that deal with signs*.[48]

This essentialist but syntactical conception of logical truth dispersed the clouds of psychologistic and Platonist mysteries that had always enshrouded the notion of logical necessity.[49] Logical necessity, Wittgenstein thought, was merely a consequence of the inevitable nature of the logical syntax for the compounding of propositions. And the only genuine (express-

[48] Wittgenstein, *Tractatus*, 6.124, 6.126.
[49] Only in the 1930s did he shed the essentialism to produce a conventionalist account of necessity. Hobbes, in *De Corpore*, and Berkeley, in his private notebooks later published as *Philosophical Commentaries*, had similar inklings. But neither developed or attempted to demonstrate this thesis. The *Tractatus*, however, inspired the conventionalism of the Vienna Circle.

ible) necessity is logical.[50] His bold thesis of analysis (viz. that every proposition has a *unique* analysis into truth-functional combinations of elementary propositions), his truth-tabular definitions of the logical connectives and his demonstration that the propositions of logic are tautologies and that all inference is mere tautological transformation, led to a major reorientation of the conception of logic.

Unlike Frege, Wittgenstein insisted that one can draw inferences from false, unasserted, propositions. He objected to Frege's presentation of logic as an axiomatic system resting on a privileged set of self-evident axioms. 'All the propositions of logic are of equal status: it is not the case that some of them are essentially primitive propositions and others essentially derived propositions.'[51] All the propositions of logic follow from operations generating tautologies out of tautologies; which is selected as the starting point is entirely arbitrary. Whether a proposition is a tautology is settled conclusively by the decision-procedure of the truth-table method. Proof in logic, in which a logical truth is 'derived' from premises which ultimately rest on axioms, is merely an expedient for recognizing complicated tautologies, which can be done by direct inspection of truth-tables. Logic is not a science resting on self-evident axioms, but the manipulation of signs determined by rules of logical syntax. 'If we know the logical syntax of any sign-language, then we have already been given all the propositions of logic'.[52] Logic has no grounds. It must, Wittgenstein insisted, 'take care of itself'.

It is not only logic, but philosophy itself that emerges from the furnaces of the *Tractatus* in a new mould. The analysis of the underlying structure of language brought to light the nature of logical necessity. It also purported to clarify the essential limits of what can be said in a language. The cardinal propositions of philosophy, conceived since the dawn of the subject as revealing ultimate truths about the nature of reality, the metaphysical structure of the world, transpire to be ill-formed propositions which violate the rules of logical syntax. They are not bi-polar, since they are conceived as *necessary* truths about reality. But only bi-polar propositions picture reality; and only tautologies are necessary truths, and

---

[50] Metaphysical truths such as abound in the *Tractatus* itself were clearly conceived as necessary, but, according to Wittgenstein, could not be expressed in language save by nonsensical pseudo-propositions that violate logical syntax. He later relinquished the idea that grammatical rules (logical syntax) mirror the essence of reality, arguing instead that the apparent structure of reality is merely the shadow of grammatical conventions.

[51] Wittgenstein, *Tractatus*, 6.127.

[52] Ibid., *Tractatus*, 6. 124.

they say nothing about the world. The typical philosophical 'propositions' employ illegitimate categorial concepts (substance, property, concept, etc.) as if they were genuine names, but analysis reveals them to be variables, not names. Consequently these metaphysical pronouncements are no more than pseudo-propositions. What task then remains for philosophy? Philosophy is a critique of language. By logical analysis of language it makes clear the legitimate empirical propositions correctly expressed in the confusing garb of the surface grammar of a natural language, and it demonstrates the illegitimacy, the nonsensicality, of putative philosophical propositions. There are, and can be, no genuine philosophical propositions. Philosophy is not a body of doctrine, but an activity of clarification.

From this highly compressed sketch of *some* of the main theses of the *Tractatus* it is worth extracting a list of fundamental principles most of which were to play a pivotal role in subsequent developments in philosophy:

(i) Ordinary language is in good logical order.

(ii) The essential function of a language is depiction (description): the representation of a state of affairs, which may or may not be realized.

(iii) Assertions, questions, commands, optations contain a descriptive component (the unasserted proposition, later called 'the propositional-radical'). It alone, the differences being relegated to psychology, is of concern to logic.

(iv) Every proposition has a unique analysis. The surface grammar of a sentence conceals its logical form; logical analysis reveals its underlying structure.

(v) All elementary propositions are logically independent of each other. They are the last (propositional) product of analysis.

(vi) The elementary proposition is isomorphic with the state of affairs it depicts, and is internally related to it.

(vii) The sense of an elementary proposition is a function of (the meanings of) its constituent names and its mode of composition.

(viii) Knowledge of the meanings of constituents of propositions (names and forms) suffices for understanding the sense of any proposition. This is how it is possible to understand without fresh explanation sentences never encountered before.

(ix) Every compound proposition is a truth-function of elementary propositions (thesis of extensionality). Hence every meaningful proposition is constructible by a series of operations on elementary propositions.

 (x) The sense of a compound proposition is given by its truth-conditions, i.e. the expression of agreement and disagreement with the truth-possibilities of its constituent elementary propositions.

 (xi) All entailments are consequences of inner complexity of propositions. One proposition entails another if the truth-grounds of the first include those of the second. Logical analysis will lay bare the logical powers of propositions.

 (xii) A language is, *au fond*, a calculus of signs. A correct function-theoretic logical calculus reveals the essential structure of any possible language.

 (xiii) Speakers of a language possess tacit knowledge of the underlying forms and elements of a language which are concealed by surface grammar. Enormously complicated tacit conventions are presupposed by everyday speech.

 (xiv) All necessity is logical necessity; logical necessity is a consequence of syntactical rules for the use of signs requisite for any system of representation by a symbolism.

 (xv) Philosophy is the activity of clarification of a language by logical analysis.

Wittgenstein's successors, first the logical positivists and then theorists of meaning, accepted at least a *version* of most (though not all) of these principles. Wittgenstein himself was later to repudiate most (though not all) of them. Ironically, those he retained tended to be precisely those which philosophers, toiling along the paths plotted out by the *Tractatus*, repudiated. Like Captain Nolan at Balaclava, Wittgenstein tried to warn his followers from galloping headlong in the direction which he had wrongly pointed out to them. And like Nolan's, his warnings went unheeded.

CHAPTER 2

Sense and Force:
the Evolution of the Species

1 The background environment

Inspired by the *Tractatus* and taking encouragement from the writings of Tarski and Carnap, troops of philosophers have charged off in the direction of elaborating theories of meaning for natural languages on the foundation of the principle that the meaning of a sentence is its truth-conditions. They conceive of such a theory as a finite array of axioms (the definitions of the primitive terms of the language) and a finite set of principles (specifications of how each of the formation- and transformation-rules which suffice to deliver all well-formed type-sentences contributes to determining the meaning of a complex expression from the meanings of its parts). Together these are thought to constitute a deductive system the theorems of which give the meanings of the well-formed sentences by stating, in a canonical form, their truth-conditions. Such a theory is also held to specify the meaning of any subsentential expression (including the primitives) by clarifying its contribution to the truth-conditions of any sentence in which it may occur. The fundamental achievement is advertised as a demonstration of how the meaning of a sentence depends on its structure and the meanings of its constituent words, for this makes transparent 'how finite resources suffice to explain the infinite semantic capacities of language'.[1]

Philosophers have been reinforced in this crusade by legions of theoretical linguists. They labour in the faith that a language is a system (or a system of systems). The task of anything worthy of the label 'a semantic *theory*' must be to expose general features of well-formed expressions

[1] D. Davidson, 'Semantics for Natural Languages', in *Linguaggi nella Società e nella Tecnica*, ed. B. Visentini (Edizioni di Comunità, Milan, 1970), p. 177.

which have systematic effects on the determination of the meanings of those expressions. Many linguists apparently consider that the best hope to achieve such a theory lies in exploiting the identification of the meaning of a sentence with its truth-conditions. On this basis a flourishing branch of linguistics seeks to 'account for the meaning of each expression on the basis of a patterned exhibition of a finite number of features'.[2]

The effort and enthusiasm lavished by philosophers and linguists on truth-conditional semantic theories is most remarkable. So too is the convergence of ideas and purposes between these two very different groups of theorists. To anybody who conceives of the construction of a semantic theory as an enterprise *au fond* scientific, the convergence itself fosters the conviction that both packs must be hot on the scent of the truth. Surely, it seems, the framework of investigation must be sound, and any residual conundrums will ultimately be removed by progressive sophistication and refinement of accepted concepts and principles.

On the other hand, the bystander must immediately be struck by the precariousness of the theorists' position. Indeed, they seem to be threatened with a complete rout once battle is joined. The reason for this is simple. The meaning of any expression is taken to be its contribution to the truth-conditions of any sentence in which it occurs. But many sentences are not expressions of anything that can be evaluated in the dimension of truth and falsity. It would be nonsense to declare that what the sentences 'When was the battle of Hastings fought?' or 'Turn out the light before you go to bed!' express is true or false. Yet, if such sentences cannot be characterized as true or false, would it not follow that it is nonsense to speak of their *truth-conditions*? More well-formed sentences of a natural language apparently fall outside the scope of such a theory of meaning than fall within it. Consequently, as a *general* theory of meaning, it is a non-starter. It must be declared bankrupt before it has even started trading. Could anybody seriously contend that questions, requests, and commands have no meanings? Or that their constituent words are deprived of meanings in these sentence-frames? Would it be any better to claim that individual words have *different* meanings in non-assertoric utterances?

In the face of this threat, some protective reaction seems required. The standard manoeuvre is to introduce a distinction between the *sense* of a sentence and its *force*. Different theorists draw such a distinction in different ways, or more accurately, they draw many different distinctions among which there is a complex set of interrelationships. But they are

---

[2] Ibid., p. 177.

guided by a number of principles which generate kinship among the *forms* of the various sense/force distinctions. To a first approximation, a sense/force distinction distinguishes within type-sentences components, features, or aspects which are bearers of sense and force and which meet the following constraints:

(i) *Every* type-sentence has both a sense and a force, i.e. both a 'sense-conveying component' and a 'force-indicator'.

(ii) The force of a sentence determines (at least in part) what *speech-act* is performed by an utterance of this sentence, e.g. whether a question is asked, an assertion made, or an hypothesis aired.

(iii) Only a *complete* type-sentence has a force. (A half-sentence cannot be used to perform any such speech-act.)

(iv) There is a *high degree of freedom* in combining senses with forces. Almost any sense can be attached to any given force, and almost any force can be linked to a given sense. In particular, any sense whatever can be endowed with assertoric force. (Equivalently, there is a great latitude in combining 'sense-conveying components' with 'force-indicators'.)

(v) The sense of a sentence is a *bearer of truth-values*. Hence it can be ascribed *truth-conditions*. The force of a sentence has no connection with truth and falsity, and therefore it has no bearing on the specification of truth-conditions. (Accordingly, a 'force-indicator' must lack sense and a 'sense-conveying component' must lack force.)

The role of a sense/force distinction is to relate the uses of non-assertoric sentences systematically to entities (the senses of sentences) which are exhaustively characterized by reference to truth-conditions. A theory of force would embroider on the following simple model: a speaker understands the sentence 'Is it raining?' if he knows that it is typically uttered to ask a question and if he can identify that what is asked is whether the proposition that it is raining (viz. the same proposition which is asserted in the sentence 'It is raining') is true.

A viable distinction between sense and force would justify a division of labour. Truth-conditional semantics will be confined to specifying the senses of sentences, leaving the clarification of any principles concerning force to another science (pragmatics). Provided that every meaningful sentence, whether or not what it expresses is open to assessment as true or false, is systematically related to something which bears truth-values and hence can intelligibly be held to have truth-conditions, and provided that this transformation does not map sentences obviously different in meaning on to the same entity, then the possibility emerges of arguing that truth-conditional semantics does offer a complete theory of meaning for the sentences of a language. This possibility would be realized, it seems, by the construction of a theory which specified how systematically to determine the force of a sentence and how systematically to relate its force and its truth-conditions to its actual use in communication.[3] Such a theory could then be applied to block derivation of the theses that non-assertoric utterances have no meaning and that words differ in sense in assertoric and non-assertoric utterances. Protected by unlimited drawing rights on an hypothetical theory of force, truth-conditional semantics, apparently solvent again, is suddenly back in business. Without this support it would apparently have to wind up. No wonder a philosopher declares 'It is difficult to see how a systematic theory of meaning for a language is possible without acknowledging the distinction between sense and force, or one closely similar.'[4] The sense/force distinction is widely held to be a *sine qua non* of truth-conditional semantics, hence indirectly of the analysis of the logical structure of language and the essential nature of human understanding. 'We should not have the least idea,' it is alleged, 'how such a theory of meaning might be constructed if we were not familiar with the distinction, introduced by Frege, between sense and force.'[5] The idea has an independent appeal to theoretical linguists. They can elaborate the notion of force into a theory of pragmatic performance, viz.

a theory about how speakers and hearers figure out the utterance-meaning of sentences used in non-null contexts on the basis of their knowledge of grammatical principles and information about the contexts . . . The conception of a theory of pragmatic performance is introduced only to provide a theoretically motivated distinction between the domains of semantics and pragmatics that will enable us to keep questions about the use of sentences out of semantics.[6]

---

[3] M. A. E. Dummett, 'What is a Theory of Meaning? (II)', in *Truth and Meaning*, ed. G. Evans and J. McDowell (Oxford University Press, Oxford, 1976), p. 74.

[4] M. A. E. Dummett, *Truth and Other Enigmas* (Duckworth, London, 1978), p. 450.

[5] M. A. E. Dummett, 'What is a Theory of Meaning?', in *Mind and Language*, ed. S. Guttenplan (Clarendon Press, Oxford, 1975), p. 72.

[6] J. J. Katz, *Propositional Structure and Illocutionary Force: A Study of the Contribution of Sentence Meaning to Speech Acts* (Harvester, Sussex, 1977), p. xiii; but some linguists, e.g. G. Gazdar, follow philosophers in defining pragmatics simply as what lies outside truth-conditional semantics.

The sense/force distinction thus offers a fresh justification for a traditional division of labour within theoretical linguistics.

Distinguishing sense from force is not merely an artificial manoeuvre promising strategic advantages, but rather an idea enjoying strong intuitive support. Two independent lines of thought converge on it. One takes rise from nomenclature of traditional European grammar. Different moods are differentiated in the conjugation of verbs: indicative, imperative, subjunctive, and (in some languages) optative. Also, sentences are classified into different forms: declarative, interrogative, and imperative. These terms indicate relations between the forms or constituents of sentences and their standard uses. A simple declarative sentence whose verb is indicative is typically used to make an assertion, an interrogative sentence to ask a question, and an imperative to issue an order or request. In the standard classification of verb-forms and sentence-structures we seem to be already familiar with the rudiments of a theory of force. Of course, the correspondence between grammatical characterizations and the uses of sentences is only rough and approximate (e.g. an interrogative sentence may be used on occasion to make a statement, i.e. as a 'rhetorical question'), but modern linguists and philosophers might well be able to refine these intuitions into a precise theory for each particular language. It is also noteworthy that traditional grammar adumbrates systematic relations between different sentence-forms. Common school exercises concentrate on transforming declarative sentences into corresponding sentence-questions, positive imperatives into corresponding negative ones, etc. Standard classifications are linked with a simple network of rough correspondences, which once again look like raw materials for building rigorous theories. Moods and basic sentence-forms provide a gateway into a theory of force.

The second source of inspiration for differentiating sense from force is reflection on the patterns of reports in indirect speech. If a speaker addresses the sentence 'What time is it?' to a passer-by, we would record what he did by saying 'He asked what time it was'; if he responds to a request for a weather-forecast by saying 'It will rain', we might make the report 'He predicted that it would rain', etc. Four features of such reports are noteworthy. First, there are more or less systematic methods for generating statements in *oratio obliqua*, methods which are often taught and learned in language-classes. Secondly, reports in indirect speech fall into two parts: the specification (more or less precise) of what act the speaker performed by uttering a sentence (e.g. 'he *asserted* that . . .' or 'he *promised* that . . .') and the identification of the object of this act (e.g. 'What he asserted was *that nitrogen liquifies* at −179 °C' or 'What he asked was *what time it was*'). The main verb typically indicates the act performed, the indirect statement (indirect question, etc.) the object of this act. Thirdly, this articulation makes perspicuous the facts that different speech-acts (e.g. assertion, conjecture, and supposal) may have the same object and that the same act may have different objects. There are two independent dimensions in which to describe what speakers do by uttering sentences, and this gives rise to multiple possibilities for describing connections between utterances. Finally, indirect statements are the typical grammatical subjects of predications of truth and falsity. If, e.g. I utter the sentence 'Herodotus understood ancient Persian', then what I have asserted (viz. that Herodotus understood ancient Persian) is false. Consequently, the expression specifying the object of an assertion, prediction, conjecture, etc. is apparently the designation of a bearer of truth-values. These four features of indirect speech mesh with some of the requirements for a theory built on distinguishing sense from force. Paraphrasing utterances into *oratio obliqua* makes explicit what speech-act the uttered sentence was used to perform, and at the same time it offers a systematic way of extracting from the uttered sentence another expression (the corresponding indirect statement) which expresses something true or false and thus is capable of being characterized by its truth-conditions. The indirect statement can therefore be regarded as a formulation of the sense of the sentence whose utterance is reported in *oratio obliqua*. And since the identification of the speech-act performed in uttering this sentence depends on features of the uttered sentence together with relevant aspects of the particular circumstances of its utterance, the force of the sentence can be identified with the typical use of sentences displaying these features. The route from utterances to reports in *oratio obliqua* traces out a general contour-line the exact delineation of which seems to be the proper business of a theory of sense and a complementary theory of force.

The support that each of these separate considerations affords to distinguishing sense from force is redoubled, it seems, by the observation that the two lines of reasoning can be dovetailed together. The features of sentences which determine jointly with the context what are the correct reports of the speech-acts performed by particular utterances are plausibly just those familiar aspects of sentences distinguished in traditional grammatical classifications of sentence-forms and the moods of verbs. Hence somebody who introduced a sense/force distinction on the basis of *oratio obliqua* reports would be led to attend to the same fundamental features of sentences as somebody who began from the traditional correspondences between grammatical aspects of sentences and the typical uses of these sentences. Even more impressive, however, is the fact that differences in mood and sentence-forms can be directly matched in sentences exploiting the resources of indirect speech. Instead of uttering the sentence 'Hydrogen is lighter than oxygen' to make an assertion, I could instead utter the sentence 'I assert that hydrogen is lighter than oxygen'; instead of saying 'What time is it?' to ask the time, I might say 'I wonder what time it is' or 'I would like to know what time it is'; and instead of saying 'Shut the door' to give somebody an order, I might say 'I order you to shut the door'. In the case of each of those paraphrases, the corresponding report of the utterance in indirect speech exactly matches the structure of the sentence uttered, and hence it seems that each of these paraphrases contains a phrase ('I assert . . .', 'I wonder . . .', 'I order . . .') which makes explicit the use to which the utterance is actually put. The possibility of transforming sentences into ones of this general form seems to put the sense/force distinction beyond question. For, in each paraphrase, the prefix apparently indicates what the force is (and nothing but the force), while the indirect statement, question, or command states what the sense is (and nothing but the sense). Clarifying how the distinction between sense and force is to be drawn for sentences of a given natural language will apparently be tantamount to explaining how to determine whether particular paraphrases of this form are correct or not. Everything seems to point to the possibility and importance of distinguishing sense from force and of applying this distinction in constructing a theory of meaning for a language.

It is altogether unsurprising to find that part of the standard procedure of theorists of meaning is to do just this. Indeed, so standard has this become that the performance is fully ritualized. Frequently no explanation at all is supplied of how the terms 'sense' and 'force' (or their equivalents) are to be employed. It is supposedly enough for a theorist to announce that he intends 'to analyze all sentences, declarative or non-declarative, into two components: a *sentence-radical* that specifies a state of affairs and a *mood* that determines whether the speaker is declaring that the state of affairs holds, commanding that it hold, asking whether it holds, or what'.[7] Every competent theorist is presumed to understand and to accept the intended distinction; no major uncertainty is envisaged, and no doubts are canvassed or countered. Apparently there is universal agreement about a

---

[7] David Lewis, 'General Semantics', in *Semantics of Natural Language*, 2nd edn, ed. D. Davidson and G. Harman (Reidel, Dordrecht, 1972), pp. 205f.

unique distinction between sense and force. This underpins a clear division of labour between semantics and pragmatics, and it transforms a seemingly insuperable objection to truth-conditional semantics into a vindication of this general framework for investigating the notion of meaning.

2 Phylogenesis

A distinction of sense from force can be used to turn the tables against the most obvious objection to the thesis that the meaning of a sentence is its truth-conditions. The argument, which we have just sketched, to a considerable degree recapitulates the evolution of the modern versions of this distinction.

The idea that the typical use of a sentence corresponds to such conspicuous features of it as the mood of the main verb and its syntactic form is an ancient one among grammarians, logicians, and philosophers. For example, the Port-Royal *Grammar* suggested that the different moods of the verb signify different 'movements of the soul' (affirmation, desire, and command); the indicative was thought to manifest the attitude of judgment towards thoughts, while the subjunctive, optative, and imperative were held to manifest different volitive attitudes.[8] The authoritative status accorded to the works of the Port-Royal school guaranteed that these doctrines remained part of the conventional wisdom of educated men down to very modern times. Frege shows the influence of these ideas in his convictions that the assertoric force of an utterance is bound up with the indicative mood of the verb[9] and that the assertoric utterance of a sentence is the outward counterpart of a psychological act of judging a thought to be true. So too does Russell in his claim that the three sentences 'Beggars are riders', 'Are beggars riders?', and 'Beggars shall be riders' each present the same proposition, adding that in the first this is asserted, in the second presented as the object of a doubt and in the third as the object of a volition.[10] Even Wittgenstein accepted a similar doctrine at the time of the *Tractatus*, for he characterized the difference between judgments (assertions), commands, and questions as merely psychological, and hence he denied any proper place in logic to Frege's judgment-stroke which was

---

[8] *Grammaire Générale et Raisonnée*, chs XIII and XVI.

[9] G. Frege, *Posthumous Writings*, ed. H. Hermes et al. (Blackwell, Oxford, 1979), pp. 2, 129, 139, 149, 194, 198, 252; 'The Thought', in *Philosophical Logic*, ed. P. F. Strawson (Oxford University Press, Oxford, 1967), p. 22.

[10] B. Russell, 'Theory of Knowledge' (unpublished typescript, 1913), p. 196.

introduced to represent assertoric force.[11] All these authors suggest that a general correspondence holds between grammatical distinctions and different uses of sentences, and all three follow tradition in relating the different uses of sentences to differences in mental acts, states, or attitudes.

Frege is widely thought to have made a decisive advance on this conventional wisdom. A distinction between sense and force is commonly catalogued among his major achievements, and he is universally hailed by modern theorists as the ultimate source of inspiration for their own sense/force distinctions. What support is there for these dramatic claims? His rather perfunctory remarks about sentence-forms in natural languages hardly seem to merit any accolade. Others had noticed rough correspondences between uttering declarative sentences and making assertions, between uttering interrogative sentences and asking questions, etc. And so too had they suggested that different speech-acts manifested different relations of speakers to common objects (ideas, propositions, contents). Where was Frege's originality? It is all tied up with his concept-script. He introduced a special symbol (the 'judgment-stroke' or 'assertion-sign') to express the act of judging something to be true.[12] In the conviction that the clear representation of this act is essential to judging the cogency of an inference in concept-script, he prefaced this symbol to every separate stage of a proof, i.e. to every premise, to every intermediate conclusion, and finally to the proposition to be proved. Hence every line of a proof in concept-script has the general form

$\vdash A$

Here the vertical bar signals the act of judgment, while the rest of the formula (the 'content-stroke' or 'horizontal' and the other symbols) merely expresses the proposition, thought, or idea which is judged to be true. It is this articulation of Frege's symbolism which has so inspired later theorists.

Although he introduced his notation in *Begriffsschrift* with an explanation that mentioned his intention to symbolize the act of judgment and 'judgeable-contents', he later altered his terminology and referred to 'assertoric force' and 'thoughts' (i.e. 'senses of sentences'). Apparently he

---

[11] L. Wittgenstein, *Notebooks 1914–16*, ed. G. H. von Wright and G. E. M. Anscombe (Blackwell, Oxford, 1961), p. 96; *Tractatus*, 4.023, 4.442.

[12] G. Frege, *Begriffsschrift*, tr. T. W. Bynum, in *Conceptual Notation and related articles* (Clarendon Press, Oxford, 1972), §2; *The Basic Laws of Arithmetic*, vol. 1, tr. and ed. M. Furth (University of California Press, Berkeley, 1964), §5.

held that the addition of assertoric force is necessary to make the expression of a thought into an assertion, and therefore the 'judgment-stroke' could be viewed indifferently as symbolizing assertoric force or the act of assertion. Since the rest of a well-formed line of a proof in concept-script is the mere expression of a thought, a distinction between *sense* and assertoric *force* is transparent in the articulation of his symbolism. Frege also stressed that these two elements are independent of each other. Any thought expressed with assertoric force can also be expressed without it, and any true thought expressed without assertoric force may legitimately be combined with this force. In particular, he harped on the thesis that the antecedent of a conditional expresses a thought without assertoric force. This case he cited as conclusive proof that any thought may be expressed without being asserted to be true. Finally, he distinguished the judgment-stroke from another symbol in concept-script which expressed a different act, viz. the 'double-stroke of definition ⊩'. This can be prefixed only to a well-formed formula whose principal logical constant is the identity-sign; it is not used to express a judgment, but rather to lay down a rule that a newly introduced symbol is to have the same content or sense as an already understood symbol.[13] Hence he apparently included a contrasting pair of force-indicators in his concept-script as well as symbolizing the difference between presence and absence of assertoric force.

The excitement derived from these explanations is enhanced by some important asides. One is a late observation about interrogative sentences. Frege declared that a declarative sentence and the corresponding sentence-question 'contain the same thought'; they differ in that the first 'contains an assertion', while the second 'contains a request'.[14] He did not, however, suggest that imperative or optative sentences express the same thought as corresponding declaratives, indeed he explicitly denied that they express thoughts at all. The other noteworthy observation is that the introduction of the judgment-stroke into concept-script is grounded in the 'dissociation of assertoric force from the predicate'.[15] This has the ring of a decisive repudiation of the venerable dogma that the indicative mood of the verb or the copula is what effects the act of assertion. And this in turn makes possible a definitive dissolution of philosophical puzzles about deductive inference. It seems, for example, that *modus ponens* involves a *petitio*, since the conclusion that *q* is already asserted in the premise that if *p* then *q*

[13] Frege, *Begriffsschrift*, §23; *The Basic Laws of Arithmetic*, vol. 1, §27.
[14] Frege, 'The Thought', p. 21.
[15] Frege, *Posthumous Writings*, pp. 185, 198.

(hence independently of knowing whether it is true that *p*). By distinguishing assertion from predication, Frege allegedly cleared up this confusion. Predication is relevant to sense alone, while assertion is a matter of force.

This whole case for honouring Frege as the founder of what is now understood to be a sense/force distinction rests on misinterpretations of his writings and on turning a blind eye to defects and confusions in his thinking. His own explanation of his formal symbolism is arguably incoherent and certainly sabotages the purpose for which we might wish to use it. In the background of his exposition are two mistakes. One is the claim that inference is possible only from judgments or assertions, i.e. from thoughts actually advanced as true. This is the ultimate rationale for the need to symbolize the act of assertion (or assertoric force) in concept-script. And it is, by modern lights, an obvious blunder. The second misconception is that the predicate of a declarative sentence *is* what *carries* assertoric force. Since he deliberately abandoned subject/predicate structure in the symbolization of judgments in his concept-script, he had to invent a special symbol to serve as the *vehicle* of assertoric force; otherwise any formula in his notation would necessarily lack assertoric force, and hence it would be inadmissible in any cogent proof. 'Dissociation of assertoric force from the predicate', far from repudiating it, actually reaffirms the doctrine traditional in earlier grammar and logic. If either of these misapprehensions had been corrected, Frege's entire case for introducing the judgment-stroke would have collapsed. Moreover, without a commitment to a quasi-mechanical conception of assertoric force, even conceding that inferences must hold among assertions need not justify his notation; his purpose would have been served as well by the stipulation that every independent line in a proof is to be taken to have assertoric force.

The more immediate purpose of Frege's novel symbolism diverges from the rationale for modern sense/force distinctions. He intended to mark in his notation the distinction between a judgment (a judgeable-content or thought judged to be true) and a mere judgeable-content (or mere thought).[16] But his point was not to contrast the use of a complete sentence to make an assertion with the use of the same (or another) complete sentence to perform another speech-act (e.g. formulating a conjecture or framing a supposition), but rather to contrast the use of an expression as a complete sentence to make an assertion with the use of the same expression as a clause in a compound sentence (e.g. a conditional or disjunction)

[16] Ibid., pp. 11n., 185, 198.

where it is not used to perform any speech-act at all (or at least none coordinate with making an assertion, asking a question, etc.). These are altogether different issues. In the first case, the alternative to having assertoric force is having some other force (e.g. imperative or interrogative), whereas in the second it is having no force at all. The second case can in fact be dealt with by a single completely general principle, viz. it makes sense to ask what speech-act is performed by uttering an expression (or what force this expression has) only if the expression uttered is a *complete* sentence (i.e. not part of some more complex sentence). It may be important to note that no clause ever is used to make an assertion – important at least for avoiding philosophical confusions. But this simple point can be established without any general investigation of speech-acts. That strategy was the one that Frege followed. He strove to make clear that a thought may occur unasserted as part of a thought which is asserted. In such cases, he held (misleadingly) that a speaker 'expresses a thought' without judging it to be true. Relatively late he cited an actor's declaiming on the stage and someone's uttering a sentence-question as further instances of expressing a thought. But his purpose was not to investigate these speech-acts; it was to prove that 'it is possible to express the thought without laying it down as true'.[17] In fact he conflated two distinct issues under the label 'to express a thought' (below, pp. 101–2), and hence this putative proof is fallacious.

More detailed inspection of his writings renders even more absurd the contention that Frege introduced a sense/force distinction along modern lines. His suggestion that sentence-questions express the same thoughts as the corresponding declarative sentences was strictly limited. He did not claim that word-questions express thoughts, and he denied that imperatives and optatives do. This rules out any possibility of using his distinction of sense from force to encompass all sentence-forms within a framework of analysis based on truth-conditions. Moreover, he refrained from referring to interrogative force.[18] His conception of sentence-questions has clear precedents, and in any case it is not even consistent with his own analysis of *oratio obliqua* (because the sense expressed by a declarative sentence is designated by an indirect statement while that expressed by a sentence-question is designated by an indirect question; but a corresponding such pair of expressions are not intersubstitutable *salva significatione*, let alone *salva veritate*, hence they cannot be co-designative). Finally, his symbolism for concept-script does not exploit the possibility of contrast-

---

[17] Frege, 'The Thought', p. 21.
[18] Still less did he broach the issue of the 'force' of the lines spoken by an actor on the stage!

ing assertoric force with any other. Although the assertion-sign has an apparent foil in the double-stroke of definition, the latter cannot be construed as attaching some non-assertoric force to a thought for the simple reason that the formula to which it is prefixed does not yet have any sense at all. Almost none of the distinctive principles informing modern sense/force distinctions are satisfied by Frege's representation of sense and force.

Russell and Wittgenstein moved somewhat closer to modern forms of a sense/force distinction. Russell envisaged that a common 'proposition' could be filtered out of appropriately related declarative, interrogative, imperative, and optative sentences. This 'proposition' he held, might be expressed in a form denuded of force, viz. a verbal noun. So the proposition common to 'The cat is on the mat', 'Is the cat on the mat?', 'Would that the cat were on the mat' is expressed by 'The cat's being on the mat'. He did not develop this curious idea. His purpose was eliminative: he wished to brush aside those aspects of sentences which do not bear on the act of grasping a proposition which alone is the proper subject-matter of logical investigation. Wittgenstein had a parallel negative aim: he banished the distinction between assertions, commands, and questions from the domain of logic in order to focus exclusively on the 'unasserted proposition'. Neither had a theory of force.[19] Both in effect declared force to be irrelevant to logic, and both left in the dark the question of how to settle whether different sentences (or utterances) expressed the same proposition.

It was the growth of truth-conditional semantics which supplied as it were the genetic impulse favourable to the development of modern versions of a sense/force distinction. In the hands of the logical positivists, the basic principle of truth-conditional semantics was transformed into the principle of verifiability: the meaning of a sentence is the method or conditions of its verification. Non-declarative sentences were pushed to the sidelines as cognitively meaningless, and so too were many declarative sentences. Pronouncements in metaphysics, religion, and morals were widely condemned. Moral utterances were likened to imperatives or to ejaculations of approval and disapproval (e.g. 'Up with honesty' or 'Murder – ugh!'), and they were held to be beyond the pale of logic and rational deliberations (so that 'practical *reasoning*' was considered a misnomer). The influence of logical positivism was widespread immediately before and after the Second World War.

[19] Any more than Frege had a theory of modality (cf. *Begriffsschrift*, §4); indeed their attitude to force resembles his attitude to modality.

The modern notion of force first made a conspicuous appearance in writings *critical* of this form of truth-conditional semantics. The leading figure of this reaction was J. L. Austin. As early as 1946 he suggested that philosophers, under the influence of logical positivism, begin many investigations of concepts by committing the 'descriptive fallacy'.[20] Epistemologists go astray in this way. They consider that a sentence such as 'I know that it is a goldfinch', because of its declarative form, must be used to make a statement; they then enquire into what would make it true, thereby treating it as a description of the speaker's performance of 'a specially striking feat of cognition, superior, [but] in the same scale as believing and being sure'.[21] According to Austin's diagnosis, this generated nonsense. The expression 'I know', like 'I promise', is really used, he argued, not to describe or report anything, but to *do* something, or to *perform* an act. Hence he dubbed these expressions 'performatives' and sentences containing them 'performative utterances'. He originally argued that such utterances cannot be assessed in the dimension of truth and falsity at all and that they lack truth-conditions because they are not descriptions. Therefore a proper account of what they mean, how they are used, and what constitutes a successful performance of these speech-acts (the 'felicity-conditions' of promising, ordering, etc.) lies beyond the scope of truth-conditional semantics. A full account of the utterances of a natural language requires a further supplementary theory for non-descriptive utterances. This will give a philosophical analysis of what it is for an utterance to *have the force* of a promise, order, request, greeting, etc. The variety of forces that utterances may have, i.e. the variety of distinct speech-acts that they may be used to perform, is enormous, whereas truth-conditional semantics is capable of clarifying only those expressions which are used to make statements or give descriptions.

Austin soon expanded his critical remarks into the outline of a novel positive theory[22] which was meant to embrace both performative utterances and assertions (or descriptions). He suggested that every utterance (and its constituents) has a more or less definite sense (and reference), and in addition that it is used to perform some particular 'illocutionary act' (e.g. asking or answering a question, giving a warning, announcing a verdict). Alternatively, he said that every utterance has a particular illocutionary force, which is the speech-act actually performed by its

[20] J. L. Austin, 'Other Minds', *Philosophical Papers*, 1st edn (Clarendon Press, Oxford, 1961), p. 71.
[21] Ibid., p. 67.
[22] J. L. Austin, *How to Do Things with Words* (Clarendon Press, Oxford, 1962).

production. If uttered with the appropriate intention in the proper circumstances, 'There is a bull in the field' may have the illocutionary force of a warning, or in a different situation, the force of a description (of the landscape). On this view, force is a feature of particular utterances, not of type-sentences, and there are as many distinct forces as there are different speech-acts. Although Austin ascribed both sense and force to every utterance, he left wholly unexplained what the sense of a sentence is. In particular, he gave no hint about how to specify the sense of a *Wh*-question or an imperative, and consequently it is unclear whether he thought that every sense could be expressed with assertoric force or that every force could be combined with any given sense. He apparently aimed to produce a general theory which would analyse assertion as a species of the genus of speech-acts and which would exhibit truth and falsity as merely one out of a range of equally important dimensions for assessing the 'happiness' of utterances. But he did not live to work out such a theory in any detail.

A parallel movement of thought leading in a different direction is visible in the work of R. M. Hare in moral philosophy. He took exception to the framework of analysing moral utterances advocated by logical positivism. The primary role of such typical moral pronouncements as 'A person ought to keep his word' or 'It was an evil act of yours to . . .' is not to describe anything, but rather to *evaluate* something, e.g. to *commend* it, to *condemn* it, or to *prescribe* the doing of some deed. Consequently, according to *The Language of Morals*, the proper method for clarifying the meanings of such expressions as 'good', 'ought', and 'right', is to focus on their role in bestowing commendatory, prescriptive or evaluative force on utterances rather than on the loose and variable descriptive content which they have. 'Good' is declared to have an 'evaluative meaning [which] is constant for every class of object for which the word is used', and whatever descriptive meaning it bears in a particular utterance is 'secondary to the evaluative meaning'.[23] Hare urged making 'a distinction between the meaning of the word "good" and the criteria for its application';[24] the latter determine its variable descriptive content, but the former fixes its constant force of commendation. Logical positivism went off on the wrong track because it failed to acknowledge the fundamental importance of the observation that to call something 'good' is to commend it. Once again the initial thrust of this reasoning is that truth-conditional semantics is too narrow in scope to embrace an analysis of the meaning of all utterances (in this case, of moral utterances).

[23] R. M. Hare, *The Language of Morals* (Clarendon Press, Oxford, 1952), p. 118.
[24] Ibid., p. 102.

Hare moved on from this negative point in the direction of building a more general positive theory very different from Austin's. His purpose was to develop the analysis of the speech-act of commending far enough to show that logical positivism was mistaken to deny the possibility of practical reasoning and so to impugn the rationality of morals. Hare carried out this programme by accepting in a modified form the identification of moral judgments with commands which had been suggested by some logical positivists. He then urged that there is a logic of imperative inference parallel to the logic of assertoric inference. The raw materials for this are what he called 'neustics' and 'phrastics'.[25] Imperative and indicative sentences may, he suggested, be about the same thing. They differ in such a case in that one commands the bringing about of a state of affairs, whereas the other describes it. 'Shut the door!' and 'You are going to shut the door' are both alleged to be about your shutting the door shortly. The verbal noun 'your shutting the door in the future' indicates what both are about, and this expression Hare called the 'phrastic'. The connection between the order and the assertion is then made transparent by so paraphrasing both that they share this phrastic. Hare transformed the command into 'Your shutting the door – please' and the assertion into 'Your shutting the door – yes'. The expressions 'please' and 'yes', as used in these paraphrases, he called 'neustics'. The neustic marks the speech-act performed by uttering the corresponding unanalysed sentence, in particular differentiating commands from assertions. On this slender basis he gave an account of imperative inference and thus, indirectly, of practical reasoning. The logic of imperatives simply boils down to the logic of phrastics together with the principle that at least one premise must have imperative force if the conclusion does. Or, more accurately, Hare aimed 'to reconstruct the ordinary sentential calculus in terms of phrastics only, and then apply it to indicatives and imperatives alike'.[26]

The Language of Morals did not use the apparatus of neustics and phrastics to construct a general theory of meaning. No neustics other than 'yes' and 'please' are considered, and no claim is made that all speech-acts can be analysed into assertion and command (e.g. asking a question). Moreover, Hare's purpose is served by the comparatively weak thesis that every command has a counterpart assertion (not requiring the converse). But in response to criticisms of his analysis of moral utterances, he later moved further in the direction of a general theory, adding 'tropics' to his

---

[25] Ibid., pp. 17ff.
[26] Ibid., p. 26.

equipment of 'neustics' and 'phrastics', generalizing to the claim that every utterance has a phrastic, neustic, and tropic, and analysing questions into imperatives (commands to fill in blanks or to assign truth-values to sentences).[27]

A flood of theorizing has sprung forth from the work of Austin and Hare. For various different reasons theorists have sought to prove that every utterance or sentence can be analysed into a neustic and a phrastic, a force-indicator and a descriptive content, and recently the main motivation for this enterprise has been to show that truth-conditional semantics, by explaining descriptive content, provides the foundation, when supplemented by a theory of force, for a complete explanation of how language works or of how communication is possible. We will review two branches of this torrent of work in philosophy and theoretical linguistics.

The first directly focuses on logic. It is now believed that Frege and Wittgenstein introduced a purely semantic conception of validity for inferences involving assertions: an argument is valid provided that the satisfaction of the truth-conditions of the conjunction of its premises guarantees the satisfaction of the truth-conditions of its conclusion. Since this explanation has no immediate application to sentences not used to make assertions, it becomes a moot point whether a distinction between valid and invalid can be drawn for non-assertoric reasoning and also whether such reasoning, assuming its possibility, obeys the same logical principles as assertoric inference. A distinction between sense and force is now commonly exploited to demonstrate the possibility of valid non-assertoric reasoning and to work out the basic principles of the 'logic of imperatives' and the 'logic of questions'. Emulating Frege's use of the assertion-sign to mark assertoric force and his practice of attaching this to the mere expression of a propositional-content, modern philosophers introduce symbols for other forces, e.g. '!' to mark commands and '?' to mark sentence-questions. They produce such formulae as '$?(p \land q)$' or '$!(p \to q)$', and they propose such rules of inference[28] as

$$\frac{!\,(p \lor q)}{!\,p} \qquad \frac{!\,p}{\vdash (q \to p)} \qquad \text{and} \qquad \frac{?\,p}{?\,\neg p}$$
$$\phantom{\frac{!\,p}{\vdash (q \to p)}}\!\! !\,q$$

[27] R. M. Hare, 'Meaning and Speech Acts', *Philosophical Review*, LXXIX (1970), pp. 3ff.

[28] Cf. A. J. P. Kenny, 'Practical Inference', *Analysis*, 26 (1966), pp. 72ff,; A. J. P. Kenny, *Will, Freedom and Power* (Blackwell, Oxford, 1975), p. 70; F. Waismann, *Principles of Linguistic Philosophy*, (Macmillan, London, 1965), p. 405.

Their general strategy is to relate codifications of intuitively acceptable non-assertoric reasoning systematically to the relations among the truth-conditions of the unasserted propositional-contents. In this way they aim to vindicate the thesis that the underlying principles of valid reasoning are everywhere the same, superficial appearances to the contrary notwithstanding. Separating sense from force is indispensable to carrying out this project.

The second stream of work tries to use a distinction between sense and force or neustic and phrastic as the gateway into a general theory of meaning. This strategy was explicitly pioneered by E. Stenius in his study of the *Tractatus*. His motive was to argue that Wittgenstein's *Philosophical Investigations* was not intended to be a root-and-branch repudiation of the *Tractatus*, but rather a modified and defensible version of the picture theory of meaning. The basis for this argument was a distinction between 'semantic mood' and 'sentence-radical'.[29] The common component in sentences bearing different forces, i.e. what Hare had called 'the phrastic', Stenius relabelled 'the sentence-radical' to emphasize that this entity, like a radical in chemistry (e.g. the hydroxyl group), cannot occur on its own, i.e. cannot be used to 'make a move in the language-game'. He represented the sentence-radical by an indirect statement (a 'that'-clause). This expresses the entire descriptive content of a type-sentence; it shows the state of affairs which the sentence describes. In paraphrasing a sentence, the sentence-radical must be completed by affixing to it a 'functional component'. This signals the 'semantic mood' of the sentence to be paraphrased. It makes explicit in paraphrase what communicative act the original sentence performs by specifying the role played by the sentence-radical in presenting a state of affairs. Stenius argued that the picture theory of the *Tractatus* could stand intact as a theory of the meaning of the sentence-radical. But it must be supplemented by a theory of semantic moods to account for the different uses of sentences in various 'language-games'. His apparatus of six mood-operators was intended to give a precise form to this programmatic claim allegedly presented in the *Philosophical Investigations*.[30]

A similar ambition is evident in many modern speech-act theories of meaning. They attempt to embroider upon Austin's distinction of sense and illocutionary force. By characterizing both the sense and the illocution-

[29] E. Stenius, *Wittgenstein's Tractatus* (Blackwell, Oxford, 1960), ch. ix.

[30] This is a grotesque misinterpretation of the *Philosophical Investigations*; cf. G. P. Baker and P. M. S. Hacker, *Wittgenstein: Understanding and Meaning* (Blackwell, Oxford, 1980), pp. 110ff.

ary force potential of every sentence, they hope to give an exhaustive account of the workings of a natural language. Modern suspicion about abstract objects has tended to motivate a purge of Platonic entities such as senses or propositional-contents. Instead, it is frequently claimed that there is a basic type of 'propositional act' which is an ingredient of every complex type of speech-act, and that a particular propositional act may be a common component of different speech-acts of asserting, commanding, questioning, etc.[31] Understanding an utterance consists in grasping what propositional act the speaker performed as well as what illocutionary act he effected (making an assertion, issuing an order, etc.). It is assumed that such understanding must be derived at least in part from features of the type-sentence uttered by the speaker. Hence it is assumed that

[w]e can distinguish two (not necessarily separate) elements in the syntactical structure of a sentence, which we might call the propositional indicator and the illocutionary force indicator. The illocutionary force indicator shows how a proposition is to be taken, or, to put it another way, what illocutionary force the utterance is to have; that is, what illocutionary act the speaker is performing in the utterance of the sentence.[32]

A complete theory of meaning would give a perspicuous representation of every type-sentence by indicating both what propositional act and what illocutionary act would typically be effected by its utterance. This enterprise is thought to be furthered[33] by paraphrasing sentences into a formal notation.

We can represent these distinctions in the following symbolism. The general form of (very many kinds of) illocutionary acts is F(p), where the variable 'F' takes illocutionary force indicating devices as values and 'p' takes expressions for propositions. We can then symbolize different kinds of illocutionary acts in the forms, e.g.

$\vdash$ (p) for assertions	!(p) for requests
Pr(p) for promises	w(p) for warnings
	?(p) for yes–no questions.[34]

---

[31] Cf. J. Searle, *Speech Acts* (Cambridge University Press, Cambridge, 1969), pp. 22–6, and J. Lyons, *Semantics*, vol. 2, (Cambridge University Press, Cambridge, 1977), pp. 735ff.

[32] Searle, *Speech Acts*, p. 30.

[33] Kenny (*Will, Freedom and Power*, pp. 39ff.) suggests that connections between utterances which are disguised beneath ordinary expressions can be highlighted with such a notation, e.g. internal relations among the expressions of mental states.

[34] Searle, *Speech Acts*, p. 31.

The propositional act common to different speech acts can itself be analysed in terms of referring and predicating. But, of course, these are just the matters which truth-conditional semantics claims to account for. Hence, if that claim were acknowledged, the clarification of the truth-conditions of the 'proposition' expressed by a sentence would be the major part of the business of a general theory of meaning for a language. The exact contours of the theory of illocutionary forces and force-indicators would remain to be worked out.

These developments in philosophy have caught the attention of theoretical linguists, and a distinction between sense and force (under various labels) is commonly thought to be of decisive importance for the empirical study of languages. One reason for this transfer of ideas is that philosophers have tended to trespass into the area that linguists had staked out as their distinctive territory. Speech-act theorists speak of illocutionary-force-indicating devices in sentences of a natural language which enable a competent speaker of a language to recognize what il-locutionary act is performed by the utterance of a sentence. But empirical semantics addresses itself to the essentially psychological question of how speakers and hearers 'figure out' the utterance-meaning of sentences used in a given context.[35] Hence, to a theoretical linguist, there is no possibility of erecting a purely philosophical speech-act theory of meaning. Either what speech-act theorists have sketched is an acceptable general framework for an empirical semantic theory or it is rubbish. The first alternative is inherently more attractive. Theoretical linguists secure the widest scope for further research if they maintain that speakers calculate the meanings of utterances by combining contextual information with their knowledge of grammatical principles and word-meanings. Apparently speakers must *recognize* a given utterance as an instance of a type-sentence the sense and illocutionary force potential of which are alike derivable from knowledge of grammar and word-meanings, and then they must 'contextualize' this calculation to yield knowledge of what was said and the illocutionary act performed by the utterance. (The operation of this mechanism is, to be sure, *very* fast!) Philosophers, pontificating from their armchairs, may have outlined the proper research programme for linguistics, but any further progress requires gathering empirical knowledge about grammatical depth-structures which only the linguist is qualified to provide.

The other motive for linguists' taking an interest in philosophical discus-

---

[35] Katz, *Propositional Structure and Illocutionary Force*, p. xiii.

sions of sense and force arose from the growth of transformational-generative grammar following in the footsteps of Chomsky. The distinction between *la langue* and *la parole* is safeguarded by drawing a sharp line between semantics and pragmatics. Pragmatics is held to encompass the 'uses and effects of signs within the behaviour in which they occur', whereas semantics requires that one 'abstract from the user of the language and analyze only the expressions and their designata'.[36] Consequently the focus of linguistics on semantics (and syntax) had been considered, since Saussure, to demand the exclusion from attention of such matters as what entity (if any) is referred to by a particular token of a context-dependent expression or what speech-act is effected by the utterance of a sentence on a particular occasion. Linguists had to take note of the syntactical differences between declarative, interrogative, and imperative sentences, but they relegated the study of correlations between sentence-forms and speech-acts to the separate (and unesteemed) science of pragmatics. This way of demarcating pragmatics had the effect of licensing linguists to ignore most issues about the moods of verbs or the forms of sentences in building semantic theories.

Chomsky's work did not remove the inclination to insist on a sharp boundary between semantics and pragmatics; on the contrary, his distinction between *competence* and *performance* called for this form of defence. But his description of syntax in terms of transformations did suggest an awkwardness in the traditional way of drawing this boundary. Transformations can be described which carry direct statements into indirect speech, or assertions into the antecedents of counterfactuals, etc. And Chomsky suggested that an adequate semantic theory would take the form of assigning meanings to simple expressions and then explaining how this meaning is passed through transformation-operations to the infinite variety of well-formed sentences of a natural language. But transformations are also available to carry assertions into sentence-questions, into *Wh-*questions, and (often) into imperatives. Hence the general thesis that meaning is transmitted through grammatical transformations presupposes that non-assertoric sentences have meanings falling within the purview of semantics, and a semantic theory based on transformational-generative grammar achieves a fully integrated and elegant shape if the syntactic differences between declarative, interrogative, and imperative sentences are mirrored in semantic differences. This obvious desideratum has been accomplished in a straightforward way by a draft on speech-act

---

[36] Quotations from Lyons, *Semantics*, vol. 1, p. 115.

theories propounded by philosophers. To semantics is now allocated not
only the analysis of whatever expresses the propositional content of a
sentence, but also the study of force-indicating devices which are conceived to fix the illocutionary-force *potential* of the sentence.[37] A Choms-
kian theory of competence embraces the study of the knowledge that an
ideal speaker-hearer has of the information about illocutionary-force
potential which is present in the grammatical structure and lexical components of a sentence. But it stops short of considering the actual use made of
uttered sentences. This study is allocated to pragmatics. For it is held that
the actual use or force of an utterance is *inferred* by speakers from
combining knowledge of its illocutionary-force potential with knowledge
about the circumstances of its utterance. Pragmatics is thus thought to deal
with 'the various mechanisms speakers use to exploit the richness of
context to produce utterances whose meaning in the context diverges
predictably from the meaning of the sentences of which they are tokens'.[38]
Pragmatics thus provides principles for bridging the gap opened up by
theoretical linguists between understanding a type-sentence and understanding what is said by uttering a token of it.

Distinguishing sense from force has become an entrenched strategy in
modern theories of language. It has removed the major embarrassment of
truth-conditional semantics. Indeed, it has converted an objection into a
vindication of this framework for the analysis of meaning. In the course of
so doing, however, it has transformed what apparently began as a series of
familiar observations about moods of verbs and syntactical types of sentences with familiar discourse functions, and about ordinary conventions
of indirect speech and the uses of verbs of speech into something altogether
unfamiliar. The ordinary mundane uses of language suddenly take on
different aspects, and the mind whirls. Do all sentences really *contain* a
phrastic in the form of a verbal noun? Are imperative sentences, interrogatives, optatives, really instruments for expressing true or false propositions
(in addition to issuing orders, asking questions, expressing wishes)? Do we
really, without noticing it, 'figure out' the meaning and force of an utterance on the basis of our knowledge (only now revealed to us) of principles
of depth-grammar concerning illocutionary-force potential and of principles
of pragmatics? We might wonder whether sense/force theories are not
appropriate objects for Dr Johnson's observation:

[37] W. P. Alston, *Philosophy of Language* (Prentice-Hall, Englewood Cliffs, NJ, 1969),
pp. 36ff.
[38] Katz, *Propositional Structure and Illocutionary Force*, p. 15.

Wheresoe'er I turn my view
All is strange, yet nothing new.
Endless labour all along,
Endless labour to be wrong.

3 Lateral radiation

The march of history has led to an apparent consensus.

What seems essential is that we should have some division of sentential utterances into a determinate range of categories, according to the type of linguistic act effected by the utterance; that there should be some notion of the sense of a sentence, considered as an ingredient in its meaning and as capable of being shared by sentences belonging to different categories; that the notion of sense be such that, once we know both the category to which a sentence belongs and the sense which it carries, then we have an essential grasp of the significance of an utterance of the sentence; and that, for each category, it should be possible to give a uniform explanation of the linguistic act effected by uttering a sentence of that category, in terms of its sense, taken as given. I do not think that we have, at present, any conception of what a theory of meaning for a language would look like if it did not conform to this pattern.[39]

A somewhat more attentive and critical review of the underlying history, however, reveals that this apparent consensus is a sham. Seeming agreement masks fundamental disagreements as well as deep unclarities. Some hints about these problems have been dropped in the previous survey, but the issues must now be put under the spotlights.

The first rift among theorists concerns the identification of the entities described as having senses and forces. One main branch characterizes sense and force as features of type-sentences. The force of a sentence is fixed by conventions about the significance of such force-indicators as the mood of the verb, syntactic structures, and the occurrence of explicit performatives such as 'I promise'; typically a type-sentence is thought to have a single invariant force, upon which the determination of the illocutionary act performed in uttering it partly depends. Similarly, sense is held to be fixed by general conventions about the use of expressions in references and predication, and what an utterance expresses is determined by the interaction of the sense of the uttered sentence with features of the

[39] M. A. E. Dummett, 'Can Analytical Philosophy be Systematic, and Ought it to Be?', in *Truth and Other Enigmas* (Duckworth, London, 1978), p. 450.

context of utterance. On the other hand, some theorists openly apply a sense/force distinction not to type-sentences, but to particular utterances. Frege held this view. The sense of different tokens of a single type-sentence may differ. And his critical thesis that the indicative mood and declarative sentence-form is at best a fallible guide to assertoric force makes sense only if he restricted assertoric force to utterances of a sentence actually used to assert the thought expressed. Austin too explicitly ascribed illocutionary force to utterances, conceding the possibility that tokens of a type-sentence may differ in illocutionary force (e.g. an utterance of 'There is a bull in the field' might have the force of a warning or of a description). Others follow this tradition.[40] What it makes sense to say about sense and about force depends on which of those two approaches a theorist adopts.

A related conceptual disagreement is associated with the term 'force' (and its congeners). On one view, force is a feature of a type-sentence which may restrict the range of possible speech-acts that can be performed by utterances of this sentence and which partially determines what speech-act is actually performed by a particular utterance. Here force is held to be related to the actual use of a sentence as potentiality to actuality. Force may thus be conceived to characterize the *typical* use of utterances of a sentence, although the circumstances of a particular utterance may cause the actual use to diverge from the typical one. Accordingly, a sentence-question may be ascribed invariant interrogative force even though particular utterances of sentence-questions may be used (and understood) to perform other speech-acts (e.g. to make a request or, as a 'rhetorical question', to make an assertion). On another, antithetical, view force is a feature of an utterance which characterizes the actual use of a sentence on a particular occasion. Accordingly, there is no such thing as divergence between force and use. Hence an utterance correctly classed as a rhetorical question would have assertoric, not interrogative force, and 'Can you pass the butter?' has the force of a request not of a question. On this view, what are picked out as 'force-indicators' in sentences, e.g. moods of verbs and even explicit performatives, are at best fallible guides to the force of an utterance, for it is expressly conceded that declarative sentences or 'performative utterances' may be used to effect a variety of different speech-acts. Once again, what it makes sense to say about force depends on which explanation is given of this term of art.

The diversity of the concepts of force which are in play among theorists

---

[40] e.g. Alston, *Philosophy of Language*, p. 37, and D. Davidson, 'Moods and Performances', in *Meaning and Use*, ed. A. Margalit (Reidel, Dordrecht, 1979), p. 17.

is most conspicuous in respect of the treatment of the identification and differentiation of forces. Some maintain that there are but two, the assertoric and imperative (the 'fiat mood'[41]), arguing that the whole gamut of different speech-acts can be reduced to these simple elements.[42] Others wish to add another force or two to this primitive stock, because, for example, they refuse to assimilate questions to imperatives, or they consider expressions of intention to differ fundamentally from both assertions and commands (in particular, such sentences as 'I'll go' or 'I'll do it' are not to be assimilated to self-addressed imperatives). Yet others identify more distinct forces or 'moods'.[43] Finally, some might argue that the attempt to reduce the diversity of speech-acts to the operation of a handful of 'moods' of sentences 'on analysis' or 'in depth-grammar' is misguided. Rather are there as many distinct forces as there are speech-act verbs which differ in meaning.[44] In short, theorists of force are in radical disagreement, not merely about the facts of language and speech they purport to describe and explain, but about *the very concepts* they should use in so doing.

An exactly parallel ambiguity besets the term 'sentence-radical' (and its cousins). On one view, a single sentence-radical is associated with each unambiguous type-sentence. On another, different sentence-radicals may

[41] The term 'mood' is systematically misused in current debates, its nexus with the morphology of the verb being altogether abandoned.

[42] Kenny, *Will, Freedom and Power*, pp. 38ff.; cf. Hare 'Meaning and Speech Acts'. Kenny distinguishes the 'assertoric mood' from the 'fiat mood' by reference to the 'onus of match' between a sentence and the state of affairs it describes. If the state of affairs described does not obtain, do we fault the sentence or the world? If the former, then the sentence is in the assertoric mood, if the latter, it is in the mood of fiats. This test is more problematic than it appears to be. The dichotomy of 'faulting' the sentence or 'faulting' the world is neither clear nor evidently exhaustive. Its application to normative sentences is opaque, e.g. 'You ought to φ', 'You must φ', 'You have a duty to φ', 'You have a legal obligation to φ'. What state of affairs do these sentences describe? – the addressee's φing, or his being required to φ? In these cases, if the addressee does not φ, do we fault the sentence or the world? So, too, 'Promises ought to be kept', 'All men have a right to freedom of speech' present problems. But even in the simple imperative case, if a commander issues a rash order, or an infelicitous order (e.g. to shut a shut door) and the 'state of affairs it describes' does not obtain (because, e.g. the troops get killed trying to obey it, or the addressee, unsurprisingly, cannot shut shut doors) do we fault the sentence or the world? We certainly fault the commander! So too in the declarative case, if a speaker asserts that the φer ψs, and there exists no φer, do we fault the sentence for lacking a truth-value or the world for lacking a φer? Note that the one thing one *cannot* do here is to appeal to the notions of truth and falsity since *both* assertoric sentences and fiats are held to possess 'semantic' truth or falsehood.

[43] For example, Stenius, *Wittgenstein's Tractatus*, pp. 163, 175, recognizes at least five.

[44] This apparently is Austin's conception of illocutionary force in *How to do Things with Words*, pp. 149ff.

be correlated with different utterances of an unambiguous type-sentence. If we focus for simplicity on a declarative sentence used to make an assertion, the first view is natural if the sentence-radical is taken to express the meaning of the sentence, whereas the second fits better with the idea that it expresses what is asserted by the utterance of this sentence (its 'sense' in Frege's terminology). The difference is clear and crucial in investigating sentences containing indexical expressions.

Also noteworthy is another ambivalence about how to use the terms 'sentence-radical', 'phrastic', 'descriptive content', etc. Many theorists so explain these terms that they designate kinds of *expressions*. Hare calls the verbal noun 'your shutting the door in the immediate future' the phrastic of the sentence [sic!] 'Your shutting the door in the immediate future, please'.[45] Stenius proposes to identify the sentence-radical as a 'that'-clause, i.e. as an indirect statement.[46] These explanations seem appropriate to an attempt to extend truth-conditional semantics to non-assertoric utterances, for it is declarative sentences (expressions) which are standardly held to have truth-conditions and hence it should be expressions (other than the sentences themselves) which have truth-conditions in the case of non-declarative sentences. So far, the terminology makes sense. But this often ceases to be so as theorists proceed to apply these terms of art. Hare immediately speaks of the phrastic (and neustic) as being *in* the unparaphrased sentences, e.g. arguing that the word 'not' is part of the phrastic in the sentence 'Do not shut the door'.[47] Stenius, in a similar fashion, claims that 'we must distinguish between two components in a sentence: the *sentence-radical* (i.e. the "phrastic") . . . and the *functional* component (the "neustic" . . .)'.[48] This is unintelligible. No verbal noun occurs in the sentence 'Do not shut the door', and therefore the question of whether 'not' is part of the phrastic in this sentence does not arise, according to Hare's own explanation of 'phrastic'. Similarly, it would be absurd to suppose that defective eyesight prevents my finding a 'that'-clause in the *sentence* 'You live here now', and consequently the generalization that every sentence contains a sentence-radical is obviously false according to Stenius's explanation of 'sentence-radical'. This difficulty is not trivial, for it threatens to undermine the fundamental thesis that the sentences 'Shut the door' and 'You will shut the door' have a common phrastic or sentence-radical. To make sense of such a claim, these technical

[45] *Language of Morals*, pp. 17f.
[46] *Wittgenstein's Tractatus*, p. 164.
[47] pp. 20f.
[48] p. 161.

terms must be understood to stand for a proposition or some such non-linguistic entity which is indicated (designated? expressed?) by a verbal noun or an indirect statement. *Pari passu*, the 'force-indicator', 'neustic' or 'functional component' of a sentence cannot be a symbol, but must be some (mysterious!) abstract entity. But now nonsense breaks out afresh. What would it be for such a Platonic object to occur in a sentence or to be a *component* of a sentence? And what would it be for it to indicate what speech-act the utterance of a sentence is used to perform? Moreover, non-declaratives would compel a theorist to abandon the claim that *expressions* have truth-conditions, since the sentence-radical (which is claimed to be the proper object of analysis for truth-conditional semantics) would not be an expression at all. This issue about the status of 'phrastics' and 'neustics', 'sentence-radicals' and 'semantic mood indicators', etc., is not one about which theorists are in open disagreement with each other, but one about which each seems chronically unclear and hence liable to fall into inconsistency and nonsense.

This danger is exacerbated by the jargon of 'depth-grammar' and 'deep structures' introduced by Chomsky and now endemic in philosophy and linguistics. A sophisticated theorist is likely to claim that sentence-radicals and force-indicators are not separate components or aspects visible in the surface-forms of sentences in a natural language, but rather distinct components to be found in the 'depth-grammar' of well-formed sentences. The 'base structure' of any sentence might be thought to take the form

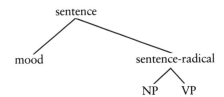

and the rider will be added that it is doubtful whether the sentence-radical can be 'represented on the surface at all',[49] whether it corresponds to any well-formed expression of English, German, etc. Alternatively it might be 'discovered' that in the deep structure of any sentence there is an explicit performative verb; simple sentences without performative verbs are then explained as the result of applying an optional rule of performative-deletion![50] A similar thesis is that

[49] Lewis, 'General Semantics', p. 206.

[50] Cf. J. R. Ross, 'On Declarative Sentences', in *Readings in Transformational Grammar*, ed. R. A. Jacobs and P. S. Rosenbaum (Ginn-Blaisdell, Boston, 1970), pp. 222–72.

in the deep structure underlying imperative sentences there is an abstract imperative predicate . . . [which] is a 3-place predicate two of whose arguments are fixed.
The agent is expressed always by the first-person pronoun, and the dative by the
second-person pronoun (or an NP coreferential with it). The third argument is the
content of the command, and in it the second-person pronoun must occur as an
agent.[51]

Accordingly, an imperative sentence such as 'Take these clothes to the
laundry' is held to hide a deep structure analogous to the surface structure
of the sentence 'I order you to take these clothes to the laundry', and
interrogative sentences are argued to contain in their deep structure 'an
abstract interrogative predicate corresponding to the overt predicate *ask*
in the sentence "I ask whether . . ."'[52]

All of these accounts of deep structure, being completely untestable,
should arouse suspicion. Do they have any more legitimate a place in an
empirical science of language than 'vital force' in biology? This suspicion
can be sharpened by asking an apparently elementary question: are the
items in the deep structures of sentences symbols or not? If they were,
linguists should be able to exhibit them. For what could prevent theorists
from producing symbols? Could there be symbols that could not in principle
be instantiated? And how could there be room for doubt whether a
'that'-clause represents a sentence-radical?[53] How linguists speak of deep
structure seems inconsistent with taking symbols to have any place in deep
structures. Some sort of abstract entities are required. But this supposition
too generates intractable problems. What sense does it make to assert that
expressions (sentences) *contain* abstract entities in their deep structure?
Would this not be as absurd as claiming that the symbol ' ⊢ ' contains the
act of assertion[54] or that a sentence contains a propositional act? Deep
structures were originally introduced to serve as the bases for the transformations envisaged by transformational generative grammar. Instead of
regarding the sentence 'Is this a dog?' as produced by applying a transformation of subject/complement inversion to the kernel sentence 'This is a
dog', we are to view both of these as the products of transformations

[51] D. Terence Langendoen, *The Study of Syntax: the generative-transformational
approach to the structure of American English* (Holt, Rinehart and Winston, Inc., New York,
1969), p. 123.
[52] Ibid., pp. 122ff.; note the ensuing distortions, e.g. the prayer 'Give us this day our daily
bread' has the deep structure of 'I order You to give us this day our daily bread'.
[53] Lewis, 'General Semantics', p. 206.
[54] Cf. Frege, *The Basic Laws of Arithmetic*, vol. 1, §5.

applied to a terminal string in depth-grammar. But how can a transformation *analogous* to the first yield a sentence when applied to something which is not an expression at all? If a symbol is generated by an alteration in structure, must the input not be a symbol? Now it appears that linguists' chatter about deep structure is inconsistent with denying that symbols are the constituents of deep structures. This makes clear that incompatible demands are made on deep structures. Items in deep structure must have the role of symbols, but at the same time be abstract, imperceptible, impalpable; not signs, but rather the souls of signs. To cash the terminology of 'sentence-radicals', 'phrastics', etc., in terms of items in deep structures is to exchange a more obvious form of incoherence for a less obvious one. No substantial improvement is effected, even if many casual bystanders are hoodwinked by the manoeuvre.

This catalogue by no means exhausts the unclarities and disagreements that are present among theorists advocating a sense/force distinction. But it should suffice to shatter the illusion that there is a high degree of consensus on a body of clear doctrines. There are many different possible ways to draw a sense/force distinction, and there are even more ways to waffle on about sense and force while saying nothing at all intelligible. Far from it being obvious that philosophers and linguists are hot on the scent of truth, it is starting to appear possible that both packs are following the same red herrings.

One moral to be extracted is that many theorists fail to draw crucial distinctions and consequently lapse into grotesque inconsistency. The question whether force and sense are characteristics of type-sentences or particular utterances seems fundamental and clear. But many an influential discussion leaves it quite opaque which view its author takes. On one page it may be claimed that an illocutionary-force-indicator is an element in the syntactical structure of a type-sentence, while on the very next page it is held that illocutionary-force-indicating devices symbolize different kinds of illocutionary acts performed in uttering sentences.[55] The price of extensive unclarity is extensive nonsense. It is impossible to establish what theorists are talking about, and correspondingly doubtful whether any of their pronouncements make any sense, let alone whether they are true.

A second important moral is that discrepancies between different ways of distinguishing sense from force turn on disagreements, overt and covert,

---

[55] Searle, *Speech Acts*, pp. 30f. (quoted above on p. 65); thus if '$w(p)$' symbolizes the illocutionary act of warning, and '$\vdash p$' symbolizes assertion, then 'The bull is in the field' will be represented as '$w(p)$' if shouted as a warning, and by '$\vdash p$' if asserted, even though the two utterances are of one and the same type-sentence.

about how concepts are to be explained and used. There is not one concept of sense and one concept of force in the field, but many. According to one theorist, the sentence 'An utterance lacking assertoric force is here used to make an assertion' will be self-contradictory, while another will regard it as exemplified by a rhetorical question. One theorist may (officially) take a sentence-radical to be an expression such as an indirect statement, whereas another may take it to be what is expressed by the expression of a judgment. And so on. These discrepancies cannot be removed by theory-construction or the gathering of data about uses of sentences in natural languages, for they concern the very concepts used in building theories and in describing the data. Reconciliation must be a matter of various theorists coming to a joint *decision* about how to explain their distinctive termin-ology. Furthermore, the fact that what one theorist says is apt to be nonsense according to the explanations used by many others proves that the idea that different theories may gradually converge on the truth is an illusion, since there is no successive approximation to truth *via nonsense*! Neither the fact nor the importance of the conceptual divisions between sense/force theories has been clearly realized, for the muddle and disagree-ment about basic concepts is typically seen to consist in a gradual sorting out of elusive and recalcitrant facts about language.

4 Suspicions of genetic defects

At this point somebody who has followed our discussion may be torn between two opposite reactions. One would be that preliminary clarifica-tion amounts to a sweeping and unwarranted criticism, apparently de-manding a denial of the legitimacy of certain well-entrenched ideas and intuitively plausible theses. The other would be that the initial clarification has opened up a vast range of possibilities for constructing a sense/force distinction and a corresponding theory of force, with the corollary that any definitive criticism must now face the Herculean task of proceeding separately against each of those possibilities. Both reactions must now be blocked.

Sketching in the diverse ways of drawing a sense/force distinction obviously does not condemn any of them, and even the odd inconsistency or confusion is not utterly damning. We may have given the impression that there is nothing to be salvaged from existing theories. Surely, it will be objected, advocates of a sense/force distinction build on unshakeable foundations. Competent speakers of a language do perform a variety of speech-acts. Typically they recognize what these are, and they agree about these identifications. It seems a truism that some features of an uttered sentence together with features of the context of its utterance must provide the justification for claiming that in uttering it the speaker performed a particular speech-act. There are various criteria for identifying speech-acts. Similarly, speakers typically recognize and agree about what it is that somebody has said; there are criteria for correctness of reports in indirect speech. Finally, there is a large measure of consensus about how to paraphrase utterances into forms which exploit the syntax of *oratio obliqua*. What somebody says may be expressed in other words, and often it will be conceded that some of these acceptable rephrasings will have such forms as 'Is it the case that . . .?' or 'I assert that . . .' or 'It is true that . . .'. But this array of platitudes seems to constitute a conclusive rebuttal of any *radical* root-and-branch criticism of introducing a sense/force distinction. For are the various attempts to build theories of force not merely extensions of these data? Even if the various theories contain important errors, how could these be shown to be *fundamental* without calling into question all of those underlying truisms?

Though natural, the reasoning is fallacious. There is a world of difference between the cited platitudes and the theses propounded by theorists of language. Truisms are subtly and swiftly *inflated* into propositions which are far from platitudes, often into propositions which do not obviously even make sense. This sleight of hand is no less apparent among linguists than among philosophers. Somehow we must be swept along into accepting some such doctrine as that in *every* type-sentence there is a component or feature which describes a state of affairs, expresses a thought, bears a truth-value, etc., and another component or feature which simply signals the speech-act typically performed by uttering the sentence. Such a claim is *not* a platitude, and it in no way follows from the basic 'data' adduced in support of a theory of force. We may well fail to notice this, as indeed the theorist of force himself typically does. For the inflation of a platitude into a dubious doctrine exploits various deeply ingrained propensities to fall into conceptual confusion. These are worth cataloguing in the hope that awareness of them may have some prophylactic value.

First, from the ability to identify speech-acts and their objects we are inclined to infer that there must be a mechanism of understanding; a theory is apparently needed to explain *how* a competent speaker recognizes that another has asked what time it is, declared an intention to leave the room, etc. Secondly, we are prone to transfer terminology applicable to one expression to another expression on the ground that the second offers an *analysis* of the first; in particular, we find little difficulty in 'discovering' components in a sentence which in fact are visible only in a purported analysis (e.g. 'phrastics' or 'sentence-radicals'). Thirdly, we fall easily into the supposition that internal relations must be mediated by *shared entities*; hence we infer from the fact that the utterance 'Smith is drunk' answers the question 'Is Smith drunk?' that the two utterances must have something (viz. a 'proposition' or 'sentence-radical') in common (other than the shared words). Fourthly, we readily suppose that the multiplicity and apparent *defeasibility* of criteria for performing particular speech-acts (and hence too of criteria for correctness of reports in *oratio obliqua*) reflects some ignorance or unclarity about the phenomena of making assertions, asking questions, etc.; hence we are disposed to accept that a proper theory might replace these criteria with complex and sophisticated accounts of the conditions necessary and sufficient for performing each such speech-act. Finally, we tend to conceive of speech as the mere production of signs which must themselves be endowed with *powers* to express thoughts and to make assertions, ask questions, etc.; hence we infer from the ability to use the sentence 'Five is a prime number' to make an assertion that this sentence must be endowed with assertoric *force*, in the absence of which its utterance would merely express a proposition. If it could be demonstrated that these five ideas were all fundamentally confused, then the thesis that speculations about a sense/force distinction are solidly grounded in truisms about speech would be shown to be a sham. To expose the incoherences endemic in theories of force does not repudiate any basic conceptual truths about speech-acts.

It is equally easy to construct a case that our discussion has ruled out the possibility of criticizing a distinction between sense and force. Different theorists make fundamentally different claims by deploying very different concepts. One theorist maintains that forces are features of particular utterances and specify the actual speech-acts performed on those occasions, while another contends that forces are features of type-sentences and characterize the typical uses of those sentences. Likewise one maintains that descriptive content is expressed by a verbal noun, another by an indirect statement, yet another by a declarative sentence. And so on. Consequently criticisms apposite for one theory simply pass another by. How then can one hope to eliminate every current variant of a theory of force, let alone all possible ones which may be thrown up by future progress in the science of language? The task seems futile.

This despair is not warranted. Theories of force are not parallel to competing scientific explanations of natural phenomena. We are moving within the domain of convention, and the task is to describe what the conventions of languages in these respects are, and, in particular, to unravel the internal, conceptual, relations set up by our linguistic conventions. This conceptual task involves clarifying the relationships between what is queried by questions and what is asserted by corresponding answers, between what is ordered by commands and what is stated by reports of compliance. It must elucidate the internal relations between speech-acts and their objects, between what a sentence of a certain kind means and what a correlative sentence of a different kind means. *This* is not an empirical phenomenon. (That we *have* these conventions is a matter of fact, of course; but that given these conventions, such-and-such internal relations obtain, is not.) Introduction of technical terminology is not illicit provided that the explanations of it are coherent. But, unlike applications of technical terminology in physics, a misdescription of the problematic 'phenomena' will result, not in contingent falsehood, but in nonsense. For a misdescription of a conceptual articulation will traverse the bounds of sense.

A critical scrutiny of theories of force will move on two parallel planes. On the one hand it must examine the intelligibility and coherence of explanations of the fundamental terms introduced by the theorist. On the other, it must investigate, not which one of the competing 'theories' gives the most economical account of the 'workings of language' (as if the theory were an investigation into natural phenomena of physics) but rather whether any of them *makes sense*. The crucial issue is whether any such theory, harnessed to *some* concepts of sense and force, does not traverse the bounds of sense.

Scope for manoeuvre in the enterprise of explaining the fundamental terminology of sense and force is much restricted. Indeed, there are only three strategies to pursue, each of which is familiar from existing writings. The first tries to explain 'sense' in terms of some such concept as description or information. The second attempts to capitalize on possibilities for paraphrasing utterances within a language. And the third seeks to draw conclusions from the structures of reports in indirect speech. These can be carefully scrutinized one by one, as we shall proceed to do. If each one leads to a clear débâcle, then we may treat the theory of force as a subject on a par with the psychology of water droplets or the algebra of monads.

CHAPTER 3

Sense and Force:
the Pathology of a Species

1 Descriptive content

Any theorist of force is committed to the thesis that every sentence (or utterance) of a natural language has a double aspect. It has a sense and a force. Moreover, different senses can be fairly freely combined with different forces. Therefore it is held that there are sets of sentences (or utterances) which are identical in sense and differ only in force, e.g. 'The door is shut', 'Shut the door!', 'Is the door shut', and 'Would that the door were shut!'. Such expressions are thus thought to have something in common (a sense) over and above the recurrence of various constituent words. This is immediately puzzling. For is there anything common which is visible (or audible) in such expressions apart from the verb 'shut' (in different forms) and the phrase 'the door'? The obvious retort is that what these expressions have in common is not itself an expression, but rather part of what is expressed. Every sentence (or utterance) expresses a sense, and sentences differing in 'mood', such as the four quoted above, express the same sense. The sense of a sentence is thus an abstract entity, not a symbol, and hence it may be shared by symbols having little or nothing in common *qua* symbols.

This strategy for discovering something common beneath apparent disparities among sentences avoids one problem, but raises another. For how is it to be explained what the common abstract entity is? What is its nature? And what difference does it make whether its existence is affirmed or denied? Theorists are ready with a panoply of explanations. Some identify the sense of a sentence with its *descriptive content*;[1] they contend

[1] M. A. E. Dummett, *Frege: Philosophy of Language* (Duckworth, London, 1973), pp. 305ff.

that 'any sentence whatever can be regarded as – *inter alia* – a description of a state of affairs',[2] and they single out its sense as something which (perhaps together with the context) determines which state of affairs it describes.[3] Others claim that sentences have the same sense if they are *about the same thing*.[4] Some stipulate the requirement that they *express one and the same proposition*.[5] Others prefer the explanation that they must convey the same information;[6] on this view, 'Someone will eat the cookies', 'Who will eat the cookies?', 'Eat the cookies', and 'I promise (warn, allow) you to eat the cookies' have as their shared sense the information that somebody eats cookies in the near future. Such explanations are meant to put beyond question the truth of the principle that different sentences (or utterances) may share the same sense and differ only in force.

Alas! far from establishing this thesis, these explanations do not even succeed in making it intelligible. We will focus criticism on the notion of descriptive content. We aim to demonstrate that the thesis that sentences in different 'moods' may share a descriptive content is either nonsensical or vacuous. Consequently appeal to descriptive content cannot legitimately be used to explain the technical term 'sense'. Precisely parallel objections can be marshalled against the other favoured explanations of 'sense'. The theses that sentences in different 'moods' may express the same proposition, may be about the same thing, or may contain the same information are severally either nonsensical or empty. We shall leave the reader to construct these parallel arguments on the model of our discussion of descriptive content. If all of these putative explanations of 'sense' (and its cousins such as 'phrastic', 'sentence-radical', 'proposition') are radically defective, then the theorist has not succeeded in explaining what the sense of an expression is, and he has not made comprehensible the thesis that something (apart from some words) may be common to sentences in different 'moods' (or to the different syntactical transformations of a given sentence).

In reflecting on the claim that all sentences describe a state of affairs, we might best start by reminding ourselves of what we ordinarily understand by 'describing' and 'a description'.[7] Describing is an activity performed by

[2] A. J. P. Kenny, *Will, Freedom and Power* (Blackwell, Oxford, 1975), p. 38.
[3] E. Stenius, *Wittgenstein's Tractatus* (Blackwell, Oxford, 1960), p. 161.
[4] R. M. Hare, *Language of Morals* (Oxford University Press, Oxford, 1952), p. 22.
[5] J. Searle, *Speech Acts* (Cambridge University Press, Cambridge, 1969), p. 29.
[6] I. Katz, *Propositional Structure and Illocutionary Force* (Harvester, Sussex, 1977), p. 11.
[7] Cf. K. Baier and S. Toulmin, 'Describing', *Mind*, XLI (1952).

the use of symbols, typically by uttering sentences in a language. It is an activity with an object, i.e. it is always in order to ask 'What (or whom) did A describe?', and the answer may identify as the object of description a wide variety of kinds of things: artefacts, persons, events, activities, processes, scenery, weather, etc. A typical description of something consists of more than one sentence; one would rarely try to give a description of St Peter's, Michelangelo's *Last Judgment*, or the ceremony of the Catholic mass with a single sentence. Furthermore, not every sentence which is about something which might be an object of description is itself either a description or necessarily a part of a description. 'That ↑ is St Peter's', 'St Peter's is a cathedral', 'Michelangelo's *Last Judgment* is in the Sistine Chapel', 'Mass is at 10.15 a.m.' are not descriptions of their subjects. To identify something, to say what sort of thing it is, to say where it is, to specify the time of an event, etc. is not to describe anything. It is true that we speak not only of descriptions of things, but also of describing something *as* a so-and-so; e.g. we may describe someone as a distinguished man of letters, an artefact as a masterpiece of its kind, an event as a catastrophe of the first order. But to say where a given object is, when an event took place, how an action was done, is not to describe object, event or action *as* an anything.

Descriptions are of many different kinds with many different purposes. Contrast a description of *how to bake* a gateau ('Take six eggs. Mix with 6 oz of . . .') with a description *of* a gateau, or the description of an accident given by the driver with those given by the policeman, the road-engineer, the bystander, and the victim. The virtues and vices of descriptions are various, depending on the kind of description and its purposes. Descriptions can be accurate, detailed, graphic, lively, exciting or moving; or they may be inaccurate, rough, crude, hurried, laboured, dull, or insensitive. Describing an X as a Y may be charming, delightful and appropriate, or unjust, grotesque, and uncalled for. Descriptions and describings stand in *contrast* to other speech-activities and their products. The Hansard record of what happened in Parliament is not (usually) a description of what happened. A musical score is not a description of the piece of which it is the score, and a map is not a description of a landscape. Descriptions are contrasted with prescriptions, recommendations, predictions, explanations and justifications. So much for preliminary reminders.

The claim that any sentence is or can be regarded as a description of a state of affairs is either false or empty. If 'sentence', 'description' and 'state of affairs' are here being employed in their ordinary sense, then it is false. If, however, the theorist contends that these expressions are being employed in a special 'philosophical' sense, the claim is empty. We shall sharpen the first horn of the dilemma first.

One can indeed describe states of affairs. But not every object of description, e.g. Leonardo da Vinci, Michelangelo's claw-chiselling technique, or the competition in the Palazzo Vecchio, is a state of affairs. Innumerable declarative sentences are employed assertorically for purposes other than description. 'John is at the door' describes neither John nor the door; nor does it describe who is at the door (but rather identifies that person) or where John is (but states or specifies that). 'It is two o'clock' does not describe the time, '2 + 2 = 4' does not describe the sum of two and two; and 'A bachelor is an unmarried man' defines rather than describes what a bachelor is.

It is true that non-declarative sentences can occur in descriptions. Examine, for example, De Quincey's famous description of Piranesi's *Carceri*:

Some of these represented vast Gothic halls; on the floor of which stood mighty engines and machinery, wheels, cables, catapults, etc., expressive of enormous power put forth, or resistance overcome. Creeping along the sides of the walls you perceived a staircase; and upon this, groping his way upwards, was Piranesi himself. Follow the stairs a little farther, and you perceive them reaching an abrupt termination, without any balustrade, and allowing no step onwards to him who should reach the extremity, except into the depths below. Whatever is to become of poor Piranesi at least you must suppose that his labours must now in some way terminate. But raise your eyes, and behold a second flight of stairs still higher, on which again Piranesi is perceived, by this time standing on the very brink of the abyss. Once again elevate your eye, and a still more aerial flight of stairs is described; and there again is the delirious Piranesi, busy on his aspiring labours: and so, until the unfinished stairs and the hopeless Piranesi both are lost in the upper gloom of the hall.[8]

This admixture of imperative and declarative sentences is wholly legitimate. It does not indicate that de Quincey alternates between describing states of affairs and issuing orders, but rather, that the typical unit of description is more than a sentence.[9]

Of course, the most common use of imperatives, optatives, interrogatives and exclamations is not as parts of a description; and occurring on

[8] T. de Quincey, *Confessions of an English Opium Eater*, revised edn (1856), part III.

[9] Indeed, this platitude can be generalized. For making a statement, issuing an order or asking a question are commonly acts performed by uttering *many* sentences, not just one sentence per speech-act.

their own they are not typically descriptions. *Wh*-questions, for example, do not normally describe anything; 'Who did what to whom when?' is not a description of someone doing something to someone sometime. Equally, the request 'Describe someone doing something at sometime!' is satisfied neither by the reply 'Who did what when?' nor by 'Did Piranesi etch the *Carceri* in 1750?' Sentence-questions are typically used to query, ask, enquire, entreat, but not to describe. 'Did Columbus discover Africa?' does not describe Columbus's discovering Africa, nor does it *contain* a description of Columbus discovering Africa (indeed, it is far from evident that anything could constitute a *description* of Columbus's discovery of Africa). Likewise exclamations and ejaculations, e.g. 'So be it!', 'What a day!', 'How frightful!', 'Angels and ministers of grace, defend us!' are not descriptions. Imperative sentences are typically used to order, command, request, plead or instruct. 'Shut the door, please!' describes neither you nor the door, nor does it *describe* what to do, although it is used to tell you what to do.[10] Finally, optative sentences 'Would that it were day' or 'If only it would rain' are typically used to express one's wishes and longings but neither describe them nor their objects. Inasmuch as 'describe' is used in its ordinary sense, the thesis that every sentence describes a state of affairs is false. Equally ludicrous is the thesis that every sentence *contains* a description, i.e. an expression which is used to describe something.

Let us now turn to the alternative horn of the dilemma. Some theorists may concede that in the ordinary sense of 'describe' the thesis is indeed false, but insist that they are introducing a special philosophical sense of 'describe'. Even if we disregard qualms about the intelligibility of special 'philosophical senses' of words, this move avails them little. The thesis that every sentence is or can be regarded as a description of a state of affairs is empty if it involves a stipulation that every meaningful sentence is to be called 'a description' and that a state of affairs is what 'corresponds' to such a sentence. This merely records an arbitrary decision not to call anything 'a sentence' which one does not also call 'a description', and to call whatever satisfies a description 'a state of affairs'. Hence we will have to say that '$2 + 2 = 4$' describes the state of affairs in which $2 + 2 = 4$, that 'One ought to keep one's word' describes the state of affairs which consists in having the obligation to keep one's word, that 'Is it raining?' is, *inter alia*, a description of the state of affairs which consists of its raining, and

---

[10] Of course, the request 'Would you describe carefully exactly what I am to do?' is perfectly in order. A correct response will involve giving detailed instructions involving careful descriptions. It does not, however, follow that every instruction contains or involves descriptions, let alone that every imperative sentence contains one.

'Shut the door!' of the state of affairs which consists of your shutting the door. This is merely to say that we have here a *form*, viz. ' ". . ." is a description of the state of affairs which consists of . . .' into which many typical sentences can, with more or less strain, be fitted.

This legislation recalls a related philosophical thesis, namely that every word names an object.[11] Here too we have a form, viz. 'The word "W" signifies W', which entitles us to say that the word (name) 'John' signifies John, that the word 'table' signifies a table, the word 'red' signifies the colour red, the word 'two' signifies the number two, the word 'north' signifies the direction north. But this does not make the logical differences between the uses of proper names, sortal nouns, adjectives, number words, etc. any the less great. So too, the stipulation that every sentence is a description does not make questioning, requesting, ordering, asking, exclaiming, etc. any the more like describing. It merely *masks* the differences by means of a form of words, a mould into which many different kinds of sentence can be poured, which conceals the diversity of use amongst different types of sentences. What initially seemed to be a discovery about the nature of sentences and their meanings transpires to be a piece of legislation. No matter how we now try, we cannot use a sentence without describing a state of affairs, nor even invent a language the sentences of which are not, or do not contain, descriptions. What we now have is a new way of talking about sentences and their significance.

The crucial question is what purpose this serves. We shall revert to this point later. For the moment let us merely note three things. First, 'by a new notation no facts of geography are changed';[12] adopting a new form of representation for discourse about language no more alters the linguistic facts than adopting Mercator's method of projection for drawing maps altered the geographical facts thus represented. Secondly, *this* use of 'describe' and 'description' forces us to introduce a new pair of words to do the work currently done by these two, for we still need to *distinguish* what we ordinarily call 'describing' from the various other speech-activities with which it is contrasted. Thirdly, similar considerations apply to the notion of a state of affairs, for it too is here stretched out of all recognition. We would normally *contrast* states of affairs with events, processes, activities, actions, abilities, etc. States of affairs obtain, but do not occur; events occur but do not obtain. Moreover, the competent speaker of English would be little inclined to say that *states of affairs* corresponded to these sentences:

[11] Cf. L. Wittgenstein, *Philosophical Investigations* (Blackwell, Oxford, 1953), §§10ff.
[12] L. Wittgenstein, *The Blue and Brown Books* (Blackwell, Oxford, 1958), p. 57.

If a player crosses the line before the whistle blows, the kick-off is replayed.
If the Moors had won the battle of Poitiers, England would not have been Christian a millennium later.
Nothing can be red and green all over.
Two and two make five.

Logical truths and self-contradictions pose a particularly acute problem here. Theorists ascribe senses to them if only because they can appear in compound sentences which have senses and also in cogent proofs (e.g. in indirect proofs). On the other hand, if possession of sense is equated with describing a state of affairs, then 'Two is even and two is not even' must, in virtue of having a sense, correspond to a state of affairs. But, of course, this state of affairs must be impossible. How can a theorist avoid falling into the absurdity of claiming that a self-contradiction describes an impossible possibility? The cost of over-stretching the terms 'describe' and 'state of affairs' is that tears open up in the fabric of our language, and the harder one strives to close them the more rents open up in adjacent spots.

Our argument has focused on the idea of *descriptive* content. The thesis that every sentence is *inter alia* a description is either absurd or vacuous, and so too is the claim that every sentence contains a description. At this juncture, a theorist is apt to make a tactical retreat. He will abjure the word 'description', perhaps conceding that he has previously misapplied it in setting up his distinction between sense and force. But provided that parallel arguments can be brought against similar explanations of what different syntactic transforms of a given sentence 'have in common' in terms of 'information', 'being about the same thing', 'expressing the same proposition', etc., then *all* attempts to give such an informal explanation of theoretical terms such as 'sense', 'sentence-radical', 'phrastic' will founder on the reef of the correct uses of the explanatory expressions. Consequently we must recognize that the basic vocabulary of the theory is so far *unexplained* if all accounts in terms of descriptions, information, etc., are withdrawn. At best we are faced with a serious lacuna. The theorist must be made to take us back to the drawing board.

Investigation of the notion of descriptive content also raises a further worry. The idea that various sentences with different structures (or different moods) have something in common over and above certain recurring words necessitates taking descriptive content to be not a symbol, but what is expressed by certain symbols. Otherwise most identifications of common descriptive contents by theorists would be patently absurd. On the other hand, truth-conditional semantics is standardly built on the thesis that *sentences* (symbols or expressions formed in certain ways) are what have the properties of being true or false, and truth-conditions are therefore normally ascribed to symbols. This generates a strategic dilemma. If a theorist wishes to defend the competence of truth-conditional semantics to account for the use and meaning of all sentences of natural languages, then it will not be cogent for him to extract descriptive contents, which are not symbols, from sentences and to argue that these abstract entities have truth-conditions; for then he must abandon the tenet that symbols are the primary bearers of truth-conditions. If, on the other hand, he retains this fundamental principle, then his quest for a common bearer of truth-conditions in sets of sentences differing only in 'mood' will be thwarted from the start. A theorist who was clear about these matters would see that nothing could satisfy his requirements. Terms such as 'description' and 'information' help to shield this incoherence from view since they are sometimes used to refer to expressions, sometimes to what is expressed. Their Janus-faced character no doubt accounts for their popularity in informal expositions of sense/force distinctions.

2 Overlapping paraphrases

The second common method for explaining the technical terms intended to denote the entity allegedly common to corresponding assertion, question, order or wish (or to their appropriate linguistic vehicles) is to exploit the possibilities of certain (more or less artificial) paraphrases. The theorist groups together sentences which are related to each other by simple syntactical transformations of the kind described in traditional grammar (e.g. a declarative sentence, the corresponding sentence-question, the counterpart imperative sentence, etc.). Then, by adopting an appropriate system of paraphrase, he aims to represent the sense common to these unanalysed sentences by a shared constituent in the corresponding paraphrases. The paraphrases will be so contrived that they have in common complex expressions which can plausibly be taken to exhaust what the paraphrased sentences say.

This general strategy for exhibiting something in common beneath apparent diversity is venerable. In particular, it is standardly employed to make clear that 'sentence-connectives' form statements which express relations among unasserted propositions or thoughts. The logical relation between

Two is a prime number.

and

Two is not a prime number.

is thought to be made perspicuous if the second sentence is rephrased as

It is not the case that two is a prime number.

This paraphrase is held to show that negation should be construed as an operation on an (unasserted) proposition (e.g. what is expressed by 'two is a prime number' in the sentence 'It is not the case that two is a prime number'). Although logicians think both of the original sentences express the same proposition, only the paraphrased denial reveals an isolated expression which expresses this proposition, and hence the paraphrase makes transparent something hidden beneath the varied ways of expressing denials in English.

Sense/force theorists typically offer paraphrases in accord with one of the three following models:

(i) The room is cool.   → It is the case   that the room is cool.
     Is the room cool?   → Is it the case   that the room is cool?
     Cool the room!   → Make it the case   that the room is cool!

Here the common component in the paraphrases is an indirect statement ('that'-clause).

(ii) The room is cool   → The room's being cool.   Yes.
      Cool the room!   → The room's being cool.   Please!

Such paraphrases contain a verbal noun in common.

(iii) The room is cool → My next utterance is an assertion.
                                              The room is cool.
       Is the room cool? → My next utterance is a question.
                                              The room is cool.
       Cool the room!   → My next utterance is an imperative.
                                              The room is cool.

These paraphrases overlap in a declarative sentence (which Davidson calls the 'indicative core' of the unparaphrased sentence).[13]

[13] D. Davidson's analysis (in 'Moods and Performances', in *Meaning and Use*, ed. A. Margalit (Reidel, Dordrecht, 1979), pp. 9–20), differs from other sense/force theories in arguing that the common constituent of different transforms of an 'indicative' sentence is the

Before trying to assess the interest of these paraphrases, we should pause to consider *what* is taken to be paraphrased. There are two obvious possibilities which differ radically from each other. First, what is paraphrased is a type-sentence. On this view, the paraphrase will be applied uniformly to every token of any type-sentence; indeed, the model paraphrase for a sentence-question will be applied to all sentence-questions whatever, the model paraphrase for an imperative to all imperative sentences, etc. Provided that the theorist does not lose sight of the facts that declarative sentences may be used to give orders, ask questions, etc., that sentence-questions may be used to issue requests or to make assertions, etc., he will not maintain that the force-indicator in his paraphrase by itself settles what speech-act any particular utterance of that sentence performs. He will not claim that there is a one-to-one correspondence between sentence-forms and the uses of sentences, but rather that there is a correspondence between sentence-forms and their *typical* uses. Hence, the circumspect theorist who paraphrases type-sentences may commit himself to nothing stronger than the thesis that his paraphrases make transparent the *standard* employments of various distinguishable syntactic forms. The second alternative possibility is to paraphrase not type-sentences, but individual utterances. On this view, the theorist is at liberty to offer different paraphrases of utterances of tokens of a single type-sentence. What looks like a translation of a declarative sentence (e.g. 'The room is cool') is really meant to paraphrase any utterance used to make a particular *assertion* (viz. that the room is cool), whatever syntactical form the sentence uttered may have (e.g. even if the speaker uttered the words 'Isn't it cool in here?'). In this case, the force-indicator in the paraphrase is meant to pin down the actual (generic) speech-act performed by the speaker in making the utterance which is to be paraphrased. Here again the circumspect theorist will acknowledge that there is no one-to-one correspondence between sentence-forms and their actual uses.

---

indicative sentence itself. Moods other than the indicative are revealed by semantic analysis to consist of an 'indicative core', which is a sentence, and a 'mood-setter' which 'function[s] semantically as [a] sentence' (p. 19) and says (but does not assert!) that the core has the specified illocutionary force. Both constituents, on this bizarre analysis, have truth-values, although their conjoint utterance does not. The move is strikingly similar to Ross's and Langendoen's grammatical theories (above, p. 74) save that revelations of 'semantic analysis' do not, apparently, require such prestidigitations as 'deletion operations' in depth-grammar. This gain, however, is obtained only at the cost of the complete obscurity of how 'semantic analysis' can show any such thing!

Although these two interpretations of the models of paraphrasing are fundamentally different and yield discrepant results, most sense/force theorists fail to clarify this aspect of their work. They seldom state *what* they are paraphrasing, and hence they do not explain how their model paraphrases are meant to budget for the looseness of fit between sentence-forms and speech-acts performed by uttering them. We all know that a sentence, declarative in form, can be used not only to assert, but also to order (e.g. 'You will φ' or 'I should like you to φ' or 'I order you to φ') to question (e.g. 'I wonder whether p', 'I should like to know whether p') to express wishes (e.g. 'I wish it would rain') and to exclaim (e.g. 'She has arrived!'). Similarly, interrogatives can be used not only to question but also to assert (as in so-called rhetorical questions), to order ('Will you be quiet!', 'Would you leave the room, please!') to exclaim ('Isn't she charming?', 'Wasn't it a marvellous concert?'), and to express wishes ('Who will rid me of this turbulent priest?', 'Will it ever rain?'). Further, tokens of one and the same type-sentence may be used on different occasions to perform speech-acts of wholly different categories. 'You will go to London' may in one context be a prediction, in another an order. 'I would like to φ' may be a statement (as in answer to the question 'Who would like to φ?'), a request, or an exclamation. These are all platitudes about English. Nonetheless, it is not clear that they do not constitute insuperable obstacles to building any intelligible general account of sense and force on these paraphrases. Sense/force theorists have an inclination to maintain both that force is a characteristic of a type-sentence *and* that its force determines how tokens of it are used in speaking. In so far as a theory rests on the notion that the grammatical form of a sentence is a *definitive* guide to its use, this theory must be written off as ludicrous.

Theorists who wish to build on the possibilities of a paraphrase normally proceed as if they were drawing attention to certain ways of rephrasing type-sentences, tokens of which might be used by a speaker in typical situations to clarify what he has said. In discussion with a student who seems disposed to accept the conclusion of Zeno's paradox (viz. that Achilles cannot overtake the tortoise if the tortoise has a head start), I might say with an expression of incredulity 'So it is impossible to overtake another car on a motorway', intending to pose a question, and should he fail to respond, I might clarify my purpose by saying 'I'm not stating that this is impossible, rather asking you whether it follows that it is impossible to overtake a car', or again I might say 'I mean: is it the case that this is impossible?' The model paraphrases simply apply such strategies generally. Putting all questions in such a form as 'Is it the case that . . .?' might be thought to make the intention to pose a question somewhat less easy to mistake than it would be in certain other cases (e.g. uttering a declarative sentence with interrogative intonation contour). So too would perspicuity be attained by phrasing all assertions in such a form as 'It is the case that . . .' and all orders in such a form as 'Make it the case that . . .'

At first sight such paraphrases seem universally available. They generate in a systematic way sentences that are roughly synonymous with the sentence to be paraphrased; 'Is it the case that the Eiffel Tower has collapsed?' seems, e.g., to be interchangeable with 'Has the Eiffel Tower collapsed?' Moreover, they seem to meet the desiderata of the sense/force theorist. Each one can apparently be split into two expressions one of which expresses the entire 'sense' or 'content' of the sentence to be paraphrased, the other of which indicates the 'force' and nothing but the 'force' which the original sentence bears; e.g. an indirect statement en-capsulates the content, while the prefixes 'It is the case', 'Is it the case' and 'Make it the case' are pure force-indicators. Of course, such force-indicators do not specify the actual use of an utterance on a particular occasion; instead, by indicating the typical use of the sentence paraphrased (or its use in the 'null-context'), they enable an addressee to work out from features of the context what speech-act my particular utterance of this sentence performs. Everything in the strategy of paraphrase seems plain and straightforward.

Further reflection might raise a few doubts. Perhaps the foremost would concern the suggestion that any of the preferred methods of paraphrase amounts to a *clarification* of our ordinary, diverse forms of expression. It would be quite mistaken to think that an unparaphrased sentence typically leaves it a matter for 'guesswork' what speech-act is performed by a particular utterance of it.[14] There are familiar criteria for whether an assertion is made, a question asked, etc., and an overwhelming consensus about the verdicts of applying them to particular utterances. This leaves no scope to effect any general clarification of a natural language by adopting methods of paraphrase (through of course individual methods may be useful in particular cases to remove actual confusions). On the contrary, wholesale paraphrase will exacerbate the extent to which use is concealed beneath form by superimposing a superficial uniformity over fine-grained differences in forms. Declarative sentences have many different uses and even different forms, but this will scarcely be made more conspicuous by prefixing every such sentence with the phrase 'It is the case that . . .' Consider the following results of such paraphrasing:

[14] As Frege seems to suggest (*Begriffsschrift*, §3).

It is the case that one ought to keep one's promises.
It is the case that $2 + 2 = 4$.
It is the case that the chess queen stands on her own colour.
It is the case that I would love a cup of tea.
It is the case that it is time to go.
It is the case that I promise (warn, insist, etc.) . . .
It is the case that it is the case that it is raining.

The apparent uniformity of these sentences may encourage us to neglect the differences between formulating rules, stating mathematical truths, expressing desires, making promises, etc., but these differences will be no less important despite their being masked by this form of paraphrase. If these differences are, as they are often held to be, differences of 'logical form', then this method of paraphrase imposes a spurious uniformity upon sentences of markedly different logical form. Confusion seems to be a more probable outcome than clarification.

The advocate of paraphrasing might recast his claim. The clarification he seeks, he might argue, is not practical; it does not bear on the elimination or reduction of actual doubts about what speech-acts speakers perform in particular circumstances. Rather, it is *theoretical*; it concerns the representation of sentences in such a way that the internal relations among utterances of different sentences are made perspicuous. Just as we might map out the internal relations among colours by identifying shades with points on a solid octahedron, so we might use a method of projecting sentences on to paraphrases to plot out the internal relations among their utterances (relative to a fixed context). Consequently, paraphrasing into indirect statements preceded by force-indicators ('It is the case', 'Is it the case', etc.) makes perspicuous that somebody who says 'It's raining' in response to the question 'Is it raining?' has answered this question, or has asserted what the questioner wished to know; and similarly, somebody who says 'It isn't raining' can be seen to have denied exactly the same thing as somebody else asserts in the same situation by saying 'It's raining'. Such explanations will be particularly prized by anybody who presupposes that internal relations must be mediated by shared entities. For the expression in common to the paraphrases of different sentences may be construed as the designation of such an intermediary (a 'proposition', a 'thought', etc.).

Admiration for this achievement might be diminished by noting that the paraphrase seems either redundant or powerless to establish any internal relation. We must be presumed able to recognize that 'Is it raining?' poses exactly the same question as 'Is it the case that it is raining?' Moreover, it must be *perspicuous* that this internal relation among questions holds in spite of there being no shared expression (apart from certain words) in these two syntactically related sentences. For if this were not so, then the perspicuous relation between 'Is it the case that it is raining?' and 'It is the case that it is raining' would not establish any *perspicuous* connection between 'Is it raining?' and 'It's raining'! But, if this possibility is conceded, then the well-known syntactic relation between 'It is raining' and 'Is it raining?' (viz. that one is the interrogative transform of the other) should suffice to make perspicuous the internal relation between utterances of these sentences *without any appeal to paraphrases*. If, on the other hand, it were conceded *not* to be perspicuous that 'Is it raining?' and 'Is it the case that it is raining?' pose the same question, then shared constituents among paraphrases would be useless for establishing internal relations. Both horns of this dilemma are threatening to the thesis that paraphrase effects any general clarification of the internal relations among utterances of sentences.

Once again the advocate of paraphrasing might shift his ground. His aim, he might claim, is not systematically to produce a sentence in some canonical form which is roughly equivalent with any given sentence. Rather, he seeks an *analysis* for each sentence of a natural language, a reformulation from which its entire significance and all of its internal relations with other sentences can simply be read off. Or, in a more avant-garde idiom, he searches for a representation of the *deep structure* of every well-formed sentence. If he succeeds in this enterprise, then the so-called 'paraphrase' of a sentence will actually exhibit what is *in the sentence* itself, or at least it will represent the items *in its depth-structure*. At this point, the theorist has plunged into an elaborate mythology about symbols. The obvious consequence is nonsense. The expressions contained in the analysis are typically not contained in the sentence to be paraphrased, and the notion that a sentence has a hidden syntactic structure, not to mention a structure consisting of non-linguistic entities, is ludicrous. Moreover, there is something perverse in the idea that canonical paraphrases reveal the essential structure of sentences. For the limited variety of forms allowed in any system of paraphrasing makes the analysed forms of a language more uniform in appearance than the unanalysed sentences, and this exaggerates the difficulty of explaining how differentiating among the uses of sentences is related to differences among sentence-forms. The theorist who builds on paraphrases seems in dire straits if he is driven to defend his proceedings by reference to incoherent explanations of 'analysis' and 'depth-structure'.

3 Shortage of logical space

These probings suggest that there is less strength to the theory of force and more nonsense to the theory of sense than might at first be supposed. We might wonder whether the paraphrastic schemata really *clarify* anything, indeed, whether there *is* anything in need of clarification. It is not a perspicuous description of linguistic phenomena, let alone an explanation of baffling puzzles, that confronts us, but rather frantic attempts to satisfy the bogus requirements of a misguided theory of meaning and a confused theory of understanding. This scepticism can be nurtured by a more critical examination of the alleged possibilities and purposes of paraphrase, particularly with respect to imperatives and interrogatives.

   Confusion in the description of the use of imperative sentences is common. Kenny, for example, suggests that 'directives are commonly second-person sentences and can be issued only in a single tense, the future',[15] but also contends that 'the felicitous utterance of an imperative . . . actually presupposes that the sentence-radical it involves is descriptively false; for only if it is false can it be made true'.[16] This is inconsistent. It is true that one can only command a person to bring about that which can be brought about, hence there are indeed no 'past-tense' commands. But, of course, it does not follow that English sentences used to issue commands are in the future tense. Typically we use imperative sentences for this purpose, and the imperative mood in English lacks tenses altogether. Similarly, the suggestion that commands are descriptively false is a distortion of a simple truth, namely that what a command requires or orders to be done should not, when the command is issued, already be done (or be believed to be). Thoughts or propositions are commonly conceived to be given by specification of their truth-conditions, but there is nothing we commonly conceive of as a condition for a command to be true. The language-theorist might introduce a parallel notion of an 'obedience-condition', viz. what an addressee must do if he is to count as having obeyed a command. To understand an order one must indeed know what will count as compliance with it. But this is confusedly expressed by equating it with knowing what thought it expresses (since it expresses none). By obeying an order to shut the door, one does indeed bring it about that the sentence 'The door is shut' (or 'N. N. shuts the door', etc.) now expresses a true thought, whereas if

---

[15] Kenny, *Will, Freedom, and Power*, p. 39.
[16] Ibid., p. 87.

previously uttered, it would not have done so. But this too is wrongly represented by identifying it with making a thought true. An imperative sentence used to give a command *does not express a proposition which is identical with the proposition expressed by an assertion of an addressee's compliance with the command given* although there is an internal relation between the command and what fulfils it (see below).

The instruction that all imperatives are to be paraphrased on the model of transforming 'Cool the room!' into 'Make it the case that the room is cool' has the virtue of being succinct, but it has the defect of leaving the aspiring translator in the lurch when confronted by many familiar kinds of expression. Consider the mechanical application of this transformation to the following imperatives:

(1) Go!	(1′) Make it the case that you will go.
(2) Be gone!	(2′) Make it the case that you will have gone.
(3) Somebody open this door!	(3′) Make it the case that somebody will open this door.
(4) Everybody take a deep breath!	(4′) Make it the case that everybody will take a deep breath.
(5) If it rains, place a bet on Plodder!	(5′) Make it the case that, if it rains you will place a bet on Plodder.
(6) Don't go!	(6′) Make it the case that you will not go.
(7) Let's go![17]	(7′) Make it the case that we will go.
(8) Let me go!	(8′) Make it the case that I will go.
(9) Let who will go.	(9′) Make it the case that who wills will go.
(10) Let A be an isosceles triangle!	(10′) Make it the case that A is an isosceles triangle.
(11) Let the heavens fall!	(11′) Make it the case that the heavens fall.

Many of the proposed paraphrases are problematic. Several of them obscure who the addressees are; e.g. (4′) masks the fact that the command is addressed to everybody. Some border on the anomalous; e.g. (10′) and (11′) could be addressed only to somebody with God-like powers. Some introduce spurious differences; e.g. (1) and (2) seem equivalent, but they

---

[17] Not to be confused with 'Let us go!' = 'Permit us to go' which is the ordinary second-person imperative of 'let' as a transitive verb.

Sense and Force

are differently represented by (1′) and (2′). Others disguise important differences; e.g. (5) is a conditional command, whereas (5′) is an unconditional command to make a conditional true, and (6) is a negative order, not a command to make a negative statement true (e.g. by shooting myself in the head). Finally, some paraphrases clearly misrepresent what is paraphrased; e.g. (8′) would be an equivalent of 'Make me go!' which is used very differently from 'Let me go!', and (9), a third-person imperative, is wholly distorted by the anomalous (9′). This cursory survey shows that what is seemingly a straightforward method for paraphrasing imperatives into sentences of the form 'Make it the case that . . .' runs up against a variety of serious difficulties. And similar problems arise in the case of other proposed paraphrases, whether of declarative sentence, sentence-questions, imperatives, or optatives. At the very best, the methods of paraphrase need to be made much more subtle and sensitive to the nuances of our expressions. But then it must be conceded that the initial model-paraphrases supplied by sense/force theorists are radically defective. Instead of rushing ahead with the comment 'Oh yes, I see what you mean', we should hang back and say 'No, I don't see at all; please explain what you mean'. Our scruples would clearly be justified.

In fact, the range of difficulties raised by the listed paraphrases of a handful of imperatives suggest a number of deeper objections to the idea that a sense/force distinction can be vindicated by procedures for systematically paraphrasing sentences within a natural language. Though many of these objections are obvious, they are seldom noticed at all.

First, proposed paraphrases produce much nonsense and many anomalous expressions. In some cases they produce utter nonsense and nothing but nonsense. This is true of paraphrases of sentences into verbal-nouns together with such 'force-indicators' as 'Yes' or 'Please'. Somebody who said to his opponent in tennis 'Your serving first. Please. . . . Your hitting a good shot. Yes. . . . My not being ready yet. Yes. . . .' might be understood, though his prowess at speaking English would be under the gravest suspicion. But somebody who said 'Tom Sawyer's being cleanly and neat's being less likely than his being mud-caked and dressed in rags. Yes' would have little chance of being understood at all. The fact that such a method of paraphrase yields *no* English *sentences* seems to make it a non-starter as a way of paraphrasing sentences within English! Other proposals for paraphrasing often yield significant English sentences, but sometimes generate expressions which are anomalous or ridiculous. For different reasons this would be true of both the following translations of the question 'Are you leaving now or not?'

My next utterance is interrogative. You are leaving now or you are not leaving now.
Is it the case that you are leaving now or you are not leaving now?

No available method of paraphrase is immune from such difficulties. Yet this objection of general and ramifying gross distortion, anomalousness and generation of nonsense is *fatal* to the programme of founding a sense/force distinction on the general possibility of systematic paraphrasing within a natural language.

A second telling objection is that the proposed paraphrases, if significant expressions at all, are in many cases not (even roughly!) synonymous with the sentences subject to rephrasing. Truth-conditional semantics advances a very strict criterion of synonymy for statement-making sentences, viz. that two sentences differ in meaning if there are any circumstances in which they may be used to make assertions differing in truth-value. The analogous requirement for non-declarative sentences would exclude taking any standard paraphrase and the original sentence to have the same meaning in many cases, and therefore it would undermine the presupposition that any proposed method of paraphrase is uniformly meaning-preserving. This point is readily established. Consider this pair of sentences:

(1) I would like to know whether p.
(2) Would I like to know whether p?

(2) is the interrogative transformation of (1). But (1), while it is *not* an interrogative sentence (but rather contains an indirect question as a subordinate clause), is typically used to question, not to assert something. Yet the question it would usually be used to ask is *not* the question which would be expressed by the normal use of (2). On the other hand, if (1) is uttered in response to the question 'Who would like to know whether p?', then it *is* used to assert. In this second case, the paraphrase of (1) into 'It is the case that I would like to know whether p' and of (2) into 'Is it the case that I would like to know whether p?' might be thought to clarify an internal relation that holds between some utterances of (1) and some (possible) utterances of (2). Yet in other cases the paraphrasing of (1) into 'Is it the case that p?' would be natural and would highlight the use of (1) to ask a question. The problem is that each of these paraphrases undermines the case for treating the other as producing a synonymous sentence *according to the theorist's own conception of synonymy*. Similar difficulties arise in many other cases. The question 'Is this gin or cyanide?', for example, is

typically quite different from the question 'Is it the case that this is gin or cyanide?'; or still more obviously, the question 'Is he breathing or not?' is standardly not the (trivial) question 'Is it the case that he is breathing or not breathing?' Such platitudes raise an awkward dilemma: *either* the proposed paraphrases are condemned as unacceptable because they do not preserve the significance and typical patterns of use of the paraphrased sentences *or* they are useless for methodically clarifying the significance and use of the paraphrased sentences because the acceptability of a paraphrase is divorced from any requirement that it *generally* preserves the significance and pattern of use of what is paraphrased. (This dilemma can be avoided, but only by abandoning the conception of synonymy as invariable equivalence which is one of the pillars of truth-conditional semantics.)

Both of these objections to proposed general methods of paraphrasing sentences have the same ultimate source. Any expression entitled to be called a paraphrase of an English sentence must itself be a well-formed and intelligible expression in English. It must not be nonsensical, and it must not be devoid of any significance (since then an *independent* explanation would be needed of what the 'paraphrase' is to mean). But a well-formed, intelligible expression is one for which competent speakers have a potential use; there are already criteria for its correct (and incorrect) use, and it is an expression understood without the need for any fresh explanations. Consequently, the theorist who invokes paraphrases to support a sense/ force distinction must respect the already established uses of these expressions. He cannot impose novel requirements on them since the logical space which they occupy, as it were, is already completely filled. If he claims that paraphrases formed out of imperatives by such phrases as 'Make it the case that . . .' or 'Bring it about that . . .' illuminate some important aspects of the use of imperatives, then he must presuppose that we have a prior understanding of sentences of these particular forms, and hence he has no business modifying what is to be understood by laying down novel fiats about these forms of expressions. He cannot legislate that 'It is the case that . . .' makes no difference to what is asserted, or that this sentence-form is a more perspicuous guide to the use of expressions than the variegated forms of declarative sentences found in English. A theorist such as Davidson may maintain that a sentence-question may be paraphrased into a 'mood-setter' (e.g. 'The following utterance is interrogative') coupled with an 'indicative core' (e.g. 'The Battle of Hastings took place in 1066'). But then he must accept the consequence: the adequacy of his paraphrase must be assessed according to what is understood by these sentences. Who is he to declare that an utterance of 'The Battle of Hastings took place in 1066' after the 'mood-setter' is not to be understood to make an assertion? What right has he to proclaim that an utterance of 'The following sentence is interrogative' asserts nothing at all (because it has no content)? By what divine dispensation can he override the verdict that the utterance of 'The Battle of Hastings took place in 1066' is simply *not* an interrogative utterance? Even God has no power thus to tamper with the boundaries of logical space. Moreover, the open attempts of a theorist to do so completely undermines the claim that there is anything to be learned from the existing possibilities of paraphrasing provided within natural languages.

A third objection comes from a different quarter: far from clarifying them, proposed methods of paraphrase distort and misrepresent the internal relations among patterns of use of sentences and among speech-acts performed by uttering sentences. The notion that a canonical method of paraphrasing brings out all of these internal relations is an obstacle to acknowledging those not made apparent by a single form of representation, and it is also a stimulus for theorists to persuade themselves that dubious forms of paraphrase are legitimate. At the same time, preferred methods of paraphrase may suggest the existence of internal relations where there are none, and hence they may lure theorists into espousing obvious absurdities. In so far as the *raison d'être* of a sense/force distinction is the clarification of internal relations among sentences and speech-acts, the sins of omission and of commission which are to be charged against proposed paraphrases seem to debar paraphrasing from providing the proper foundations of a theory of force.

Instances where methods of paraphrase threaten to screen out obvious internal relations are readily found. One already mentioned is the typical equivalence between utterances of a sentence of the form 'I wonder whether *p*' and utterances of the corresponding sentence-question '*p*?'. Another is the relation between a sentence-question and the corresponding declarative sentence which constitutes an answer. A theorist may claim that the paraphrases 'Is it the case that Harold died at Hastings?' and 'It is the case that Harold died at Hastings' make clear that the question 'Did Harold die at Hastings?' is *answered* by the sentence 'Harold died at Hastings'; the paraphrase apparently reveals that what is queried is just what is asserted. But this claim is mistaken; for, what is asked is *whether* Harold died at Hastings, while what is asserted is *that* Harold died at Hastings, and the paraphrase fails altogether to establish any relation between these 'entities'.

Of course, no sense/force theorists will be prepared to lose such central internal relations from their accounts. Some protective reaction will be initiated. This might take the form of modest observations (e.g. that to ask *whether* Harold died at Hastings is to ask whether it is the case *that* Harold died at Hastings) and some sleight of hand (e.g. that the indirect statement 'that Harold died at Hastings' gives the substance of the indirect question). Alternatively, the reaction may be a more elaborate proposal for paraphrasing. This strategy is pursued in the treatment of W*h*-questions. It is manifest that saying 'Harold died in 1066' is to answer the question 'When did Harold die?', but theorists have great difficulty in explaining this fact within the parameters of their theories. The typical solution to this difficulty is to construe W*h*-questions as 'concealed' imperatives. Analysis reveals, it is said, that interrogatives are really orders to fill in a blank in a sentence-frame to yield a true statement. So, for example, 'What time is it?' is allegedly equivalent to some such form as 'Fill in the blank in "It is —o'clock" ' to yield a true statement. Since the sentence-radical of the imperative 'Do φ!' allegedly has the underlying form: 'that you (the addressee) φ at t', this assimilation of W*h*-questions to orders to complete a 'sentence-frame' to yield a truth transforms a question why, when, who, how, etc. into a 'description' of the addressee's truly completing the sentence-frame. Accordingly the sentence-radical of 'When was Hastings fought?' is expressed, say, by 'that you fill in the blank in "Hastings was fought in —" ', and the complete analysis of the question adds an imperative force indicator, e.g. 'Make it the case', to this expression. The explanation of the connection between the W*h*-question and the answer to it is that somebody who says 'Hastings was fought in 1066' has complied with the instruction to fill in the blank in 'Hastings was fought in —'.

Such explanations of obvious internal relations should be judged to be defective by the theorist's own lights. His theory demands that every internal relation among sentences or speech-acts be represented by exhibiting a shared sentence-radical or a shared mood-indicator. But his paraphrases of W*h*-questions do not accomplish this purpose! If the sentence-radical of 'When was Hastings fought?' is expressed by 'that you fill in the blank in "Hastings was fought in —" ', then the *corresponding* assertion must not have as its sentence-radical what is expressed by 'that Hastings was fought in 1066', nor even by 'that the blank in "Hastings was fought in —" is filled by "1066" ', but rather by 'that I fill in the blank in "Hastings was fought in —" '. Yet that would not be an appropriate paraphrase for any expression which counted as an *answer* to the W*h*-question! A W*h*-question is typically used to request information from the addressee, but never to report or describe his answering the question. The imperative-analysis of W*h*-questions should also be objectionable to the theorist because it *mentions* an incomplete sentence and therefore renders the analysed form of any W*h*-question language-specific. The instruction to fill in the blank in 'It is – o'clock' is distinct from the instruction to fill in the blank in 'Il est – heures', and hence it follows that what a speaker asks in English could never be what another asks in French. This is absurd. In addition to these internal inconsistencies in the theorist's analysis of W*h*-questions, there are other objections. The analysis proposed is modelled on multiple-answer examination questions, in which a box is ticked or a single word inserted. But it would be ridiculous to expect a question requiring an essay as an answer, e.g. 'In what sense was Hume a sceptic about induction?', to commence uniformly with the sentential clause 'Hume was a sceptic about induction in the sense that . . .' Finally, the proposed analysis loses sight of the aim to present the sentence-radical of a question as *what* is asked in uttering the analysed sentence. This is properly expressed for W*h*-questions by the corresponding indirect question; e.g. 'when Hastings was fought' specifies what is asked by somebody who says 'When was Hastings fought?' By contrast, the phrase 'that you fill in the blanks in ". . ." ' is not an indirect question and hence cannot fulfil this role at all. The constraints of a sense/force distinction seem to generate the 'problem' of explaining how W*h*-questions interlock with their answers and also to exclude the possibility of any satisfactory answer.

At the opposite extreme, paraphrases yielding expressions with shared constituents are liable to generate illusions about internal relations. Some sham relations may be very local, seldom noticed, and comparatively insignificant. This might be true of the apparent connection between 'I wonder whether *p*' and 'Do I wonder whether *p*?' which is suggested by standard paraphrasing of declarative and interrogative sentences. But other illusions about internal relations seem widespread and of momentous importance for breeding confusions. One of these is integral to the use of paraphrases in supporting a sense/force distinction. A theorist who, for example, makes much of the fact that various paraphrases share a single indirect statement cannot readily concentrate on some instances of overlap and ignore others. He is inclined to argue that such overlap *always* signals some important internal relation mediated by a shared entity corresponding to the indirect statement (e.g. a 'proposition'). He insists that such paraphrases as 'It is the case that Harold died at Hastings' and 'Is it the case that Harold died at Hastings?' show sentence-questions and corresponding declarative sentences to express common propositions. In conformity with the practice of most logicians, he probably discerns the same propositions to be expressed in the sentences 'It is not the case that Harold died at Hastings' and 'It is possible that Harold died at Hastings'. Of course, it is essential to note that these propositions are not asserted to be true by a speaker who seriously utters these latter sentences (or the sentence-question). Hence the theorist emphasizes that a proposition must be taken, *ceteris paribus*, to be unasserted, or that the act of expressing a proposition must not be confused with the act of making an assertion. Some theorists, eager to avoid the accusation of Platonism, have built theories of speech-acts around the concept of a basic act of expressing a proposition. Others have simply assumed that expressing a proposition is something that the components of molecular sentences (negations, disjunctions, conditionals) have in common with non-declarative sentences, thereby viewing the logic of non-declarative utterances as a smooth extension of the propositional calculus.

This reasoning is misguided. There is indeed a range of performances correctly described as somebody's 'expressing a proposition (thought, idea)', and it is compatible with so describing an utterance to add that the speaker has not made an assertion. But the theorist distorts the concept of expressing a proposition in claiming that *every* utterance is used to express a proposition, and he further distorts this concept by frequently mis-characterizing *what* proposition is expressed. It is ludicrous to say that I have expressed any proposition if I telephone the airport and ask 'Has the morning plane from Timbuctoo arrived yet?' It is equally nonsensical to claim that I have expressed the proposition that π is rational if I state 'If π were rational, then so too would π^2 be rational' – still more absurd if I state 'π is *not* rational'. Logicians and speech-act theorists blatantly abuse the concept of expressing a proposition (thought, idea, etc.). Were they openly to acknowledge that they are introducing a technical expression as part of a theory, it would become obvious that the act of expressing a proposition is a figment of their manufacture designed to defend their attribution of supreme importance to the occurrence of indirect statements in complex sentences of natural languages. But that would put the onus of proof on them to justify the need for and the interest of their theories. And it would require a clear explanation of how they propose to use the expression 'express a proposition'. Without this they must be diagnosed to be labouring under a delusion generated by their drawing false conclusions from possibilities of paraphrase.

We have now formulated three fundamental objections to founding a viable sense/force distinction on methods of paraphrasing within a natural language. The only plausible candidates for straightforward systematic paraphrase are few, and none of them comes even close to satisfying the constraints adumbrated by sense/force theorists on expressions of sense and expressions of force. The verdict must be that it is impossible now to justify a sense/force distinction by appeal to possibilities of paraphrase. This is an important conclusion, and it cannot properly be brushed aside by a vague optimism that some day somebody may come up with a better and hitherto neglected form of paraphrase. It is one thing to develop a theory without any strong evidence in favour of its truth, but quite another to 'theorize' without any ground for thinking that any part of the 'theory' is even intelligible! The hurdle that a sense/force theorist must surmount is to explain what he is talking about, and *he has not succeeded in doing so.*

Many theorists, however, will not be impressed by the distinction between their activities and those of chemists exploring the structures of amino acids, and hence they will be able to work for decades on a diet of a Macawberish faith that something might turn up. We wish now to prove this optimism to be indefensible. The argument is simple. The general requirements placed by theorists on the concepts of sense and force make inconsistent demands on *expressions* for sense and force, and therefore no expressions available in a natural language could be a satisfactory basis for explaining a sense/force distinction. In short, it is no accident, and no defect of imagination, that proposed paraphrases are found wanting. The sentence-radical, a phrastic, an indicative core, etc. (taken as lexical items) expresses the entire 'descriptive content' of the sentence to be paraphrased; it must express a proposition which may be true or false. It must also specify what is asserted in uttering the paraphrased sentence to make an assertion (or what is queried, what ordered, etc.).[18] Finally, it must be totally purged of force; this is most naturally construed to mean that it cannot be used without supplementation by a force-indicator to *say* anything at all, e.g. to make an assertion. These requirements are incompatible. Only an expression that can be used to say something can be said to express a proposition. Indeed, to express a proposition is to say something (e.g. to formulate an hypothesis, to air a possibility, to make a conjecture), though not necessarily to make an assertion. Yet the theorist cannot easily drop the thesis that (an expression for) a sentence-radical cannot be used by itself to say something, because this threatens to remove the possibility of isolating separate expressions in a paraphrase which

---

[18] Otherwise there would be no hope of employing shared entities to account for internal relations among speech-acts.

express only the descriptive content and indicate only the force attached to it. In any case, there is a further inconsistency: the demand that the sentence-radical express the proposition expressed by a declarative sentence conflicts with the demand that it specify what is asserted in uttering this sentence. Only a sentence fulfils the first demand, whereas the second calls for an expression which designates what is asserted (standardly an indirect statement). In English (and in many other languages) expressions of these two types systematically differ in structure. This is enough to rule out the possibility of 'discovering' some unsuspected form of paraphrase which would provide a less inadequate justification for a sense/force distinction than methods of paraphrase commonly advocated.

At this point advocates of paraphrase may fall back on a new argument. They may concede that no expressions in English can be used systematically to paraphrase sentences in such a way that a clear and consistent separation of sense from force is visible in the symbols of the paraphrase. Yet nothing prevents one, they may continue, from introducing a novel form of symbolism in which their requirements on paraphrases are manifestly met. Careful legislation may supply the deficiencies of discovery-procedures. The theorist may use a notation in which letters represent descriptive contents and in which force is indicated by special operators (e.g. '⊢', '?', '!' or 'Est-' and 'Fiat-'). He might hold this symbolism to make perspicuous something obscured by the surface-forms of natural languages. And his well-formed formulae such as '⊢p' or 'Fiat-q' cannot be criticized on the grounds of torturing English as other methods of paraphrase do. Does he not have the freedom, like Humpty Dumpty, to make his symbols mean what he pleases?

This strategy too is futile. First, no such symbol has the status of a *paraphrase* at all. It is not an expression in English, and it has no independently understood use. Its constituent parts are all symbols standing in need of explanation, whereas the role of a paraphrase is to express what is said in other terms which are already intelligible. Although possibilities of paraphrase into a canonical form of sentences in English might plausibly be thought to reveal something about what a speaker already (perhaps 'tacitly') understands, much less plausibility attaches to drawing the same conclusion from the possibility of devising an artificial notation. Secondly, sense/force theorists who employ formal notations regularly forget that their symbols have no pattern of use apart from their explanations of how to use these expressions. Hence they fall into ridiculous confusions. Philosophers debate about whether the assertion-sign can come within the scope of logical operators (e.g. whether '¬ ⊢ p' is well-formed) or about whether a conditional command should be written as '$p \rightarrow !q$' rather than '$!(p \rightarrow q)$'. They agonize about whether it makes sense to write '$?p \rightarrow ?q$' or '$\vdash p \rightarrow !q$'. As if there were real principles laid up on High which governed the possibilities of combining logical connectives with force-operators! This is an exemplary illustration of the generalization that philosophers are often like children who first scribble some arbitrary lines on a piece of paper and then ask the grown-ups 'What is this?'.[19] Finally, appeal to an artificial notation to illuminate a sense/force distinction presupposes that the notation itself has been made intelligible, and this in turn presupposes that the requirements imposed on the invented symbols are compatible with each other. But the first of these tasks was what possibilities of paraphrase were to establish, and the second is precisely what the examination of paraphrases within natural languages puts in doubt. The claim that English obscures something important which is perspicuous in an artificial symbolism requires clear explanations of these symbols and the support of a proof that the stipulations of how to use them are consistent. Otherwise founding a sense/force distinction on the articulations of these symbols has all the virtues of theft as opposed to honest toil. To the advocate of such 'paraphrases', the obvious reply is

We might just as well say this: among numbers hitherto known there is none which satisfies the simultaneous equations

$$x + 1 = 2$$
$$x + 2 = 1,$$

but there is nothing to prevent us from introducing a symbol which solves the problem.[20]

The question in any such case is whether there is any room for the envisaged legislation.

Here we have finally checkmated the advocate of explaining a sense/force distinction in terms of possibilities of paraphrasing with natural languages. His tactics are flawed. He cannot actually produce any systematic paraphrases that meet all of his requirements, and his demands themselves are under suspicion in respect of their consistency. This is a damning verdict. But it can be further strengthened. His strategy is also misguided. Even if it were possible to produce satisfactory paraphrases, what reason would there be for holding this to indicate anything other

---

[19] L. Wittgenstein, Big Typescript, p. 430.
[20] Frege, *The Foundations of Arithmetic*, §96.

than this possibility itself? Explaining a method of paraphrase (e.g. into sentences of the form 'It is the case that . . .', 'Is it the case that . . .?' etc.) is comparable to teaching a painter fixed-point perspective. Suppose that a pupil, having mastered this technique, reports to his instructor that he has made a splendid discovery: viz. that rhombi and rectangles *really* have the same shape! Suppose, too, that he criticizes his instructor for having differentiated among the shapes of three-dimensional objects according to the usual criteria. Should one not reply: the pupil has adopted a method of representing three-dimensional objects according to which rhombal and rectangular surfaces may alike be projected on to rhombi; it is integral to this method of perspective drawing that rhombal and rectangular surfaces have the common property that they may be projected on to the same shape in the plane; consequently this common property cannot be defined independently of this method of representation, but is solely the *product* of adopting this method. Paraphrase is similar. If a pair of sentences can be so paraphrased that they share an indirect statement, why should one conclude anything more exciting than that these sentences have in common the property that they can be projected by certain translation-rules on to a pair of sentences sharing an indirect statement? What room is there for the important discovery that they have the same descriptive content? Or that the relation between them is mediated by an abstract entity designated by the indirect statement? If these 'deep' conclusions were licensed, would we not also have to concede that every declarative sentence contains a question because of the possibility of rephrasing assertions on the model of transforming 'It is raining' into 'Is it raining? Yes.'?[21] A sense/force theorist seems to have no justification for treating possibilities of paraphrase as *revelations* of anything else. Without this his strategy of calling attention to paraphrases is altogether futile. Even if he woke to find his dreams realized, he would discover that paraphrases could not fulfil his aspirations.

4   An indirect approach via indirect speech

The third standard method for explaining the terms 'sense', 'sentence-radical', etc., and the correlative terms 'force', 'mood-indicator', etc., is to draw attention to the form of typical reports in indirect speech, e.g. 'He asserted that (asked whether, promised to) . . .' In all these cases there is a

---

[21] Wittgenstein, *Philosophical Investigations*, §22.

verb which specifies what speech-act a speaker has performed, and there is a noun-clause (indirect statement, question, or command) which specifies what the speaker has said (what he has asserted, predicted, asked, requested). The theorist then explains that the sense of the utterance reported in *oratio obliqua* is what the noun clause designates, while the force of the utterance is the speech-act specified by the verb of saying. The separability of sense from force is transparent in the articulation of reports in *oratio obliqua*, and so too is the large degree of freedom in combining the same sense with different forces and the same force with different senses. This seems an incontrovertible basis for distinguishing sense from force and for clarifying these theoretical concepts.[22]

The most straightforward way to develop this idea is to treat sense and force as features or aspects of particular utterances of expressions. The force of an utterance is the actual speech-act performed by a speaker on a particular occasion, while its sense is the specific content of this speech-act. This seems the obvious corollary of the fact that reports in *oratio obliqua* are typically descriptions of particular speech-acts. Yet it is open to doubt whether this interpretation will satisfy the central requirements of theorists who seek a sense/force distinction.

One immediate difficulty concerns the propriety of speaking of *the* sense and *the* force of a given utterance. There is no unique canonical method for rendering utterances in indirect speech. Typically the speech-act performed can be described in different ways, more or less specific (e.g. 'He declared that . . .', 'He stated his firm belief that . . .', 'He affirmed with the utmost conviction that . . .'). So too can what is said. Indeed, if the uttered sentence contains indexical expressions, the corresponding indirect statement, question, or command may differ systematically with the context in which *it* is uttered. There is typically much latitude in what counts as a correct report of what is said, and the criteria of correctness depend on the purposes for which reports in *oratio obliqua* are offered. Consequently, accepted methods for framing and judging reports in indirect speech give no justification for ascribing a *unique* sense or force to any utterance according to this proposed explanation of the sense/force distinction. A second objection is that the idiom of reports in indirect speech does not suffice to make perspicuous even the most basic internal relations among

---

[22] Searle contends that the common propositional content of different transforms is 'what is asserted in the act of asserting, what is stated in the act of stating' (*Speech Acts*, p. 29); Kenny argues that 'There is no need to think of optation as distinct from proposition. Both correspond to the *content* of a speech act; this is the same in both the assertoric and imperative case' (*Will, Freedom and Power*, p. 44).

utterances. As previously noted, indirect questions, indirect commands, and indirect statements have different syntactical structures in English (and most other languages). Consequently, the proposed explanation of 'sense', by restricting shared sense to utterances correct reports of which in indirect speech have a shared noun-clause, cannot account for the fact that the question *whether* $\sqrt{2}^{\sqrt{2}}$ is rational is answered by the statement *that* $\sqrt{2}^{\sqrt{2}}$ is rational (and also by the statement *that* $\sqrt{2}^{\sqrt{2}}$ is *not* rational!). Indeed, it is doubtful whether this explanation of 'sense' allows for the possibility that *any* question has a sense in common with *any* assertion, even though this possibility (and the parallel possibilities of shared sense between statements and commands and between commands and questions) is a cornerstone of all theories erected on a sense/force distinction. A theorist who builds this distinction rigorously on the forms of report in indirect speech seems to be squaring up to shoot at his own goal.[23]

    A third difficulty concerns the relevance of the sense/force distinction applied to utterances for a theory of meaning of the sentences of a natural language. Truth-conditional semantics is usually thought to seek to account for the meanings of type-sentences, and the assignment of truth-conditions to type-sentences is often argued to be the foundation of a theory of understanding. The reporting of particular utterances in indirect speech appears to have no direct bearing on these matters. The fact that different utterances of a single unambiguous type-sentence may correctly be reported quite differently in *oratio obliqua* seems to imply that the meanings of type-sentences fall outside the scope of any theory erected in the proposed explanations of 'sense' and 'force'. The only obvious way to connect the two theories would be to explain exactly how the correctness of reports of utterances in indirect speech depends systematically on features of the type-sentence uttered (together with the circumstances of its utterance). In this case the focus of a semantic theory incorporating a sense/force distinction is not on utterances (and how they are reported in indirect speech), but on type-sentences. Hence the theorist is led towards reintroducing the terms 'sense' and 'force' to specify features of type-

---

[23] Of course, he can always try to save the day by 'discovering' a goal-keeper in the 'depth-grammar'. Thus, for example, Searle is disturbed that in 'I promise to come', unlike 'I promise that I will come', 'the surface structure does not seem to allow us to make a distinction between the indicator of illocutionary force and the indicator of propositional content' (*Speech Acts*, p. 30), but, *mirabile dictu*, 'if we study the deep structure of the first sentence, we find that its underlying phrase marker, like the underlying phrase marker of the second, contains "I promise + I will come" '. Dr Pangloss would be relieved to find that all is for the best in the best of all possible depth-grammars.

sentences that are thought, together with circumstances of utterance, to determine what is said and what speech-act is performed. This indicates a need for some less straightforward way to develop a sense/force distinction on the basis of reports in indirect speech.

Many theorists follow a natural route to connect reports of particular utterances in indirect speech with a sense/force distinction applicable to the type-sentences uttered by speakers. They postulate (or deduce?) the existence of a mechanism of recognition whose operation presupposes such a distinction. The argument rests on three truisms. The first is that there is overwhelming agreement among competent speakers as to whether a given report in *oratio obliqua* is correct or incorrect. The second is that understanding an utterance is often incompatible with inability correctly to identify what speech-act the utterer has performed (e.g. whether he has made an assertion or asked a question). And the third is that features of a type-sentence (e.g. interrogative structure) play a role in the identification of the speech-act performed on a particular occasion by a speaker who utters this sentence. Together these truisms seem to adumbrate the shape of a rigorous theory of understanding. Agreement on the identification of speech-acts must be explained by the hypothesis that speakers systematically exploit features of type-sentences which, together with the circumstances of a particular utterance, determine what constitutes a correct report of somebody's utterance in indirect speech. Moreover, since the idiom for indirect speech separates out what is said from what is done in saying it, a theory of understanding should distinguish those features of a type-sentence which bear on what is said (its sense-conveying component) from those features which bear on what is done in saying it (its force-indicator). A full theory would reveal how one recognizes what another has said and what speech-act he has performed on the basis of the ability to discriminate sense-conveying components and force-indicators within type-sentences. Such a theory presupposes that understanding an utterance is a complex, multistage *process* which breaks down into various feats of *recognition* and sundry activities of *computation*. A sense/force distinction applied to type-sentences is held to be an integral part of the operation of this mental mechanism.

For numerous reasons, this strategy is flawed. It rests upon a mythology of psychological processes of understanding. Through a misconception of what it is to understand an utterance, it postulates acts of recognition and computation that are fictitious. This matter will be investigated in detail later.

We will try to diminish the forcefulness of this mythology by drawing attention to some familiar mundane features of exceedingly elementary communicative acts which do not cohere with the preferred picture. We often communicate at least in part by gestures and facial expressions. Many of these 'concrete symbols' have institutionalized significance; their meanings can, and, for a foreigner, need to be explained. In some cases, a gesture alone may support a complete report in indirect speech, e.g. if I make a thumbs-up gesture to a friend to indicate having won a game, I may be reported as having signified (perhaps even asserted) that I won; a shrug of the shoulders (particularly by a Frenchman) may, in an appropriate context, be reported as signifying that one does not care about such-and-such. But do such *gestures* decompose into a force-indicator and a sense-conveying component? Does a thumbs-down gesture have a similar force-operator? And does a threatening throat-slitting gesture have a different one? When one politely steps aside and holds the door for a lady, does one's *gesture* decompose into a phrastic 'Your entering first' and a neustic 'Please!'? These suggestions are ludicrous. Reflection on such facts may have the same prophylactic effect on advocates of a sense/force distinction as it had in moving Wittgenstein to reconsider his conception of language in the *Tractatus*.

Wittgenstein and P. Sraffa, a lecturer in economics at Cambridge, argued together a great deal over the ideas of the *Tractatus*. One day (they were riding, I think, on a train) when Wittgenstein was insisting that a proposition and that which it describes must have the same 'logical form', the same 'logical multiplicity', Sraffa made a gesture, familiar to Neapolitans as meaning something like disgust or contempt, of brushing the underneath of his chin with an outward sweep of the finger-tips of one hand. And he asked: 'What is the logical form of *that*?' Sraffa's example produced in Wittgenstein the feeling that there was an absurdity in the insistence that a proposition and what it describes must have the same 'form'. This broke the hold on him of the conception that a proposition must literally be a 'picture' of the reality it describes.[24]

The phrase 'broke the hold . . . of the conception' is singularly apt. For, of course, Sraffa's point was not an argument. Rather was it an indication of an incongruity. So too reflection on the use of nods and headshakings, winks and wry grimaces, quizzical looks and raised eyebrows, gestures to come or go, etc. should be a preliminary warning against theories which

[24] N. Malcolm, *Ludwig Wittgenstein: A Memoir* (Oxford University Press, Oxford, 1967), p. 69.

contend that every utterance contains a force-indicator and sense-conveying component.

We can, perhaps, build upon this seemingly minor objection. The idea informing this version of the theory is that we understand what is said by an utterance and hence can report it in indirect speech only because we recognize an utterance as a token of a type which decomposes into a force-indicator and sense-conveying component, which we duly anatomize and then, by invoking our knowledge of pragmatics, contextualize. This theory is especially favoured by linguists supposedly engaged in the *empirical* study of natural language, keen to explain how a hearer can 'figure out' what is said by an utterance. If the theory is indeed an explanatory scientific hypothesis (as linguists suggest), then its claims about the deep structure of sentences, about the existence of a common object of assertion, command and question, etc. must be merely contingent, empirical claims. But, reflecting on examples of communication by gestures, can we not envisage, indeed *invent*, possible languages and uses of language in which assertions, questions and commands do *not* 'have something in common', in which questions do *not* have a 'descriptive content' and in which commands are not given by, nor represented by, sentences with a mood-operator distinct from that possessed by sentences used assertorically? If we cannot, however hard we try, then it seems the claims cannot be empirical ones. But if we can (and, indeed, it is easy enough) then it seems evident that we must raise questions about the nature of assertion, the relations of speech-acts, the structure of inferences, etc. which arise both within common human languages and *within* the different, envisaged, languages. These questions will not be answerable by the sense/ force theorist. Yet it is these questions, about the nature of assertion, question or command, about the internal relations between assertion and question, between command and description of its compliance, that were the original issues to be clarified.

This objection points to a deep flaw in the reasoning of theorists who pursue a theory of understanding along the lines adumbrated, namely a confusion of conceptual investigations with empirical ones. This is manifest in two further ways. First, these theorists confuse normative (conceptual) explanations of what *counts* as making an assertion, what it *means* to ask a question, with putative causal investigations about mechanisms of understanding. Compare the question 'How does one recognize that A's utterance "Shut the door" is an order to close the front door?' with the question 'How does one recognize that a shape is a square?' One might try to answer the latter question by spelling out

recognitional *cues*, viz. the shape must have four right-angles, it must be a
four-sided equilateral, it must enclose a space. Surely, this is how one
knows. And one knows that 'Shut the door!' is an order to close the door
by a similar process of recognizing the sentence as an imperative, analysing
it into components, etc. But this is a muddle! The putative recognitional
cues for a shape to be a square are simply the defining features of a square,
the features which determine what counts as a square. To know these is
not to know '*how* to recognize squares', but to know what the word
'square' means, to possess the concept of a square. To 'be able to recognize
squares' one must indeed possess the concept (and that includes being able
to apply it). But that is grossly misrepresented when it is claimed that one
must use a range of (perhaps only tacitly known) recognitional cues,
externally related to the concept of a square. Similar considerations apply
to the understanding of what is said by an utterance. How I know that A's
utterance of 'Is it raining?' is a question is (typically) answered by saying
that I know what it is to ask a question. I know what kinds of criteria
determine (defeasibly) whether a sentence is used to query. The theorist
misrepresents mastery of a concept as a recherché psychological process of
recognition and computation.

A second manifestation of a confusion of the conceptual and the empirical
is evident from the insistence that a speaker *must* have 'recognitional cues'
in order to understand what is said. For, it might be said, if the investigation really is a causal one, and if causal connections are contingent, then it
may well turn out that people understand what is said *without* recognizing
utterances as tokens of types, decomposing them into illocutionary-force
potential and sense, and then contextualizing them. If the theorist insists
that that is *impossible*, that the contrary *must* be the case, it should be
pointed out, first, that he is in effect offering us a bogus 'transcendental
deduction' of the necessity of a sense/force distinction – bogus because
there can be no transcendental deduction of contingent truths. And secondly,
if it seems that it *must* be so, that is only because a gross misconception of
understanding, of concept-mastery, distorts our vision (see below).

Finally, this last variant of sense/force theory does not answer the
already noted objection that conventions of indirect speech, far from
supporting the thesis of a common object of assertion and parallel question, order or wish actually counts *against* the acknowledgment of any
such entity (sense, descriptive content, or abstract sentence-radical). Conventions of *oratio obliqua* show, unsurprisingly, how to report what is
said. They do *not* point beyond to the elements of a theory of sense and
force.

5 Diagnosis

The various theorists in logic, philosophy of language, the theory of practical reasoning and theoretical linguists who have invoked a distinction between force and sense each perceive some general problem and construct a *theory* as a solution to it. The key to success in each case has appeared to be the recognition or postulation of certain entities, whether mental, linguistic or abstract, the existence of which will explain the puzzling phenomenon. To the uninitiated the resulting theories have the appearance of myths. For the idea that there is an intentional act of entertaining a proposition or thought that is a common ingredient in every use of a sentence is not an empirical discovery delivered by introspection or by experimental psychology. The thesis that different transforms of a given sentence all express a common sentence-radical which describes, in each case, the same state of affairs and bears truth-values is not derived from careful inspection of natural language. The claim that every sentence contains a force-indicator which signifies the force or potential force with which a thought or proposition is propounded does not rest on empirical evidence. It is 'an idea not an experience'. The fact (if it is a fact) that all (or most) sentences *can* be represented by paraphrase into, e.g. a noun-clause plus a prefix, is *not* theoretically significant. It is not, as proponents of the doctrine contend, a revelation of unity underlying diversity, but rather an *imposition* of a unity in form. The purported descriptions of the norms and articulations of ordinary language transpire to be not a description of the facts, but a new form of representation in the deceptive guise of a discovery about depth-grammar or real logical form.

An historical parallel might highlight this novel form of mythology. It is striking that contemporary philosophers are educated to have a disdain for pre-Fregean logic. The doctrine that every judgment consists of subject and predicate strikes us as *obviously* false, as does the thesis that the copula is the indispensable glue of predication and bearer of assertoric force. For we can cite dozens of types of sentence-structures which do not fit this Procrustean mould. If it is pointed out that traditional logicians were perfectly aware of these 'deviant' sentence-types, but that they *paraphrased* them into forms which did satisfy the demands of subject/ predicate patterns of reasoning, we react with contempt. For these paraphrases are not *discoveries* of 'underlying depth-structures', but impositions of a normal form in the name of an idea. Yet in contemporary analyses of sentences into neustic and phrastic, semantic mood-operator

and expression of a sentence-radical, force-indicator and sign of propositional content, we engage in exactly the same kinds of prestidigitations,
producing similar illusions and distortions.

Having examined a wide range of theories of sense and force, and found
them all wanting, a quite different kind of response to them may cross our
minds. We might wonder whether there is really anything in need of a
'theoretical explanation' of this kind at all. For the existence of the very
problems which the theories are designed to solve is itself open to question.
They are taken for granted rather than demonstrated by the theory
builders, who bundle us quickly through the entrances of their workshops
to confront us with a display of the intricacies and articulations of their
theoretical machinery. We might pause at the door to ask whether there is
really any task for this Heath-Robinsonian machinery to perform. Upon
reflection the central problems may simply disappear.

Consider first the philosopher's primary reason for constructing a
theory of force. Allegedly explanations of meaning instruct us on how to
use expressions only in assertable sentences by clarifying their contribution to the truth-conditions of such sentences in which they occur. This is a
perversion of the truth about what we normally count as explanations of
word-meaning. For whether verbal or ostensive, they are not restricted to
the use of words in assertable sentences. Rather, they typically have the
form of more or less complex substitution-rules, and they license substitutions in sentences of any form whatever. A standard dictionary definition,
e.g. of 'triangle', can be applied *immediately* to occurrences of the
definiendum in questions or commands. So too can an ostensive definition;
e.g. if 'red' is explained by saying 'Red is this ↑ colour [pointing to a red
sample]', then the question 'Is the pelmet red?' can be transformed into 'Is
the pelmet this ↑ colour? [pointing to the sample]'. There seems to be no
problem about ordinary explanations of meaning that a theory of force is
needed to solve. At least, there is no problem for a non-philosopher.
Philosophers, by contrast, have standardly adopted the view that explanations of meaning are *really* or *essentially* explanations of how words
contribute to the truth-conditions of sentences. It is this piece of
philosophical *theory* which generates the problems which the theory of
force is conjured up to solve. Rather than plunging into the business of
theory construction, we might do better to stand back and clear the ground
of these houses of cards (below, chapters 5 and 6).

The situation is broadly similar in respect of constructing 'logics of
questions' or 'logics of commands', for which the separation of the
sentence-radical from the force is held to be essential. Modern logic is built

on the presupposition of the sharp separability of syntax from semantics. Semantics is developed on the basis of the idea of truth-conditions. Truth-table definitions of propositional connectives and the standard definitions of quantifiers explain these logical constants directly in terms of their contributions to the truth-conditions of sentences in which they occur. Consequently, the whole apparatus of logical semantics is applicable only to the analysis of arguments each component of which can be assigned a truth-value. Viewed from this perspective, any piece of reasoning involving imperatives or interrogatives must appear problematic. For imperatives and interrogatives do not apparently bear truth-values, and consequently any embedded sentential connective or quantifier must have a different meaning in these contexts. The apparent triumph of the logical analysis of assertions, questions, and orders as operations on sentence-radicals, is to reveal that logic, being the codification of relations between sentence-radicals, really is uniform, e.g. that 'not', 'if . . . then . . .', 'or', are to be interpreted univocally as truth-functional connectives.

This is an exemplary case of running hard to stay in the same place. Here again the necessity for the favoured distinction between sense and force is a consequence of an antecedent theory, not of the natural phenomena of language. If the planets revolve around the earth on crystalline spheres, we must investigate of what adamantine crystal the spheres are made. But we might instead question the premise. Likewise we might question what led philosophers in the first place to think that 'not', 'if . . . then . . .' 'or' etc. are truth-functional connectives (below, pp. 170–9), or to think that all inference proceeds from assertion to assertion or potential assertion to potential assertion. Is it only by invoking a theory of sentence-radicals that we can assure ourselves that 'if . . . then . . .' is univocal in 'If it is raining then the window is shut' and 'If it is raining then shut the window!'? These sentential connectives do not require fresh, separate, explanations for use in sentences used to assert and in sentences used for other purposes, e.g. to order. The same principle of inference is indeed applied in the inference 'If it is raining, the temperature is above − 10 °C; it is raining, so the temperature must be above − 10 °C' as in drawing a conclusion ('So I must turn on my windscreen wipers') from a conditional instruction ('If it is raining, turn on your windscreen wipers') when the antecedent is fulfilled (when it is raining). The only reason for doubting that, and for erecting a complex theoretical structure to ward off the doubt, is a philosophical theory. It is *this* that should be questioned and investigated.

General theories of speech-acts are typically constructed on some version of a sense/force distinction. They delineate the 'logical geography' of a vast

range of distinguishable speech-acts by analysing particular acts of saying
something, or particular utterances, or even the sentences uttered, into
combinations of elements which may recur in different combinations. It is
unclear exactly how theorists conceive of this enterprise. They might
consider it to be a clarification of concepts (e.g. the concepts of making an
assertion, predicting something, asking a question, etc., or the concepts of
a question, a command, etc., or the concepts of a declarative sentence, an
interrogative sentence, etc.). Or they might take themselves to be investigating very general features of the phenomena of speech (e.g. engaging in the natural history of the 'workings of language'). Or they may fail
or refuse to make any such differentiation. This renders the status of their
theories indeterminate. Still less clear is the *point* of the resultant theories.
What central questions are they designed to answer? Little attention is
directed to this issue. But from the products of theorizing about speech-
acts, we can infer that there are two primary motivations for this activity.
The first is a desire to exhibit the complex network of relations among
speech-acts by analysis of these acts into simpler components some of
which must be shared by any internally related complex speech-acts.
Common senses and common forces of sentences or utterances (or perhaps
common 'propositional acts' and common 'illocutionary acts') are the
metaphysical or psychological mechanisms which establish the crucial
relations among speech-acts. This conception becomes more conspicuous
the more overtly a theorist pursues a programme of analysis. It is most
clear when the resulting theory claims to effect some form of reduction;
e.g. when a theorist argues that every speech-act contains a propositional
act itself decomposed into acts of reference and of predication,[25] or when a
theorist claims that all different illocutionary forces can be analysed into
combinations of a single pair together with suitable tense-operators.[26] The
second motive is to clear up certain confusions or uncertainties in the
concepts (or phenomena) of speech-acts. Everyday explanations of what it
is to make an assertion, to express a wish, etc., seem rather rough and
ready. They may serve for ordinary practical purposes, but they seem to
leave us in the lurch when we seek a rigorous, 'scientific' account of the
conditions under which a speaker by uttering a particular sentence
performs the speech-act of making an assertion, expressing a wish, etc.
The theorist tries to remedy this defect. He seeks for a precise list of
conditions individually necessary and jointly sufficient for performing any

[25] e.g. Searle, *Speech Acts*, pp. 23ff.
[26] e.g. Kenny, *Will, Freedom, and Power*, pp. 38ff.

given speech-act. Armed with his analyses of the 'happiness conditions' of making a promise, giving a description, asking a question, etc., we could in principle reach a *definitive* verdict about the correct characterization of the speech-act(s) performed by somebody who utters any given sentence. This would be an advance on our everyday procedures which may give no verdicts in many (unusual) cases or only provisional verdicts subject always to revision in the light of further information. The twin aims of a general theory of speech-acts seem to be the clarification of the nature of the various speech-acts and of the complex network of relations among them.

To many these aims would seem not merely sane and comprehensible, but also highly reputable and important. None the less, both grow out of a seed-bed of philosophical misconceptions.

The aim of explaining internal relations by inventing (or discovering?) shared intermediate entities is coeval with philosophy itself. It has yielded many noteworthy products, ranging from Plato's theory of forms to Chomsky's deep structures (and innate capacities). But this fact does not justify the strategy. On the contrary, the postulation of intermediate entities is gratuitous. It stems from a misguided attempt to *explain* matters which are *already perspicuous*, to provide some sort of metaphysical support for what is already self-supporting. And in doing so, philosophers and linguists generate confusions or unclarities.

The defects of this strategy are patent in general theories of speech-acts. It is true that different speech-acts and propositional attitudes *may* have the same object. For one may assert, suppose, hypothesize, declare, insist, avow *that* it is raining, as well as know, believe, remember or forget that it is raining. Similarly one may ask, enquire, query, investigate *whether* it is raining, as well as doubt or wonder whether it is raining. But to explain this triviality we need not postulate any entities. The common object is the product of grammatical conventions (for *oratio obliqua* and for reporting propositional attitudes), not a grammatical reflection of an extra-linguistic entity. It is simply what is said in reply to the question 'What did he assert, suppose, hypothesize?', and it may indeed be the case that what A asserted was identical with what B supposed and what C hypothesized (although not with what B asked or C ordered). The answer to each question is the same, i.e. the same *indirect statement*. But this platitude does not justify the philosophical thesis that assertions, suppositions, and hypotheses, let alone questions and commands, may constitute different relations of speakers to a common Platonic object. That contention is altogether superfluous.

Indeed, a theory invoking Platonic entities corresponding to indirect statements, questions, and commands creates difficulties for itself. If differences between these grammatical forms are held to reflect differences between the corresponding types of entities, the theory will be unable to account for important internal relations among speech-acts or among sentences uttered in performing them. It is true, for example, that an order is internally related to a description of its fulfilment. But what intermediate entity can be produced to forge this link? It is a myth that the order 'Open the door!' (addressed to X) and the report 'X opened the door' share a common descriptive content. Moreover, the corresponding reports in indirect speech have no common noun-clause, since an indirect command differs in form from an indirect statement. The notion that they share a common propositional act is also absurd, since the two sentences are used neither to refer to the same subject (the imperative is addressed to X, but refers to nobody) nor to predicate a common predicate of something (the imperative does not predicate anything of anything). The quest for an intermediate entity leads to an impasse.

The moral to be drawn is not that a bolder postulation of yet more sophisticated Platonic entities is required. Still less should we conclude that there really is no internal relation between an order and a description of its execution. Rather, we should take to heart that this internal relation, like all others, is forged in Everyman's explanations of the concepts of an order and of the execution of an order. The order to open the door, addressed to X, is the order the execution of which consists in X's opening the door, i.e. the order the fulfilment of which is correctly reported by the description 'X opened the door'. This is a tautology. It could be rephrased in the formal mode: viz. 'The order to open the door, addressed to X' $=_{def.}$ 'The order that is executed by X's opening the door'. This link is already firmly forged without the help of any third entity; *nothing* remains to be done. The whole apparatus of senses and forces is redundant. *A fortiori* the puzzlements which it generates do not deserve to be resolved by the creation of further epicycles in the operation of this transcendental machinery.

The other aim of general theories of speech-acts is equally awry. The explanations of such expressions as 'make an assertion', 'ask a question', etc., which competent speakers of English give and acknowledge to be correct are not first approximations to lists of conditions individually necessary and jointly sufficient for performing these various speech-acts. Rather, they lay down the *grounds* which justify claiming that somebody has made an assertion, asked a question, etc., and in so doing they *definitively* delineate an important aspect of our concepts of making an assertion, asking a question, etc. The fact that these grounds may prompt us to conflicting verdicts in particular cases is something expressly envisaged in the practice of giving these explanations; hence it is *built into* the concepts of various speech-acts, not something to be regretted and avoided in 'more perfect' explanations of these concepts. The *defeasibility* of inferences from the forms and circumstances of utterances to the identification of the speech-acts performed is constitutive of the concepts of making an assertion, asking a question, etc. Recognizing this defeasibility does not indicate that our explanations of these concepts are defective. On the contrary, it is an essential part of a proper grasp of these very concepts. The theorist who seeks to 'improve' our concepts by eliminating the defeasibility of such inferences does not deepen our understanding of 'how language works'. Rather, he presents in the misleading guise of discoveries about the nature of various speech-acts a refusal to acknowledge as correct the patterns of explanation which alone give meaning to such expressions as 'make an assertion', 'ask a question', etc. In each case 'what he rebels against is the use of this expression in connection with *these* criteria. That is, he objects to using this word in the particular way in which it is commonly used. On the other hand, he is not aware that he is objecting to a convention'.[27] The resultant theories of speech-acts are manifestations of this confusion, not intelligible answers to any coherent questions.

The theoretical linguist has another, but no less suspect, reason for introducing a sense/force distinction. Since he is primarily interested in symbols, he considers the distinction to be applicable to type-sentences. His purpose is to elaborate a general psychological theory about how speakers work out from a symbol and the context of its utterance what has been said and what speech-act has been performed. Sense and force, as features of sentences, are thought to be the appropriate theoretical concepts for elucidating the mechanics of the process of understanding. Under these two headings he intends to list those aspects or components of sentences which play a role in the explanation of how speakers recognize what is said and what speech-act is performed by an utterance. As already noted, this whole enterprise rests on a fundamental confusion about the concept of understanding and a misconception about recognition. A conceptual mythology is the drive-shaft of the theoretical linguist's machinery. Wheels turn with much noise and hubbub, and engineers dispute about how to make the engine more efficient. But the whole mechanism does no work at all.

[27] Wittgenstein, *The Blue and Brown Books*, p. 57.

Even though there is scope for more detailed probing into the *theoretical* motivation for current endeavours to construct a theory of force, enough has already been said to raise doubts about the *intelligibility* of any such theory. Nothing is *refuted* by our observations. There is no such thing as refuting *a picture*, but only persuading one to abandon it. Indeed, it must be admitted that to each offensive move we have made, defenders of various theories can be imagined to make piecemeal ripostes, lay down local smokescreens, engage in tactical feints. Amidst the alarums and noise of controversy, it may not be noticed that there is in fact no central citadel under siege, no decisive strongpoint to be captured. Perhaps the task of definitively undermining the theory of sense and force is not merely difficult but impossible. The walls, bastions and keeps of a blueprint cannot crumble under assault. One cannot lay siege to castles in the air. What we have done is to point out that the planned defences have no force and that the central design lacks sense.

CHAPTER 4

Truth-Conditions:
Origins and Evolution

1 The present position

Critical examination of theories of sense and force has shown their incoherence. However this is unlikely to dislodge the dream of some such theory from the hearts and minds of modern theorists of meaning. If a sense/force distinction is viewed as a *precondition* for the construction of a theory of meaning of the favoured type, the whole enterprise must surely be doomed to failure. But if the essential skeleton of a successful explanatory theory of meaning can indeed be constructed out of independent materials, and if such a theory then requires a sense/force distinction for its completion, then, it may seem, *some* such theory *must* be possible. According to this conception the burden of proof lies with the construction of an underlying theory of meaning of which a sense/force distinction is merely the keystone of the arch.

By common consent there is little to debate. Philosophers and linguists alike seem to be virtually unanimous in adhering to the principle that the meaning of a sentence is its truth-conditions, as well as to the corollary that the meanings of subsentential expressions are to be explained as their contributions to the meanings of sentences in which they occur. These ideas are intoned on every side: '. . . to give truth conditions [i.e. necessary and sufficient conditions for the truth of a sentence] is a way of giving the meaning of a sentence'.[1] A theory of meaning for a natural language is claimed to be a theory of truth, i.e. 'a set of axioms that entail, for every sentence in the language, a statement of the conditions under which it is true. . . . An acceptable theory should . . . account for the meaning (or conditions of truth) of every sentence by analyzing it as composed, in

---

[1] D. Davidson, 'Truth and Meaning', *Synthese*, 17 (1967), p. 310.

truth-relevant ways, of elements drawn from a finite stock.'[2] Somebody who does not know 'the conditions under which it would be true' does not know 'the first thing' about the meaning of an English sentence; consequently, 'semantics with no treatment of truth-conditions is not semantics'.[3] It is 'part of the received wisdom among philosophers' that 'a grasp of meaning consists in a grasp of truth-conditions'.[4] Indeed, it is even argued that 'under any theory of meaning whatever . . . we can represent the meaning (sense) of a sentence as given by the condition for it to be true, on some appropriate way of construing "true": the problem is not whether meaning is to be explained in terms of truth-conditions, but of what notion of truth is admissible'.[5] Truth-conditions provide the apparently unassailable foundations of semantics.

This conception is not peculiar to philosophers. Though not the sole available paradigm for semantic theories among linguists, it is widely exploited in their investigations. So-called 'model-theoretic semantics' is one of the most active branches of modern linguistics and it is built on the concept of a truth-condition.

Furthermore, the identification of sentence-meaning with truth-conditions is not a latter-day brainstorm. Allegedly it is 'explicitly contended for by Frege'.[6] Though this interpretation of Frege is radically mistaken, the direct lineage of truth-conditional semantics certainly includes Wittgenstein's *Tractatus*. There we find clear definitions of logical constants in the form of truth-tables, definitions which are put to use to demonstrate that certain formulae are tautologies (logical truths) and that certain inferences are valid in virtue of their logical forms. There too is an explicit identification of sense with truth-conditions in the case of molecular propositions.[7]

By direct derivation from Wittgenstein's reflections, the same conception dominated the thinking of the Vienna Circle. Indeed the notorious principle of verification seems to be a straightforward reformulation of the identification of meaning with truth-conditions which incorporates the

[2] Davidson, 'Semantics for Natural Languages', in *Linguaggi nella Società e nella Tecnica*, ed. B. Visentini (Edizioni di Comunità, Milan, 1970), p. 178.

[3] Lewis, 'General Semantics', in *Semantics of Natural Language*, ed. D. Davidson and G. Harman (Dordrecht, Reidel, 1972), p. 169.

[4] Dummett, *Truth and Other Engimas* (Duckworth, London, 1978), p. xxi.

[5] Ibid., xxii.

[6] M. A. E. Dummett, 'What is a Theory of Meaning? (II)', in *Truth and Meaning*, ed. G. Evans and J. McDowell (Clarendon Press, Oxford, 1976), p. 67.

[7] Wittgenstein, *Tractatus*, 4.431.

restrictive gloss that only those conditions are admitted among truth-conditions which can in principle be established by observation or experiment.

> ... it is simply impossible to give the meaning of any statement except by describing the fact which must exist if the statement is to be true ... The statement of the conditions under which a proposition is true is *the same* as the statement of its meaning. ... And these 'conditions' ... must finally be discoverable in the given.[8]

This conception was compressed into the slogan 'The meaning of a sentence is the method of its verification', and members of the Vienna Circle[9] erroneously tried to foist this notion of truth-conditions on to the *Tractatus* in order to demonstrate Wittgenstein's allegiance to the cause of logical empiricism.

Although the principle of verification soon fell into disrepute, the strategy of explaining sentence-meaning as truth-conditions has not merely survived, but even flourished after the demise of logical positivism. Transformed and extended in the work of Tarski and Carnap, the conception has become firmly entrenched in a distinctive form. A sharp distinction is drawn between object language and metalanguage, or between use and mention of expressions. The modern norm for various versions of truth-conditional semantics is to use equivalences in some metalanguage to formulate the truth-conditions of a sentence which is mentioned. Theorists tend to embroider on Tarski's famous paradigm:

'Snow is white' is true if and only if snow is white.

The truth-table explanations of sentence connectives can be recast in this form; e.g. ' $\neg p$ ' is true if and only if it is false that p. So too can the standard semantic explanations of quantifiers; e.g. '$(\forall x)\ \varphi x$' is true if and only if every object in the domain of quantification has the property φ. The crucial feature of these formulations of truth-conditions is that they consist of biconditionals one side of which mentions an expression (in the object language) and the other side of which uses an expression (in the metalanguage). Only in this way is it apparently possible to make precise and general statements about the relation of language to the world.

[8] M. Schlick, 'Positivismus und Realismus', in *Gesammelte Aufsätze* (Georg Olms Verlag, Hildesheim, 1969), p. 90.

[9] Aided and abetted by Wittgenstein's developing ideas (cf. *Philosophical Remarks*) which were communicated to the Circle by Schlick and Waismann; cf. F. Waismann's 'Theses' in *Ludwig Wittgenstein and the Vienna Circle*, conversations recorded by Friedrich Waismann, (Blackwell, Oxford, 1979), pp. 233ff.

Moreover, this conception holds out at least the prospect of giving 'an account of how the meanings of sentences depend on the meaning of words',[10] i.e. of achieving the goal of giving 'the meanings of all independently meaningful expressions on the basis of an analysis of their structure'.[11] A semantic theory elaborated on this model will capitalize on the identification of sentence-meaning with truth-conditions, since for each sentence in the object language it will make explicit in the metalanguage the conditions under which this sentence is true.

Although this impressive pedigree and the current widespread agreement among theorists is eloquent testimony in support of the contention that the meaning of a sentence is its truth-conditions, this conception also speaks for itself. In fact, it seems self-evident and hence unassailable. Is it not a platitude that somebody who understands an assertion must know what would be the case if what is asserted were true?[12] There seems no point to attack. Any serious attempt at criticism evokes a reaction of bewilderment or incredulity: how could anybody be so perverse or misguided? The defender of truth-conditional semantics may then launch a counterattack: the standard form of explanations of meaning, especially in dictionaries, is the listing of conditions necessary and sufficient for truly applying the defined word, and therefore any *general* criticism of truth-conditional semantics must challenge the legitimacy of this established practice. Somebody who explains that 'triangle' means 'three-sided plane rectilinear figure' specifies the contribution that the predicate 'triangle' makes to the truth-conditions of sentences in which it occurs, and he thereby demonstrates his allegiance to truth-conditional semantics. Consequently, the critic is represented as pitching battle against Everyman in a cause that is utterly absurd. His task seems altogether unlike that of somebody who challenges a typical scientific theory. For, in that case, there is a limited identifiable body of its supporters, and there are acknowledged possibilities of alternative theories. Everything and everybody seems to speak in favour of truth-conditional semantics (at least when it is put under attack).

The existence of this broad consensus supplies the background for singling out and consolidating what are now perceived to be some of the basic insights of the last hundred years of philosophy. These include Frege's context principle, viz. that 'only in the context of a sentence has a

---

[10] Davidson, 'Truth and Meaning', p. 304.

[11] Davidson, 'Semantics for Natural Languages', p. 177.

[12] And, we might add in the spirit of Tweedledee, he must know what is the case if it is true, what is not the case if it is false, and what might be the case if it were possible for it to be true!

word a meaning' ('probably the most important philosophical statement Frege ever made',[13] since it elucidates the primacy of the sentence in a theory of meaning); the idea that language is deeply systematic ('the meaning of a word is its role in the calculus' and 'if anyone utters a sentence and *means* or *understands* it he is operating a calculus according to definite rules');[14] the contention that the predicate calculus exposes a structure hidden beneath the variegated vocabulary and syntax of expressions of generality in natural languages (since in light of this formal notation 'we can return to ordinary language and see, as never before, what has been happening all along'[15] or a significant aspect of 'the working of language');[16] and the legitimacy of contextual definitions (e.g. Russell's celebrated theory of definite descriptions). Without the fecund soil of truth-conditonal semantics, these apparent seeds of truth would have fallen on stony ground and hence failed to fructify in the garden of knowledge.

The same background of consensus also makes sense of the main controversies dividing theorists of meaning. One such dispute is the opposition between realism and anti-realism; this turns on the twin issues of bivalence (whether every significant sentence must be either true or false in any fully specified circumstance) and effective decidability of truth-values (whether the truth-conditions of a sentence must necessarily be conditions whose satisfaction or non-satisfaction we are in principle capable of determining in a finite time). This dispute constitutes a disagreement about the general contours of a theory of meaning only in the context of a prior agreement that the meaning of a sentence can be specified by a metalinguistic formulation of its truth-conditions. The same point holds in respect of other prominent controversies. One is the legitimacy (or significance) of appealing to *possibilities* of truth and falsity in elucidating truth-conditions (e.g. the admissibility of 'possible worlds' into a semantic theory). Another is the question whether the role of an expression in determining the truth-values of sentences in which it occurs exhausts the meaning of a word or phrase, or whether on the contrary a full philosophical analysis of the workings of language requires some further aspect to be taken into consideration (e.g. the 'sense' of an expression in addition to its

---

[13] Dummett, 'Nominalism', in *Truth and Other Enigmas*, p. 38.

[14] Wittgenstein, *Philosophical Investigations*, §81.

[15] W. V. Quine, 'Logic as the Source of Syntactical Insights', in *The Ways of Paradox and Other Essays* (Random House, New York, 1966), p. 44.

[16] M. A. E. Dummett, *Frege: Philosophy of Language* (Duckworth, London, 1973), p. 80.

'reference' or 'semantic role'.)[17] Yet another is the question whether metalinguistic equivalences on Tarski's model actually connect expressions with reality or whether, on the contrary, they merely constitute a translation manual for rendering expressions in the object language into other expressions in the metalanguage.[18] Perception of what the main problems in semantics are is shaped by the conviction that sentence-meaning is a matter of truth-conditions. Indeed, somebody of a cynical bent might conjecture that the problems are altogether the product of this modern conception of meaning.

2   Logical semantics

The original home of the notion of a truth-condition was the elucidation of the logical constants within systems of formal logic. We are now inclined to identify Frege's explanations of his logical primitives as paradigms of what it is to formulate truth-conditions for the expression of a thought. As earlier argued, this distorts his thinking by overlooking his insistence that logical primitives are function-names and his correlative thesis that the True and the False are objects. The 'truth-condition' of a sentence[19] is a specification of exactly how a complex expression in concept-script presents the True as the value of a function for an argument. It is also noteworthy that those stipulations apply only to well-formed formulae in his concept-script. In effect what he attempted to elucidate is the significance of such formulae as '$\neg p$', '$p \rightarrow q$', and '$(\forall x) Fx$'. Frege offered no parallel definitions for sentence-connectives of German, though he suggested rough correspondences (and disanalogies) between some forms of German sentences and corresponding formulae in concept-script.

Wittgenstein did undeniably introduce truth-table definitions of the propositional connectives occurring in the formalization of logic in *Principia Mathematica*. Moreover, the *Tractatus* explained the expression 'truth-condition' by explicit reference to truth-tables: viz. the truth-conditions of the molecular proposition '$p \rightarrow q$' are those combinations of states of affairs (truth-possibilities) under which it takes the value 'T' in the truth-table. Consequently a truth-table is the very paradigm of the formulation of the truth-conditions of a logical formula. Indeed, since the

[17]   Ibid., pp. 83ff.
[18]   M. A. E. Dummett, 'What is a Theory of Meaning?', in *Mind and Language*, ed. S. Guttenplan (Clarendon Press, Oxford, 1975), pp. 98, 103f.
[19]   Frege, *The Basic Laws of Arithmetic*, vol. 1, §32.

Tractatus erroneously gave a truth-tabular explanation of the universal quantifiers by reducing generalizations to conjunctions, Wittgenstein then regarded a truth-table[20] as the only possible form for 'giving the truth-conditions' of a proposition. By contrast, later logicians would admit the standard semantic definitions of the quantifiers among the paradigms of framing the truth-conditions of a logical formula.

The origin of the notion of a truth-condition in systems of formal logic is of crucial importance. Equally so is the enormous prestige that it soon acquired as a consequence of its fruitful application to the investigation of formal systems. These applications now seem to most logicians to mark the watershed between primitive prescientific logic and the sophisticated logical theories of the present day. From the modern point of view, logic came of age only when it achieved a clear grasp of the concept of a truth-condition.

Modern expositions of formal logic differentiate sharply from the outset between the *syntax* and the *semantics* of formal systems. Logical syntax is concerned with three fundamental questions about a formal system: what counts as a well-formed formula (the formation-rules), which formulae (or schemata), if any, constitute distinguished formulae (the axioms), and what operations are admissible in deriving one formula from others (the transformation-rules). Together these rules determine whether any given formula can be derived as a theorem within a fully specified formal system. This question is held to be syntactic since its answer is wholly independent of any knowledge about what, if anything, any well-formed formula means. In contrast to these questions about logical syntax are issues in logical semantics.[21] The fundamental notion here is the semantic characterization of the validity of an argument, viz. an argument is valid if and only if it is impossible for all of its premises to be true and its conclusion to be false. The corollary of this definition is the conception of a law of logic as a statement which cannot be false. These venerable principles are given definite content in modern logic by appeal to the standard '*semantic*' definitions of the logical constants,[22] viz. truth-tables for sentence-connectives and the standard explanations of the quantifiers.

---

[20] Strictly speaking, he exhibited truth-conditions in terms of the operation of joint negation which could take even an infinite set of propositions for its argument.

[21] Originally these matters too were considered, especially by Wittgenstein and Carnap, to belong to logical *syntax*, (below, pp. 140–2).

[22] These are contrasted with implicit syntactic definitions in terms of axioms and transformation-rules (e.g. introduction- and elimination-rules in systems of natural deduction).

Consequently, a set of formulae in the propositional calculus constitutes a valid argument if and only if every assignment of truth-values to its sentence-letters which the truth-tables show to make each of the premises true is also shown by the truth-tables to verify the conclusion. And a formula is a logical truth if and only if it is true under every possible assignment of truth-values to its constituent sentence-letters (i.e. if and only if it is a tautology).

Parallel accounts are offered for the predicate calculus. Here logicians introduce the notion of a 'model' or an 'interpretation'. An interpretation for a formula of the predicate calculus is an assignment of some non-empty set of entities (the domain of quantification) to serve as the values of the individual variables, an assignment to each predicate-letter of a property or relation defined over objects in this domain, and an assignment of a truth-value to each sentence-letter. A formula is satisfiable if it has some model in which it is true according to the standard definitions of the quantifiers and the sentence-connectives; e.g. the formula '$(\forall x)(\exists y)Rxy$' is satisfiable since it is verified if the domain is taken to be the integers and 'Rxy' is correlated with the relation $x < y$. An argument in the predicate calculus is valid if and only if every model in which all of its premises together are satisfied is a model in which its conclusion is also satisfied, i.e. if and only if there is no interpretation under which its premises are true and its conclusion is false. Similarly, a formula of the predicate calculus is a logical truth if and only if it is true under every interpretation. Like the truth-tables for the propositional calculus, the standard semantic definitions of the quantifiers are held to give an objective criterion for validity and logical truth which is altogether independent of appeals to self-evidence or intuition. That the argument-schema '$(\forall x)(\exists y)Rxy \vdash (\exists y)(\forall x)Rxy$' is fallacious (invalid) can be conclusively proved by showing that the premise, but not the conclusion, is satisfied in the model where the domain is the integers and the relation $x < y$ is associated with the binary predicate 'Rxy'. Logical semantics, unlike logical syntax, depends essentially on the significance of the logical constants as stipulated by the semantic definitions of these symbols.

The key to the possibility of building both proof theory and model theory has been the exploitation of the recursive specification of what counts as a well-formed formula in the predicate calculus. A complex symbol is well-formed if and only if it can be shown to be built up by the application of one of a listed set of operations out of elements which themselves are well-formed. Consequently, provided that there is some procedure to settle what are the atomic well-formed formulae, the question whether any finite sequence of symbols constructed out of the vocabulary of the predicate calculus is well-formed has a determinate answer which can be discovered mechanically by appeal to specifications of the admissible operations for constructing complex formulae out of simpler subformulae. Although the set of well-formed formulae in the predicate calculus is infinite according to this account, there is an effective decision procedure for determining well-formedness. This rests on the fact that every well-formed formula has a completely definite and perspicuous structure; also on the fact that there is a strictly circumscribed set of operations for building up complex formulae. The recursive definition of well-formedness is the foundation for the further mathematical investigations of proof theory and model theory. In particular, the notion of an interpretation is so constructed that it meets the requirement that what is assigned to any complex formula as its interpretation can be systematically derived from the interpretations of its primitive elements by exploiting its overt structure. Model theory incorporates the demand that the semantic value of a complex expression must be completely determined by its structure and the semantic values of its constituents. Logical semantics is a viable branch of mathematics because various correlations of symbols in the predicate calculus with mathematical structures do conform with this demand.

The terminology of 'model', 'interpretation', and 'satisfaction' has gained wide currency among philosophers. It is important to note that these terms were originally applied in the analysis of formalizations of logic. Moreover, they obtained definite content from the same background (truth-tables and the standard definitions of the quantifiers) which gave content to the expression 'truth-conditions'. In fact, definitions of entailment and logical truth can readily be formulated expressly in terms of truth-conditions, as they were in the *Tractatus*. One formula entails another if and only if the truth-conditions associated with the first are a subset of the truth-conditions of the second, and a formula is logically true if and only if its truth-conditions are all-embracing (i.e. if and only if the set of truth-conditions of its negation is empty). Modern logical semantics for the predicate calculus is built solely on the basis of truth-conditions, whether expressly or only by implication.

Wittgenstein's attempt to characterize entailment and logical truth by a decision-procedure was the catalyst for a major transformation of formal logic. It suggested the possibility of a rigorous mathematical science of formal systems based on interpretations of formulae in terms of systems of logico-mathematical entities (e.g. numbers, sets, truth-values). It served as midwife to the birth of metalogic,[23] and it triggered off in the next decade investigations which yielded a series of fundamental results about the characteristics of logical systems and attempted formalizations of arithmetic.

The leading thoughts of the *Tractatus* can be highlighted by comparisons with ideas informing the pioneering work of Frege in the invention of the predicate calculus. Frege considered that the only justification for holding a formula to express a law of logic was that it could be derived from primitive truths (axioms) certified by immediate inspection as self-evident according to rules of inference that were self-evidently truth-preserving. This is a far cry from the conception of the *Tractatus*. Similarly he was prevented from reaching the present-day semantic account of validity by his unshakeable and often repeated conviction that an argument could be cogent only if it proceeded from true premises. And he poured scorn on Hilbert's contention that there could be any formal science establishing the consistency of a set of axioms; in his own view, any axiom, whether of logic or geometry, formulated a generalization with a definite content, and hence the only demonstration of consistency of a set of axioms would be that each one expressed something actually known to be true. Even if Frege's formulations can now be used as proper semantic definitions of his primitive logical constants, he did not use them to break away from traditional ideas. He thought his explanations to be *elucidations*, not formal *definitions*, and he appealed to them not to construct *proofs* that his logical axioms were unconditional truths, but rather to fortify his readers' intuitions so that they would apprehend his primitive formulae to express *self-evident* generalizations.[24] By contrast, Wittgenstein exploited the truth-table definitions of the logical constants to castigate these fundamental misconceptions in Frege's presentation of formal logic. Subsequent logicians have devoted much effort to constructing 'scientific' answers to questions which Frege scorned or of which he never even dreamt.

A precise calculus of 'models' or 'interpretations' erected on the foundation of truth-tables and the standard definitions of the quantifiers was immediately attractive to mathematicians. The most immediate, and least

[23] This consequence seems ironic, since Wittgenstein thought that attempts to formulate doctrines or theses about the logical syntax of language inevitably produce nonsense.

[24] This conception of the role of semantic definitions of logical constants survived even in Tarski's seminal early contributions to logical semantics (A. Tarski, 'The Semantic Conception of Truth', in *Readings in Philosophical Analysis*, ed. H. Feigl and W. Sellars (Appleton–Century–Crofts, Inc., New York, 1949), p. 67).

revolutionary, idea was to capitalize on such a theory to establish theorems of logic wholesale, as it were. An early instance was the principle of duality; it is readily shown that any theorem in the propositional calculus expressed wholly in terms of the constants ' ¬ ', ' ∧ ', ' ∨ ' is correlated in a systematic way with another formula (its 'dual') which is expressed wholly in terms of the same repertoire of constants and whose negation is also a theorem of logic. Deeper results flowing from the calculi now called 'logical semantics' were proofs of the independence and consistency of sets of axioms for the propositional and predicate calculus. But the most impressive results concerned completeness. An axiomatization of logical laws is said to be complete provided every logical truth of the appropriate form can be derived as a theorem within the system. And a set of rules of inference is called complete if every valid argument of the relevant form can be exhibited as a sequence of correct derivations employing only these primitive transformation-rules. The axiom system for the propositional calculus in *Principia Mathematica* is complete provided that every tautology is a theorem of the system. Within a decade of apprehending the possibility of such completeness proofs, mathematicians succeeded in demonstrating the completeness of the first-order predicate calculus with identity as presented by Frege and in *Principia*, and Gödel produced a celebrated proof of the impossibility of simultaneously demonstrating the consistency of any axiomatization of arithmetic exploiting only the logic of *Principia*. The notion of truth-conditions let loose a torrent of novel *mathematical* results. It changed the focus of formal logic, diverting mathematicians from the enterprise of deriving theorems within logical systems to the task of formulating and proving theorems about logical systems (metalogic). Truth-conditional logical semantics conspicuously justified itself by its works.

This success story had an impact on philosophical reflections related to formal logic. It reinforced the inclination to suppose that principles of correct reasoning are both systematic and essentially mathematical. It fostered the notion that formal proofs may contribute definitive solutions to what appear to be general and insoluble problems. Finally, it overturned an age-old dogma. Philosophers had commonly argued that there could be no such thing as a justification for the fundamental laws of logic. Any attempt to demonstrate the tenability of any logical law would have to employ some principles of reasoning, and therefore a proof of any axiom of logic would be viciously circular. This point was often trotted out in arguing that any justification of inductive inference would constitute a *petitio principii*. Logical semantics, as now conceived, has stood this reasoning on its head. Rules of inference, even the most basic ones, can be vindicated by proofs of their validity, and the axioms of a logical system can be justified by proofs that they are tautologies or unconditional truths. Precise formal arguments apparently fill a lacuna previously occupied by mere dogmatic insistence that certain formulae expressed basic logical laws. The previous conviction that some logical principles were at rock-bottom in the analysis of rational thought suffered defeat in a trial by battle. Logicians have employed the notion of truth-conditions to open up a deeper level of explanation. The concept of a truth-condition came into the consciousness of philosophers and linguists trailing clouds of glory generated by its miracle-working powers in formal logic. Its welcome outside the circle of formal logicians was ensured by its earlier prize-winning performances.

3   Truth-conditions domesticated: applications to natural languages

At least three crucial developments have intervened between the introduction of the concept of truth-conditions into formal logic and the present-day employment of this concept in building theories of meaning. The most remarkable of these changes is the least often remarked – and the most difficult to pin down: namely, the direct application of 'truth-conditions' to expressions (sentences) in natural languages. Whereas logicians earlier spoke of truth-conditions only in respect of formulae in their formal systems (e.g. '$p \rightarrow q$' or '$(\forall x)(Fx \rightarrow Gx)$'), philosophers now, without any feelings of incongruity, address themselves to the problem of formulating the truth-conditions of such sentences as 'If the brakes had not failed, the car would not have crashed'. Terminology previously applied to specimens found only within the restricted and exotic habitat of the predicate calculus is now used to characterize familiar entities that strut about in Everyman's intellectual backyard. This radical change deserves careful scrutiny. Is there evident here an undetected equivocation on the term 'truth-conditions'? Or have meaning-theorists discovered that the predicate calculus begins at home?

What is perhaps the earliest and ultimately the most influential aspect of this evolution is very subtle. It is something readily dismissed as trivial and unworthy of attention. We will call it the Principle of Equipollence. This can be elucidated by a comparison. Modern logic texts abound in expressions combining symbols drawn from natural languages with symbols taken from formal notations. An analysis may be given of such an expression as

'[Cobalt is present ∧ the flame is blue] → nickel is absent]'

or of such an expression as

'p unless (q only if r)'.

and a familiar problem posed to novice logicians is whether the expression '$p \to q$' has the same meaning as 'if p then q'. By contrast, Frege would have judged the exemplified expressions and this standard question to be nonsense. He viewed his formal notation as a novel *language*, self-contained and disjoint from every natural language. Consequently, he scrupulously avoided mixing his special symbols with expressions in German. This very deliberate practice indicates that he would have set his face against the obvious argument in defence of the modern practice. He would urge that the letters occurring in such a formula as '$p \to q$' are understood by him to be the expressions of thoughts (e.g. 'p' might express the thought that any integer is the sum of four squares), and therefore we conclude that his own explanation of the logical constant '$\to$' is directly applicable to assign significance to any expression where '$\to$' stands between expressions of the same thoughts (e.g. 'any integer is the sum of four squares $\to$ . . .'). But Frege did not accept the contention that all expressions of a thought are on a par with each other, i.e. that any is interchangeable with every other one in the context of a formula of his concept-script. He rejected this Principle of Equipollence. His conception of a well-formed formula of concept-script is much more restrictive than what is countenanced in modern logic.

Probably more by inadvertence than design, *Principia Mathematica* made free use of expressions combining logical notation with English words (e.g. citing the expressions 'φx' and 'x is hurt' as examples of propositional functions). This convenient practice is now so firmly established that few logicians can imagine any alternative conception or even recognize its presence in Frege's exposition of his concept-script. The Principle of Equipollence is enshrined in modern terminology: well-formed formulae are called 'sentences', while the letters in ' $\neg p$', '$p \to q$', '$p \wedge q$', etc., are called 'sentence-letters' and taken to be replaceable by 'sentences' couched in any symbolism whatever. *Pari passu*, sentence-letters are employed together with sentence-connectives of a natural language (e.g. 'It is not the case that p', or 'If p, then q') to represent sentence-forms and to express generality (e.g. the argument-schema 'If p, then q; p; so q').

This apparently innocuous phraseology has an important consequence: it legitimates direct comparisons between expressions in natural languages and certain logical symbols. Since the expression 'grass has chloroplasts $\rightarrow$ grass is green' resembles the expression 'If grass has chloroplasts, then grass is green' in being well-formed, it is natural to compare the 'sentence-connective "$\rightarrow$" ' with the conjunction 'if . . . then . . .' in respect of their meanings. Moreover, since a truth-table is the canonical form for explaining the meaning of the first sentence, a comparison of the meanings of these sentence-connectives is driven into the form of an enquiry into whether 'if p, then q' can be given a truth-table definition, in particular whether the same definition applies both to 'if p, then q', and '$p \rightarrow q$'. The upshot is the many arguments familiar from courses in elementary logic. Some authors maintain, others deny, that some of the sentence-connectives 'and', 'or', 'if . . . then . . .', 'not only . . . but also . . .', '. . . although . . .', 'but', are truth-functional, i.e. that their meanings can be fully specified by truth-tables. Most stand prudently on the sidelines urging that there are in many cases close parallels, but always minor discrepancies, that truth-tables clarify much but not all of the meanings of these expressions. Similar discussions rage around expressions of generality such as 'any', 'each', 'every', 'all', 'some', 'there is a . . .'. Here too there is a general consensus that many minor differences prevent any outright identifications of the meanings of these expressions with those of the quantifiers as explained in logical semantics, but that the predicate calculus illuminates much about the workings of these expressions (e.g. scope-differences between 'any', 'each', and 'all'). For present purposes we are not directly concerned with these vexed questions (below, pp. 170–9). Rather, we wish to draw attention to the fact that the term 'truth-conditions' has undergone a transformation in the very raising of these questions. Whereas a truth-table was originally conceived as a specification of the truth-conditions of a formula such as '$p \rightarrow q$', we must now admit the *intelligibility* of offering a truth-table in explanation of the sentence 'If grass has chloroplasts, then grass is green'. Concomitantly, we must contemplate the possibility that a truth-table might afford the genuine, proper definition of the subordinating conjunction 'if' even though earlier generations of competent English-speakers had no inkling of this fundamental truth.

Even this major extension of the concept of a truth-condition does not encompass the whole of the territory now thought to fall under its sway. This point is obvious, though easily overlooked. First, if sentences of the form 'If p, then q' were not susceptible of truth-table explanations, then we would be driven to conclude that 'If p, then q', unlike '$p \rightarrow q$', had no truth-conditions. Secondly, although it might make sense to assign truth-conditions to the sentence 'Grass is green and grass has chloroplasts', it would make no more sense to ask 'What are the truth-conditions of "Grass has chloroplasts"?' than to ask 'What are the truth-conditions of "*p*"?' In short, the concept of truth-conditions borrowed from logical semantics is applicable only to molecular sentences formed with the aid of truth-functional connectives (and to generalizations constructed out of expressions conforming to the standard semantic definitions of the quantifiers). Yet philosophers now deem it wholly appropriate to investigate the 'truth-conditions' of sentences falling outside this restricted class. Nobody thinks it to be *absurd* to lay down the truth-conditions of 'This snow is white' or even of 'Columbus believed that the earth was round'. Here too we must acknowledge a dramatic change.

The origins of this transformation appear to lie in the notion of analysis which came to fruition in the logical atomism of Russell and Wittgenstein. Much of Russell's early work was a refurbishment of classical empiricism in conformity with the improved logic first developed by Frege. The kaleidoscope picture of the mind Russell reformulated as an account of empirical discourse. This produced his celebrated principle of acquaintance: every proposition which we can understand is composed wholly of constituents with which we are acquainted. The ultimate ground, not merely of knowledge, but even of language, is experience (though Russell held abstract objects, universals, and even logical forms to be objects of experience). The notion of analysis is then invoked to protect this position against obvious attack. It seems plain that not every significant expression can be correlated with something confronted in experience, e.g. the phrase 'round square'. Russell admitted this objection, but then argued that his principle applied only to fully analysed expressions. Although the phrase 'round square' wears a preliminary analysis on its sleeve, this is not true of all expressions capable of analysis (e.g. 'unicorn' or 'prime (number)'). The proper analysis of expressions may be difficult to discover, but once found and used to transform sentences of natural language into their fully analysed counterparts, the principle of acquaintance would be visibly demonstrated to hold universally. In a fully analysed sentence each expression would stand for something immediately presented to us in experience. However, this project could, in Russell's view, only be carried out by someone versed in the 'New Logic'. Analysis would have to exploit all the resources of the predicate calculus.

The *Tractatus* took over this conception of analysis. But Wittgenstein purified Russell's account of its epistemological motivation and its ties with classical empiricism, elaborating his logical atomism as a doctrine about the conditions for the intelligibility of any possible system of signs (language). Moreover, he reformulated the principle of analysis in a very strict form: every proposition is a truth-function of elementary proposi-tions. In other words he held that any significant sentence could be exhibited as equivalent to the output of truth-functional operations ap-plied to some members of a determinate stock of elementary propositions. Such a sentence could be transformed by analysis into a truth-function of elementary propositions. (In accord with Wittgenstein's later repudiation of the account of generality in the *Tractatus*, this thesis would need reformulation. It would become the principle that every significant sentence can be transformed by analysis into a well-formed sentence constructed solely by truth-functional operators and quantifiers out of the set of elementary sentences.) The procedures of analysis were taken to expose the true hidden structures of the sentences of natural languages and of the thoughts (propositions) expressed by these sentences, even though it was left for future discovery what the forms and constituents of the elementary propositions might be.

The explanation of 'truth-condition' in the *Tractatus* can be applied in a straightforward manner to any well-formed expression which is con-structed by truth-functional operators, *a fortiori* to any formula which combines elementary sentences with the primitive logical constants of *Principia*. A truth-table can, in the simplest cases, be employed to exhibit the truth-conditions of a molecular sentence. The method for deriving the truth-conditions of such a formula from the formula itself are purely mechanical. Matters stand altogether differently with respect to singular sentences of a natural language. In the *sentence* 'Paris is a city in France', there is no logical constant at all, and therefore no question of extracting its truth-conditions on the model of using a truth-table to yield the truth-conditions of '$p \rightarrow (q \vee r)$'. On the other hand, the *Tractatus* did not acknowledge such a sentence to be elementary; analysis would reveal it to be equivalent to a truth-function of elementary sentences; and this equiva-lent formula would have truth-conditions in virtue of being molecular. What could be more natural than to characterize the resultant truth-table as expressing the truth-conditions of the original sentence 'Paris is a city in France'? Parity of reasoning seems to license talking of the truth-conditions of almost all, if not all, sentences of any natural language. (And any residual cases could be encompassed by allowing 'degenerate cases' of truth-conditions.) Consequently, the thesis of analysis can be rephrased as the claim that every significant sentence of any possible language has determinate truth-conditions (expressible solely in terms of the symbolism of the predicate calculus and the resources provided by a fixed stock of elementary sentences). In this way, the range of applicability of 'truth-conditions' is greatly extended: whereas previously the question 'What are its truth-conditions?' could intelligibly be raised only about a sentence having a definitely circumscribed structure, it can now be raised about *any* sentence whatever.

Although this movement of thought is very natural, it also poses a danger of misinterpretation. What in fact has taken place is a dramatic redrawing of the boundaries of the concept of a truth-condition. By a bit of linguistic legislation something previously regarded as nonsense has been transmuted into the expression of a truth, e.g. the statement ' "Paris is a city in France" has truth-conditions'. This is plain from the fact that the original explanation of the term 'truth-condition' must be altered to make this new use *comprehensible*. The danger (to which Wittgenstein and Russell both succumbed in their logical atomism) is to misconstrue this change in the rules for the use of 'truth-condition' as a discovery of an important fact, hitherto unrecognized, about the nature or essence of sentences of natural language. As if the more restricted application of 'truth-condition' were based on mistaken beliefs! Far from this being so, this earlier use was indubitably correct when judged by the appropriate standard, viz. the explanation of 'truth-condition' in terms of truth-tables and standard definitions of the quantifiers. By revising the explanation of this term, no facts are changed, but only our way of (correctly) talking about the facts. The expression 'analysis' is well-suited to obscuring this important aspect of the extension of the application of 'truth-conditions'. It seems as if what analysis exposes in a sentence must really always have been present, on analogy with the atomic structure of matter, whereas, in fact, by appealing to 'analyses' of expressions, philosophers take themselves to be authorized to make statements that were previously held to be unintelligible. It is not the apparatus of logical semantics that shows every sentence to have truth-conditions, any more than it is Russell's theory of descriptions that licenses the representation of the sentence 'Paris is a city in France' by the formula '$(\exists x)((\varphi x \wedge (\forall y)(\varphi y \rightarrow y = x)) \wedge \psi x)$'.[25]

Clarity on this point has considerable importance since it might forestall further conceptual confusion. Accustomed to a practice of using 'truth-conditions' in application to any sentences whatever, we may be tempted to conclude from scrutiny of its origins in the *Tractatus* that we can divorce the concept of truth-conditions from Wittgenstein's set of doctrines about logical analysis. This would be catastrophically misguided. The concep-

[25] In this connection a distinction has often been drawn between 'same level' and 'different level' logical analysis.

tion of analysis in the *Tractatus* is not separable from the explanation of
the term 'truth-condition' which supports its applicability to every sentence of a natural language. There is therefore no fall-back position, in
particular no prior explanation which itself legitimated this extension. To
jettison the doctrine of logical analysis is to restore the *status quo ante*
according to which the general applicability of the term was unintelligible.
Without some fresh explanation, the statement ' "Paris is a city in France"
has truth-conditions' is an empty formula, signifying nothing at all.

Another danger from failing to appreciate the role played by the notion
of analysis in giving content to the concept of a truth-condition is the
generation of a mythology of symbolism. A well-formed formula such as
'$p \wedge ((q \rightarrow r) \vee (\neg r \rightarrow s))$' can be described as a truth-function of the
propositions p, q, r, and s; it is built up from the sentence-letters 'p', 'q', 'r',
's' and the logical operators '$\neg$', '$\rightarrow$', '$\wedge$', '$\vee$'. But suppose that this
formula is produced as the analysis of the sentence 'Paris is a city in
France'. Neither the listed sentence-letters nor the listed logical operators
occur in this *sentence*, even though both the sentence and the formula
make the same statement *ex hypothesi*. None the less, if the equivalence of
these expressions is to justify the claim that the *sentence* has truth-
conditions, and if these truth-conditions are to be expressed by the truth-
table corresponding to the logical formula, then it seems that the sentence
itself must really contain these constituents even if this is not apparent. Its
superficial grammatical form must disguise a more complex logical
structure. Any correct description of the formula constituting a proper
analysis of a given sentence in natural language can be applied to the
original *sentence* itself. Consequent paradox is dissolved by bearing in
mind that the description is really applicable to the logical form of this
sentence, not to its grammatical form. From a logical point of view, every
sentence or formula capable of expressing a given proposition must have
the same structure and constituents. For only on this (bizarre) assumption
would the putative possibility of analysing the sentence 'Paris is a city in
France' into a truth-function of elementary propositions show that this
sentence itself has any truth-conditions (unless it were acknowledged that
the product of 'analysis' is in fact a novel extension of the concept of a
truth-condition). Philosophers trained to this species of double-think have
no difficulty in finding the negation-sign and a universal quantifier in the
sentence '2 is a prime number'.[26] (And with practice they also learn to find
a force-indicator and a sentence-radical in the *sentence* 'What is the largest

[26] Because they take its logical analysis to be expressed by the formula '$(\forall x)((x < 2) \wedge \neg (x = 1) \rightarrow \neg (\exists y)(yx = 2))$' where the quantifiers range over positive integers.

prime factor of 857,863?') A powerful myth here overpowers sound common sense. Confusion about the concept of logical form and the concept of a truth-condition then manifests itself in the idea that the nature of language is profoundly mysterious, that there is a vast gulf between appearance and reality in respect of the simplest utterances of natural language.[27]

The practice of speaking of the truth-conditions of arbitrary sentences of natural languages was widespread among philosophers most immediately inspired by the conception of analysis in the logical atomism of Russell and Wittgenstein. In particular, it is characteristic of the writings of members of the Vienna Circle. They followed Wittgenstein in taking the task of philosophy to be the logical analysis of statements of 'science', including everyday predictions and reports of observations, and likewise they took this task of clarifying meaning to require revealing for every sentence its method of verification. They investigated sentences as diverse as 'There is a book on top of the cupboard', 'Seitz has been elected mayor', 'Caesar crossed the Alps', 'An electron is negatively charged', and 'He is depressed'. In every such case

whenever we ask about a sentence, 'what does it mean?' what we expect is instruction as to the circumstances in which the sentence is to be used; we want a description of the conditions under which the sentence will form a *true* proposition, and of those which will make it *false*. . . . stating the meaning of a sentence amounts to . . . stating the way in which it can be verified (or falsified).[28]

This explanation of the basic methodology of logical positivism obviously presupposes that every significant sentence can be said to have truth-conditions. Correlative with this conception was acceptance of the notion that *sentences* of natural language have logical forms made explicit in formal notations. Familiar words are, as it were, the flesh put on an invisible 'logical skeleton'.[29] Finally it was standard to argue that some,

---

[27] Philosophers are readily bewitched by this difference in considering language (cf. Waismann, *Ludwig Wittgenstein and the Vienna Circle*, p. 48).

[28] Schlick, 'Meaning and Verification', in *Gesammelte Aufsätze*, p. 340. It is noteworthy that this quotation simultaneously offers three distinguishable accounts of sentence-meanings. The meaning of a sentence is said to consist of the circumstances for its correct *use*, the conditions for its *truth*, and the method of its *verification*. Failure to draw sharp distinctions between these characterizations is typical of the work of the logical positivists, and it frustrates the attempt to subsume logical positivism under the aegis of 'anti-realism'.

[29] R. Carnap, *The Logical Structure of the World*, tr. R. A. George (Routledge & Kegan Paul, London, 1967), §46.

but not all, sentence-connectives of natural language could be properly defined by truth-tables. Against the background of contrary ideas emerging in Wittgenstein's reflections, Carnap proclaimed a general faith that there is no difference in principle between 'formalized languages' and natural languages, and he therefore advocated that sophisticated mathematical techniques have fruitful applications to the analytical description of natural languages. All of these modern ideas were in place by the early 1930s, although they were then supported by a conception of analysis that has officially passed out of favour.

4 Forging links between language and the world

A second transformation in the notion of a truth-condition was equally dramatic and influential. It was initiated by Tarski in his famous essay 'The Concept of Truth in Formalized Languages' (1935). This provided the catalyst for a comprehensive but subtle metamorphosis of the conception of what is now called 'logical semantics'. This change can be best clarified by contrasting the general conception of logic which Carnap and other logical positivists extracted from the *Tractatus* with the conception now prevalent among logicians.

Wittgenstein held the explanations of logical constants by truth-tables to belong to what he called the 'logical *syntax*' of language. Carnap put a particular gloss (arguably incorrect) on this opaque phrase. According to his interpretation, truth-tables provide translation-rules for replacing well-formed formulae of *Principia Mathematica* by matrices filled with arrays of 'T's and 'F's. Tautologies are then picked out by the feature that under this syntactic transformation a matrix is generated in which 'T' stands in each row under the main connective. Since a formula expresses a logical truth if and only if it is a tautology, logical truth is a matter only of the logical syntax of language, i.e. something independent of any explicit consideration of truth and falsity. (For the purpose of identifying tautologies, one need assign no meanings to the symbols 'T' and 'F').

The early ('classical') phase of the growth of what we now call 'logical semantics' was dominated by this conception. Investigations (including Gödel's sophisticated and celebrated work) into the consistency, independence, and completeness of axiomatizations of logic and arithmetic were considered to be developments of the logical syntax of formal languages. Carnap formulated this general view in his book *The Logical Syntax of Language* (1934). Its central contentions are that logic is the science of linguistic expressions (not of abstract entities such as judgments or propositions) and that precise statements can be framed only about the syntax of sign-systems (not about their meanings or designations). He strove to prove that 'the logic of science is nothing other than the logical syntax of the language of science'[30] – a rephrasing of what he took to be the programme of the *Tractatus*. In particular, he advanced the thesis that 'the logical characteristics of sentences (for instance, whether a sentence is analytic, synthetic, or contradictory . . .) and the logical relations between them (for instance, whether two sentences contradict one another or are compatible with one another; whether one is logically deducible from the other or not . . .) are solely dependent on the syntactical structure of the sentences'.[31] Essential to Carnap's vindication of this thesis was a precise formulation of the meanings of the logical constants of his system by statements of truth-conditions of sentences in which they occur; viz. by truth-tables and the standard explanations of the quantifiers.[32] The presence of these definitions and their essential role in his reasoning did not, in his view, conflict with the claim that logic is solely concerned with syntax.

The significance of this conception of logical syntax is difficult to apprehend (especially because acceptance or rejection of it has no direct implications for the conduct of metalogic). The most important aspects of the matter escape detection because they are remote and negative. The *Tractatus* was taken to exclude the possibility of making any significant statements about the meanings of signs. Some symbols can of course be defined, but definitions were construed as syntactic (substitution-) rules. The process of analysis must ultimately terminate in truth-functions of elementary sentences, each of which is composed of symbols incapable of further analysis. Meaning is assigned to these 'indefinables' by their direct association with simple objects through 'elucidations'. These methods of projection cannot be described in language. Arguably what Wittgenstein had in mind as the foundation of language, the terminus of analysis, was the form of explanation which was later singled out under the label 'ostensive definition'. It is entirely natural to picture this procedure as lying on the limits of language and as effecting an ineffable connection between symbols and the world.

The Vienna Circle extracted this picture from the *Tractatus* and combined it with the empiricist tenet that experience provides the raw ma-

[30] R. Carnap, *The Logical Syntax of Language*, tr. A. Smeaton (Routledge, London, 1937).
[31] Ibid., p. 2.
[32] Ibid., p. 20.

terials for concept-formation. The result was a conception of ostensive
definition characteristic of logical empiricism.[33] On this view, explanations of meaning can be divided into two mutually exclusive types: intra-
linguistic verbal definitions (or analyses) and extralinguistic ostensions of
'indefinables'. Ostensive definitions alone carry the entire empirical content of language since they alone mediate between a calculus of symbols
and the reality described by its formulae. They alone connect symbols with
the world and thereby make the difference between a mere game of
manipulating signs and speaking a language. This picture incorporates a
host of important misconceptions. But for present purposes the one of
paramount interest is the idea that meanings are at bottom ineffable. In
giving an ostensive definition one steps outside language.[34] Evidently 'our
ordinary verbal language must be supplemented by pointing to objects and
presenting them in order to make our words and sentences a useful means
of communication'.[35] The proverbial problem of explaining colour-words
to the congenitally blind man is offered to confirm the principle that all
explanation 'must end by some demonstration, some activity'.[36] Schlick
went so far as to connect this conception of ostensive definition with the
doctrine of the *Tractatus* that philosophy is an *activity* of clarifying
meaning; for, he noted, 'the final giving of meaning always takes place . . .
through *deeds*'.[37] He also drew the consequence that meaning is ineffable,
claiming that the meaning of a word cannot ultimately be stated, but 'must
in the end be *shown*, it must be *given* . . . by an act of indication or
pointing'.[38] According to this conception, all of those aspects of specifying
word-meaning which can be formulated at all in language (viz. explicit
definitions) belong to the province of logical syntax. Hence whatever is left
over from this science of symbolism is not susceptible to being stated, *a
fortiori* it does not lie within the sphere of any possible science. Semantics
falls within the domain of the ineffable.

This was the background to Carnap's reception of Tarski's invention of
a theory of truth for a formalized language. Tarski set out a recursive
definition of the expression 'true sentence' in the logical calculus
elaborated in *Principia Mathematica*. This exploited the truth-table explanations of the logical constants of the propositional calculus and the

---

[33] This conception is carefully anatomized (and criticized) in G. P. Baker and P. M. S.
Hacker: 'Wittgenstein and the Vienna Circle: The Exaltation and Deposition of Ostensive
Definition'; *Teoria*, 1984.

[34] Waismann, *Ludwig Wittgenstein and the Vienna Circle*, p. 246.

[35] Schlick, 'Form and Content', in *Gesammelte Aufsätze*, p. 194.

[36] Ibid., p. 129.   [37] Ibid., p. 36.   [38] Ibid., p. 90.

standard explanations of identity and the quantifiers. The essential trick was to lay down in some appropriate metalanguage the conditions for the truth of each atomic formula: viz. to stipulate that 'φa' is true if and only if the object correlated with 'a' has the property correlated with 'φx', that 'Rab' is true if and only if the pair of objects correlated with 'a' and 'b' stand in the relation correlated with 'Rxy', etc. Then the explanations of the logical constants can be so interpreted that they suffice to calculate the truth-value of any molecular formula from the truth-values determined by the stipulations for the components of the atomic formulae. Carnap seized eagerly on Tarski's machinery for carrying out this programme. He noted the general form of the explanation of the truth-condition of a formula: viz. 'p' is true if and only if p. But he gave this a novel interpretation, quite contrary to Tarski's avowed intentions. Carnap saw in this schema the possibility of circumventing the conclusion that meaning is at bottom ineffable. For even if a sentence, whether in a natural language or a formalized language, has no analysable components, it must still have some complexity, and hence its meaning can be non-trivially *stated* by an appropriate metalinguistic statement of the form ' "p" is true if and only if p' (e.g. 'Rabc' is true if and only if a, b and c stand in the relation R). This transformed his whole outlook on logic and language. The bounds of intelligible discourse about expressions seemed to be suddenly pushed back, and a mighty science (logical semantics) seemed to be already in place on ground where it had previously seemed that there was no room for significant statements at all!

Carnap was not alone in making this *volte-face* (though he was in the vanguard). The idea also appealed to other logical positivists who had accepted the same conception of the grounding of logic in syntax and the same conception of ostensive definition as forging the fundamental links between language and the world. Many philosophers were intoxicated by the prospect of using Tarski's formal machinery to construct the science of semantics – the rigorous explanation of the relation of language to the world. The core of this enterprise is the stipulation in a metalanguage of the *truth-conditions* for every well-formed sentence of the object language. *Mirabile dictu*, the very same concept that had earlier seemed to enclose the scientific investigation of language within syntax now appeared to open the gate to rigorous formal semantics.

The key to this seeming paradox is another shift in the explanation of the term 'truth-condition'. What masquerades as a substantial discovery about language is in fact a revised way of speaking about sentences. The original explanation of 'truth-condition' involved truth-tables or definitions of the quantifiers. One of Tarski's T-sentences (viz. a metalinguistic statement of the form ' "*p*" is true iff *p*') is not of an appropriate form even to be a candidate for an explanation of the truth-conditions of a sentence. No such equivalence could be viewed as stating truth-conditions. Even if Wittgenstein's scruples about the intelligibility of metalinguistic statements were brushed aside, a truth-table can at best be regarded as a transformation of one metalinguistic statement into another. The truth-table for '*p* ∧ *q*', e.g., states an equivalence between the metalinguistic statement ' "*p* ∧ *q*" is true' and another metalinguistic statement, viz. ' "*p*" is true and "*q*" is true'. Similarly, the explanation of '(∀*x*)φ*x*' states that ' "(∀*x*)φ*x*" is true' if and only if every sentence of the form 'φ(A)' is true. The only way to subsume ' "*p*" is true iff *p*' under the label of 'specifying the truth-conditions of "*p*" ' is to pass some novel linguistic legislation. The need for this redefinition is masked for two reasons. One is that the earlier explanations of the logical constants play a pivotal role in Tarski's formal semantics (though they are reinterpreted). The other is that a sentence of the form ' "*p*" is true iff *p*' can plausibly be claimed (at least in many cases) to state a condition for the truth of the sentence '*p*'; one may mistakenly infer that it states a 'truth-condition of "*p*" ' by forgetting that 'truth-condition' is a technical term. The metamorphosis of logical syntax into logical semantics rests on a novel extension of the term 'truth-condition'.

In one respect the applicability of the term is greatly extended. Every well-formed formula, whether atomic or molecular, has truth-conditions. The truth-conditions of the formula 'φ*a*' would be stated in the metalanguage as the requirement that a (the object designated by '*a*') have the property φ (the property correlated with 'φ'). The articulation of the truth-conditions in the metalanguage matches the articulation of the formula in the object-language. Moreover, the thesis that every sentence of a formalized language has truth-conditions is cut free from any presupposition that it can be analysed into a molecular formula. Hence the naive extension of Tarskian semantics to sentences of natural language is not encumbered with the millstone of any doctrines about philosophical analysis.

In another respect, however, the application of 'truth-condition' is narrowed. According to the earlier conception, a truth-table does actually specify the truth-conditions of a molecular formula, and so too does the explanation that '(∀*x*)φ*x*' is true if and only if every formula of the form 'φ*a*' is true. But now, since every atomic formula has its own truth-conditions, these explanations do not complete the specification of the truth-conditions of any molecular formula. Rather, they are considered to state the truth-conditions of molecular formulae *relative to* the truth-conditions of their constituents. On this view, e.g., the truth-table for '$p \rightarrow q$' determines how to calculate the truth-conditions of this formula from statements of the truth-conditions for 'p' and 'q'. Whereas such a truth-table had previously served as a paradigm for the specification of truth-conditions, its fresh interpretation presupposes an independent explanation of how to apply 'truth-condition' to atomic formulae.

On this conception of a truth-condition, Tarski inaugurated the science of formal semantics, the study of the relations between formalized languages and their interpretations (or models). His ambitions were precise and narrowly circumscribed. He held that a formal definition of truth in a language could be constructed only for a formalized language, since only symbols in such a system would have fully determinate syntactic structures capable of supporting a recursive specification of truth. Moreover, he presupposed that it was possible to give precise mathematical characterizations of the entities involved in the interpretation of the symbols of the object-language. In both respects his caution has gone out of fashion. The attraction of model theory now is that it is conceived to be 'the study of the relations between languages and the world'.[39] This manifests radical confusions.

One such confusion is the supposition that a natural language has a determinate syntactic structure on the basis of which a calculus could be constructed parallel to the formal semantics of a formalized language. This supposition no doubt seemed unproblematic to logical empiricists. They were already committed to it in analysing the logical syntax of language, since this was to be 'the systematic statement of the formal rules which govern [language] together with the development of the consequences which follow from these rules'.[40] But given that any genuine rules of syntax must actually guide the behaviour of speakers, there is no calculus of syntactic rules for any natural language, and also no possibility of postulating one (or more) such systems. A mythology about normative phenomena is a precondition of extending truth-conditional semantics to sentences of a natural language.

Another set of confusions shrouds the idea of a connection between language and the world. The distorted conception of ostensive definition

---

[39] Cf. T. Potts, 'Model Theory and Linguistics', in *Formal Semantics of Natural Language*, ed. E. L. Keenan (Cambridge University Press, Cambridge, 1975), p. 241.
[40] Carnap, *The Logical Syntax of Language*, p. 1.

among logical positivists was symptomatic of some deep misunderstanding. How could anybody think that such explanations of meaning would settle all aspects of word-use or be immune from the possibility of misinterpretation? Who would suppose that no word open to a verbal definition could properly be explained by ostension, and vice versa? Yet the positivists embraced these absurd theses in defence of their conception of how language hooked on to experience. Instead of clarifying this conception, the advocates of Tarskian semantics accepted it and then argued that metalinguistic statements (and only metalinguistic statements) could accomplish what the positivists had wrongly considered to be impossible. All the underlying misconceptions soldiered on. The notion of an 'indefinable' was not examined, nor the idea of what it is to *say* what an expression means. There was no room for samples among the instruments of communication, or even for gestures; this indicates confusion about the alleged boundary between symbols and what is symbolized. Most importantly, both logical empiricism and Tarskian semantics accepted the idea that explaining meaning is at root a matter of correlating words with entities of suitable types. Both were captivated by the Augustinian picture of language. If that is a distorting mirror for reflections on language, then nothing but a grotesque will be produced in either workshop.

It seems strange that a diet of T-sentences can produce a form of intoxication in philosophers. No doubt much of this effect is the consequence of noting the possibilities for mathematical sophistication in devising systems of formal semantics. Set theory, abstract algebra, and topology are all brought to bear. But it should not be forgotten that this rich growth of formal calculi does not guarantee the intelligibility of any of the terminology of formal semantics, and that it does not show that model theory sheds any light on philosophical problems about natural language. The conceptual foundations of this new set of applications of the term 'truth-conditions' seem to be very problematic. But the inertia of the movement of formal semantics diverts attention on to other issues which are heatedly debated by contemporary theorists of meaning. One characteristic controversy concerns the question whether T-sentences are mere translation-manuals for rendering expressions of the object-language into equivalent expressions of the metalanguage (which might be another natural language such as French) or whether on the contrary they can in principle really clarify the workings of language by revealing how symbols are correlated with reality (or with the behaviour of speakers of the object-language). Another similar debate centres on whether a semantic theory presupposes metaphysical principles (and hence might transgress the bounds of sense) or whether, on the contrary, metaphysical questions are really reducible to questions about the nature of semantic theories (and hence might be settled conclusively by investigating the use of expressions). Tarski's revolution brought about a decisive change in the course of modern philosophy, but perhaps it did not steer philosophers into investigating those issues most urgently in need of conceptual clarification.

The upshot of Tarski's work was a permanent reorientation about the tools of logical semantics and the nature of logical truth. Truth-tables and the standard logical elucidations of the quantifiers were now acknowledged to belong to semantics, not to be transformation-rules belonging to logical syntax. They were now held to afford the basis for a purely semantic conception of validity and of logical truth. Thanks to Tarski, Carnap had the revelation that 'logical truth in the customary sense is a semantical concept'.[41] An appropriate 'informal characterization of logical truth . . . [is] *truth based on meanings*'.[42] And the proper explication of this concept in formal semantics is that a sentence in a semantical system is 'L-true' if and only if the semantical rules of this system suffice for establishing its truth.[43] Only as a result of Tarski's work did philosophers succeed in putting what is now taken to be the correct interpretation on the formal calculus that had yielded proofs of consistency and completeness of axiomatizations of logic. Only then did logical semantics spring properly into view and deliver a wholly semantic definition of validity.[44]

5 Cutting language free from actuality

A third transformation of the concept of a truth-condition was brought about by the invention of 'intensional logic'. Several distinct streams of thought converged to prompt this major development. Carnap's book *Meaning and Necessity* (1947) is the seed from which possible-worlds semantics has sprung in all its multifarious forms. A fresh conception of truth-conditions provides the foundations for modern intensional logics.

[41] R. Carnap, 'Intellectual Autiobiography', in *The Philosophy of Rudolf Carnap*, ed. P. Schilpp (Open Court, La Salle, Ill., 1963), p. 64.

[42] Ibid., p. 916.

[43] R. Carnap, *Meaning and Necessity* (Chicago University Press, Chicago, 1947), pp. 7ff.

[44] Just as in the case of Frege's devising quantification theory, here too a sophisticated and elaborate formal calculus arose on the basis of general conceptions now held to be irremediably defective or even incoherent. In both cases an important moral is to be drawn about the relation of formal systems to their putative 'philosophical foundations'.

Much of the impetus for this development derives more or less directly from the prior growth of truth-conditional semantics. These ideas have a trajectory that leads naturally to further philosophical theory-building and hence to the requisite conceptual innovations. A clarification of the distinction between extension and intension will, as a by-product, make intelligible an important aspect of the evolution of modern logic.

Carnap's reflections on semantics represent an attempt to marry the account of logical truth in the *Tractatus* with Tarski's definition of truth for a formalized language. From Wittgenstein he accepted that truth-tables and model theory constituted a procedure for determining whether any fully analysed sentence expressed a logical truth; this had earlier persuaded Carnap to argue that logical truth was purely a matter of the logical syntax of language. But now from Tarski he accepted that truth was a semantic concept belonging to the same family as designation, reference, and satisfaction. This obviously suggested that truth-tables, properly viewed, belonged to semantics, not to syntax: they are 'semantical truth-rules in the form of diagrams'.[45] That conclusion in turn prompted the thesis that logical truth is a semantic property of a formula or sentence. Carnap indeed adopted as a leading thesis the claim 'that logic is a special branch of semantics, that logical deducibility and logical truth are semantical concepts'.[46] He set out to construct a semantic theory to vindicate this claim.

One technical problem raised an immediate obstacle to further progress. He followed Tarski and Hilbert in distinguishing sharply between speaking in a language and speaking about a language. He characterized a semantic system as a set of rules formulated in a metalanguage which lay down a truth-condition for every sentence in the object-language, i.e. a necessary and sufficient condition for its truth.[47] Consequently he held that logical truth would be exhibited as a semantic concept only if it could be defined in the metalanguage for a given object-language. But the straight-forward procedure would be to define a logical truth as any sentence of the object-language such that the statement that it is true can be derived solely from the semantic rules for the object-language. This formulation, in virtue of mentioning derivations from semantic rules, must belong to the meta-metalanguage, not to the metalanguage itself. Hence, strictly speaking, it fails to define logical truth as a semantic property![48] The very same distinction between language and metalanguage which underpins Tarski's

---

[45] R. Carnap, *Introduction to Semantics* (Harvard University Press, Cambridge, Mass., 1961), p. 30.

[46] Ibid., p. 56.   [47] Ibid., p. 22.   [48] Ibid., pp. 83f.

definition of truth seems to forestall employing his idea to give a precise semantic definition of logical truth and logical validity.

Carnap addressed this crisis as Russell had tackled the parallel difficulties generated by the theory of types. He adopted the tactics of judiciously relaxing the full rigours of semantic ascent from language to metalanguage. He assumed that the metalanguage contained an operator 'N' which in combination with a sentence ' "s" is true' of the metalanguage stated exactly the same thing as the sentence in the meta-metalanguage ' " 's' is true" is true solely in virtue of semantic rules of the object language'. Hence, 'N ("s" is true)' is a statement framed in the metalanguage which asserts that 's' is a logical truth. The intended interpretation for 'N' is the expression 'It is a necessary truth that . . .' or 'Necessarily . . .'. Clearly Carnap's strategem is successful only if the operator 'N' is not conceived to attribute a property to a sentence (since 'N("s" is true)' would then belong to the meta-metalanguage); it must be conceived as an operator on propositions, i.e. on what is designated by a sentence (in the metalanguage), and hence Carnap held propositions to be part of the ontology essential to logical semantics. The requirement that discourse incorporating logical modalities be intelligible was also integral to his programme.

Having waded so deep into modality, Carnap was induced to consider whether he could give a semantic analysis of modal statements themselves. On reflection, he found that he had already introduced the requisite resources. State-descriptions or possible states of affairs allowed a simple system of semantics for modal statements on the basis of Leibniz's conception of necessary truth as truth in all possible worlds. Possible states of affairs afforded the entities needed for the semantic interpretation of generalizations over possible worlds. Hence Carnap was able to state truth-conditions for a sentence of the form 'Necessarily . . .' by the metalinguistic stipulation: 'Np' is true if and only if 'p' is true in every possible state of affairs. With this system of semantics for modal statements, Carnap undertook a semantic analysis of the axiomatizations of modal logic proposed and developed by Lewis, and he even thought that he could prove one of these to be correct, the others mistaken, on the basis of his explication of logical necessity. He introduced the concept of intension to simplify his exposition of semantics: the intension of a sentence is a determination of its truth-value in every possible world. Necessary truths are then instances of the limiting case in which the intension of a sentence is all-encompassing, and the logical validity of an argument can be expressed as a simple relation among the intensions of its constituent sentences. The framework of possible worlds allowed the construction of a formal system of semantics which embraced not only the predicate calculus but also modal logic, and thus it constituted the foundations of the semantic analysis of sentences containing operators or connectives which are not truth-functional ('intensional discourse').

According to the idiom established by the *Tractatus*, it was the truth-conditions of a molecular sentence, as expressed in truth-tables and the model-theoretic explanations of the quantifiers, which established whether it expressed a logical truth and what its entailment-relations were. Since Carnap took the intension of a sentence to assume these roles in his extended semantical system, his protégés have been tempted to redefine 'truth-condition' and to use this term as a synonym for 'intension'. This conception has become definitive of one main branch of philosophical semantics, usually called 'possible-worlds semantics'. Here 'truth-condition' is so understood that 'a truth-condition specifies truth-values for a sentence; but in all possible worlds, not just in whichever world happens to be actual'.[49] Accordingly the truth-condition of a sentence is held to be a *function* from possible worlds to truth-values.[50] Alternatively it can be identified with a subset of the set of all possible worlds (consisting of those worlds in which it is true). The notion of a possible world is thus an essential component in the explanation of this concept of a truth-condition.

This revised concept had to meet one further constraint to win a place in the semantics of a formal system: intensions must be invented for the constituents of well-formed formulae in such a way that the intension of any sentence can be derived systematically from the intensions of its constituents and its syntactic structure. Fortunately this problem had an immediate solution. What is required in the case of an individual constant (name), a predicate letter, a quantifier (or predicate symbol of second-level) is something which stands to an object, a property or relation, or a second-level property, as the intension of a sentence stands to its actual truth-value. Hence, it suffices in the case of a name to correlate some object with it in each possible world, in the case of a predicate to correlate some set with it in each possible world to serve as its extension, etc. The intension of a name can therefore be defined as a function from possible worlds to objects; the intension of a predicate as a function from possible

[49] D. Lewis, *Convention: A Philosophical Study* (Harvard University Press, Cambridge, Mass., 1969), p. 171.

[50] Lewis, 'General Semantics', p. 174.

worlds to properties (or sets of objects), etc.[51] Then the truth-value assigned to 'φA' in a given possible world W can be calculated from the intension of 'φ' and the intension of 'A'; viz. 'φA' is true in W if and only if the object designated by 'A' in W belongs to the set correlated with 'φ' in W. A generalization of this consideration shows that the semantic value of a formula depends systematically on the semantic values assigned to its consitituents under the new definition of 'truth-condition'.

The formal adequacy of Carnap's extended system of semantics was reinforced by arguments in favour of its philosophical importance. One of these was the claim that the definition of logical validity in terms of truth-conditions constitutes a valuable *explication* of the intuitive conception of the cogency of a deductive argument which is encapsulated in the principle that the conclusion of a cogent argument *must* be true if the premises are jointly true. In other words, the semantic definition of validity makes precise a somewhat vague notion traditionally associated with the use by logicians of the words 'cogent', 'valid', 'sound', 'demonstrative', or 'conclusive'. For, in Carnap's system, an argument is 'logically valid' only if there is no possible world in which all of its premises are true and its conclusion false. Intensions are tailor-made to yield this principle.

A second supporting argument was that the concept of an intension is a good explication of the intuitive conception of meaning. Carnap described a semantical system as

A system of rules . . . [which] determine a truth-condition for every sentence of the object language . . . In this way the sentences are . . . made understandable, because to understand a sentence, to know what is asserted by it, is the same as to know under what conditions it would be true. . . . [T]he rules determine the *meaning* . . . of the sentences.[52]

Moreover, the rules are so designed for sentence-constituents that 'the truth-condition for every sentence is determined by the rules for the expressions of which it consists'.[53] In both respects Carnap's system of semantics is claimed to meet the criteria of adequacy for explanations of meaning. Although the everyday conception of meaning includes a rather indeterminate range of features not related to the determination of the truth-values of sentences, the concept of intension captures the core of this

[51] Lewis, *Convention*, p. 172.
[52] Carnap, *Introduction to Semantics*, p. 22.
[53] Ibid., p. 23.

allegedly vague concept of meaning and thereby is vindicated as an explication of a concept itself unsuitable for scientific investigation.

A third argument attempted to harness Frege as a draught-horse to put
Carnap's wagon in motion. Frege had invented the concept of sense
allegedly to solve a puzzle about the informativeness of identity statements, and he had then used it to break new ground by analysing statements incorporating non-extensional sentence-operators (e.g. 'Columbus
believed that . . .', 'I fear that . . .'). Carnap proposed his concept of
intension as a clarification of Frege's concept of sense, and he then went on
to correct and improve upon some of Frege's analyses of intensional
discourse (e.g. introducing 'intensional isomorphism' into the analysis of
belief-statements). He invoked Frege's authority for his own project without conceding that Frege had already arrived at a proper conception of
logical semantics and its full range of applications.

All three of Carnap's philosophical arguments in support of his semantical system have been influential. They are points of widespread, although
not universal, consensus. Recognition that logical validity is a purely
semantic concept is thought to be the very basis of the great progress in
modern formal logic.[54] The details of Carnap's treatment are open to
question, but his general conception of validity is above suspicion. Similarly, his relating the concept of meaning to his notion of intension may be
mistaken in detail, but it captures many points of fundamental importance. It differentiates sharply between the intension and extension of an
expression in every case (since even a function whose value is uniform over
all possible worlds must be distinct from this value itself), and hence it
differentiates the meaning of an expression from what it stands for (its
sense from its reference). Carnap recognized and tried to explain the fact
that the meanings of compounds are built up from the meanings of their
constituent parts; he thereby identified the fundamental problem of semantics. Finally, he built a theory in conformity with the principle that 'A
meaning for a sentence is something that determines the conditions under
which the sentence is true or false';[55] he thereby isolated the primary
subject-matter of semantics. What philosophers and linguists alike would
call a theory of *meaning* for a language would be something directly
comparable with the system Carnap raised on the foundation of the
concept of intension. He also established an orthodoxy in the interpretation of Frege's philosophy. Attempts to fill the lacuna of criteria of identity

[54] In fact, model theory is conceptually (and historically) independent of this particular
philosophical interpretation.
[55] Lewis, 'General Semantics', p. 173.

of sense invariably start from Carnap's proposal that identity of sense is necessary identity of reference even though this idea is ludicrous in relation to Frege's own declarations (e.g. that '$2^2 = 4$' differs in sense from '$2 + 2 = 4$') and inappropriate for his purposes. Modern interpreters are also obsessed with the conviction that Frege intended the concept of sense to clarify the notion of meaning, and they consequently neglect the mathematical rationale for Frege's sense/reference distinction as well as the multiple connections between the concept of sense and the notion of a function.[56]

Whether these philosophical components of Carnap's semantics are flawless is debatable. But our present purpose is simply to note that his conception of intension is the one at the centre of the cluster of contemporary versions of truth-conditional semantics. This prominence of his ideas has a ready explanation. He combined together in an elegant synthesis the main components of earlier explanations of 'truth-condition'. Truth-tables, the methods of model theory, and T-sentences were used jointly to demonstrate that semantics is the basis of pure logic. Every sentence was shown to have truth-conditions without support of any dogmas about analysis, and its truth-conditions are never trivial (since its intension is always a function defined over possible worlds). Logical relations depend only on truth-conditions. Provided that all entailments are formal, model theory, exploiting the definitions of the logical constants, suffices to identify any valid inference. Once again the engine of change is not some fresh discovery about the real nature of truth-conditions, but rather a new stipulation for the term 'truth-condition'.

6 Diaspora

The stream of ideas which gradually accumulated from the works of Frege, Wittgenstein, and Tarski and which gushed forth in Carnap's system of semantics has now diversified into many rivulets spread out over a wide delta. Comparison of each of the main branches of modern semantics with Carnap's system is a convenient way to map out the terrain, and it is facilitated by the fact that many theorists have used this very method to plot their own positions. We shall undertake a brief survey, ignoring detail wherever possible.

---

[56] These themes are elaborated in G. P. Baker and P. M. S. Hacker, *Frege: Logical Excavations* (Blackwell, Oxford, 1984).

Two different dimensions of dispersion are detectable. The first is variation in the scope and techniques of semantic analysis. The other is the significance of the resultant theories. Disagreements of the first type influence the shape and structure of semantic theories, whereas those of the second type do not directly do so. This independence generates a considerable spectrum of possible semantic theories. Most of these possibilities have been realized.

Disagreements about the scope and tools of semantic theories can be plotted as different interpretations of the thesis that the meaning of a sentence is its truth-conditions. We shall outline three points of divergence.

(i) Since syntax, semantics, and pragmatics are held jointly to exhaust the phenomena of any language, the scope of semantics depends on how the boundaries between syntax and semantics and between semantics and pragmatics are drawn. Both boundaries are controversial. Semantic theories for formal systems take for granted the prior discrimination of expressions into the class of those with sense and the class of the nonsensical. This dichotomy is effected by purely syntactic principles that can be mechanically applied to decide whether a complex symbol is well-formed. The same assumption is often made about the scope of semantics for sign-systems in general, including natural languages. It may be held that it is strictly the business of syntax to determine the boundary between sense and nonsense, while semantics is concerned only with specifying what meaning an expression has which is independently certified to be meaningful. According to this conception, we may find it difficult to construct rules for deciding whether 'The teapot smiled' is meaningful, but if this were established, then a semantic theory might deliver its meaning in the T-sentence ' "The teapot smiled" is true if and only if the teapot smiled'[57] or the theory might declare this sentence to have vacuous truth-conditions and hence to be necessarily false. But the opposite view is also common, viz. that some of the rules for differentiating sense from nonsense belong to semantics. On this conception, a semantic theory for English must show that such syntactically well-formed sentences as 'The number three is happy' or 'Red is higher in pitch than green' make no sense because they violate certain meaning-rules governing the constituent expressions (type-restrictions). An account which is not patently ludicrous is notoriously difficult to construct (below, pp. 336–9). The axioms of a semantic theory would take different forms depending on whether they do or do not incorporate type-restrictions.

[57] Cf. Davidson, 'Semantics for Natural Languages', pp. 185f.

The boundary between semantics and pragmatics is even more controversial. Two matters usurp attention, viz. context-dependence and illocutionary force, but others have been noted (e.g. the status of background assumptions and of principles relating to speakers' purposes in communication). One view excludes both force and context-dependence from semantics; here its meaning is taken to be a feature of an (unambiguous) type-sentence and to be fully explained in terms of general directions for its correct use on any occasion of its utterance, while principles for determining its actual use (e.g. to make an assertion) or the reference of context-dependent terms (e.g. indexicals such as 'I' or 'this') are the proper business of another science (pragmatics). Another view holds the principles for determination of reference of context-dependent expressions to belong to semantics since nothing short of this would provide the basis for connecting language fully with the world or for determining the truth-value of an uttered sentence.

(ii) Explaining sentence-meaning in terms of truth-conditions amounts to a clarification of meaning only on the supposition that the concept of truth itself is clear and unproblematic. This point is now a focus of dispute. Dummett has contended that the most crucial general problem in semantics is to settle 'what notion of truth is admissible',[58] and his powerful advocacy of this view has put the conflict between 'realism' and 'anti-realism' at stage-centre in current philosophy of language.[59] The debate turns on how properly to relate truth to verification. On the one hand, it is maintained that the question whether we have any means to determine the truth or falsity of a proposition has no bearing whatever on the question of whether this proposition is true or false. Truth, according to this conception, is said to be 'verification-transcendent'; it makes sense to suppose a proposition to be true although there is in principle no method available to us to ascertain its truth. Dummett calls this position 'realism' since it treats truth as an objective property of propositions, independent of human cognition. On the other hand, it is argued that there is no such thing as a truth which cannot in principle be known to be true. This connection of truth with verification is held to be fundamental to the explanation of 'true', i.e. to how this word is taught and learned. The notion of verification-transcendent truth is therefore held to be incoherent – the product of slovenly analogical thinking. Dummett calls this position 'anti-

[58] Dummett, *Truth and Other Enigmas*, p. xxii. He presupposes that truth is a *theoretical* concept.

[59] The seminal texts are Dummett's 'Truth' and 'The Reality of the Past' (reprinted in *Truth and Other Enigmas*).

realism' since he claims that it ultimately removes, for some propositions, any distinction between being true and being thought to be true; such fundamental propositions are made true by conditions the obtaining of which, if they obtain, we can recognize. Viewed through Dummett's spectacles, the principle of verification espoused by logical positivists rested on an anti-realist conception of truth, and investigation of anti-realism has resurrected this principle from the dead. Many philosophers now behave as if they followed Dummett in considering the issue between realism and anti-realism to be 'one of the most fundamental of all the problems of philosophy'.[60]

This rift in the conception of truth has potential consequences for the shape of semantic theories and the criteria of adequacy for them. This stands out in two respects. First, the justification of an anti-realist notion of truth is often held to turn on a general requirement that knowledge of sentence-meanings be something that can be fully manifested in a speaker's behaviour.[61] This in turn is thought to be possible only if meaning is explained ultimately in terms of capacities for verification. Consequently, according to anti-realism, any acceptable specification of the meaning of an expression in a semantic theory must be something knowledge of which can be determined from behaviour. Precisely what this requirement amounts to is difficult to say, but it certainly has a natural affinity with well-known scepticism about the legitimacy in semantics of any appeal to the notion of logical possibility or to the distinctions between analytic and synthetic or *a priori* and empirical truth. Anti-realism would seem to be an uneasy bed-fellow for some familiar versions of truth-conditional semantics. The second impact of anti-realism centres on the proper explanation of the various logical connectives. Dummett has suggested that anti-realism is coherent if and only if the rules of inference are taken to be those sanctioned by intuitionistic logic, not those associated with classical logic as presented by Frege, *Principia*, and the *Tractatus*.[62] The appropriate conception of validity is not captured by the classical explanations of sentence-connectives by truth-tables. These presuppose the principle of bivalence, viz. that every significant sentence is either true or false. This assumption is not open to the anti-realist. Hence his explanations must

---

[60] Dummett, 'Truth', p. 24; but compare Schlick's observation, quoted above, p. 139.

[61] Dummett discusses this argument at length in 'What is a Theory of Meaning? (II)', pp. 76ff.; cf. 'The Philosophical Basis of Intuitionistic Logic', in *Truth and Other Enigmas*, pp. 224f., and *Elements of Intuitionism* (Oxford University Press, Oxford, 1977), pp. 376ff.

[62] Cf. Dummett, 'The Philosophical Basis of Intuitionistic Logic', pp. 225ff., and 'Is Logical Empirical?', p. 288, in *Truth and Other Enigmas*.

take the different form of specifying in what conditions a molecular proposition is verified in terms of the conditions in which its components are verified. The classical explanations of the quantifiers must be similarly modified. The upshot is that certain classical logical truths are judged not to be logical truths (e.g. the Law of Excluded Middle) and certain classically valid inferences to be fallacious (e.g. $\neg(\forall x)\neg Fx \vdash (\exists x)Fx$). The important point to be noted is that there are coherent alternatives to the explanations of the logical connectives entrenched in the semantic theories presented by Tarski and Carnap. Different conceptions of truth ramify into conspicuous local differences among semantic theories.

(iii) Truth-conditions circumscribe potentialities or possibilities for the truth (and falsity) of sentences; indeed, truth-conditions are naturally described as truth-possibilities. But theorists come to blows about what notion of possibility should be used to clarify this principle. The range of positions is vast.

One great divide is the question whether any genuine modal notions are legitimate in a semantic theory. Quine has ridiculed the idea of *possibilia*.[63] There are allegedly no ways to individuate and enumerate possible objects, possible properties, and possible states of affairs; therefore discourse about such entities is held to be suspect, if not incomprehensible. His attitude has been influential. Many theorists have tried to banish possible worlds from truth-conditional semantics. Perhaps the most obvious way to accomplish this and yet to preserve an element of generality in specifications of truth-conditions is to focus on context-dependent sentences expressing empirical propositions and to construe stipulations of their truth-conditions to state generalizations about the actual occasions (past, present, and future, here, there, and elsewhere) on which they are held to be true by competent speakers. Quine and Davidson have pioneered this strategy of building semantics around the analysis of occasion-sentences.[64] By contrast, other prominent philosophers have made free use of modal notions in the manner of Carnap. Kripke introduces two forms of modality into his account of proper names and names of natural kinds,[65] while Lewis offers an analysis of counterfactual conditionals incorporating quantification over possible worlds.[66] Various forms of possible-worlds semantics flourish in the present philosophical climate.

[63] W. V. Quine, 'On what there is', in *From a Logical Point of View* (Harper & Row, New York, 1963), pp. 3ff.

[64] W. V. Quine, *Word and Object* (MIT Press, Cambridge, Mass., 1960), pp. 35ff; Davidson, 'Truth and Meaning', pp. 319f.

[65] S. Kripke, *Naming and Necessity* (Blackwell, Oxford, 1982).

[66] D. Lewis, *Counterfactuals* (Blackwell, Oxford, 1973).

In addition to these controversies about the scope and tools of semantics, there are two very general disputes that colour a philosopher's interpretation of what is achieved even by a theory he considers successful. These issues are not always brought out into the open, but burying them under piles of detailed argument does not diminish their importance.

The first general issue is what it is for a semantic theory to be correct. The most naive conception is that any language, natural or formalized, is governed by a definite system of semantic rules (at least at each instant of its evolution), and that a semantic 'theory' is correct if and only if it consists of exactly these rules. The 'theory' simply attempts to describe an aspect of a language and is true if it fits the facts. Indeed, the term 'theory' is misleading except in so far as it suggests an axiomatic structure of propositions which allows the derivation of the truth-conditions of any sentence from its structure and the semantic rules governing its constituents. A system of semantics, on this view, describes a language just as Euclidean geometry was once thought to characterize space. Such an idea is altogether natural. Carnap expressed its analogue for syntax by explaining 'the logical syntax of a language . . . [to be] the systematic statement of the formal rules which govern it together with the development of the consequences which follow from these rules.'[67] The vision of a unique factually correct set of syntactic and semantic rules must hover before the eyes of any theorist who hopes to uncover the mental mechanism of grasping the meaning of any meaningful utterance in English.

This naive account of correctness is no longer officially in circulation. It has been replaced by an account which takes rise from the dogma that any theory is underdetermined by the data. Just as any number of distinct smooth curves can be drawn through any finite number of points, so also it is argued, any consistent set of observations can be subsumed under indefinitely many different explanatory theories. Why should systems of syntax or semantics for a natural language be any exception to this generalization? (Formal languages are thought to differ from natural languages precisely because their rules of formation and interpretation are explicitly stipulated.) On this view, the adequacy of a theory is assessed by how well it squares with the data. No irrefutable confirmation is possible, and nothing can exclude the possibility that several very different theories will square exactly with all the available data. The idea that a natural language has a determinate semantic structure remains intact, but no set of data will whittle the set of possible theories down to a single member. The

---

[67] Carnap, *The Logical Syntax of Language*, p. 1.

multiplicity of viable theories mirrors the fact that human knowledge is never complete.

This popular account of correctness of semantic theories has itself faced criticism and now seems obsolete to many philosophers. Its most celebrated critic is Quine, and its replacement is what he called the thesis of the indeterminacy of translation.[68] Quine accepted the view that a semantic theory will consist of statements in a metalanguage correlated with judgments that certain sentences of the object language are true. But he suggested that this procedure was equivalent to translating quoted sentences into indirect speech; e.g. 'In saying "Es regnet" he asserted that it was raining'. He then produced a number of different arguments to support the claim that there is no uniquely correct way to effect such a translation, even within a single natural language. The sole method for judging the adequacy of a translation into a metalanguage is allegedly to consider whether it forms part of a theory of semantics for the entire language which is coherent and as simple as possible. A theory must be assessed in its entirety, not piecemeal. On Quine's view, there are no semantic data at all. Every semantic statement is theoretical; there is no fact of the matter to make it true. Widespread acceptance of this view might be expected to put an end to semantics. For, if there is no such thing as a determinate set of semantic rules for a natural language, how is it possible to build a science about such non-entities? In fact the typical response is to recommend a method of bold postulation. We are urged freely to invent systems of semantic rules and then to explore these creations. What the point of these flights of fancy may be is left to our imagination. The resemblance between this activity and scientific theorizing seems rather strained and remote.

The net effect of this 'progress' in the conception of semantic theories is to insulate the products of philosophical research against criticism. Within the limits of coherence, any 'theory' deserves examination, if not respect. The explanation of the meaning of counterfactual conditionals in terms of a metric of proximity imposed on the set of possible worlds[69] seems initially neither intelligible nor plausible, but many philosophers consider it all the more admirable for this reason. Our propensity to take 'theories' seriously is prodigious. Perhaps we are often duped by nonsense. Are there really no facts about meanings? Is there even any room for erecting any explanatory theories about meanings? Is the underdetermination of scien-

[68] Cf. Quine, *Word and Object*, pp. 27, 72ff., and *Ontological Relativity and Other Essays* (Columbia University Press, New York, 1969), pp. 1ff.
[69] Lewis, *Counterfactuals*, pp. 8ff., 48ff., 91ff.

tific theories by observational data relevant to any investigation into meaning? The ready tolerance of pluralism of semantic theories should be replaced by close scrutiny of these questions.

The second general issue about semantic theories is the question of their psychological (or even physiological) reality. There is official disagreement about this, but perhaps more underlying convergence of view than commonly acknowledged. Philosophers and linguists alike are inclined to incorporate truth-conditions into an analysis of successful communication. Knowledge of truth-conditions is often represented as an intermediate stage in a process of recognizing what a speaker has said. In broad outline, it is held that an assertoric utterance is understood in a series of stages: first it is identified as a token of a type-sentence, then a set of truth-conditions is correlated with this type-sentence, and finally knowledge of the circumstances of utterance is used to determine what is asserted. In this way, knowledge of truth-conditions is an essential step on the route to knowledge of the truth or falsity of what is said.

At this point there is an overwhelming inclination to build semantic theories into the putative mechanism of understanding. Indeed, a theory of meaning seems to be at root a theory of understanding: it explains what otherwise seems to be an intractable puzzle, viz. how it is possible to understand an infinity of sentences. Wittgenstein[70] and Carnap offered this account: 'we understand a compound [expression] because its meaning is determined by the meanings of the component [expressions] and the logical structure of the compound expression'.[71] Many others have followed their lead. What above all makes semantics alluring is the prospect of finding the answer to the question how it is possible to understand infinitely many sentences including wholly novel ones. For a semantic theory will explain how we derive the truth-conditions of a sentence from the meanings of its components and its structure, how we recognize its meaning from recognizing the meanings of its constituents.

We shall defer consideration of whether a semantic theory affords a coherent answer to an intelligible question. What deserves immediate attention is philosophical qualms about the committing the sin of 'psychologism' in relating semantics to understanding. Frege urged that logic should be kept free of any incursions of psychology, and under this banner he waged a campaign to evict from logic most considerations about knowledge, mental imagery, actual patterns of inference, and even under-

[70] Wittgenstein, *Tractatus*, 4.024ff.
[71] Carnap, *Meaning and Necessity*, p. 20.

standing. The *Tractatus* followed suit.[72] Psychologism became something to be forsworn. Hence it is scarcely surprising to find some philosophers taking pains to disavow the claim that a semantic theory should have some psychological reality, that it describes mental mechanisms and hence is open to confirmation (or disconfirmation) by psychological experiments.[73] By way of contrast, many linguists have no feelings of guilt about offering theories involving psychological hypotheses and manifesting ambitions to give psychological explanations. Typically they see semantic theories as attempts to reconstruct some of the mechanisms of the production and processing of speech (the contents of a black box), in particular the rules for deriving the understanding of a sentence from an understanding of its constituents.

Although there is apparently a sharp division about the psychological implications of semantics, there is more agreement than commonly acknowledged. Philosophers espousing anti-psychologism evidently consider understanding to be a mental process or a state achieved as a result of such a process, even one which it is the business of semantics indirectly to illuminate.[74] Adherence to anti-psychologism thus takes a distinctive form: the well-educated philosopher admits that understanding is a mental process, but instead of investigating this process itself, he tries to duplicate the process in the form of derivations within a formal calculus of semantic rules (an 'abstract model' of this putative process) and then elicits philosophical conclusions somehow from the scrutiny of these calculations. The justification for this procedure is far from transparent. Moreover, the anti-psychologism is very superficial. What is accomplished

---

[72] Wittgenstein held that every significant sentence expresses a thought; the sentence itself is given a sense by its projection in thought on to the world. The thought backing a meaningful sentence must have the same complexity as the analysed sentence; it must have constituents which correspond to the words of language, and these 'psychical constituents' must have 'the same sort of relations to reality as words'. These ideas reveal that the *Tractatus* rests on important presuppositions about meaning something by an expression, about understanding, and about the relation of thought to expressions of thoughts, even if these presuppositions were relegated to the cupboard of the unmentionable. Modern discussions of the 'language of thought' might be viewed as attempts to fill in the unwritten doctrines of the *Tractatus* (or as locating the skeleton in its cupboard).

[73] Cf. Lewis, 'General Semantics', p. 170; Dummett, 'What is a Theory of Meaning? (II)' p. 70; and D. Davidson, 'Theories of Meaning and Learnable Languages', *Proceedings of the 1964 International Congress for Logic, Methodology and Philosophy of Science* (North Holland, Amsterdam, 1965), p. 387.

[74] Cf. Dummett, *Frege: Philosophy of Language*, p. 4; also Davidson, 'Truth and Meaning', p. 311.

is merely avoidance of any *detailed* investigation of psychological concepts; the barest outline is thought to suffice for philosophical purposes. This may secure the worst possible outcome. If it is a confusion to treat understanding as a process at all (below, pp. 347–56), then the philosopher's first move already damns everything that follows, while his refusal to consider any details will help his misconceptions to persist. Anti-psychologism may be nothing but a device for reconciling mortal sin with sincere protestations of innocence. In spite of controversy about the psychological reality of semantic theories, we will argue that theorists of meaning have not penetrated to the heart of the matter. A more radical and efficacious form of anti-psychologism would challenge the presumption that understanding is a mental process or state, and it would root out the confusions which thrive in this contaminated soil.

The point of this survey is to convey some impression of the *vast* range of theories subsumed under the label 'truth-conditional semantics'. These theories make use of diverse semi-technical concepts and formal techniques, and they put radically different glosses on their results.

7   The evolution of a concept

This conspectus of the gradual transformations and the increasing ramification of the concept of a truth-condition is a source of valuable insights. But it may equally foster its own forms of fresh confusion. It may seem to many philosophers to narrate the growth of an explanatory theory, comparable to the evolution of classical physics: numerous piecemeal advances in knowledge ultimately fitted together into a powerful system. We should make a brief attempt to forestall this misconception.

There is a temptation to conflate conceptual changes with discoveries. Mathematicians and logicians are especially prone to it. A mathematician expounding real analysis may offer as a provisional explanation of what it is for a function to be continuous that its graph can be drawn without lifting the pen from the graph-paper; this is provisional because he has in mind a precise definition in terms of multiple quantifiers which he will later formulate. But, reflecting on the history of real analysis, he is then apt to claim that his precise definition is a discovery of what 'continuous' *already meant* in the work of earlier mathematicians who formulated only naive and inadequate explanations of the term. He may even *correct* their judgments about which functions are continuous by reference to his precise definition. Finally he may claim that his scientific definition unfolds to students who have grasped only the provisional explanation what they themselves *really mean* by 'continuous'. All of these theses are dubious: each presupposes that what a term means may differ radically from what a person who is said to understand it is able to explain. The issue is whether meanings stand to explanations of meaning as the nature of rocks stands to (current) knowledge in geology. For logicians this issue takes the form of such questions as whether it makes sense to claim that Frege *discovered* the meanings of sentence-connectives and expressions of generality and thereby *discovered* the general logic of generality.

The inappropriateness of likening conceptual change to discovery is transparent from a close examination of the evolution of the use of the term 'truth-condition'. Given that the sole original explanation of this term referred to truth-tables for molecular propositions in a formal notation, nothing could possibly reveal that, contrary to earlier beliefs, the atomic formula '*p*' or the atomic sentence 'That is a birch tree' have truth-conditions, nor could something demonstrate that the sentence ' "Snow is white" is true if and only if snow is white' formulates the truth-condition of the sentence 'Snow is white'. The evolution of the use of 'truth-condition' is a series of transformations of when it makes sense to ask 'What are the truth-conditions of the sentence ". . ."?' and of what it makes sense to give as an answer. Internal connections between truth-conditions and truth-tables are first stipulated, then abrogated, and finally re-established in altered forms. What is illustrated here is not gradual approximation to the truth, but a series of motivated changes in a concept which are evident in alterations in what is acknowledged to be a correct explanation of the term 'truth-condition'. What must be digested is not a set of reports of novel facts unearthed on the frontiers of knowledge, but various reasons offered to persuade philosophers to change their minds about what to understand by, and how to explain, an expression already in currency. We have taken pains to highlight this feature in the history of truth-conditional semantics.

This makes obvious the fact that divergences between alternative semantic 'theories' cannot be resolved by the methods appropriate to testing and choosing between competing theories in physics. There are no observations and no predictions, but rather different proposed ways of representing some aspects of the use of expressions in a language. The crucial issue is not truth or adequacy to the facts, but the *purposes* served (and also those thwarted) by opting for one form of description rather than another. The point of constructing a particular semantic theory is what deserves careful scrutiny – and seldom receives it. Philosophers might profitably compare semantic theories with mathematical ones and then reflect on why the notion of an infinitesimal first supported the development of the calculus, then was discarded, and has recently been revived as the basis of 'non-standard analysis'. So high may the tide of fashion rise, and so low may it ebb in the *a priori* sciences! This might instil some salutary scepticism about how much real light emanates from the notion of a truth-condition.

One corollary of distinguishing conceptual change from empirical discovery is a recognition of the dramatic discontinuity in the evolution of truth-conditional semantics. Apparent seeds of truth are mixed with quantities of nonsense. Frege's definition of the universal quantifier cannot be separated from his conviction that it names a second-level function; hence it cannot be prised off his view that a well-formed formula (sentence) is a proper name of a truth-value and that a concept-word literally designates a *function* from objects to truth-values. Similarly, the thesis of the *Tractatus* that every sentence of a natural language has truth-conditions cannot be isolated from a conception of analysis which incorporates a host of (indefensible) doctrines in metaphysics and logic. And so on. In retrospect, each stage in the evolution of truth-conditional semantics is fundamentally different in many ways from what is now perceived to make sense. Points of contact are superficial since the frameworks of thought informing apparently identical remarks are so distant from one another. *And there is no such thing as a successive approximation to the truth via nonsense.* It is salutary to examine the seminal works of Frege, the young Wittgenstein, Carnap, Tarski, *et al.* to remind ourselves how much of their thought is riddled with fallacious argument. (Of course, this does *not* demonstrate that their ideas were unaccountably primitive or that we have made great progress in the last few years.)

A second corollary is the essentially historical character of understanding the product of a succession of conceptual changes in philosophy. In the sciences, it is often thought, a variety of routes of observation and conceptual innovation will converge on a successful theory that will explain and predict the facts. Knowledge of the history of its development is commonly held to be irrelevant to grasping the developed theory. Be that as it may, the understanding of concepts introduced by philosophers in order to clarify the conceptual structures with which they are concerned is radically different. Appreciating the routes to modern conceptions of truth-conditions is not readily divorced from grasping these conceptions themselves. Moreover, if viewed ahistorically, the suggestion that the meaning of a word is exhausted by its contribution to the truth-conditions of sentences in which it occurs seems *prima facie* ludicrous, since we are sensitive to the idea that a proper explanation of the meaning of a word must not be restricted to its occurrence in expressions of truth and falsehood. However, the sources of the modern conception of a truth-condition lie in a different intellectual milieu, and the original concept was introduced in the course of confronting different problems from ours.

Frege thought the subject-matter of logic to be judgments (or judgeable-contents), which were bearers of truth and falsity, while Wittgenstein held logic to be concerned only with descriptions of states of affairs, viz. something true or false. Consequently, a truth-table (or something similar) appeared to them to be a *complete* explanation of a logical constant. Having built on this foundation some apparently substantial results, they and their successors naturally tried to protect their prior investment in the face of changed intellectual circumstances. At this point, when philosophers began to take non-statement-making discourse seriously, it made sense to defend the heartland of logical semantics by introducing an auxiliary theory of force. By a series of such tactical steps, each of which seemed entirely natural and creditable at the time, the concept of a truth-condition has evolved in a way neither forseen nor intended. Even if present ideas have all arisen out of a form of natural selection, there is no guarantee that they are not in conflict with one another or that any one of them is now a viable organism. In any case, what must be assessed cannot be comprehended independently of its origins. Many of the deepest aspects of a form of representation are invisible until revealed by judicious staining by dyes refined from historical surveys. What might be reckoned an ornament to expositions of scientific theories should be counted among the indispensable tools of analysis of philosophical conceptions.

A third corollary is a clarification of the nature of philosophical criticisms of truth-conditional semantics. It is a mistake to judge that criticism is justified only if it constitutes a cogent *refutation* of a theory, for the fundamental thesis that the meaning of a sentence is its truth-conditions does not have the status characteristic of a *theory* at all. It rests not on identifiable observations whose interpretation is open to debate, but on various preconceptions about the nature of symbols, truth, meaning, understanding, and explanations of meaning. Whereas scientists typically envisage one theory as being in competition with radically different, alternative explanations of a body of data, theorists of language may proclaim that no general alternative to truth-conditional semantics is even conceivable. This should arouse suspicions about the content of such a so-called '*theory* of meaning'. At the same time, this imperviousness to refutation makes excellent sense if the core of truth-conditional semantics is the invention and development of the *concept* of a truth-condition. It makes no sense to challenge the explanation of a technical term as being false or incorrect. Criticism must rather turn on whether this concept is useful, e.g. whether it promotes perspicuity or on the contrary leads to antinomies and confusions. But in the end it is a matter of decision whether to retain or to jettison the proposed explanation. Philosophical criticism may steer someone in the direction of abandoning certain concepts, but it should not be expected to necessitate anyone's performing an act of renunciation.

Truth-conditional semantics is a powerful myth in the guise of a scientific theory. This myth gains some shallow, but important, support from the mere fact that the term 'truth-condition' is in circulation among theorists of meaning. Surely, it seems, they must mean *something* by this term, and what they call 'truth-conditions' must have *something in common* (vocabulary has not lost its power to generate myths even among enlightened modern intellectuals!). In virtue of its kinship to an intellectual myth, truth-conditional semantics is as difficult to budge as a building constructed on a large number of deeply driven piles. To make it topple, a demolition expert must dig down in many different and seemingly unrelated directions. What is visible above ground will withstand any amount of direct battering.

The point of describing truth-conditional semantics as a myth is to pinpoint its role in modern thought. An archetypal theory does admit genuine alternatives, and it is to be surrendered in the light of accumulated disconfirming data. Moreover, it is weakened to the extent that it generates unresolved problems or leaves relevant data unexplained, and it is annihilated by internal contradictions or antinomies. A myth differs in all of these respects; it portrays what must be so, and hence it thrives despite recalcitrant experiences and despite raising insoluble problems and leading to paradoxes.[75] Whereas adversities wound and ultimately kill off theories, they are food to myths. The defenders of truth-conditional semantics cheerfully concede that they face 'a staggering list of difficulties and conundrums',[76] and they may admit that they have made very little positive advance in explaining the workings of language.[77] But far from sinking

---

[75] Cf. P. Ernst, 'Nachwort' in Grimm's *Kinder und Hausmärchen* (1910), pp. 275f.

[76] Davidson, 'Truth and Meaning', p. 321.

[77] Cf. Dummett, *Frege: Philosophy of Language*, p. 82.

into despair, they find here occasion for the renewal of faith. They behave like members of millennarian sects whose commitment is redoubled in the face of failed predictions of the Second Coming. Truth-conditional semantics enshrines a vision which is immune to those forms of rational criticism fatal to scientific theories. It does not follow that such a myth is immortal. It may fall victim to other ills.[78] If the putative insights that it vouchsafes can be shown to be illusions, and if its leading principles are revealed to harbour deep confusions, it may cease to command allegiance. Rational criticism may sap the *will* to adhere to this vision. Like a shadow, a myth may seem unassailable – but with more light it can sometimes be made to vanish.

---

[78] Its adherents may simply drift away, captivated by some novel and more alluring vision. Or it may cease to make any new recruits and die out with the Old Believers.

CHAPTER 5

Truth-Conditions:
Flaws in the Foundations

1 Targets

The previous chapter has made clear how problematic it is to undertake any general philosophical investigation and criticism of what is labelled 'truth-conditional semantics'. We have sought to establish two main points of difficulty. The first is that there is no single concept of a truth-condition but many different ones. Hence too there is not one theory, nor even a number of directly comparable theories, but a range of different ways of representing speech and languages which are constructed out of different kinds of conceptual building-blocks. Different versions of truth-conditional semantics succumb severally to very different criticisms: one may be taken to task over the intelligibility of quantifying over possible worlds whereas another may be required to defend the thesis that sentence-meanings are properly specified by metalinguistic statements of the form ' "*p*" means that *p*'.[1] One might well conclude that to defeat an armada there is no alternative to searching out and sinking each individual ship. The second difficulty is that there appears to be no key target to attack. The flagship of the armada is a phantom, impervious to critical gunfire. It is a vision, a diffuse faith about the hidden systematic character of speech and languages. Since this does not rest on any definite set of observations and is not substantiated by any determinate arguments, it cannot be challenged in the way appropriate to scientific theories.

[1] A view propounded by D. Davidson (cf. 'Semantics for Natural Languages', in *Linquaggi nella Società e nella Tecnica*, ed. B. Visentini (Edizioni di Comunità, Milan, 1970), p. 184) and M. A. E. Dummett (cf. 'What is a Theory of Meaning?', in *Mind and Language*, ed. S. Guttenplan (Clarendon Press, Oxford, 1975), p. 105). But the sentence 'I'll have a drink' does *not* mean that I shall have a drink, although my uttering it may mean that I've had a hard day at the office and would like to unwind over a gin and tonic.

In face of this pair of difficulties, must we abandon hope of carrying out any satisfactory philosophical criticism of truth-conditional semantics? This conclusion would be too precipitate. The first difficulty could be met if the various theories could be confronted wholesale, and this might be accomplished by an indirect approach. The second depends on a particular conception of the nature of philosophical investigation, and hence it might disappear if a different purpose were taken to inform the enterprise of scrutinizing semantic theories. Instead of trying to sink each ship in the armada, it might be possible to take the wind out of their sails, leaving them becalmed far from the sea-lanes of intellectual commerce.

One guideline for this programme is to focus on very general pre-suppositions common to most, if not all, versions of truth-conditional semantics. We have already thoroughly criticized one such indefensible presupposition, the distinction between sense and force. In this chapter we shall concentrate on other issues, viz. the meanings of logical constants, the nature of truth and falsity, the idea of conditions of the truth of a sentence, and context-dependence. In each of these cases we shall demon-strate that deep conceptual flaws run through the foundations of the common programme as well as the various executions of it.

Our other guideline is to focus on conceptual issues, not empirical ones. This does not insulate avowedly empirical theories from philosophical criticism. Conceptual confusions may vitiate the pronouncements of a soi-disant scientist. This charge has been laid against many theses in psychology and psychoanalysis. We shall lodge the same accusation against various theories about languages even if their proponents offer them as studies of 'the biologically necessary properties of human language'[2] or as clear and testable theories about the pairing of expressions with their meanings.[3] In particular, we shall concentrate on how theorists deploy their distinctive vocabulary, e.g. 'true', 'truth-value', 'truth-condition', 'meaning', 'give the meaning of', 'concept'. Hence the crucial question is not whether their practice does or does not coincide exactly with Everyman's speech-patterns (though manifest divergence is a ground for suspicion), but rather, whether they have succeeded in giving coherent explanations of how these expressions are to be understood in the context of their theorizing. Their use of expressions is not exonerated, but put in the dock, by accepting their own claims that these expressions are to be construed as technical terms with specialized uses in their theories.

---

[2] N. Chomsky, *Rules and Representations* (Blackwell, Oxford, 1980), p. 29.
[3] D. Davidson, 'Truth and Meaning', *Synthese*, 17 (1967), p. 320.

2   Semantic analyses of logical constants

We have noted that the origin of the term 'truth-conditions' in the *Tractatus* is inseparable from the truth-table definitions of the formal propositional connectives. If a truth-table is constructed for a molecular proposition, the lines in which the symbol 'T' is correlated with the main connective together exhibit the truth-conditions of the given proposition. Moreover the standard semantic definitions of the quantifiers and identity allow a generalization of this account to embrace any well-formed formula of the predicate calculus with identity. Such a formula takes the value T provided that certain conditions are met, e.g. the formula '$(\forall x)(Fx \rightarrow Gx)$' takes the value T if and only if for any arbitrary object a in the domain of quantification the formula '$(Fa \rightarrow Ga)$' takes the value T. The historical origins of the concept of a truth-condition lie in these definitions of the primitive symbols of modern formal logic. This makes the semantic analyses of logical constants into a topic of fundamental importance for truth-conditional semantics, and therefore this is a singularly natural place to begin our philosophical investigations.

One preliminary concession must be made: current conceptions of truth-conditions are not fettered tightly to their ultimate progenitor. This is obvious in two respects. First, Wittgenstein's original idea that universal quantification can be reduced to conjunction (and existential quantification to disjunction) has been abandoned. Secondly, many modern theorists hold that a truth-table contains only a statement of relative truth-conditions, not absolute ones; according to this view, the truth-conditions of '$p \wedge q$' is not that 'p' and 'q' are both true, but rather the truth-table shows how to determine the truth-conditions of '$p \wedge q$' from a specification of the truth-conditions of 'p' and those of 'q'. None the less, neither of these points eliminates the centrality of the semantic definitions of the formal constants in the modern accounts of truth-conditions. Truth-conditional semantics without these definitions would be inconceivable.[4]

A second point must also be noted: although debate about these definitions has taken place, it has assumed a peculiar form. Because of the Principle of Equipollence, theorists freely mix the symbolism of logical

---

[4] This is a slight exaggeration. 'Truth-conditional semantics' is sometimes so construed that intuitionist explanations of logical constants are excluded, but sometimes so interpreted that they are admissible. In the latter case, it is an analogue of a truth-table that is used to explain the formal constants of the propositional calculus.

calculi with expressions of natural language in complex symbols which are presumed to be intelligible (above, pp. 132–8). This encourages the illusion that an invented form of representation is a discovery about the inner nature of our language. In particular, it suggests that the proper analyses (and real explanations) of sentence-connectives of English such as 'and', 'or', 'if', 'but', 'although', etc. might be truth-tables (and similarly that the real accounts of the use of such expressions of generality as 'every', 'each', 'all', 'some', 'any', 'exists', etc. might be isomorphic with the semantic definitions of the quantifiers). Logicians are tempted to suppose that parts of the calculus of logical semantics reveal something about the workings of natural languages. Hence they are prone to conduct investigations into whether certain expressions in English, German, etc., can be correctly *defined* by truth-tables. This question has been a locus of controversy. (And so too has the analogue for expressions of generality in natural languages.) The argument is conducted by noting analogies and disanalogies between certain 'sentences', especially in respect of truth-value. A simple case is the comparison of 'He died and was buried' with 'He died ∧ he was buried'. Order-indifference of the 'conjuncts' in the second case is not matched in the first, and then it is disputed whether or not this establishes a difference in meaning between the two connectives. Within the camp of truth-conditional semantics, there are many such scuffles.

These local quarrels typically have one of two outcomes. The first is to acknowledge important discrepancies between formal operators and sentence-connectives (or expressions of generality), but to categorize these discrepancies as irrelevant to logic or semantics. Some contemporary philosophers construct sophisticated theories to defend the thesis that the semantic definitions of formal logical constants actually hold for expressions in English which appear to behave differently. Their strategy is to relegate discrepancies to pragmatics, claiming that evident 'oddities' do not amount to differences in truth-values and therefore do not bear on the meanings of sentence-connectives. Any such manoeuvre is deeply suspect. It presupposes that certain anomalies in utterances must be ascribed to violations of certain pragmatic principles. If, e.g., it were a pragmatic implication of narrative discourse that the first conjunct described an event prior to the second (as in 'He heard an explosion and phoned the police'), then it should make sense to override this implication by *marking* the second clause as describing a prior event (as in 'He phoned the police and he *had* heard an explosion'), whereas the attempt produces nonsense. Moreover, misunderstanding the sentence 'He heard an explosion and phoned the police' in the context of a detective story by taking the second clause to describe the prior event of the pair would be compatible with a perfect understanding of the meaning of 'and', since the error would be ascribed to misapprehension about a pragmatic principle. But surely such a misinterpretation of the sentence has just as good a claim to be treated as a criterion for a defective grasp of the meaning of 'and' as a failure to appreciate that the narrator has asserted that a certain person did hear an explosion. (This point does not establish that 'and' in the context of narratives always has the same meaning as 'and then'. Rather, it shows that the distinction between semantics and pragmatics is not the basis for a cogent refutation of this erroneous identification.)

The alternative strategy is to concede that there is only a *rough* correspondence between the logical constants and the corresponding expressions in natural languages. On this view, discrepancies in their respective uses do not pertain solely to 'pragmatics', but fall within the proper purview of logic. None the less, many theorists eschew the detailed investigation of the complex and subtle patterns of use of such expressions as 'and', 'but', 'or', 'if', 'every', 'any', and 'each' (the 'logic of ordinary language'), instead maintaining that the corresponding formal symbols have uses that are idealizations of the varied uses of these expressions of English. The truth-table definitions of '∧', '∨', '⌐', and '→' are held to capture the core of the meanings of 'and', 'or', 'not', and 'if', and likewise the semantic definitions of '∀x', '∃x', and '=' to capture the core of the meanings of 'every', 'some', 'exist', and 'same'. In certain cases the correspondence in meaning is thought to be closer (e.g. between '∧' and 'and'), in others more remote (e.g. between '→' and 'if' or '∃x' and 'exist'). But for the purpose of determining the validity of arguments, discrepancies are held to be insignificant.

This strategy is misconceived. The divergences between the uses of the cited English expressions and those of the counterpart logical symbols are persistently understated and misdescribed, and logicians' idealizations are guilty of obscuring the boundary between sense and nonsense. Consider the relatively favourable case of 'and'. This particle has many uses in which it is not a sentence-connective at all (e.g. 'Fish and chips is my favourite food', 'Two and two makes four', 'This film was made in black and white', 'He was hit again and again', 'New York and London are more than a thousand miles apart'). Moreover, its uses as a sentence-connective fail to square with the implications of a truth-table definition. Coordination of sentences with 'and' requires some form of association; this rules out as nonsense a sentence like 'It rained hard yesterday and unicorns do not exist'. Furthermore, the implications of coordination vary widely and depend on the content of the coordinated sentences (e.g. 'He heard a bang and looked up', 'She washed her hair and dried it', 'Frege was a mathematician and Wittgenstein a philosopher'. 'Give me a hand and I'll climb over the wall'). In both these respects, 'and' lacks the topic neutrality essential to a truth-functional connective, and in a few kinds of case (e.g. the final example) compound sentences formed with 'and' do not entail either of their constituent sentences. Finally, it is typically claimed that 'but', 'and', 'although', 'since', 'whereas', etc., share a massive common core of meaning. Frege pioneered this approach, arguing that the difference between the conjunctions 'and' and 'but' is not a matter of conceptual content, but something psychological: viz. 'the speaker uses "but" when he wishes to hint that what follows is different from what one might at first expect'.[5] Later he refined this doctrine, claiming that these conjunctions differ in colouring, not in sense, and adding the explanation that colouring turned on mental imagery which is epistemically private and in principle incommunicable. Although frequently reiterated, this account is clearly absurd, for whether 'but' is or is not correctly used does not depend on ascertaining anything about a speaker's mental imagery, nor even on establishing his intentions. The substitution of 'but' for 'and' in the role of a sentential coordinator often changes the sense or produces *nonsense*, as is evident from the following examples:

> He heard an explosion and phoned the police.
> She washed the dishes and dried up.
> Give me some money and I'll help you to escape.
> He was unhappy about it, and yet he did what he was told.
> He was eager and skilful and well-informed.
> He saved money so that he could buy a house and so that he would have enough for his old age.

Not only is the difference between 'and' and 'but' not a matter of psychology, or a matter of mere pragmatics, but the suggestion that the two expressions have a common sense is patently false.

Considerations parallel to these humdrum remarks about 'and' raise serious objections to all of the standard proposals to link the uses of expressions of English with the semantic definitions of the logical constants of the predicate calculus. Talk of 'rough correspondences' and of 'idealization' seems not at all in order in this context. It leads to a mistaken

---

[5] Frege, *Begriffsschrift*, §7.

assimilation of the very different explanations given of allegedly closely related expressions (e.g. 'and' and 'but'), to an underestimation of the varieties of explanations given for particular expressions (e.g. 'and'), and to an oversimplification of the criteria for understanding sentences containing these expressions (e.g. compound sentences formed by coordinating sentences with 'and'). It also forces the theorist to claim that these familiar expressions are highly ambiguous, i.e. actually have a great multitude of slightly differing meanings (e.g. that 'and' means 'and then' in compound sentences understood to indicate temporal ordering), whereas in fact the only warrant for this counterintuitive suggestion is the urgent desire to attribute every aspect of the meaning of a complex expression to the meanings of its parts (or its structure).

The furore over resemblances and differences between formal logical constants and expressions of natural languages consists largely of dubious generalizations and fallacious reasoning. But this is not the worst of its faults. It has distracted philosophers from attending to very general presuppositions and difficulties which are associated with the semantic analyses of the logical constants of the predicate calculus. We shall air a few.

First, what reasons are there for taking the celebrated 'semantic definitions' to be *explanations* even of the logical constants occurring in formalizations of the predicate calculus? Frege had an obvious justification for this claim: in his mature theory he viewed each of these formal symbols as the name of a function whose values were uniformly truth-values, and he thought a function-name to be fully explained provided it is specified what each compound name stands for which is formed by filling the argument-places with names of admissible arguments. But this rationale is not available if the logical constants and predicate letters are not literally function-names. The *Tractatus* offered another justification: since the sense of any sentence is expressed by a truth-function of elementary sentences, a truth-table determines the sense of any molecular sentence by relating this sentence, via the analyses of its constituents, with elementary sentences. But this account too is not open to anybody who does not commit himself to Wittgenstein's early programme of logical analysis. In absence of these arguments, what supports the contention that truth-tables explain the significance or meanings of the formal logical constants? An *ingénue* might ask what the expression '$p \wedge q$' means (or what a substitution-instance of this formula means). A logician would clarify nothing for her were he to declare:

' "$p \wedge q$" means the same as   "$p \quad q \qquad p \wedge q$" '

p	q	$p \wedge q$
T	T	T
T	F	F
F	T	F
F	F	F

unless the mode of employment of truth-tables were already known to her. (Truth-tables themselves need to be explained!) If he instead replied "$p \wedge q$" is true if and only if both "p" and "q" are true', why should she not object that he has not answered her question? She wished to know what '$p \wedge q$' *meant*, not an account of the circumstances in which this formula expresses something true. Of course, the logician could retort that his account (together with parallel ones) contains everything of interest in determining the validity of arguments couched in the symbolism of the predicate calculus, i.e. that *for certain logical purposes* the semantic definitions of the logical constants exhaust their significance. But then it is conceded that these 'definitions' are proper explanations of how to use these formal symbols only in a circumscribed context. They are not paradigmatic explanations of the meanings of symbols. Far from it: they are acceptable as explanations only when employed for a quite specific purpose. Any general thesis that the meaning of a sentence is explained by specifying the conditions under which it is true, far from being supported by truth-table definitions of formal logical constants, is presupposed by these definitions.

Secondly, qualms about whether the semantic definitions are genuine explanations of the meanings of formal logical constants are multiplied manyfold in the face of the contention that they also explain the meanings of expressions current in any natural language. They do not even seem to be *candidates* for explaining such expressions as 'and', 'or', 'if', 'every', and 'some'. All of these expressions occur in utterances used to pose questions, to issue orders or directives, and to formulate rules; since the question of truth does not arise in these cases, any attempt to explain sentence-meanings in terms of conditions of truth seems to be immediately frustrated. Yet the notion that these expressions have different meanings in such utterances is unattractive for many reasons. Likewise, the restricted purposes of the formal logician which licensed his treating truth-tables as explanations of how to use the formal logical constants manifestly do not apply to basic expressions in natural languages. A truth-table definition of the sentence-connective 'and' would obviously not explain what a sentence of the form '... and ...' *meant*, and the defence that it would constitute an explanation how to use 'and' for the purposes of determining the validity of arguments would leave a gigantic lacuna (viz. the need to explain what it meant in all other contexts) and a bizarre implication (viz. that 'and' is ambiguous). Further difficulties abound. The stipulations " '$p \wedge q$" is true if and only if "p" is true and "q" is true' and ' "$(\forall x)\varphi x$" is true if and only if every sentence of the form "φx" is true' raise no suspicion of circularity, since the metalanguage (English) is distinct from the object-language (the formalized predicate calculus). But this condition does not hold in respect of the monolingual speaker of English who is informed that 'p and q' is true if and only if 'p' is true *and* 'q' is true or that '*Everything* is extended' is true if and only if *everything* satisfies the predicate 'x is extended'. This charge of circularity cannot be set aside by the defence that the explanations could be intelligibly reformulated for a *bilingual* person in a metalanguage distinct from English! For the question whether one explanation has any function for one person cannot be answered affirmatively by citing another explanation which can be put to use by somebody else. A truth-functional definition of 'and' also raises again perplexity about how to accommodate the divergence in patterns of use between 'and' and '$\wedge$', and similar puzzles beset parallel proposals for explaining other 'logical constants' of natural languages.

Behind all these major difficulties lies the fundamental doubt whether there is any such thing as discovering the real and hitherto unknown explanation of expressions already in use in a language. This would presuppose that every speaker of a language before 1921 had *tacit* knowledge (inaccessible to his 'conscious mind') of these truth-tabular definitions, which Wittgenstein merely made explicit. This in turn presupposes that rules for the use of expressions, explanations of meaning, can act at a distance (below, p. 236–7), can constitute norms of correct use, even though no one cites them in explanations of meaning, criticisms of errors, or justifications of use. The only alternative would be to maintain that indefinitely many expressions in many natural languages suddenly changed their meanings when the *Tractatus* was published! These absurdities are readily avoided by the simple expedient of acknowledging that the semantic definitions of formal logical constants have *no* place in the established practices of explaining such expressions as 'and', 'or', 'every', 'exists', etc.

Thirdly, doubts about whether these definitions qualify as explanations of the meanings of any expressions whatever are countered by a typical manoeuvre. Instead of conceding that discrepancies between the uses of these 'definitions' and that of paradigmatic explanations proves that the semantic definitions are not genuine explanations, theorists argue that the discrepancies show that what are usually called explanations of meaning do not measure up to the rigorous standards for genuine explanations which are set by the semantic definitions of the logical constants! By this transvaluation of values, the dubious candidates are transformed into the only paradigms of genuine explanations of meaning, and the star performers are relegated to the sidelines and replaced by substitutes. True explanations of meaning must be dug out from beneath the rubbish-heap of our usual practice of explaining words in classrooms, nurseries, textbooks, and dictionaries. Our familiar and homely forms of explanation by ostension, example, exemplification, paraphrase, contrastive paraphrase, etc. are brushed aside, despite their conspicuous intelligibility and success over many millennia. They are, we are told, not 'real' explanations. This widespread misconception is altogether disastrous. It ignores the internal connection between meaning and explanation. As Wittgenstein stressed, the meaning of a word is what is explained in explaining its meaning, not something else hidden in, but not expressed by, these explanations. How a word is correctly explained is not something to be discovered by an elaborate programme of research, and hence its meaning is similarly transparent (in the practice of explaining it). By dismissing recognized explanations of meaning as merely provisional and fallible, semantic theorists ensure that the subject-matter of their research is not *meaning* at all. Moreover, the contrast between apparent and real explanations of meaning which truth-conditional semantics invokes leads straight into a mythology about symbolism. Truth-tables, being real explanations, must be superior to other explanations of sentence-connectives (e.g. by gestures, paraphrase, or contrastive paraphrase). They must be super-explanations. They alone must capture the entire essence of negation, conjunction, disjunction, etc. They must be complete in themselves, i.e. impossible to supplement without redundancy and sufficient to deliver all of the uses of the defined expressions (e.g. the cancelling-out of double-negation must flow from the truth-table for negation). They must also be immune to misinterpretation, since otherwise further explanations might be necessary in certain circumstances. But, of course, these contentions are all absurd. No explanation has any such magical powers.[6] Truth-tables are mere symbols. They provide rules for translating one form of symbolism

---

[6] Logical positivists concocted a similar mythology by deifying ostensive definitions.

into another (e.g. molecular formulae of the propositional calculus into T–F matrices). The proper employment of truth-tables can itself be explained (and typically *needs* to be explained); i.e. it is not self-evident how to use this symbolism. And this can also be misunderstood. The truth-table for negation is not an infallible delineation of the essential nature of negation even if it is an explanation of a symbol which may be readily understood and applied. (It might also, as the colour octahedron does for colour-words, render surveyable a portion of the complex, but familiar, explanations of the word 'not'.) The cancelling out of double negation 'flows from' this truth-table only for somebody who understands how to make iterated applications of this single explanation. To the level-headed the semantic definitions of logical constants (formal or non-formal) would not appear to differ in principle from any other explanations of how to use symbols.

Finally, the assumption that the semantic definitions of logical constants constitute complete explanations of their meanings is associated with a tendency to neglect logically significant differences, especially by assimilating propositions having different 'logical forms'. This modern error is exactly parallel to a venerable one. Traditional logic was built on the supposition that all judgments had subject/predicate structure, and accordingly it assigned the same logical form to what is expressed by the pair of sentences 'Socrates is mortal' and 'All men are mortal'. Following Frege's lead, modern logicians find the whole doctrine ridiculous: the subject/predicate structure of (most) declarative sentences masks an enormous diversity in the forms of propositions expressed. On this view, there is no such thing as *the* logical form of subject/predicate sentences. Yet this insight is accompanied by a novel illusion. For it seems to most modern logicians that there are such things as *the* logical form of conjunctions, *the* logical form of negation, *the* logical form of universal generalization, etc. This is no less absurd than the earlier doctrine. The truth in all these cases is that certain forms of declarative sentences (or what they express) are mapped on to certain patterns of symbols in a logical calculus, and that many differences *relevant to the cogency of inferences or the differentiation of sense from nonsense* are neglected in the process. This is obvious even in the case of sentences conjoined by 'and'. In some cases the principle of conjunction-elimination fails (e.g. 'You will pass the exam' does not follow from 'Pay me $10.00 and you will pass the exam'); internal relations between propositions have the consequence that the truth-table adumbrates impossible 'possibilities' (e.g. assigning a truth-condition to the conjunction 'A is red and A is green'); and a truth-tabular explanation of 'and' does not square with the fact that total absence of a connection between two sentences renders nonsensical their coordination by 'and' (e.g. 'Pigs cannot fly and three is a prime number').

Exactly similar observations hold in respect of generalizations. Some universal statements can be established by complete enumeration of cases, others by mathematical induction, and yet others by generalization from observed instances (inductive arguments); these differences are significant for determing the cogency of arguments. Moreover, it is a presupposition of quantification theory that the formula '$(\forall x)\varphi x$' makes sense if and only if the formulae '$(\forall x)\neg\varphi x$', '$\neg(\forall x)\varphi x$', and '$\neg(\forall x)\neg\varphi x$' also make sense; but this principle is often violated in the specification of the logical form of a statement (e.g. in discerning the form '$(\exists x)(\varphi x \wedge \psi x)$' in the statement 'Some sense experiences are hallucinations'). It may be no exaggeration to claim that there are as many different logical forms of generalization as there are different logical forms of subject/predicate sentences.[7] Failure to acknowledge this point multiplies confusion. Instead of acknowledging that generalizations over the natural numbers have a distinctive logical form and that mathematical induction is *sui generis*, logicians follow Frege in redefining the expression 'natural number' to encapsulate in this concept the cogency of mathematical induction, or they follow the Intuitionists and formulate a novel explanation of generality that directly licenses mathematical induction as a special case. These contortions could all be avoided by recognizing that logical forms are both more numerous than and different from those envisaged in the predicate calculus. This would also relieve the pressures to conceive of logical forms as hidden essences discoverable by mathematico-logical techniques, as opposed to familiar, but not readily surveyable, aspects of our uses of expressions.

Truth-tables and the semantic definitions of the quantifiers are not worthless. They are just misunderstood. Their real significance is as elements of a formal calculus (model theory). They there supply the foundations for formal derivations. But logicians invested them with more regal trappings. They are unduly held to provide the true justification for familiar patterns of deductive inference as well as the real explanations of the grammar of certain expressions in natural languages. It is in these roles that they are presented as the centrepiece of truth-conditional semantics. But this putative sterling silver turns out to be base metal. They are counterfeit explanations of meaning, and they have distorted philosophical activity by driving sound currency out of circulation.

[7] L. Wittgenstein, *Philosophical Grammar*, ed. Rush Rhees (Blackwell, Oxford, 1974), p. 269.

3   Truth and falsity

Truth-conditional semantics accounts for the meanings of subsentential
expressions in terms of their contributions to the meanings of sentences,
and it treats the concepts of truth and falsity as pivotal in giving the
meanings of sentences. This pair of concepts lies at rock-bottom of the
whole enterprise. For 'to know what it is for a sentence – any sentence [of a
language] – to be true ... amounts ... to understanding the language'.[8] The
programme for a theory of meaning for a language is to specify the
conditions in which each well-formed sentence is true (and perhaps too the
conditions in which it is false). A successful search would result in a
so-called 'truth-definition' for this particular language. Tarski originally
introduced this concept in connection with 'formalized languages' (logical
calculi): he sought for such a language 'the definition of truth . . . [i.e.] a
materially adequate and formally correct definition of the term "true
sentence" '.[9] In modern truth-conditional semantics the restriction to
formalized languages has disappeared. The quarry is a truth-definition for
any language whatever, or, conspicuously among philosophers, the sketch
of a procedure for arriving at such a definition for any particular language
(i.e. the form of a correct truth-definition). This will constitute at least the
essential core of any acceptable theory of meaning for a given language.

The uninitiated might feel utterly bewildered at this point. What has a
truth-definition to do with his understanding of the word 'true'? Is his
grasp of this familiar English word defective unless he can give a truth-
definition for English? Must his understanding of the thesis that the
meaning of a sentence is its truth-conditions be accordingly just as imperfect? Does the correct interpretation of this thesis await the construction of a truth-definition? And how would such a definition mesh
with his employment of the term 'true'? Would any of his bewilderment be
alleviated by dissociating understanding 'true' from truth-definitions?
Would anything become clearer when he encountered the thesis that a
Tarskian truth-definition would not yield a complete explanation of the
concept of truth?[10] Or the thesis that the definition of truth is impossible in
respect of any natural language?[11]

[8]   Davidson, 'Truth and Meaning', p. 310.

[9]   A. Tarski, 'The Concept of Truth in Formalized Languages', in *Logic, Semantics, Metamathematics* (Clarendon Press, Oxford, 1956), p. 152.

[10]   M. A. E. Dummett, *Truth and Other Enigmas* (Duckworth, London, 1978), p. xxi.

[11]   Tarski, 'The Concept of Truth in Formalized Languages', pp. 153, 165.

Two suggestions are offered to clarify these matters. One is that the term
'true' is vague, ambiguous, and perhaps incoherent. It is allegedly applied
sometimes to physical objects (e.g. sentences), sometimes to psychological
phenomena (e.g. beliefs), sometimes to abstract entities (e.g. propositions);[12] it carries different connotations, especially evident to philosophers;[13] and it generates antinomies (e.g. the antimony of the liar).[14]
Consequently we may be urged to construct a concept of truth which is
precise, unequivocal, and paradox-free to serve as the solid foundation for
semantic theory. The second suggestion is that the concept of truth is a
theoretical concept. According to this view, Everyman's employment of
the term 'true' reflects his groping towards the construction of a semantic
theory. He is attempting to build or refine a theory about how a language
works, and assessments of truth and falsity are one of the parameters in
this exercise. But, since he (tacitly) seeks the best theory available, he may
have good reason to concede that some theorist (a Tarski, a Davidson, a
Dummett, a Katz) has met with better success than he himself did by using
his native wit. Hence he might rationally replace his original 'theoretical
concept' with one based on a rigorous truth-definition.

Though initially reassuring, both of these suggestions give way to deeper
perplexity. The case against the everyday use of the term 'true' turns on
fabricated evidence. The actual applications of this word are perhaps less
diverse than they are alleged to be. Beliefs and judgments are not properly
characterized as psychological objects, and sentences are dubious candidates for being physical objects or being subjects of truth-predication.
Moreover, somebody who says 'It is true that grass is green' has not
obviously predicated truth of a Platonic object (a proposition), though he
has obviously predicated green of a stuff (grass). Finally, the antinomy of
the liar might reveal, not the incoherence of the concept of truth, but the
absurdity of taking an expression used to refer to *other* expressions (e.g.
'this sentence') to refer to itself. The fact that the use of 'true' does not
match a philosopher's preconceptions does not render the concept of truth
vague, ambiguous, or incoherent. Likewise, the idea that truth is a
theoretical concept is ludicrous. 'True' and 'false' are basic in elementary
English; their use is learned relatively early, and it is widespread in adult
speech on a vast range of topics. Any reason for classifying them as
theoretical terms would apply equally well to 'red', 'sweet', and 'heavy'.

[12] A. Tarski, 'The Semantic Conception of Truth', in *Readings in Philosophical Analysis*,
ed. H. Feigl and W. Sellars (Appleton–Century–Crofts, New York, 1949, p. 53.

[13] Tarski, 'The Concept of Truth in Formalized Languages', p. 153.

[14] Ibid., pp. 157ff.

But what conceivable gain would there be in calling all adjectives, or indeed all words whatever, 'theoretical terms'? The truth is that certain philosophers look on 'true' and 'truth' *as if* they were intended to be the technical jargon of an explanatory theory, but this is a source of distortion rather than insight.

Provisionally shelving these general scruples, let us scrutinize the programme of constructing a truth-definition for a language. It is assumed from the outset that truth is (or can be considered) a property of sentences. Tarski explicitly aimed to characterize the totality of true sentences of a formalized language, and all generalizations of his logical semantics seek a recursive specification of the true sentences of a given language.[15] Likewise, any attempt to explain meaning in terms of truth-conditions presupposes that what have meanings and what are true (or false) are the very same entities (sentences).[16] Considerations about conditions of their truth are to be exploited to pair sentences with their meanings. Consequently truth will be directly relevant only if it is a property of sentences. The attribution of truth to sentences is essential to truth-conditional semantics.

This thesis is supported in various ways. Sometimes it is admitted that 'true' is not standardly used as a predicate of (quoted) sentences, but rather as a predicate attached to noun-clauses (indirect statements in English or Latin); none the less, for theoretical purposes, 'true' can be transferred from statements to sentences by an obvious stipulation (viz. ' "Grass is green" is true' means the same as 'It is true that grass is green'). Sometimes application of 'true' to sentences is argued to be a regularization of a chaotic pattern of usage. And sometimes this is urged to be the primary use of 'true'; sentences such as 'That grass is green is true', which appear to predicate truth of some abstract object designated by an indirect statement (a 'proposition'), can be analysed into such a sentence as ' "Grass is green" is true', which makes clear that truth is really a property of sentences. We shall ignore the stronger claims and focus for the present on the weakest possible thesis, viz. that 'true' can be given a coherent explanation as a predicate of quoted sentences which is sufficient for the purpose of explaining sentence-meanings (at least as conceived within truth-

[15] In fact, Tarski and his followers vacillate on this issue. Sometimes they claim that what 'true' is predicated of in a truth-theory is not sentences, but structural descriptions of the sentences of a given language (e.g. Tarski, 'The Concept of Truth in Formalized Languages', p. 157, and Davidson, 'Truth and Meaning', p. 309). This opens up another divergence with the usage of the term 'true', which we will charitably ignore.

[16] We disregard here objections which arise from the use of non-declarative sentences to issue orders, make requests, ask questions, etc.

conditional semantics). This minimal thesis is more problematic than commonly realized.

Initial clarification is needed about what the truth-theorist counts as a *sentence*. For the claim that sentences are true or false is open to various competing interpretations. On one view, it would apply to type-sentences (to word-patterns that may be exemplified on many different occasions and in different media (speech and writing)); on another, to token-sentences (so that, e.g., the activity of a class of students each of whom copied down 'grass is green' from a blackboard would increase the number of truths). But should token-sentences themselves be considered as physical objects, as well as being instances of a pattern? To escape any suspicion of invoking abstract entities, some theorists treat truth as a property of inscriptions (physical objects, either visual or auditory). This has absurd implications. Does it make sense to count the number of true objects that are strewn on the surface of my desk? Or the number of truths located on the shelves of the British Museum? In erasing a pencilled inscription, might I annihilate a truth? And did truths go up in smoke when the library at Alexandria burned? Might a signpost inscribed 'London 65 mi. →' become a false object if turned around or moved to another location? Matters stand even worse. The very same inscription can be re-used (e.g. I might write letters partly by a technique of collage using entire sentences, and the banner 'The President is a fascist' might be used recurrently for years by Rent-a-Crowd), and it might then make different statements, some true and some false. Unless the same inscription is allowed to be both true and false, truth must be relativized to particular utterances of a given inscription, but then the criteria of identity and difference for the bearers of truth and falsity diverge from the identity-conditions for physical objects.

Problems arise on another front. Philosophers and linguists alike take type-sentences to be the primary bearers of meanings, and therefore any straightforward explanation of sentence-meaning in terms of the conditions under which a sentence is true requires that type-sentences be the bearers of truth and falsity. This would eliminate some of the absurdities raised by treating truth as a property of inscriptions, since type-sentences, being abstract entities, seem proof against destruction by negligence and arson. But fresh difficulties abound. In particular, the possibility of using different tokens of the same type-sentence for different purposes appears to license the ascription to a suitably chosen type-sentence of all three of the predicates 'true', 'false', and 'neither true nor false'. Alternatively, and equally absurdly, this circumstance could be taken to debar the ascription of truth to a type-sentence in spite of the fact that it may properly be used to say something true. It is obvious that the doctrine that truth is a property of sentences needs to be clarified, and it is not at all obvious that any coherent explanation will be forthcoming.

The shifting and purpose-relative boundary of a language raises further problems for theorists seeking a truth-definition. Assertions may be made not only by uttering or writing words, but also in whole or in part by gestures, diagrams, samples, and signals. How should this matter be dealt with? Should one argue that the signal lantern hung in the belfry of the Old North Church in Boston to inform Paul Revere that the British were marching on Lexington was a *true* instrument of assertion, but not a *sentence* of English and hence irrelevant to a theory of meaning for English?[17] But this reasoning would not apply to the *repertoire* of gestures available to native speakers of English. Should these uniformly be relegated to 'pragmatics'? By what principles? The standard exposition of the rationale for ascribing truth to (wholly verbal) sentences applies equally directly to utterances incorporating gestures or samples. Moreover, like words, they are commonly viewed as having meanings; they can be explained (e.g. standard gestures of disgust or surprise), and there are criteria for understanding them. All of these considerations together with the interpenetration of speech by gestures suggest that the boundary of the term 'sentence' in truth-conditional semantics should be drawn generously enough to include certain concrete objects and bodily actions as well as verbal symbols. But now other difficulties arise. How are concrete symbols to be processed to fit into the framework of truth-conditional semantics? What is the analogue of direct quotation for such symbols? How does the theory represent what the predicate 'true' is predicated of? How can a concrete object or action belong to a calculus which constitutes a recursive specification of the true sentences of a language?[18] Truth-conditional theorists proceed as if the only institutionalized instruments of communication were wholly verbal symbols; to correct this howler generates intractable problems.

To characterize truth as a property of sentences is not merely unclear, but also implausible. 'True' and 'false' are commonly employed as adjectives modifying such nouns as 'statement', 'assertion', 'belief', 'conjecture', 'wish', 'conviction', etc., and also as adjective complements of

---

[17] This riposte raises acute difficulties about the bounds of a language (below, pp. 376–78).

[18] Perhaps a description of this object or act constitutes part of the 'structural description' of a sentence (or utterance).

indirect statements (e.g. 'That grass is green is true') or indirect questions (e.g. 'What he suspects about Smith's motives is true'). In these roles, 'true' and 'false' are merely two out of a family of closely related expressions which include 'accurate', 'right', 'wrong', 'exaggerated', 'exact', 'clear', 'certain', 'refuted', 'well-founded', 'vague', 'obscure', and 'definite' as well perhaps as 'faithful' (e.g. of descriptions or accounts), 'literal' and 'metaphorical' (e.g. of statements or descriptions). If a theorist affirms the utility of treating 'true' and 'false' as predicates of sentences, does he mete out the same treatment to all of their cousins? Here he confronts a dilemma. Should he deny that a parallel treatment makes sense, he would be committed to arguing that 'true' and 'false' are not as closely related to these other expressions as they are thought to be. But has he any telling grounds independent of his proposed reform to suggest that we have here stumbled on a hitherto unknown category difference? If, on the other hand, he condones 'transferring' these adjectives and employing them as predicate complements of quoted sentences, he is apt to breed patent nonsense or confusions arising from conflicts with established patterns of usage.[19] An archivist might well say of a sentence in a manuscript that it was clear, but this would be a comment on the orthography (not a characterization of its content). What would one make of the claim that a sentence was well-founded or solidly supported? (Perhaps that part of an inscribed architrave was not in danger of collapsing?) Can a *sentence* be exaggerated, refuted, or even metaphorical?[20] (Perhaps a kick in the shin might be reckoned a (metaphorical) sentence or utterance, just as a savage rebuke might be

[19] Logicians run a parallel risk in redefining 'arguments' as ordered sets of sentences. To describe an argument as well-balanced is not to characterize the typographical lay-out of a text, and to call an argument clear or easy to follow is not to comment on a speaker's enunciation.

[20] The analysis of metaphor is perverted by a widespread assumption that type-sentences are intrinsically either literal or metaphorical. But nearly any sentence can be given figurative uses, and many (though not all) utterances used metaphorically can also be used to make literal statements. When Hamlet tells Laertes 'I shot my arrow o'er the house and hit my brother', he is not narrating an exploit of archery, but apologizing for having injured Laertes by unintentionally driving Ophelia to suicide; yet somebody else might use the same sentence to give a literal description of an accident. This is a typical metaphor, though of course there are type-sentences which appear to be ineradicably metaphorical because it seems impossible to describe circumstances in which they could be used literally (e.g. because they contain violations of category restrictions as in 'Architecture is frozen music'). A recognition that the literal/metaphorical distinction applies primarily to *uses* of sentences, not to sentence-*forms*, would forestall the misguided search for 'metaphorical meanings' of words or sentences as well as the investigation of the putative mechanisms by which such meanings are derived from the components and structures of sentences expressing metaphors.

counted a metaphorical kick in the shin?) There is little sense, no evident point, and great danger of confusion in 'transferring' adjectives coordinate and contrasting with 'true' and 'false' from propositions, statements, beliefs, etc., to sentences. This suggests that the treatment of truth and falsity as properties of sentences is motivated solely as a precondition of constructing truth-conditional semantics.

Doubts can be further reinforced by reflecting on parallel manoeuvres grounded in arguments exactly similar to those supporting the contention that truth is (or should be) treated as a property of sentences, not of assertions, statements, beliefs, etc. Philosophical qualms about apparent reference to abstract objects and about apparent quantification over such objects arise not only for assertions, propositions, etc., but also for numbers, rules, possibilities, geometrical figures, etc. Should we uniformly adopt the strategy of 'transferring' properties apparently predicated of such entities to corresponding concrete objects? Natural numbers are commonly characterized by the predicates 'even', 'odd', 'prime', 'composite', etc., and quantification over numbers is widespread. Would the science of arithmetic rest on firmer foundations were we to replace the sentence '11 is prime' by a sentence explicitly referring to a numeral (viz. ' "11" is prime')? We could perhaps learn to speak in this bizarre manner, to translate elementary arithmetic into this odd idiom. But even here there would be risk of confusion, since the term 'composite' might well be applied to the numerals '101', '11', and '12' alike, in differentiating them from the numerals '0', '1', '8', '9' (which would be called simple). And a multitude of manifest incoherences, already pointed out by Frege, follow in the wake of any such 'reform'.[21] Parallel difficulties arise from other parallel proposals. Since rules are expressed by rule-formulations, one might 'transfer' properties of rules to rule-formulations. We speak of rules being enacted, repealed, confirmed, cancelled, overturned, etc. But cancelling a rule need not consist in cancelling a rule-formulation. Overturning a rule is not a matter of turning an inscription upside down. Endless absurdities arise in pursuing as a general strategy the pattern of reasoning which supports the scientific definition of truth as a property of sentences in truth-conditional semantics. What ground have we for supposing that a tree which bears so much rotten fruit produces anything wholesome?

These considerations together indicate that the attribution of truth to sentences in semantic theories is far more obscure and problematic a

---

[21] G. Frege, *The Basic Laws of Arithmetic*, vol. 2, §§86–137, in *Translations from the Philosophical Writings of Gottlob Frege*, ed. P. T. Geach and M. Black (Blackwell, Oxford, 1960), pp. 182–233.

suggestion than it seems at first sight, and they intimate too that deep confusions may be not far below the surface. We shall elaborate this hint.

First, the application of 'true' and 'false' to sentences abrogates many of the internal connections among the network of related concepts which give the concept of truth its point. The properties of truth and falsity are incompatible. But if a semantic theory follows the standard practice of taking type-sentences to be the bearers of meaning, and if it clarifies their meanings in terms of the conditions for *their* being true or false, then it breaches this principle. For a sentence containing indexical expressions can be used in some contexts to make true statements, in others to make false statements, and in yet others to make no statement at all (e.g. because referential presuppositions are not fulfilled). Even a context-independent unambiguous sentence can be used to make different statements (e.g. if used ironically or metaphorically).[22] But the preferred explanation of what it means to ascribe truth to a sentence would require in such cases that both the predicates 'true' and 'false' be predicated of the same type-sentence! Even retreat to token-sentences or concrete inscriptions would not eliminate this antinomy. Should we then drop the incompatibility of truth and falsity? Further difficulties abound. What is true is worthy of belief and fit to be asserted (*ceteris paribus*!). But this object of a belief is not a sentence, rather is it what a sentence expresses (represented typically by an indirect statement). Similarly, what is asserted is not a sentence, but a statement or proposition (though, of course, a sentence may be uttered in making an assertion). What is proved is true, while what is refuted is false. But a geometer proves *that* the square on the hypotenuse equals the sum of the squares on the other two sides, not a sentence; and a skilful debater may refute what his opponent maintained, not the sentence that he uttered. Truth is internally related to belief, assertion, knowledge, certainty, proof, evidence, etc. To honour those relations requires a denial that truth is a property of *sentences*. Yet to turn our backs on them would be to make our new 'technical concept' of truth both vacuous and point-less. Truth-conditional semantics here confronts an insoluble dilemma.

Another route leads to a similar impasse. Truth-conditional theories owe us a clear explanation of the terms 'true' and 'false' in application to

[22] A sentence such as 'Pickwick visited Rochester', though used literally, may make different statements too. By its utterance in different contexts a speaker might make a true assertion about a fictional character or a false assertion about nineteenth century tourism. The answer to the question 'Is it true that Pickwick visited Rochester?' depends upon the identification of the *purpose* of the enquiry. Purpose-relativity of truth-assessments is neglected by semantic theorists, though it is a noteworthy feature of many statements (e.g. rough generalizations or approximate descriptions such as 'France is hexagonal').

sentences. Presumably this will take the form of an account relating the familiar use of these adjectives to characterize beliefs, statements, conjectures, etc. (or what is believed, what is stated or asserted, etc.). The simplest proposal (give or take a few local difficulties about context-dependence and the forms of indirect statements) would be that ' "*p*" is true' means the same as 'It is true that *p*' (or '(The statement) that *p* is true'). But this would not serve the purposes of truth-conditional semantics. For, according to this explanation, every sentence of the form ' "*p*" is true if and only if *p*' would be *trivially* true, since it would be a disguised instance of the truism 'It is true that *p* if and only if *p*'. It is essential to Tarskian semantics, however, that ' "*p*" is true', being a sentence of the metalanguage, has a meaning different from the meaning of any sentence in the object-language, *a fortiori* from that of '*p*'. This point is standardly substantiated by the argument that sentences of the form ' "*p*" is true' behave differently under translation from those of the form '*p*' (or 'It is true that *p*'); or equivalently, by noting that the metalanguage might differ from the object-language (e.g. that one might be English, the other French). Obviously this claim undermines the proposed explanation of how to apply 'true' to sentences. *That* explanation gives no warrant for maintaining that 'Trois est un nombre impair' is true if and only if three is an odd number, since it says *nothing* about how to predicate 'true' of sentences in any language other than English. Of course, this lacuna could be filled. A revised explanation might read thus: ' "*p*" is true' means the same as ' "*p*" states that *q* and it is true that *q*'. Yet now a fresh hydra-head rears up. How can such an explanation have a proper place in a theory which purports to give an explanation of the meanings of all meaningful sentences of a language? For if we knew for any sentence what it stated and therefore were in a position to apply this explanation of 'true', we would not require a 'truth-theory' in order to erect a theory of meaning in the first place. That would presumably be effected by whatever enables us to say of any given utterance of a sentence '*p*' that it states that *q*. Contrariwise, if we were (absurdly) ignorant about what sentences stated, the definition of 'true' would be impossible for us to make use of. Consequently this revised explanation of 'true' must be either unintelligible or useless for the purposes of building a theory of meaning.

In these dire straits, should a truth-theorist subscribe to the doctrine that truth is a simple, inexplicable property of sentences? This proposal hardly recommends itself as the basis for introducing a technical term in the construction of a rigorous scientific theory. Introducing technical terminology or redefining current expressions for particular expository purposes is permissible, but such expressions must be clearly and coherently explained. For to concede that certain uses are technical is to agree that the only appropriate canon for judging their correctness is the explanation given by theorists themselves. If this is incoherent or lacks any clear application, then the statements containing the explained term must be judged to be nonsensical. This is the predicament of those who propose to use 'true' and 'false' as predicates of sentences. We should take their explanations seriously. Instead, from fear of embarrassment at not comprehending what others seem to find obvious, we run the risk of persuading ourselves that we understand what is incomprehensible.

Finally, the very strategy of treating 'true' as a technical or theoretical term in semantics is misguided. It subverts the intelligibility, not to mention the plausibility, of the claim that truth is the key to the clarification of the concept of the meaning of a sentence. Truth-conditional semantics builds on the compelling idea that understanding what a speaker says is often manifested in knowing what would be the case if what he said were true. But this source of insight is lost immediately if the truth-theorist then adds that he is using 'true' as a technical term (yet to be explained!) in his theory-construction, for this revokes our licence to associate his fundamental principle with this facet of our concepts of understanding and meaning. In short, his claim that meaning is a matter of truth-conditions is comprehensible and interesting only to the extent that his concept of truth (what he means by 'true') coincides with ours (what competent speakers of English mean by 'true'). The pressure to declare his concept to be a technical one arises from his recognizing important divergence in this matter. He wishes to ignore the pattern of explanation of 'true' which authorizes its use as an adjective complement to indirect statements or as a modifier of such expressions as 'belief', 'judgment', 'assertion', and 'speculation'. And he wishes to bestow on 'true' novel uses. In particular, he affirms that 'the truth predicate is a device of disquotation', i.e. it cancels the effect of quotation-marks and thereby secures that the sentence ' "Snow is white" is true' (unlike the sentence ' "Snow is white" contains three words') makes a statement about snow, not about words.[23] The truth-theorist contends that the real role of the word 'true' is to bring us back from talk of language to talk of the world,[24] to link symbols with reality. Furthermore, he applies the terms "true' and 'false' to utterances which are not properly described as saying anything

[23] W. V. Quine, *Philosophy of Logic* (Prentice-Hall, Englewood Cliffs, NJ, 1970), p. 12.

[24] D. Davidson 'In Defence of Convention T', in *Truth, Syntax and Modality*, ed. H. Leblanc (North-Holland, Amsterdam, 1973), p. 76.

true or false, e.g. sentences used to pose questions or to issue commands. He must do so on pain of being unable to account for the meanings of such (meaningful) sentences. Yet he legitimates such applications of 'true' only by introducing an extraordinary explanation of how to use this term (e.g. to introduce the technical concept of a sentence-radical and then to define 'true' as a predicate applicable to sentence-radicals).[25] The important point is that his use of the word 'true' generates nonsense according to the standards set by accepted explanations of this term. But to try to evade this awkward fact by redefining 'true' as a theoretical term deprives truth-conditional semantics of its intuitive support and threatens to make it incomprehensible.

Without the principle that truth is a property of sentences the whole project of constructing any version of truth-conditional semantics would collapse. But many independent arguments converge to show that this principle is totally indefensible. The truth-theorist who brushes aside our justified qualms by a disarming patter about making minor adjustments to our concept of truth or about a harmless transfer of truth from statements to sentences may well be persuasive. But we would fare better by cultivating sales-resistance and pressing home our objections to his procedures. Then we would discover that his entire performance of theory-building signifies nothing. This is not to deny that there is any internal connection between meaning and truth. Rather, it is to argue that truth-conditional semantics rests on fundamental distortion and oversimplification of a very intricate network of internal relations.

4 Truth-conditions

The hallmark of truth-conditional semantics is the tenet that the meaning of a sentence is its truth-conditions (or that its meaning is determined by its truth-conditions). Since the term 'truth-condition' is not in general circulation outside linguistics or philosophy, and since it has the appearance of being used as a technical term in theories of meaning, we might reasonably expect to find some explanation of it at an early stage in the exposition of semantic theories. But none is forthcoming in most contemporary discussions.

[25] Here again the theorist undermines his own official doctrine that truth is a property of sentences! Alternatively, he commits himself to the incoherent notion that sentence-radicals are kinds of expressions (rather than what certain expressions express). Neither position is tenable for him, but instead of facing up to the difficulty, he fudges the issues (above, pp. 72–5).

One explanation of this lacuna might be that 'truth-conditions', though a technical term in semantics, has become so entrenched that it has an established and familiar explanation together with an institutionalized pattern of correct use. On this view the pioneers of truth-conditional semantics gave complete and satisfactory explanations, and hence there is no point in restating the obvious. The *Tractatus*, in first introducing the term, did define it: the truth-conditions of a proposition are given by an expression of its agreement and disagreement with the truth-possibilities of its constituent elementary propositions (above, pp. 126–30). Can we not take this to be the canonical explanation of 'truth-conditions'? This would be a viable strategy only for somebody who accepted the whole doctrine of analysis presented in the *Tractatus*, since these ideas are needed in order to make sense of the cited definition. But there are few, if any, contemporary theorists of meaning who would wish to nail their colours to this mast. So they cannot legitimately avail themselves of Wittgenstein's definition, and must introduce this technical term with an explanation of their own.

The other obvious excuse for the lacuna is that the term 'truth-condition' is self-explanatory. 'The truth-conditions of the sentence "p"' simply means: 'the conditions under which the sentence "p" is true'. The expression is constructed on a familiar model. The 'fulfilment-conditions' of a command are the conditions under which the command is fulfilled; the existence-conditions of a law of the land are the conditions under which a statute is held to be in force; etc. Waiving the previous objections to the attribution of truth to sentences, we find that there is nothing in need of explanation. And the truth-theorist's use of the term 'truth-conditions' appears to be above criticism. The expression itself could be eschewed without obvious loss. The entry for 'truth-condition' in the index of Carnap's *Meaning and Necessity* takes the reader to the 'rule of truth' for atomic sentences, viz. 'An atomic sentence in S, consisting of a predicate followed by an individual constant is true if and only if the individual to which the individual constant refers possesses the property to which the predicate refers.'[26] Does it not follow that the concept of a truth-condition is altogether unassailable?

Truth-conditional semantics cannot be safeguarded by this manoeuvre. The fact that a term is deemed to be self-explanatory does not guarantee that it makes sense, and the absence of the term 'truth-condition' from the exposition of a theory does not prove that the theory does not rest on the concept of a truth-condition. The crucial question to consider is what is

[26] R. Carnap, *Meaning and Necessity* (Chicago University Press, Chicago, 1956), p. 5.

involved in the concept of a *condition*. Having clarified this concept, one can then turn to the issues of whether the expression 'the conditions for the truth of the sentence *"p"* ' makes any sense and whether particular forms of metalinguistic sentences can coherently be said to express such conditions.

For present purposes it is sufficient to note a few salient features of what are paradigm cases of *conditions*. First, a standard formulation of a condition is a conditional sentence. A lawyer might explain the conditions for there being a contract between two parties by saying 'A has entered into a contract with B to φ . . .' or '. . . *on condition that* . . .', or '. . . *provided that* . . .' or '. . . *only if* . . .' Conversely, a standard use of conditionals is to stipulate or describe conditions for something. Secondly, there is a requirement of relevance to be met by a condition. The conditions for the existence of a contract, e.g., must be circumstances relevant to determining whether or not a contract holds between two parties. This relevance-requirement is loose enough to tolerate various different relations between actions, states of affairs, circumstances, etc. Logicians often distinguish between necessary and sufficient conditions, but the spectrum of what can intelligibly be called 'conditions' is not exhausted by this pair of characterizations. Conditions may be *defeasible* both positively and negatively.[27] This is typical of the application of legal concepts;[28] e.g. the condition that a document be signed and witnessed at the bottom of the final page is normally necessary for it to qualify as a valid will, but this condition can be overridden in certain circumstances. Thirdly, the specification of a condition must be non-circular or non-trivial. A condition must be capable of being formulated independently of what it is a condition for. The existence of a contract between A and B may, e.g., be a condition for A to have a duty to deliver a specific piece of property to B, but not a condition for there to be a contract between A and B.[29] Fourthly, it must be

---

[27] Defeasible conditions for truth are not standardly considered or exploited in semantic theories (though they could be, cf. G. Baker, 'Criteria: A New Foundation for Semantics', *Ratio*, XVI (1974)). The reason is obviously that defeasible inferences are doubtful candidates for incorporation in a mechanically operated formal calculus.

[28] This claim was stressed by H. L. A. Hart, especially in his article 'The Ascription of Responsibility and Rights', in *Logic and Language: First Series*, ed. A. G. N. Flew (Blackwell, Oxford, 1960).

[29] It is improper (or at least potentially confusing) to speak here of a 'trivial condition'. This phrase is normally used to describe conditions which may be fulfilled with negligible effort, expense, or ingenuity (e.g. breathing at least once per minute). Rather, a circular specification indicates no condition whatever. (Similar confusions arise in respect of 'trivial assumptions', 'trivial provisos', etc.)

possible to establish whether a condition holds independently of establishing what it is a condition for. A condition must be capable of independent ascertainment, since otherwise it would not be available to settle anything in dispute. Absence of heart-beat, lack of breathing, a flat electroencephalogram, etc., are conditions of (medical) death, but not the parting of the soul from the body. Finally, specifications of conditions must have a degree of generality. There is no such thing as a one-off condition,[30] e.g. a condition for Fischer to checkmate Spassky in a particular encounter which would not likewise count as a condition for an arbitrary player to checkmate his opponent at any meeting. The conditions for making a valid will in England hold indifferently for any person who meets certain nationality and residence requirements, while the question of whether A has executed a valid will at a particular moment will be settled by instantiation of these general conditions. These remarks all are major components of the elucidation of the concept of a condition.

Bearing these matters in mind, let us return to the notion of a truth-condition, i.e. the concept of the *conditions* for the truth of a sentence. There are two parallel paradigms for the specification of truth-conditions. One is the truth-tabular definitions of sentence-connectives; the other what Carnap called the 'rule of truth' for atomic sentences. But each is capable of two contrasting interpretations. One might summarize the truth-table for ' $\wedge$ ' in the explanation: '$p \wedge q$' is true if and only if 'p' is true and 'q' is true. And the rule of truth might be phrased thus: the sentence 'φA' is true if and only if 'A' designates an object which possesses whatever property the letter 'φ' designates. In these cases, quoted expressions occur on both flanks of the biconditional. Alternatively, one might rephrase the explanation for ' $\wedge$ ' in this way: '$p \wedge q$' is true if and only if p and q. Likewise, the rule of truth might take this form: 'φA' is true if and only if the object A (which is what 'A' as a matter of fact designates) has the property φ (which is what 'φ' happens to stand for). On this view, the expressions on the right of the biconditional belong to the object-language and really contain no quoted expressions at all. It is this second view that prevails in truth-conditional semantics. It constructs specifications of truth-conditions within the framework of Tarski's schema: 'p' is true if and only if p. And it requires the support of the doctrine that 'true' is a device for 'disquotation', since otherwise it would be a mystery how any sentence in the object language could be used to make the same statement as the one made by predicating 'true' of an expression in the metalanguage.

---

[30] There may, of course, be general conditions which in fact are met no more than once – or even never at all (e.g. if the 'operative facts' of a legal statute are never instantiated).

Let us focus first on this interpretation of the paradigms of specifications of the *conditions* for the truth of sentences. These do meet one desideratum, viz. the formulations have the form of conditionals (indeed, of biconditionals). But do they have the other features requisite for specifications of conditions? Manifestly not. Indeed, they fall at the very first hurdle, the requirement of relevance. On the left of each biconditional stands a sentence of the form '(The sentence) "*p*" is true'; this ascribes a property (truth) to an entity (a quoted sentence). If what stands on the right is to express a necessary *condition* for the sentence '*p*' to have this property, then it must lay down requirements to be satisfied by the *sentence* (or its parts) if it is to have the property of being true; and if this also expresses a sufficient condition for the sentence to be true, then it must lay down stipulations the satisfaction of which by the *sentence* (or its parts) guarantees that it has this property. Yet what stands on the right of the biconditional is expressly claimed to say nothing whatever about any expressions of the object-language, *a fortiori* nothing at all about the sentence '*p*'![31] There is no such thing as the satisfaction of the condition that three is an odd number by the sentence 'Three is an odd number'. The idea that '"*p*" is true if and only if *p*' formulates a condition for the sentence '*p*' to be true is no less absurd than the claim that 'The sum of two odd numbers is even' frames a condition for its being the case that some blue cheeses contain penicillin. The lack of mutual relevance of the two sides of a Tarskian biconditional is masked from view by the apparent double occurrence of the sentence-letter '*p*' (once mentioned, once used). But it leaps to the eye as soon as the metalanguage is so chosen that it differs from the object-language. Consider the sentence: ' "Trois est un nombre impair" is true if and only if three is an odd number'. Could anybody mistake the right-hand side of this biconditional for the formulation of a *condition on the French sentence* 'Trois est un nombre impair'?

Exactly parallel difficulties arise about the requirement of generality. The apparent double occurrence of the dummy sentence '*p*' in the schema ' "*p*" is true if and only if *p*' gives the impression of generality which is

---

[31] Contrast with this a specification of the condition for somebody to bear the legal name 'Ebenezer Scrooge', e.g. that a duly qualified vicar of the Church of England pronounced the name 'Ebenezer Scrooge' over him in a correctly performed ceremony of baptism. The need to *mention* the sentence (or its parts) on the right of the Tarskian biconditional no doubt accounts for the temptation to formulate truth-functional explanations on the pattern ' "*p* ∧ *q*" is true if and only if "*p*" is true and "*q*" is true' as well as for the vacillation between this formulation and the official one, viz. ' "*p* ∧ *q*" is true if and only if (it is true that) *p* and (it is true that) *q*'.

conveyed by an algebraic formula such as '$(x + y)^2 = x^2 + 2xy + y^2$'. But the rigorous distinction of mention from use shows this apparent generality to be an illusion generated by our conventions for using quotation-marks. Strictly speaking, ' "p" ' is meant to be the name of an arbitrary sentence (not the name of the sixteenth letter of the English alphabet!), whereas 'p' holds a place open for the occurrence of this sentence in the formulation of a proposition (and hence for an expression which is not a name at all). Divergence between the metalanguage and the object-language annihilates any semblance of generality. For the biconditional ' "Trois est un nombre impair" is true if and only if three is an odd number' exemplifies only such a form as ' "p" is true if and only if q' or even 'A is true if and only if q'. Here the appearance of any generality has vanished. Nor can it be recaptured by supposing that each Tarskian biconditional lays down a condition which may in principle be satisfied by *every* meaningful sentence of the object-language. Since 'Three is an odd number' does not even formulate a condition which could be met by the *sentence* 'Three is an odd number', it certainly does not formulate a condition which could in principle be met by the *sentence* 'Grass is green', but which as a matter of fact is not satisfied by this sentence! Generality has disappeared without leaving any trace.

Further doubts arise about the other defining characteristics of *conditions* in connection with the Tarskian paradigms for specifying the conditions for the truth of a sentence. It might appear that the sentences on the left and right sides of such biconditionals are both logically and epistemologically independent just because the ones on the left belong to the metalanguage, the ones on the right to the object-language. But once again appearances are deceptive. The truth-theorist is eager to undermine the contrast: 'the utility of the truth predicate is precisely the cancellation of linguistic reference. . . . [D]espite a technical ascent to talk of sentences, one eye is on the world. . . . By calling the sentence ["Snow is white"] true, we call snow white.'[32] According to this conception, the sentence ' "Snow is white" is true', if used to make an assertion, makes the same statement as the sentence 'Snow is white'. Therefore the condition of non-circularity is not met by any of the putative formulations of the conditions for the truth of a sentence which exemplify the schema ' "p" is true if and only if p'. Even without this argument, the requirement of independent ascertainability would not generally be met by the so-called 'truth-conditions'. The apparent independence is conditional on the presumption of ignorance of

---

[32] Quine, *Philosophy of Logic*, p. 12.

the meaning of the sentence quoted in the biconditional. For a person who understands the sentence 'Three is an odd number' (or Trois est un nombre impair'), the question whether it is true (or whether what it expresses is true) is the very same question as the question whether three is an odd number![33] He cannot take ascertaining the truth of the left side of the biconditional to be independent of ascertaining the truth of the right side, and hence he cannot properly understand the biconditional to formulate a *condition* at all.

This volley of objections suggests that the champions of truth-conditional semantics should engage in a strategic retreat to the employment of biconditionals in which quoted expressions occur essentially on both wings. Should they advocate as a proper paradigm the schema: '$p \wedge q$' is true if and only if 'p' is true and 'q' is true? This would obviously escape objections on the score of irrelevance, since such biconditionals would clearly have sentences (or their parts) as the subject-matter of the sentences occurring on the right side. Moreover, the apparent generality indicated by dummy letters in such biconditionals would be genuine; e.g. the conditions for the truth of any substitution instance of '$p \wedge q$' can be derived by straightforward instantiation from the schema ' "$p \wedge q$" is true if and only if "p" is true and "q" is true'. On the other hand, the requirement of non-circularity can be met only in the case of sentences liable to *analysis*. Unless it contains logical constants or components susceptible to analytic definition (e.g. the term 'triangular' or 'prime (number)'), there will be nothing available to the truth-theorist apart from a formula of the form: ' "p" is true if and only if "p" is true'. Every language will contain sentences with regard to which no truth-*conditions* can be formulated according to the preferred model.[34] This catastrophe may be hidden under a patter about satisfaction: surely the theorist can always state ' "φA is

---

[33] This observation implies that radical translation, far from beginning at home, can only be carried out abroad among aliens.

[34] It might be suggested that this difficulty should be countered by postulating *ineffable* truth-conditions, i.e. by the supposition that a sentence may have genuine truth-conditions (which may be recognized as obtaining if they are fulfilled) which cannot be expressed except by using this very sentence itself (cf. Dummett, *Truth and Other Enigmas*, p. 361). This looks like a dubious sleight of hand. And it yields a dilemma: *either* the statement of the truth-conditions of such a sentence is not an explanation of its meaning at all *or* the meaning of a sentence, i.e. what we understand when we understand it, may transcend anything that might count as a complete explanation of its meaning. The first horn is untenable for truth-conditional semantics, and the second disregards a crucial internal connection between meaning, explanation, and understanding.

true if and only if "A" names an object which satisfies the predicate "φ" '. But the explanation of what it means to say that the object named by 'A' satisfies the predicate 'φ', when applied to this account, makes its latent circularity patent. Hence the theorist again faces checkmate. Unless every expression can be given an analysis within any given language, there will be no such thing as formulating for every sentence in this language the conditions for it to be true, and hence truth-conditions cannot provide a general account of the meanings of sentences.

The upshot of this investigation is the verdict that there is no intelligible interpretation of the paradigms of specifying the '*truth-conditions of sentences*' which justifies taking them to formulate the *conditions* for the *truth* of *sentences*. Nor can we fall back on some agreed definition of the term 'truth-condition', e.g. the one in the *Tractatus*. The consequence is that all discourse about truth-conditions lacks any sense; it is quite literally incomprehensible. Of course it passes muster among most philosophers and linguists in respect of intelligibility, and somebody who deploys the term astutely will be reckoned profound. Conversely, anybody who even so much as queries this fashion exposes himself to derision. None the less, it seems rational to ask for an explanation of a term whose meaning is apparently so well understood. It also seems reasonable that the explanations given should stand up to critical scrutiny. This discussion has tried to demonstrate that they conspicuously fail this test. Before jumping on the bandwagon and waving the banner emblazoned 'The meaning of a sentence is its truth-conditions', we would be prudent to insist on having a coherent explanation of what 'truth-condition' means, an account of what constitutes a statement of the truth-conditions of a sentence, and a defence of the claim that *every* sentence has truth-conditions. It seems that none of these tasks can be discharged against the background of assumptions and purposes inspiring truth-conditional semantics.

5   Context-dependent sentences

It is a conspicuous and commonly remarked feature of natural languages that a single type-sentence may often be used in different circumstances to make different assertions, some of which are true, others of which are false. This most obviously holds for sentences which contain indexical or token-reflexive expressions. Within this class fall personal pronouns ('I', 'you', 'he'), demonstratives ('this', 'that'), tensed verbs ('It is raining', 'It rained'), certain place- or time-indicators (e.g., 'here', 'now', 'yesterday', 'over there'). What is said, *a fortiori* the truth or falsity of what is said, by uttering a token of a sentence such as 'I see you now' depends more or less systematically on aspects of the *context* in which this token is spoken or written (e.g. who the speaker is, who is addressed, and when it is uttered). Theorists of meaning are inclined to consider the variation of truth-value with variation in context to be fully systematic and to subscribe to the principle that it can be assigned to variations in the reference of indexical expressions. Consequently they talk of context-dependent setences or occasion sentences. Contrasted with these are context-independent or eternal sentences which have the distinguishing mark that the utterance of one token of any of them in any circumstance necessarily makes the same statement as the utterance of any other token of the same sentence in any other circumstance, e.g. "Napoleon Bonaparte died on St Helena in 1825'.

  Context-dependent sentences pose an immediate threat to truth-conditional semantics. On the assumption that meanings are to be assigned to type-sentences (i.e. that any two tokens of an unambiguous type-sentence must have the same meaning), the occurrence of context-dependent sentences implies that the connections between meaning and truth cannot be straightforward because these bearers of meaning are not the proper bearers of the properties of truth and falsity. Since, however, the relation of meaning to truth involves truth-conditions as an intermediary, there is some scope for manoeuvre. One tactic is to incorporate a rider into a semantic theory – a rider stating that 'truth-conditions' for a context-dependent sentence must be understood to be 'relativized' to particular contexts of utterance. We are invited to view 'Truth as a relation between a sentence, a person, and a time'.[35] The other strategy is to relegate the whole business of context-dependence to pragmatics, confining semantics to giving an account of the general directions for using expressions which 'make possible' the employment of context-dependent sentences to express different statements in different contexts.[36] With some such perfunctory bow in the direction of the problem of context-dependence, the theorist of meaning hurries past in pursuit of more important business.

  These proceedings seem opaque and unsatisfactory. What is it to relativize truth-conditions to contexts of utterance? Does it make sense to view truth as a relation at all, let alone as a relation of a sentence with a person

---

[35] Davidson, 'Truth and Meaning', p. 319.
[36] This conception is presented by P. F. Strawson, *Introduction to Logical Theory* (Methuen, London, 1952), ch. 8.

and a time? And how does leaving the context-dependence of truth-values to pragmatics vindicate the thesis that *truth*-conditions constitute the meanings of type-sentences? If truth is divorced from type-sentences, must truth-conditions not be dragged away in the wake? There appear to be two options open to truth-conditional semantics. One is to take truth-conditions to parallel meanings, i.e. to be invariants associated with unambiguous type-sentences. The other is to take truth-conditions to parallel truth-values, i.e. to vary with the context of utterance of tokens of a context-dependent sentence. Both possibilities deserve brief investigation.

The first option is the more popular of the two. It holds out the prospect of identifying the meaning of a type-sentence with its truth-conditions since it explains an invariant set of truth-conditions for any type-sentence, whether it is context-dependent or not. The basic idea is to formulate the truth-conditions of a sentence such as 'I have an IQ greater than 100' by the sentence 'The sentence "I have an IQ greater than 100" uttered by x at time t is true if and only if x has at time t an IQ greater than 100'.[37] This analysis makes transparent how the truth-value of a particular utterance of this sentence depends on the identity of the speaker and the time of his speaking; it formulates a general condition for any utterance of this type-sentence to be true (to express something true). The generalization of this account to embrace all forms of indexicality seems straightforward in principle, even if intricate in detail. A formulation of the truth-conditions of a context-dependent sentence will state how the truth-value of any utterance of it depends on aspects of the context of utterance. Indeed, it is commonly thought to indicate how to calculate the referents of any indexical expressions from a specification of the relevant facts about the context of their utterance, and therefore it makes clear how the truth-value of a particular utterance depends on the referents assigned to the sentence-constituents relative to this occasion of utterance. According to this conception, the statement of the truth-conditions of any context-dependent sentence will be a generalization laying down conditions for the truth of any particular utterance of this sentence. Because no such generality attaches to formulations of the truth-conditions of context-independent sentences, context-dependent sentences provide particularly sensitive tests for the correctness of a complete theory of meaning for a natural language.[38] Indeed, the theorist can even conduct experiments by uttering

---

[37] Cf. Davidson, 'Truth and Meaning', pp. 319f.
[38] Ibid., p. 320.

context-dependent sentences in carefully controlled circumstances and 'observing' what truth-values are assigned to these utterances by competent speakers of the language under study.

Despite these evident attractions, this treatment of context-dependent sentences has a major defect. It renders unintelligible the thesis that a *type-sentence* has *truth-conditions*. The truth-conditions of the sentence 'I have an IQ greater than 100' must be the *conditions* under which *this sentence* is *true*. But the proposal concedes that truth cannot be ascribed to such a type-sentence at all, only to particular utterances of it; *a fortiori*, there is no such thing as the conditions under which *it* (the type-sentence) is true. On the other hand, there are conditions under which *utterances* of such a type-sentence are true (at least if truth can be transferred from propositions to utterances). But now it is particular utterances which have truth-conditions, whereas the goal of truth-conditional semantics is to assign meanings to type-sentences. Here again, from a fresh quarter, we encounter the difficulty of making any coherent application of the phrase 'a condition of its being true' to the entities (type-sentences) which are taken to be the primary bearers of meaning in truth-conditional semantics. The method of 'relativizing truth-conditions to contexts of utterance' hides this incoherence from view, but achieves nothing more substantial.

The second strategy embraces the idea that the truth-conditions of a context-dependent sentence will be no more invariant than the truth-conditions of its tokens. This conception explicitly contends that truth-conditions belong to particular utterances of type-sentences, and that different utterances of a single type-sentence may have different truth-conditions. If, e.g., A utters the sentence 'I have an IQ greater than 100', then this utterance is true on condition that A at the time of speaking has an IQ greater than 100, while if B utters the same sentence, then the truth-condition of his utterance is the (different) condition that B has an IQ greater than 100. The generalization of this analysis yields an account of truth-conditions for context-dependent sentences which resembles Frege's conception of sense, for he held that the thought expressed by such a sentence, not merely its truth-value, varied according to the context of its utterance.[39] The rationale for these proposals is that what is asserted by the utterance of a context-dependent sentence varies with the context of its utterance. But if this is what is true or false, then anything which counts as

---

[39] This point is often misunderstood, largely under the influence of the presupposition that what Frege meant by the sense of a sentence is closely connected with what is understood as its meaning. Cf. E. J. Lemmon, 'Sentences, Statements, Propositions', in *British Analytical Philosophy*, ed. B. Williams and A. Montefiore (Routledge, London, 1966), p. 95.

a condition for *its* being true must be specific to it and different from anything called a condition for another proposition's being true (viz. the proposition expressed by the same sentence in a relevantly different context).

This proposal has very similar defects to the first one. By severing truth-conditions from type-sentences, it forecloses the possibility of identifying the *meaning* of a type-sentence with *its* truth-conditions. Even surrendering this presupposition of truth-conditional semantics would accomplish nothing. Truth-conditions could be used to assign meanings to different utterances of sentences only on condition that context-dependent sentences are radically ambiguous, i.e. that they differ in *meaning* from context to context. But that is absurd. Moreover, we are plunged back into the difficulty of making sense of the claim that the so-called specification of the truth-conditions of a particular utterance specifies *conditions* for its being true (above, pp. 191–7), and we would face fresh difficulties in trying to work out what would be the *correct* ways to make references to speakers, times, places, addressees, etc., in framing specifications of the truth-conditions of particular utterances.[40] Assigning truth-conditions to utterances instead of type-sentences does not eliminate incoherence, but simply shifts the difficulties to new locations.

The upshot of this investigation is that the standard perfunctory methods of accommodating context-dependent sentences containing indexical expressions within the framework of truth-conditional semantics are shams. This is not the consequence of some careless error that could be rectified. The underlying problem is that inconsistent demands are imposed on the notion of a truth-condition. Truth-conditions must be directly related to meanings, and equally they must be related to truth and falsity. But context-dependent sentences show that incoherence results from supposing that what has meaning is what is true or false. If truth-conditions are ascribed to the bearers of meanings (type-sentences), they are divorced from what bears truth-values (statements or utterances), whereas if they are ascribed to the bearers of truth and falsity, they are cut off from meanings. Waffle about the boundary between pragmatics and semantics or about relativizing truth-conditions to contexts distracts

[40] This is parallel to the difficulty of giving a precise general account of the conditions under which the utterance of two different sentences may be described as making the same statement. (Both projects are futile since the criteria for correctness of reports in indirect speech are purpose-relative; but of course this cannot be conceded by this form of truth-conditional semantics.)

attention from the real problem. At best it might off-load incoherence on to pragmatics just as polemics about psychologism allow theorists of meaning to put the blame on psychologists for their own muddles about understanding.

This irreparable lacuna might be shrugged off as a trivial deficiency of an otherwise admirable framework for analysing the meanings of sentences. After all, not every sentence contains indexical expressions, and there is apparently no problem about assigning truth-conditions to context-independent type-sentences. Moreover, every statement can arguably be expressed by an eternal sentence, and therefore truth-conditional semantics is capable of giving an analysis of the meaning of every sentence belonging to a proper subset of well-formed sentences of English and totality of which has the same expressive power as the entire set of English sentences. Is this not enough to vindicate a theory of meaning for a language?

This strategy of minimizing the damage is seriously misguided. One obvious objection is that the use of indexical expressions is very wide-spread, at least in English and European languages. Indeed, if tenses of verbs are counted among indexical devices (as they usually are), then virtually every sentence of English unavoidably contains indexical expressions, even such paradigms of context-independent sentences as 'Napoleon Bonaparte died on St Helena in 1825'. One might adopt the special convention of rephrasing such sentences in the present tense and regarding the whole sentence as atemporal; but it is doubtful whether such an eternal sentence is a part of the language mastered by native speakers of English, and hence it is dubious whether every statement can properly be para-phrased into an eternal sentence of English. Indeed, it might be argued that only sentences expressing atemporal or omnitemporal propositions lack indexical expressions (verb-inflections), e.g. 'Two and three make five', 'Water is a combination of hydrogen and oxygen', or 'The pressure of an enclosed gas is directly proportional to its absolute temperature'.

Matters are even worse for truth-conditional semantics. The source of the difficulty raised by sentences containing indexical expressions is that the same type-sentence may be used on different occasions to make dif-ferent assertions. But this phenomenon arises for sentences even in respect of their containing expressions which are not standardly characterized as indexical expressions. This generates a pressure to extend the notion of context-dependence, and correspondingly the notion of the context of an utterance, perhaps to the point where both become vacuous. For it is unclear where to stop short of declaring that every conceivable type-sentence is context-dependent, and that the whole state of the universe together with its history must be taken to be the context of any utterance. This would be absurd.

First steps in this direction are motivated by reflection on proper names.[41] Consider sentences incorporating such names as 'Tom', 'Dick', or 'Harry'. These names are not on lists of indexicals, yet a sentence such as 'Tom hit a six at the Oval on 4 June 1952' can obviously be used to make different statements, some of which might be true, others false. How can truth-conditional semantics account for this fact? It might claim the type-sentence to be ambiguous (because 'Tom' has as many different meanings as there are people (and cats, dogs, parrots?) called 'Tom'); or it might claim that difference in the statements made reflect differences in the full type-sentence whose elliptical form is uttered (e.g., that 'Tom hit a six . . .' may be an elliptical formulation of 'Tom Smith, the plumber who lives at The Wicket, East Short-Leg, Salop, hit a six . . .'); or finally it might contend that 'Tom' is a context-dependent expression whose reference depends on certain features of the context of its utterance (e.g. whether there is a Tom in the house or whether a particular Tom is associated by the intended audience with the topic of cricket). None of these strategies looks inviting. The first two distort the notions of ambiguity and ellipsis, while the third removes any possibility of circumscribing the parameters or dimensions of the circumstances of an utterance which are relevant to determining the referents of uttered expressions. Moreover, the difficulty is not restricted to common proper names. John Searle named a dog 'Frege' after the great logician. Knowing this fact must we now count the sentence 'Frege published *Begriffsschrift* in 1879' as ambiguous, elliptical, or context-dependent? Moreover, even if the name 'Gottlob Frege' had never been applied up to the present except to the celebrated German logician, I would still be free to bestow this name on a dog, a book, a song, or a boat and thereby create the possibility of using a sentence incorporating this expression to make different statements. Consequently, it seems, every proper name is at least potentially ambiguous, elliptical, or context-dependent.

Proper names, appropriately misconceived, are but the beginning of difficulty. The same phenomenon arises in respect of predicates. Consider the sentence 'He put out his hand and stopped the car'. If this were used to

---

[41] There are parallels for definite descriptions in connection with such a sentence as 'The beer is kept in the cellar'. Russell's theory of definite descriptions apparently demands that we treat such expressions as elliptical (e.g. for 'The beer which is brewed according to a special formula by Brouwers Ltd is kept in the cellar of St John's College, Oxford'). A more modern proposal is to list 'the' among indexical expressions.

describe a policeman on point-duty, it would convey the information that he gave a signal that a certain car should stop.[42] But if it were used to describe a child playing with his toys, it would be understood to state that he employed his hand to impede the progress of a car and bring it to a halt. Compare the sentence 'He put out his hand and stopped the train'. Said of an engine-driver in a steam locomotive, this would assert that he pulled on the brake lever and thereby initiated a mechanical process that brought the train to a standstill. Does this comparison of cases show that the 'put out his hand and stopped the car' is trebly ambiguous? Does it really leave the hearer in each context with a choice among three competing interpretations (which of course he quickly rules out because he knows, e.g., that the kinetic energy of a moving car is too great to be neutralized by the resistance of a policeman's hand)? Or is each utterance really elliptical? Or should the predicate be considered to be context-dependent in the manner of indexicals or tensed expressions? If so, is not this notion of context-dependence both distorted and stretched beyond all recognition? Again, none of those options is very attractive in itself. And there is the prospect that nearly all predicates would turn out, on further reflection, to need to be classified by this reasoning as ambiguous, elliptical, or context-dependent.[43]

If context-dependence is the preferred method for dealing with this vast range of hard cases, we might end up wondering whether there is any such thing as a context-independent sentence at all. The multifarious possibilities for using sentences such as metaphor, irony, hyperbole, rough or approximate description, novels, reports of dreams, historical fiction, science fiction, drama, examples in grammars, etc. suggest the extreme difficulty of instancing any typical everyday empirical type-sentence which cannot be used to make a variety of statements differing in truth-value. Indeed, it is doubtful whether there is any such thing as a type-sentence which invariably makes the same statement whatever the circumstances of its utterance, and it is equally doubtful whether there are any features of the world or its history which may not be relevant to specifying what is said by the utterance of some type-sentence. If truth-conditional semantics

---

[42] Contrast this with 'He put out his leg and stopped the car': this is not in the repertoire of British policemen's signals to motorists.

[43] Another interesting difficulty arises from the use of samples in communication. If I point at a ripe tomato and say 'English posting boxes are this colour', should my gesture and the tomato (or its colour) be reckoned as parts of my utterance (as symbols)? Or rather as parts of the context of my utterance of the quoted words? Some putative context-dependence might be the result of too narrow a construal of what constitutes a symbol (sentence, utterance).

is confined to 'context-independent sentences' thus construed, it seems to be a theory of meaning for the void. The same considerations that put sentences with indexical expressions outside its scope appear to bestow the same status on all sentences of natural languages. Under its aegis the category of context-dependent sentences becomes all-embracing and the notion of the context of an utterance all-inclusive. This double nonsense is symptomatic of the vanity of attempting to marry meaning and truth through the good offices of truth-conditions. Absurd it undoubtedly is to call all sentences context-dependent, and the fault lies with the theory which drives us to this conclusion.

It is platitudinous that utterances of an unambiguous type-sentence may sometimes make true statements, sometimes false ones, sometimes none at all. Yet this observation ties truth-conditional semantics into various knots. The remedy is staightforward enough, but the sufferers from these intellectual cramps are determined not to avail themselves of it. They are attached to misconceptions about meaning and truth as well as to a picture of a simple and rigid internal connection between them. Until these are surrendered and replaced by healthier conceptions, their thinking will continue to be deformed.

CHAPTER 6

Truth-Conditions: Ramifying Defects

1 In pursuit of a mirage

Up to this point our critical attention has been turned to the immediate foundations of truth-conditional semantics. We have examined its basic concepts: sentence (the bearer of truth-values and of truth-conditions), truth, and the technical concept of a truth-condition. We have argued that its explanations of these concepts are inadequate and that the various demands imposed on them are incompatible. It is nonsense to take truth-tables to be the proper explanations of the meanings of any expressions in natural languages, and the general claim that the meaning of a sentence is its truth-conditions has not even been made intelligible in spite of the vast literature constituting the science of truth-conditional semantics. What survives this criticism is merely various formal calculi whose relevance to the clarification of understanding natural languages is altogether opaque.

We now move on to a different enterprise. This is to explore some of the central implications and presuppositions of truth-conditional semantics. On the general assumption that its formal machinery does have some bearing on the concept of the meaning of an expression, truth-conditional semantics leads directly to important theses about the notion of synonymy, the differentiation of sense from nonsense, the primacy of sentences in a theory of meaning, the nature of ordinary explanations of meaning, and the concept of understanding. These topics will be severally considered with the purpose of discrediting the initial assumption by showing that it leads to absurd consequences.

Our strategy here should be distinguished from the one pursued in the previous chapter. We do not argue that truth-conditional semantics leaves lacunae in respect of synonymy, the differentiation of sense from nonsense, etc., nor that the implied doctrines about these issues are obviously incoherent. In each case, its position is tolerably clear and its claim superficially intelligible. Our complaint is rather that it systematically distorts or misrepresents concepts internally related to the concept of meaning by virtue of its implications for synonymy, the sense/nonsense distinction, etc. We aim to demonstrate that truth-conditional semantics, far from affording important insights into these issues, darkens counsel by creating confusions, multiplying paradoxes and introducing as sophisticated technical apparatus concepts that are at worst incoherent, at best useless. Our purpose is to make the myth or vision less eligible. The fanatic can dig in and defend his faith against our objections. He may argue that he proposes to replace a loose, purpose-relative, and perhaps confused notion of synonymy by a *strict* or exact one; that he offers a *rigorous* principle for distinguishing sense from nonsense; that he subjects explanations of meaning to very *demanding standards* which are not satisfied by explanations commonly accepted to be correct in everyday life; etc. We cannot expect to prise him away from these dogmas, but rather to reveal these dogmas for what they are; houses of cards that can bear no weight nor serve any purpose relevant to understanding the nature of languages. Our arguments in this chapter boil down to a single great question: Why follow the determined defender of truth-conditional semantics down that road? If the journey promises much hardship without any prospect of real benefit, would it not be wiser to look for a different way to achieve understanding of what is puzzling about the meanings of expressions in natural languages?

2 Synonymy

It is often asserted by philosophers and linguists alike that the crucial question for a semantic theory to answer is not 'What is the meaning of a sentence?' but rather 'What is the condition for two sentences to have the same meaning?'

Different lines of reasoning converge on this methodological principle. One is the familiar anxiety among philosophers about abstract entities. The phrase 'the meaning of a sentence', appropriately misunderstood, has appeared to some philosophers to signify a Platonic object. The theorist who purports to pair every sentence of a language with its meaning seems to be 'ontologically committed' to these questionable entities. By contrast, a theorist who offers only a general account of the conditions under which any pair of sentences are synonymous has apparently abstained from any such ontological excesses. At the same time, concentration on the issue of synonymy appeals strongly to linguists and even to philosophers who seek empirically testable theories of meaning. For by choosing appropriate criteria for identity of sentence-meaning, the issue of whether two sentences of a single language (or even perhaps of different languages)[1] are synonymous could be confirmed or disconfirmed by suitable experiments. Devoting attention to synonymy seems to hold out the best hope of yielding meaningful scientific theories of meaning.

Within the framework of truth-conditional semantics, the question of the synonymy of sentences boils down to the question of identity of truth-conditions. What is to be understood by sameness and difference of truth-conditions is not something open to discovery, but rather an integral part of a clarification of the concept of a truth-condition. Indeed, for philosophers who stress the importance of criteria of identity, laying down such criteria should be a central part of any adequate definition of 'truth-condition'.[2] Consequently it is somewhat surprising that so little explicit attention is given to this issue (as if the criteria of identity and difference of conditions were clear, uniform, and completely general so that identity-conditions for conditions for the truth of a sentence could be derived by instantiation!). But it is not in the least surprising that very different stipulations are adumbrated in the different major versions of truth-conditional semantics in light of the fact that they employ different concepts of truth-conditions. Our purpose is not to assess their comparative merits, but to show how misguided all the standard explanations are as theoretical reconstructions of the notion of synonymy or sameness of meaning.

One main branch of truth-conditional semantics shuns modality and confines itself to T-sentences. The truth-conditions of any sentence 'p' are stated by a biconditional ' "p" is true if and only if p'. This account hints at a conception of identity of truth-conditions which generates paradoxical consequences when used to explicate synonymy. The intelligibility of the biconditional itself presupposes, according to the canons of such truth-theories, that the biconditional asserts the material equivalence (*de facto* identity of truth-values) of ' "p" is true' with 'p'. But the acceptability of

---

[1] Some such rider may be required according to theorists who stress the importance of the concepts of idiolects and dialects in the analysis of language.

[2] Frege's explanation of his technical term 'sense' is often criticized for failing to make explicit any criteria for identity and difference of sense, and commentators' eagerness to fill in this lacuna is motivated by the conviction that 'sense' will otherwise lack any meaning (or sense!).

this assertion will, in any instance, be unaltered provided that 'p' itself is replaced by any other sentence with the same truth-value. Therefore, this version of truth-conditional semantics must concede that the truth-conditions of 'Two plus two makes four' and of 'Grass is green' are identical. More generally, it seems that any true context-independent sentence must have the same truth-conditions as any other one. But if identity of meaning reduces to identity of truth-conditions, the absurd consequence must be drawn that any two such sentences are synonymous! Some remedy is urgently needed.

The standard manoeuvre is to claim that the bare truth of a biconditional of the form ' "p" is true if and only if p' is not enough to entitle it to a place in a theory of meaning for a language; nor, indeed, is the bare truth of *every* biconditional of this form. Rather it must be shown that every such biconditional can be derived in a particular way, viz. as a theorem within a calculus whose axioms assign meanings to the semantic primitives of the language and to the basic grammatical structures of its sentences. This requirement will weed out ' "Two and two makes four" is true if and only if grass is green' from the set of the biconditionals and exclude it from a theory of meaning for English. Among the indefinitely many true biconditionals of the form ' "Two and two makes four" is true if and only if . . .', only the one completed by the sentence 'Two and two makes four' (or a synonymous sentence) will be admitted as a formulation of the truth-conditions of 'Two and two makes four'. This restrictive legislation about 'truth-condition' appears to rehabilitate identity of truth-conditions as a proper explication of sentence-synonymy.

But difficulties re-emerge at once. The first is the implication that no two sentences of a language can have the same meaning if they differ from one another in structure or if one contains a constituent for which the other has no exact counterpart. Although many philosophers accept the notion that every meaningful sentence has a unique ultimate analysis and hence cannot be synonymous with any sentence having a different ultimate analysis, the attempt to pin sentence-meanings down to unique structures and sets of constituents is both futile and obfuscating (below, pp. 327–39). The second more obvious difficulty arises from the fact that certain pairs of subsentential expressions may be interchangeable *salva veritate* in every sentence of a form that falls within the purview of a successfully constructed truth-theory. Two predicates may be co-extensional, and two singular referring expressions may co-designate. Consequently, the axioms of a theory of meaning could be altered by substituting the definition of one of those terms for that of the other, and then this altered theory, which still meets the proffered criteria of adequacy, could be used to substantiate intuitively false conclusions about synonymy. Consider, e.g., the predicates 'creature with a heart' and 'creature with a kidney', and suppose, for the sake of argument, that they are strictly co-extensional. In respect of atomic sentences and of molecular sentences formed out of truth-functional connectives and expressions of generality, there is *ex hypothesi* no possibility of distinguishing these two predicates in terms of the truth-values of the sentences in which they occur. Hence, if the axiom governing 'creature with a heart' were altered to read ' "a creature with a heart" designates a creature with a kidney', the entire theory of meaning would remain unchanged except that it would now be possible to prove as a theorem every instance of the sentence-form ' "x is a creature with a heart" is true if and only if x is a creature with a kidney'. This would demonstrate that 'Man-o'-War is a creature with a heart' has the same truth-conditions as 'Man-o'-War is a creature with a kidney' despite the evident fact that they are not synonymous. This and similar problems about co-designating referring expressions call forth further manoeuvres from truth-theorists. These we need not elaborate or criticize here. The point to note is that the problems arise in a straightforward way out of combining a T-sentence account of truth-conditions with the claim that the meaning of a sentence is its truth-conditions. The difficulty of how to distinguish between the meanings of materially equivalent sentences does not plague Everyman,[3] even if it has become the touchstone of success in constructing one form of a theory of meaning for a natural language.

The other main branch of truth-conditional semantics embraces modal concepts with gusto, viz. the various forms of possible-worlds semantics. They formulate the truth-conditions of a sentence by specifying its truth-value in every possible world, identifying its meaning with a function from possible worlds to truth-values. This obviously accounts for the possibility that sentences may differ in meaning though having the same truth-value, and similarly for the possibility that co-extensional predicates and co-designating referring expressions differ in meaning. But another familiar paradox arises from employing this concept of truth-conditions as an

---

[3] He is not typically in the business of seeking out definitions of expressions by exploring possibilities of substitutions *salva veritate*. When he requires definitions, he looks them up in a dictionary or asks another competent speaker to give explanations of what he does not understand. Explaining words is a practice which constitutes a proper part of the mastery of a language, and this practice carries within it criteria of correctness and completeness of explanations of meaning (below, pp. 233–7). Quine's scepticism about identity and difference of meaning has no foothold here at all.

explication of the synonymy of sentences. Any two sentences which have the same truth-value in each possible world have identical truth-conditions. In particular, any two sentences which are true in every possible world ('necessary truths') have the same truth-conditions, hence the same meaning. In conformity with standard interpretations of necessity, the result seems absurd. It would make each of the axioms of Euclidean geometry and every theorem of number-theory synonymous since each would frame a non-contingent and *a priori* truth. And if truth-conditions are to underpin the proper explanation of logical validity, this would have the dramatic consequence that proofs in logic and mathematics (whose constituent sentences are necessarily true or necessarily false) are totally unlike other proofs (e.g. deductions from hypotheses in empirical science).[4] The standard response to this dilemma is to seek stricter criteria for identity of truth-conditions. One manoeuvre is to exploit a stronger notion of necessity,[5] another is to incorporate a requirement for identity of sentence-structure into the conditions for identity of truth-conditions.[6] Here again the further intricacies of possible-worlds semantics are of no immediate interest. The point to note is that these problems too arise naturally out of a specific theoretical framework. The difficulties of distinguishing among the meanings of sentences formulating different necessary truths or of explaining the cogency of proofs in Euclidean geometry are difficulties only for a theorist who has already accepted possible worlds as the key to clarifying the meanings of sentences.

Truth-conditional semantics in either main form yields disquieting results about the synonymy of sentences. Since one of its main planks is that the meanings of words are to be explained in terms of their contributions to the sentences in which they occur (by 'relativization of the truth-conditions of sentences to sentence-constituents'), these difficulties carry over immediately from the synonymy of sentences to that of words and phrases. One version has problems differentiating the meanings of co-extensional predicates and co-designating referring expressions while the other labours with similar problems about necessarily co-extensional predicates and necessarily co-designating names. These are sore

---

[4] This appeared as an overt doctrine in the *Tractatus*.

[5] Dummett ascribes this strategy to Frege in suggesting that his concept of sense is an essentially cognitive notion (M. A. E. Dummett, *Frege: Philosophy of Language* (Duckworth, London, 1973), pp. 632ff.).

[6] The *locus classicus* is the explanation of 'intensional isomorphism' in R. Carnap, *Meaning and Necessity*, 2nd edn (Chicago University Press, Chicago, 1956), §§14f.

difficulties. Attempts to find their solutions call forth a wealth of technical apparatus whose efficacy and coherence are both questionable.

Even worse problems follow close behind. Since the meanings of words (and phrases) are to be related directly to the truth-conditions of sentences in which they occur, the criterion of identity of word-meaning must involve generalizations over all sentences in which a given word can legitimately occur. It follows immediately that two words cannot possibly have the same meaning if one may occur in a sentence-frame which will not accept the other; e.g. that 'table' and 'schedule' differ in meaning since we may speak of a schedule of Saturday trains to London, but not of a 'table of trains' (rather of a 'time-table of trains'). Likewise, two words differ in meaning if there is any sentence-frame in which the substitution of one for the other, though grammatically permissible, alters the truth-value of what is stated. (Such pairs of sentences constitute the 'minimum-contrast pairs' beloved of linguists building semantic theories.) This is a very stringent condition indeed. Consider the preposition 'on' and the prepositional phrase 'on top of'. Cursory reflection might lead one to conclude that they are synonyms since, e.g., 'The *Tractatus* is on my desk' and 'The *Tractatus* is on top of my desk' seem to make the same assertion. But this illusion is dispelled once for all by noting that 'Hillary is on Everest' and 'Hillary is on top of Everest' could, in the situation that Hillary is a thousand feet below the summit, be used to make two different statements, one true and the other false. *Ceteris paribus*, a single discrepancy of this kind establishes an incontrovertible difference of meaning. According to truth-conditional semantics identity and difference of meaning is an all-or-nothing matter. It is a clear implication of this conception that there are very few synonyms at all, certainly far fewer than competent speakers of a language are inclined to believe or than a thesaurus lists. It becomes a complex and controversial question for philosophers and linguists whether *any* two expressions in *any* natural language are synonyms. Without the ability to survey all possible sentence-frames and all conceivable circumstances of their utterance, this issue seems to debar semantic theories from conclusively establishing any positive results. Synonymy is conceived to be absolute. The claim that two expressions are synonymous entails an unrestricted generalization about an indefinitely large set of sentence-frames.

Even this striking thesis does not exhaust the implications of truth-conditional semantics for the conception of identity and difference of meaning. The pattern of argument demonstrating unsuspected differences of meanings between words can be used in reverse gear to reveal undetected differences of meanings between sentences. This reasoning exploits the compositional principle which is a main part of the *raison d'être* of truth-conditional semantics. According to this idea, the meaning of a sentence can be compounded out of the meanings of its parts in accordance with its structure; its truth-conditions can be determined from a knowledge of its structure and a proper specification of the meanings of its constituents (a semantic lexicon). It is this essential complexity of the meaning of a sentence that makes it possible to understand all the utterances of a language. The corollary of this compositional principle is that two expressions differing in meaning make different contributions to the meanings of all the sentences in which they occur.[7] Hence the substitution of one of two such expressions for the other in any sentence must, barring the production of nonsense, yield another sentence differing in meaning from the original (unless this difference is neutralized by another correlative change, e.g. the cancellation of a passive/active transformation by subject/predicate inversion). In the case of minimum-contrast pairs, it follows that the two sentences cannot be synonymous. The difference in meaning earlier demonstrated between 'on' and 'on top of' will, e.g., manifest itself in an (imperceptible) difference in meaning between 'The book is on the desk' and 'The book is on top of the desk'! Not only are there a myriad of unsuspected differences in meaning between words or phrases commonly taken to be synonymous, but also these differences reappear as differences in sentences widely thought by competent speakers to be synonymous (and unconditionally interchangeable).[8] Unless this conclusion is warded off by postulating a host of ambiguities among apparently unambiguous expressions, compositionalism of sentence-meaning must be abandoned and with it a large measure of the attractiveness of truth-conditional semantics.

At this point two avenues open up. The one taken by theorists of meaning is to conclude that the question of synonymy is a recherché *theoretical* question whose solution calls for a battery of concepts and techniques not available to the competent speaker of a language. His impressions about identity and difference of meaning deserve no serious

---

[7] Frege escaped from this absurdity to the extent that he exploited function/argument decomposition in the analysis of the *senses* of sentences. For, although taking different values for a single argument demands that a difference between functions be acknowledged, it does not follow that two distinct functions must have different values for *every* admissible argument!

[8] A parallel oddity is visible in Frege's doctrine that an expression which has any borderline cases of application deprives *every* sentence in which it occurs of a truth-value. (Vagueness he viewed as a deadly contagion.)

respect; they will be superseded by precise verdicts within a rigorous theory. So too will his instancing of synonyms and his explanations of the meanings of expressions. These are all fallible indications of how he uses expressions and will be replaced by a thorough account. Support for this contention will be garnered from the fact that speakers are willing to concede that their explanations of word-meanings are not fully adequate because they do not cater for all conceivable circumstances for using expressions or for all significant combinations with other expressions. Having been softened up, the reflective speaker may agree with the theorist that synonymy must be unearthed by painstaking research and that it is not transparent even to well-informed speakers of a language. Explanations of meaning are heavily discounted, while hypotheses within theories of meaning are sold at a premium.

The opposite approach is to treat the divergence between Everyman's judgments about synonymy and the deliverances of truth-conditional semantics as a symptom of deep misconceptions among theorists of meaning. According to this diagnosis, there is a progressive sublimation of the notion of synonymy which ends in a complete distortion of this familiar concept. This is evident from the fact that the theorist must find fault not only with the individual speaker's impromptu explanations of what expressions mean, but also with the institutionalized paradigms of correct explanation, viz. dictionary definitions. These take many different forms, none of which certifies that the defining word or phrase can significantly be substituted for the defined word in *every* sentence-frame or that this substitution will in *any* sentence preserve what is said relative to any conceivable context of utterance. To explain 'black', e.g., as meaning 'of the colour of soot or coal' is perfectly correct even though it fails to account for the anomalousness of the phrase 'black light' and even though it might be incomprehensible to a person unfamiliar with either soot or coal. The suspicion of inadequacy of such a definition arises from misrepresenting the purposes of dictionaries. The criterion for adequacy is that the *definiens* should standardly be substitutable for the *definiendum*. Otherwise the definition would be useless as a general instruction about how the *definiendum* is to be used. But such a licence for substitution is *defeasible*. There are general heads of exception to legitimate substitution, e.g. in certain direct questions; the question 'Are flying foxes canine herbivores?' is not the same question as 'Are the large diurnal fruit-eating bats of South-East Asia canine herbivores?', nor is the question 'Are flying foxes bats?' the same as the question 'Are the large fruit-eating bats of South-East Asia bats?'. And there are often localized or specific heads of exception as well; e.g. in the phrase 'on schedule', the word 'time-table' or 'tabular statement' cannot be substituted for the word 'schedule' despite a high degree of interchangeability in other expression-frames. The activities of compiling and consulting dictionaries take place against this general background. The compiler has the purpose of directing a speaker on how to use an expression correctly by calling attention to generally applicable equivalences with other expressions and to significant general features of its standard applications. The speaker who understands how to make use of dictionary entries is apprised of this purpose and treats the definitions accordingly. Both rightly take dictionary entries to provide paradigms of *synonymity* (of words with words or phrases, often too of phrases with phrases or of sentences with sentences). And both recognize that these definitions do *not* indefeasibly license substitutions. Truth-conditional semantics, however, treats the conjunction of these two propositions as an inconsistency! This is manifest proof of a distortion of the concept of synonymy. The source of this perversion is the striving after generality. Accepting, as we all do, that a definition is better *ceteris paribus* the more general it is in its applicability, the theorist fixes his eye on the 'ideal' of a definition in principle completely general in its application and then condemns all actual explanations of meaning as defective by this elevated standard. But the charge of being defective sticks only if our purpose in constructing dictionaries were to attain an absolute licence for verbal substitutions (which it is not). Indeed, the notion that such an unconditional licence would be the ideal form of a definition presupposes that it makes sense to suppose oneself to possess something of the sort (which it does not). The idea of synonymy in truth-conditional semantics is nonsense masquerading as the acme of scientific rigour.

To illuminate the nature of this error we will first resort to an analogy. One main role of dictionary definitions or lists of synonyms is to facilitate paraphrasing or substitutions of certain expressions for others (e.g. to avoid inelegant repetitions or to replace a word not understood or misunderstood by a speaker). This situation is comparable to making a purchase with a pound note or to converting sterling into French francs. In both cases the activity is undertaken for specific purposes. Moreover, in cashing in one expression for another, as in buying goods or currency, the 'rate of exchange' may vary from time to time or place to place. We may legitimately speak of the purchasing power of one pound even though it might buy more eggs from a farmer than from a grocer at Land's End, more roubles on a Moscow street corner than in a bank, or fewer eggs today than last week. All of these are familiar features of the use of currency. Somebody who cited them in support of the thesis that it made no sense to speak of '*the* value or the purchasing power of a pound' or even of '*the* current rate of exchange of sterling into roubles' would make himself look ridiculous, as too would somebody who introduced a theoretical entity ('the value of a pound') which was a relation between a place, a time, two persons, and a parcel of medium-size dry goods, and hence would have variable representations or manifestations. Truth-conditional semantics is forced into one or another contortion parallel to those by its misconceptions about synonymy.

The perpetuation of absurdity can be avoided only by a fundamental reorientation in the approach to identity of meaning. It is a nearly universal preconception among philosophers and linguists that strict synonymy between any pair of expressions is a relation which must be absolute, once-for-all determined in advance, and independent of context of utterance and speakers' purposes. Any other conception is unimaginable. It is with a sense of shock that one reads this passage:

'Can he speak?' under [certain] circumstances means 'Is his throat all right?', under others (e.g., if he is a small child) it means 'Has he learned to speak?' . . . The question whether 'He can continue [the series, 2, 4, 6, 8 . . .]' means the same as 'He knows the formula $[A_n = 2n]$' can be answered in several different ways; we can say 'They don't mean the same', i.e., they are not in general used as synonyms . . .; or we may say '*Under certain circumstances* "He can continue . . ." means he knew the formula.'[9]

For identity and difference of meaning are not regarded as relative to circumstance and there are clearly situations in which utterance of these sentences would make different statements.[10] Like objections are raised against claims of sentence-synonymy. Should the thesis that 'I wonder whether Smith has come' is typically synonymous with 'Has Smith come?' be denied because the first sentence may be offered in answer to the question 'What are you wondering?' or because there is no parallel equivalence between the sentences 'He wonders whether Smith has come' and 'Has Smith come?'? In all these cases we are strongly tempted to set our faces against the idea that such explanations by paraphrase are proper explanations of the meanings of expressions. Local interchangeability of

---

[9] L. Wittgenstein, *The Blue and Brown Books* (Blackwell, Oxford, 1958), pp. 114f.

[10] Of course, it will be objected that one must distinguish utterer's meaning from utterance meaning in such contexts. We postpone criticism of this futile manoeuvre (below, pp. 222–3).

expressions, even when this holds with a fair degree of generality, seems too little to authorize identification of meanings. Here again the source of this denial is neglect of the purposes for which synonyms and explanations are sought and given. It is basic to communication that the same thing may correctly be said in different words. Dictionary definitions and the standard practice of explaining words (including ostensive definitions) do, with greater or less degrees of generality, instruct speakers on how to do this. Truth-conditional semantics, in abstracting from these considerations, imports a bogus and incoherent criterion for correctness of explanations and statements of synonymy.

It is instructive to compare this false conception of synonymy with the equally misguided notion of determinacy of sense familiar from Frege's philosophy and prominent in the *Tractatus*.[11] In both cases a familiar, purpose relative, eminently useful concept (synonymy, exactness) is distorted out of all recognition. What we ordinarily take to be an exact concept is not really so, because we can imagine circumstances in which there would be borderline cases of its application. And what we ordinarily, relative to standard contexts, take to be synonyms are not really so, because we can imagine contexts in which intersubstitution would affect sense. So, under the guise of a proper analysis of synonymity (or exactness), we are offered an improved or ideal concept. (It might even be put forward as a technical concept, useful for special 'theoretical' purposes.) Thus a concept is held to be exact only if it is determined for any possible object in any possible circumstance, whether it falls under it or not; and two terms are synonymous only if they are interchangeable in every possible context. But what we are offered as an ideal is not only not an improvement over our ordinary concept (since it does not do the same job better), but it is incoherent. There is no such thing as determinacy of sense as understood by the *Tractatus*. And so too, there is no such thing as synonymy as interpreted by truth-conditional theorists.

The consequences of this distortion ramify widely in modern philosophy. In particular, it fosters a wholly unwarranted scepticism about establishing statements of synonymy and about the worth of accepted explanations of meaning. This in turn gives succour to the modern dogmas derived from Quine, the rejection of the analytic/synthetic distinction and the thesis of the indeterminacy of translation. These do incalculable harm, diverting philosophers into the activity of constructing theories

---

[11] For a detailed criticism of the ideal of determinacy of sense, see G. P. Baker and P. M. S. Hacker, *Wittgenstein: Understanding and Meaning* (Blackwell, Oxford, 1980), pp. 367ff.

instead of clarifying the concepts (such as that of synonymy!) from which their puzzlements arise.

3 Circumstance-dependence of meaning

The misconception about the absolute nature of synonymy which typifies truth-conditional semantics is not an isolated quirk; rather it reflects a general double presupposition about meaning. First, that meanings (truth-conditions) are the property of type-sentences; even a context-dependent type-sentence is typically held to have a unique set of truth-conditions although different tokens may be used in different circumstances to make different statements.[12] Second, that the meaning of a sentence is invariant (except in cases of ambiguity); in particular, its meaning is independent of matters of fact and of all features of the contexts in which tokens of it may be produced. A competent speaker can establish what an utterance means solely on the basis of his knowledge of the semantic rules of a language, and this knowledge is in principle independent of any knowledge about the occasion of the utterance and of any general or specific empirical knowledge. Typically the truth-conditions of a type-sentence together with the context of its utterance determine what it is used to assert, and what is asserted together with the relevant facts determine the actual truth-value of the utterance. In this way, the possibilities of truth and falsity serve as the permanent backdrop to ascertaining the actual truth or falsity of speakers' statements.

This general picture of 'how language works' contains a multitude of dubious assumptions and implications. But for the moment we focus exclusively on the notion that meanings are invariants of (unambiguous) type-expressions. Despite considerable plausibility, this doctrine leads to absurdity. Its defence requires the wholesale postulation of ambiguity or else the denial that the great majority of intelligible utterances can be said to have meanings at all. Difficulties are most obviously generated by the correlative doctrine that whether a sentence has sense or is nonsensical is a distinction that can be drawn absolutely sharply and once-for-all, but other problems are not far from the surface.

The idea that meanings are invariants of type-expressions has an extensive and prestigious ancestry. It is supported by the widespread assump-

[12] Correspondingly, meanings are ascribed to type-words and type-phrases; even an indexical expression such as 'I' or 'this' is held to have a single invariant meaning although what the referent of a particular token is depends on features of the context.

tion that the meanings of words (and some phrases) are laid down by linguistic conventions or semantic rules. These are assigned definitively in advance of observations or experience. Compositionalism apparently guarantees that any well-formed expression has a meaning (or definite range of possible meanings) laid up in the totality of the meaning-rules for the semantic primitives of a language. In particular, combinatory rules can in principle be framed which will draw a precise boundary once-for-all between nonsensical and meaningful sentences.[13] Hence, according to truth-conditional semantics, a determinate set of strictly linguistic conventions generates absolute bounds of sense for all possible expressions of a language.

The *Tractatus* advanced this conception in the strongest possible form. Its doctrine of analysis had the corollary that the bounds of sense could be drawn timelessly for every possible language. Wittgenstein explicitly noted the implications that whether one sentence has a sense cannot depend on whether another proposition is true or false and that every sentence has a sense that is independent of all matters of fact.[14] Logical positivists offered a similar account, often without any overt commitment to the doctrine of the uniqueness of analysis into 'logical atoms'. Waismann emphasized the sharpness of the boundary between the semantic rules ('grammar') of a language and their applications.[15] He likened the establishment of the grammar of a language to the setting up of a system of measurement and the calibration of its instruments. This settles what it makes sense to say about the relevant measurements of objects. But the actual truth or falsity of particular propositions, like the ascertaining of the dimensions of objects, typically depends on the outcome of particular procedures of comparing objects with instruments of the metric system. In principle, the setting up of the system could be completed at an instant, but its applications would spread out indefinitely into the future.[16] Other positivists compared the assigning of truth-conditions to a sentence through semantic rules to the building of an experimental apparatus in physics, while the determination of the actual truth or falsity of this sentence parallels running the experiment and noting the result.[17] To

[13] Of course, these rules might undergo changes, in which case there would be a fresh but no less definitive reclassification of expressions into the meaningful and the nonsensical.

[14] Wittgenstein, *Tractatus*, 2.0211, 4.061.

[15] F. Waismann, *Principles of Linguistic Philosophy*, (Macmillan, London, 1965), pp. 13f., 39f.

[16] These remarks echo ideas prominent in Wittgenstein's writings in the early 1930s.

[17] Cf. M. Schlick, 'Positivismus und Realismus', in *Gesammelte Aufsätze* (George Olms Verlag, Hildesheim, 1969), pp. 89ff.

understand a sentence is to know what would be the case if it were true, and to verify it is to find out whether this possibility is realized. A full set of linguistic conventions for a language will authoritatively divide sense from nonsense.

This doctrine of meaning as an invariant of type-sentences is an explicit component of modern truth-conditional semantics. It is a perspicuous aspect of possible-world semantics since the sense or intension of a sentence is identified with a function from possible worlds to truth-values. It is likewise a feature of semantics based on Tarskian T-sentences: there it is a corollary of the compositional conception of the sense of a sentence. Such a semantic theory requires that the sense of a sentence be determined by its structure and the meanings of its constituents, for it demands that the lexicon for the primitives together with the rules for computing the semantic values of compound expressions suffice for the derivation of every sentence of the form ' "p" is true if and only if p'. Consequently a sentence is ascribed a sense in such a theory only if its truth-conditions can be computed *a priori* from a finite set of axioms and the specifications of a finite set of operations. The grip of this compositional conception of sentence-meaning is very firm. This accounts for many aspects of modern philosophy of language. Despite disagreement about how to analyse definite descriptions, there is an underlying consensus that such expressions have fixed meanings independently of whether they denote or refer to anything, presumably grounded in the observation that they are typically constructed out of meaningful components (e.g. 'the present king of France'); to suggest that such a phrase as 'the round square' lacks meaning would be heterodox.[18] Similarly, there is a common reaction of shock and indignation to Wittgenstein's account of first-person 'avowals'; we are prone to argue that 'I have a toothache' *must* have truth-conditions simply because its parts have meanings and because the parallel sentence 'He has a toothache' is typically used to make an assertion, and we are inclined to make this claim with absolute conviction in advance of investigating how the sentence 'I have a toothache' is employed and even independently of looking to see whether it has any conceivable use at all. It would be a mortal blow to faith in compositionalism to entertain the least doubt whether the intelligibility of a sentence might depend on any factors other than its mode of composition out of meaningful constituents. If meaning

---

[18] Is it meaningful because it indicates a possible entity which happens not to exist? Or does it indicate an impossible entity which is as it were a genuine possibility that is impossible?

were admitted not to be an invariant of type-sentences, the principle that the meaning of a sentence is its truth-conditions would be stone dead.

Like any powerful myth about concepts, this one is not wholly lacking in support. Apart from a strong attachment to compositionalism there are some more immediate and less suspect considerations. Perhaps the most obvious is familiarity with dictionaries. These contain entries for most type-words, and under each word there is one or more explanations of how it is to be understood or used correctly, some of which may be restricted to certain contexts. Yet, however many explanations may be listed and whatever restrictions may be mentioned, each sub-entry is meant to characterize the standard employment of a type-expression. There is no such thing as an explanation of the meaning of an expression which in principle is applicable only to a single token; it is type-expressions that are explained or defined. A related point is that explanations of meanings of words resemble rules and, like typical rules, are not beholden to the facts. Their applicability may depend on contingencies, but not their content. Since explanations are in this sense unconditional, so too is what is established by them, viz. the meanings of words. A third important consideration is the distinction between explanations of meaning and general knowledge (collateral information) about the phenomena associated with words (e.g. what is denoted or connoted by them).[19] A botanist, e.g., may know far more about trees than a layman, or a physicist may possess an optical theory about colours unavailable to a child, but it does not follow at all that the botanist understands the word 'tree' better than a trial lawyer, or that the physicist has some special insight into the meanings of the terms 'red' and 'green'.[20] The amassing of factual information is typically distinct from clarifying the meanings of expressions, and though factual discoveries may lead to a shift in meanings of certain terms, such discoveries are not themselves discoveries about the 'real meanings' of terms.

[19] Of late this distinction has been under increasing attack. It is blurred or rejected by those impressed by Quine's criticism of the analytic/synthetic distinction. Furthermore Putnam and Kripke have elaborated influential accounts of natural kinds according to which scientific research, by revealing the essential natures of things, gradually unfolds what words like 'gold' or 'horse' have meant all along. These misguided ideas all rest on ignoring the internal relations between meanings and explanations of meaning (below, pp. 235–7).

[20] It is common for theorists to borrow terms current in Everyman's discourse and to use them in accord with explicit redefinitions in the context of theory-construction, e.g. the terms 'circle' or 'parallel' in geometry or 'fruit' and 'petal' in botany. The theorist of course does have a privileged status in declaring what such semi-technical terms mean in the context of his theories, but this does not extend to the use of the same expressions in everyday parlance.

Despite this support, some genuine and some spurious, the doctrine that meanings are invariants of type-sentences is bizarre. It raises many *prima facie* objections. First, the doctrine of invariance faces a range of specific difficulties generated by familiar uses of sentences for what might be called 'secondary purposes'. These cases include irony, hyperbole, indirect speech-acts (e.g. 'It's so hot in here' uttered with the purpose of requesting somebody to open a window), and expressions half-way to becoming institutionalized idioms (perhaps, e.g., 'He is now pushing up the daisies'). Some protective reaction is required, standardly a distinction between utterer's meaning and utterance-meaning. A second idea is that dependence of interpretation of utterances on circumstances should be acknowledged in respect only of secondary uses of language and used as the distinguishing mark of such utterances. Theorists commonly differentiate metaphors from literal utterances by the putative necessity of invoking extralinguistic knowledge in order to find the appropriate 'interpretations'. It is claimed, e.g., that the utterance 'The chairman was a wolf among sheep' presupposes general knowledge or standard beliefs about animal behaviour unlike a paradigmatic literal utterance (e.g. 'The cat is on the mat'). According to this doctrine, irrelevance of circumstantial knowledge to clarifying the import of an utterance serves to isolate just those serious fact-stating uses of language the analysis of which theorists take to be their primary business.

These responses to obvious objections to the dogma that meaning is a circumstance-invariant feature of type-sentences mix much nonsense with very little sense. The first extrapolates from and distorts a distinction *sometimes* drawn between what a speaker meant by saying something and what his utterance meant.[21] In most conversational exchanges a competent speaker will be master of what his interlocutor has said (that he has asked what time it is, threatened to break off cooperation unless . . ., predicted that this government will fall, etc.), and hence somebody who asks 'What does that mean?' will probably wish to be informed what his interlocutor has said. If a French plumber tells me that he realizes that he promised to have the kitchen sink installed three weeks earlier and then adds, with a shrug of the shoulders, 'Mais il y a des ronces', my conversational *savoir faire* will hardly be improved by the information that the sentence means 'But there are briars', while it would be much furthered by somebody who told me that he was excusing his failure by saying that he was subject to many competing obligations or distractions. It is with such cases that

----

[21] Or means (timelessly).

theorists explain their differentiation of utterer's meaning from utterance meaning. The latter is claimed to be an invariant of a single unambiguous type-sentence, whereas the former may vary from token to token of such a sentence (differing, e.g., between the plumber's use of 'Mais il y a des ronces' to offer an excuse and my use of the same sentence in describing the hedge around my vegetable plot). Apparently, the paradigm for specifying utterer's meaning is an indirect statement (question, command) which fills out the sentence-frame 'He meant that . . .', 'He wished to say that . . .' ('Il a voulu dire que . . .'). In most cases this will simply be a matter of saying what the speaker said (since standardly speakers say what they mean), i.e. giving a correct report of his utterance in *oratio obliqua*, but in some cases there may be a divergence (especially if the speaker himself explains what he meant by a particular utterance). None of these humdrum observations, however, guarantees the intelligibility or the point of *theorists'* distinguishing utterer's meaning from utterance meaning and their applying this distinction to all utterances. For it is unclear how to relate utterer's meaning to the statement made by an utterance, and it is far from obvious that there is any such thing as *the* (unique) utterer's meaning for any utterance (since in most circumstances many divergent reports in *oratio obliqua* are acknowledged to be correct). Still worse, the clear separation of utterer's meaning from utterance meaning undermines the theorists' own purpose in drawing the distinction. The ostensible point of insisting on an invariant utterance meaning underlying variable utterer's meanings (e.g. of 'Il y a des ronces') is to defend the thesis that a semantic theory has as its proper concern the assignment of meanings to type-sentences. But the stronger the case for distinguishing utterer's meaning from utterance meaning (e.g. the plumber's excuse), the less plausible the contention that utterance meaning (e.g. 'There are briars') plays a crucial role in communication (in ascertaining what a speaker has said or meant to say). This is an exemplary instance of a Pyrrhic victory: the clarity of the concept of utterer's meaning is inversely proportional to its relevance to illuminating the concept of understanding.

The second response is equally misguided. It is false that factual information is important for the correct 'interpretation' only of secondary uses of language such as metaphor, irony, indirect speech-acts, etc. Such information is crucial for a proper understanding of paradigmatic literal utterances. Grasping what is asserted by somebody who says 'The cat is on the mat' rests on background presuppositions about the orientation of the mat and of the cat relative to the mat – presuppositions which would not be fulfilled in a satellite orbiting the earth. Understanding the utterance 'The policeman raised his hand and stopped the oncoming car' draws in obvious ways on knowledge of car mechanics, kinematics, and conventions about signalling. Such cases are ubiquitous. Moreover, the multiple dependencies of the 'interpretation' of literal utterances on background information accounts for the relative ease of imagining circumstances for which standard explanations of meaning are not tailored.[22] Conversely, concocting such far-fetched possibilities is a powerful method for clarifying what is taken for granted in the explanation and employment of familiar and apparently transparent expressions.

These objections suggest that the dogma that meanings are invariants of type-expressions is itself indefensible. *Prima facie* counter-arguments must be sustained. This negative conclusion can be strengthened by reflecting on an immediate corollary of the central dogma, namely that the distinction between sense and nonsense is absolute and independent of the circumstances surrounding an utterance. Although this doctrine has some initial plausibility together with the cachet of philosophical respectability, it seems to crumble away under critical reflection.

Obvious objections arise in respect of everyday uses of language. Suppose I am sitting in a room with an open door giving on to another room and that I am so placed that the north-east corner of the second room is visible. I might report 'I see Smith standing in the north-east corner of that room'. But suppose somebody else uttered this sentence with his back turned to the door or standing in a position from which he could not see into the other room at all, *must* we conclude that he said something intelligible (but false), even if he *regularly* made such bizarre utterances in all apparent good faith? Or should we allow that whether an utterance makes sense may depend on the spatial location of the speaker? Again, consider this case: I bore a hole six inches in diameter into the ground, reach my arm down the hole, and declare 'I feel water two feet down'. This assertion would obviously be intelligible, and I might support it by displaying my wet hand. But suppose I uttered the same sentence in the same situation although the arm that I thrust down the hole had been amputated at the elbow. Or suppose that I had said instead 'I feel water ten feet down'. Would these utterances make sense? What would count as evidence for or against what is stated? If *any* sentence of this form makes sense, what is the

---

[22] This point is stressed in Waismann's celebrated notion of the open texture of empirical concepts (F. Waismann, 'Verifiability', in *Logic and Language, First Series*, ed. A. Flew (Blackwell, Oxford, 1960), pp. 117ff.). Many examples are familiar from Wittgenstein's writings, e.g. the criteria for personal identity and suffering toothache in another's tooth (*Blue and Brown Books*, pp. 52f., 61f.).

connection between uttering a sentence with a sense and saying something intelligible? Or between uttering a sentence with a sense and saying something which could be true? Does it just happen that nobody as a matter of fact can use the sentence, 'I feel water 10^{10} feet down' to make a true assertion? Would it not be more cogent to maintain that whether somebody's utterance makes sense may depend on the circumstances in which it is made? On this view a person with a four-foot-long arm could use the sentence 'I feel water four feet down' to make an immediately intelligible assertion although more ordinarily proportioned human beings could not do so (in the envisaged situation). In general, whether a sign makes sense depends on the circumstances of its use. Musical notation offers an attractive illustration of this point: the fact that an oboe can play only one note at a time renders nonsensical the occurrence of a triad in the oboe part of an orchestral score, even though the same chord might be an unproblematic part of a score for guitar or piano. Again, reflect on the sentence 'I can feel a pink quartz crystal'; one can *see* pink quartz crystals, but can one *feel* one? Is this not as absurd as hearing a smell? The answer is – it depends on the circumstances. If one is told that a bag contains polished marbles and rough pink quartz crystals, and that one should insert one's hand, pick up the first object one touches in the bag, and without looking, say what one has in one's hand, then the utterance makes perfectly good sense. The idea that the sense/nonsense distinction is circumstance-relative seems altogether natural, and it avoids the contortions necessary to defend the antithetical orthodoxy.

These observations are greatly reinforced by reflecting on more complex uses of expressions. The theorist's official picture is that every utterance is an instance of a type-sentence whose meaning is laid down by unconditional rules and that what is said depends on a systematic interaction of this invariant meaning with features of the context of utterance. This leads to an absurd extension of the notion of the context of utterance and a fundamental misconception about explanation in support of a ludicrous once-for-all differentiation of sense from nonsense. Though these defects are apparent even in respect of simple literal assertions, they become more glaring in other cases. We shall consider but a few instances.

The over-extension of the concept of context becomes transparent from considering utterances manifesting certain social conventions and utterances incorporating allusions. Suppose an MP were to shout 'The honourable and gallant member is a cowardly liar!' To the uninitiated in parliamentary ritual, this might pass for a self-contradiction. But to the knowledgeable, it is a plain insult couched in the correct mode of address.

Should this sentence be accounted self-contradictory in sense and then its use on this occasion as an insult be explained by the fact that this sense is modified in this context by the presence of an operative custom of addressing others which cancels out part of its content? Allusion calls for a similar manoeuvre. Consider this remark:

I don't like dogs: I always expect them to go mad. A lady once asked me for a motto for her dog Spot. I proposed *Out, damned Spot!*, but strange enough she didn't think it sentimental enough.[23]

The joke would obviously be lost on somebody who was unfamiliar with the mad-scene in *Macbeth*. He would not fully understand the third sentence, and he would miss the relevance of the first to the third. The only alternative to allowing the *meanings* of these two utterances to depend on an implicit reference to *Macbeth* would be to treat the existence of the text of this play as part of the *context* of Sydney Smith's joke and to hold that this extrinsic factor bestows a significance in addition to its literal meaning. To pursue this general strategy would require expanding the notion of context of utterance to encompass the whole present state of the world together with its entire history. This would distort the concept of context beyond recognition. And it would be futile too, since there would be no such thing as a complete specification of the context of an utterance and hence nothing which could be used mechanically to calculate what a speaker said from a specification of the meaning of the type-sentence that he uttered.

Sophisticated descriptions of painting, music, landscapes, wines, faces, etc. exemplify a completely different form of circumstance-dependence of intelligibility. Consider this account of the painting of Piero della Francesca:

He starts his exploration from the high, bright plateau of gothic painting, whereas Vermeer emerges from the shadows of Caravaggio. The light which illuminates Piero's figures casts no dark shadows . . . and the decorative unity of the surface is unbroken; middle tones tell as darks, and very slight transitions from one light tone to another have an extraordinarily poignant effect.[24]

This whole passage would mean very little to anybody who was unacquainted with the relevant aspects of Western art. This is not simply

---

[23] Hesketh Pearson, *The Smith of Smiths* (Folio Society, London, 1977), p. 248.
[24] K. Clark, *Piero della Francesca*, 2nd edn (Phaidon, Oxford, 1969), p. 24.

because of references to Vermeer, Caravaggio, and Piero, nor even because of 'allusions' to their paintings. Rather, the crucial point is that such terms as 'gothic painting', 'the decorative unity of the surface', 'middle tones', and perhaps even 'the shadows of Caravaggio' ('chiaroscuro') are themselves to be explained only by reference to *paradigms*. In the absence of these, there would be no such thing as an explanation of these expressions. Consequently, the intelligibility of this passage is not unconditional. It directly depends on the availability of relevant paradigms (as well as on having reflected on these paradigms under appropriate critical guidance). Were the paradigms to be completely snuffed out, the passage, which now makes good sense to the properly educated, would cease to make (much) sense. Such a fall from grace has now in fact befallen many ancient descriptions of ancient art (e.g. the detailed discussion of musical harmony in Plato's *Republic*). Any explanations of meaning which incorporate paradigms introduce a form of circumstance-dependence of intelligibility which cannot be assigned to the mediation of context between the meaning of an utterance and what it is used to say. Nor can this form of explanation be ignored in any viable analysis of the concepts of meaning and understanding.

Metaphor raises the most telling obstacle to the once-for-all absolute differentiation of sense from nonsense. Although many metaphorical utterances could be used in suitable circumstances to make literal assertions (e.g. 'He is as thick as a brick'), it is a distinctive feature of many metaphors that they violate category restrictions. It makes no sense to say that one can drink laughter, yet we understand the aphorism 'Laughter is the wine of life'. One cannot quaff music, yet it is intelligibly said to be the cordial of a troubled mind. One cannot eat it, but it was correctly observed that 'generally music feedeth that disposition of the spirits which it findeth'. Artistic ingenuity and originality is manifest in the creation of such striking metaphors. If a theorist were to ascribe a sense to any sentence that might be used for some communicative purpose, it would be difficult to identify any nonsense at all and difficult to state what the sense of many expressions is. Unlikely candidates might turn out to have sense; e.g. Wordsworth used the phrase 'the marble index of a mind for ever voyaging through strange seas of thought – alone' to describe the statue of Newton in Trinity College, Cambridge, even though independently of this known circumstance it seems improbable that anybody could have indicated any situation in which utterance of this phrase would have amounted to an intelligible description of anything. On the other hand, were a theorist to concede that an intelligible metaphor might be nonsensical, he would have lost his match by scoring an own-goal. For if competent speakers can correctly specify what was said in spite of the fact that the sentence uttered lacked any sense, then their ability to do so cannot *in general* depend on their calculating what somebody has said from the sense of what he has uttered! And once non-inferential knowledge of what is said is admitted as a possibility, it is no longer clear why this possibility is not often realized even in cases where the theorist succeeds in ascribing a sense or meaning to the utterance. The fact that readily intelligible metaphors violate *prima facie* category-restrictions suggests either that knowledge of what is said need not be inferred from the meaning of a type-sentence or that the boundary between sense and nonsense depends on the circumstances in which an utterance is made. Once the first alternative is conceded, the rationale for denying the second evaporates.

The upshot of these considerations is a revelation of the patent absurdity of the picture which calls forth the doctrine of the circumstance-invariability of the meaning of type-sentences. Without this dogma the whole enterprise of truth-conditional semantics would be stopped in its tracks. But dogged adherence to this dogma brings out a widely ramifying set of compensatory misapprehensions and distortions. The proper reaction is not to deny that meaning is a feature of type-expressions, for dictionaries and grammars do explain the meanings of expression-types, not of particular tokens. Rather, the point is to recognize that a correct specification of the meaning of a type-expression need not account for the use of *every* kind of occurrence of this expression, just as an impeccable dictionary definition may leave some occurrences of an unambiguous *definiendum* unilluminated. Different explanations of an expression may be required in different circumstances without the need for one being taken to impugn the legitimacy of the other. Moreover, there are different levels of understanding, as it were different dimensions of incomprehension and misapprehension. An all-or-nothing distinction between sense and nonsense cannot do justice to this important fact about mastery of a language. The doctrine of circumstance-invariance of meaning feeds on and fosters a whole mythology. It is not an isolated and easily remedied mistake.

4 Sentence-meaning

The thesis of the primacy of the meanings of sentences over the meanings of words and phrases is a fundamental tenet of truth-conditional semantics.

Well-formed sentences have meanings, which are identified with their truth-conditions and sentence-components are held to have meanings only in so far as they make some contribution to the truth-conditions of sentences in which they occur. It is presupposed that a correct explanation or analysis of the concept of meaning can and should begin from an elucidation of what it is for sentences to have meanings.[25] The notion of a truth-condition is presumably introduced as a precise explication of something already dimly apprehended but not yet clearly articulated in the concept of meaning. Without the doctrine of the primacy of sentences over words in the analysis of meaning, semantics could not legitimately take the notion of a truth-condition to be at rock bottom.

The doctrine about the primacy of sentences in a correct explanation of the concept of meaning already raises difficulties without any psychological trappings. It must of course be conceded that we do intelligibly speak of the meanings of sentences in certain circumstances. One such case is in training designed to give facility with a second language. Up to a moderately advanced level, the usual criteria of success at translation is the production of sentences which are approximately synonymous with the ones to be translated. This criterion is rather crude; it become increasingly difficult to apply to more sophisticated tasks of translation, and at the highest level of literary, scientific, or philosophical translation it becomes altogether inapplicable. Another context for speaking of sentence-meanings concerns paraphrase, synopsis, and substitution of expressions within a single language. A paraphrase of a poem might be criticized for distorting the meanings of certain stanzas, or substitution of one phrase for another might be praised for preserving the meaning of a sentence while securing greater elegance by avoiding repetition. But it must be remembered that this everyday kind of talk about the meanings of sentences is subject to caveats that make it unfit for the purposes of theorists of meaning. For, as previously noted, judgments about sameness or difference of the meaning of sentences do not involve any rigorous universal generalizations over all possible circumstances of utterance, and a sentence may be said to have a clear and readily explained meaning in one context even though we might envisage other circumstances in which it would be deemed nonsensical. It would be absurd to deny that we can make sense of talk about the meanings of sentences, though of course not

---

[25] Dummett, *Frege: Philosophy of Language*, pp. 3ff.; D. Davidson, 'Semantics for Natural Languages', in *Linguaggi nella Società e nella Tecnica*, ed. B. Visentini (Edizioni di Comunità, Milan, 1970), pp. 177ff.

at all absurd to deny that we can make sense of what philosophers or linguists say about the meanings of sentences.

Everyday talk about meaning gives no support to the crucial doctrine of the primacy of sentence-meaning over word-meaning. On the contrary, it exposes considerable oddities about this idea. These emerge most clearly from stressing how meaning is related to explanation and understanding.

In our culture, dictionaries have an important and institutionalized status in the practice of explaining meanings. Among educated persons, recourse to a dictionary is a standard method for finding out what an unfamiliar expression means, and what an up-to-date dictionary records is generally acknowledged to settle disputes or uncertainties about meanings. But, of course, the entries in dictionaries are primarily for words, secondarily for recurring phrases, but scarcely ever for entire sentences (even if a full dictionary cites many sentences to illustrate the use of a particular word with one or more distinguishable meanings). Dictionary definitions of words and phrases serve as the fundamental paradigms of explanations of meaning, and hence it is part of the fabric of our practice of explaining expressions that explanations of the meanings of words and phrases take precedence over explanations of the meanings of entire sentences (e.g. by the method of paraphrase). The primacy of sentence-meaning over word-meaning in truth-conditional semantics must be so glossed that it does not conflict with this important fact about explanation.

Utterances of sentences may be misunderstood or not understood. But typically this arises either from ignorance about what a particular word (or phrase) means or from ignorance of what a speaker has said (e.g. whom his remark was about, or whether his observation was an insult or merely a joke in poor taste). The remedy will correspondingly be either a clarification of the meaning of a word (which may be by phrasal or sentential paraphrase) or an account in *oratio obliqua* of what the speaker said. And a request for an explanation ('What did that mean?') is commonly treated as a call for one or the other of these two remedies.

Of course, speakers do sometimes give explanations of entire sentences by the method of paraphrase, and they rightly consider this to be a correct method of explaining the *meanings* of sentences. Frequently such sentential paraphrases will rightly capitalize on context-dependent features of the puzzling or misunderstood utterance. In so doing they may provide a perspicuous and successful explanation of what was said. One would rarely attempt to achieve, and even more rarely succeed in achieving, this goal of explanation by offering a paraphrase of an uttered sentence which is intended to formulate a type-sentence with an equivalent use in *all* contexts. Despite adherence to the thesis of the primacy of sentence-meaning over word-meaning, semantic theories seldom countenance accepted paraphrases as proper explanations of the *meanings* of sentences. This reflects misconceptions about the requirements for synonymy. As if the paraphrase were an acceptable explanation of meaning only if it held in every conceivable circumstance of utterance and only if it met some appropriate standard of generality. These requirements are bogus. The concept of meaning licenses identifying the *meanings* of sentences (and words) in instances where these restrictions are not satisfied. It makes good sense to paraphrase the sentence 'I wonder whether the train has come yet' as the question 'Has the train come yet?' since sentences of this form would typically be used to pose questions, and it is no valid objection to this thesis of synonymy to note that the paraphrased sentence might also be used to answer the question 'What are you wondering?', in which case the paraphrase would be inadmissible. By exaggerating the requirements for synonymy between (type-) sentences, the theorist debars himself from recognizing explanations of sentence-meanings by paraphrase in the very cases in which they do occur.

Consideration of the internal connections of meaning with explanation and understanding shows that, in the doctrine of the primacy of sentence-meanings, theorists in various ways distort the concepts of a sentence and of the meaning of a sentence. They do so even more conspicuously in hanging psychological trappings on the notion of the meaning of a sentence. This concept is alleged to be an essential part of an explanation of how communication is possible ('how language works'). The meaning of a sentence is held to play a pivotal role, either causal or evidential, in the identification of what a speaker has said; it provides a 'means of recognizing' what is said. This claim is not treated as if it were open to empirical confirmation or refutation. For it is adhered to in the face of the evident absence of explicit inference from known formulations of the truth-conditions of type-sentences. It is unclear that any utterance could conceivably be acknowledged to be a counter-example to the causal thesis since the fact that it conveyed something would be cited as conclusive proof that it must have some meaning. On the other hand, to build into the concept of the meaning of a sentence any explicit reference to the putative causal or evidential role of sentence-meanings in communication threatens to make the concept itself vacuous, like the concept of the ether in the early theory of electromagnetic radiation. The intelligibility of everyday discourse about the meanings of sentences is not beholden in *this* way to matters of fact. And the coherence of the theoretical notion of the meaning of a sentence is rendered suspect by the reflection that successful communication can be effected by uttering expressions which would be judged to be nonsensical by the canons of truth-conditional theories of meaning or to have meanings contrary to what is communicated. These possibilities are regularly exploited in certain figurative uses of language, especially by metaphor and irony. The whole idea of incorporating the meanings of sentences into an account of how communication is possible is unnecessary because the *general* question of how speakers recognize what others have said is itself nonsense,[26] and it lures theorists of meaning into further misconceptions and conceptual confusions.

Although the humdrum concept of the meaning of a sentence is above suspicion and has legitimate use in everyday discourse about languages, theorists refine and inflate this concept into something altogether unrecognizable which has no coherent applications at all. The idea of sentence-meaning characteristic of truth-conditional semantics is not a firm foundation on which to erect any sound reflections, *a fortiori* not the Alpha and Omega of a classification or analysis of the concept of the meaning of an expression.

5   Explanation

The avowed goal of a complete theory of meaning for a natural language is to formulate the meaning of every well-formed meaningful expression of that language. More precisely, the aim is 'to give the meaning' of each simple expression together with an account of how the significance of complex expressions depends on the meanings of their constituents and their grammatical structures.[27] In this way, it will be made transparent exactly how each significant expression (and each grammatical construction) contributes to the truth-conditions of any sentence in which it occurs. And to make this clear is held to be an exhaustive specification of the meaning of any expression.

Listening to a theorist so describing his enterprise, the neophyte might expect the activity of 'giving the meanings of expressions' to bear a close

---

[26] The term 'recognize' is abused when a theorist addresses the question of how a person recognizes that a speaker who says to him 'What time is it?' has asked what time it is. I no more recognize this than I recognize what time it is when I look at the face of my watch or recognize my wife when I sit down to dinner with her of an evening. Confusions are further multiplied by failing to distinguish grounds (or reasons) from causes.

[27] D. Davidson, 'Truth and Meaning', *Synthese*, 17 (1967), p. 310.

resemblance to the familiar practice of *explaining* meanings. The ability to explain words, phrases, and sentences is basic to the mastery of a language. It is exercised frequently by parents and teachers, and not uncommonly by speakers who wish to introduce technical terms or to secure precise agreement about the significance of a term for a specific purpose (e.g. parliamentary legislation or delimiting the bounds of a scientific treatise). Moreover, understanding an expression is internally related to the ability to explain what it means; there is no such thing as a significant expression whose meaning cannot be explained, and a person's inability to explain what an expression means is a criterion for his not understanding it. The intimate connection of meaning with explanation suggests that a theorist engaged in 'giving the meanings of expressions' is in fact endeavouring to explain what they mean. This expectation is reinforced by further observations made by these theorists themselves. They often indicate that a clarification of the contribution of an expression to the truth-conditions of a sentence is a systematization and generalization of the familiar practice of explanation. It is held to encompass all of those forms of explanation which we rate as precise and rigorous such as formal definitions of terms in geometry or number theory and their counterparts in physics, biology, or the law of the land. The very paradigm of explanations of meaning is a definition *per genus et differentiam*, e.g. 'a triangle is a three-sided plane rectilinear figure'. Such a definition is incorporated directly into a semantic theory, though typically in the altered form of an open sentence (viz. 'x is a triangle' is true if and only if x is a three-sided rectilinear figure). But further forms of acceptable definition are also acknowledged, and are advertised as an improvement on a conception of explanation restricted to standard analytic dictionary definitions; in particular concepts can be rigorously defined which involve generality (e.g. 'n is a prime number' is true if and only if for any number x greater than 1 and less than n x is not a divisor of n), and 'definitions in use' can be formulated for terms otherwise relegated to the category of indefinables (e.g. Russell's theory of definite descriptions). What is called 'giving the meaning of an expression' in truth-conditional semantics is recommended as a generalization and liberalization of the concept of explaining what an expression means. This claim is especially prominent in connection with the definition of sentence-connectives by truth-tables and the semantic definitions of the quantifiers (and related expressions of generality). Here logicians pride themselves on having won through to the true explanations of expressions that had previously defied analysis. A proper semantic theory tries to capitalize on this bridgehead and to effect further radical improvements on ordinary explanations of other expressions (particularly those of philosophical or theoretical moment).

On the other hand, the very notion of improving upon accepted explanations of expressions suggests a tension between the business of 'giving the meanings of expressions' and the accepted practice of explaining their meanings. Other remarks of theorists of meaning stress the differences and attempt sharply to segregate these activities from each other. The point of this operation is to isolate the deliverances of a theory of meaning from the canons of acceptability appropriate to explanations of meaning. The need for this defensive manoeuvre is evident. Apart from analytic equivalences, the paradigm for 'giving the meaning of an expression' is the model-theoretic interpretation of primitive symbols in a logical calculus. This is accomplished by associating with each proper name a specific individual, with each one-place predicate-letter a property, with each two-place predicate-letter a binary relation, etc. Accordingly, a paradigm for 'giving the meaning' of an expression is to state ' "Socrates" designates (or stands for) Socrates'; or similarly, to declare ' "x is red" stands for the property of being red' or ' "x is greater than y" designates the relation *larger than*'. Whatever the merits of these statements, they would not count as *explanations* of the name 'Socrates' (if there is any such thing at all) or of the adjective 'red' or the phrase 'greater than'. They would be incapable of filling any of the roles of explanations for anybody who did not *already understand* these expressions, i.e. they could not tell him who Socrates is or what the property *red* or the relation *greater than* is, nor could they be used by such a person to settle whether any particular applications of these expressions were correct or mistaken. But if they lack all of the distinctive functions of explanations, they must obviously fail to constitute explanations at all.

This manifest discrepancy between paradigmatic specifications of meaning in truth-conditional semantics and standard explanations of meaning calls forth various reactions. One is that most received explanations of meaning are radically defective by the ordinary canons of acceptability of explanations; viz. they do not succeed in supplying a generally applicable criterion of correctness of application of the explained expression and hence they are evidently incomplete. Common practice sanctions, e.g., ostensive definitions of such expressions as 'black' and 'a light', but this fails to account for the fact that the sentence 'I looked out across the water at midnight and saw a black light flashing' is nonsense. A second response is to declare everything extrinsic to model-theoretic interpretations to be of merely psychological interest; viz. the roles of explanations in teaching the uses of expressions and in furnishing criteria of correctness are dismissed as strictly psychological. On this view, a so-called 'modest' theory of meaning (i.e. one incapable of explaining expressions to somebody who does not already understand them) is none the less impeccable. A third manoeuvre is to maintain that model-theoretic interpretations of expressions do capture their meanings for anybody who really understands them. Though anybody familiar with the conventions for using quotation-marks in English knows, e.g., that ' "red" designates red' makes a true statement, he will not know what this sentence states (i.e. he will not truly 'grasp the proposition' expressed by this sentence) unless he knows what red is, but in that case the axiom does express what he understands by the term 'red'.[28] Fourthly theorists sometimes argue that 'homophonic translations', e.g. ' "red" designates red', are potentially informative despite the appearance of triviality. For in cases where the metalanguage differs from the object language, an isomorphic sentence, e.g. ' "rouge" designates red', could be used to teach somebody what the defined word means. Finally, the discrepancy may be acknowledged but then cited as grounds for maintaining that a full 'theory of understanding' must contain a richer array of axioms than the model-theoretic interpretations which are sufficient to settle the cogency of arguments; in addition what is thought to be necessary is some specification of appropriate means for recognizing the referents of unanalysed expressions, or at least an account of what constitutes manifestations of the ability to recognize these referents.[29] The point of all of these manoeuvres (each of which is open to objection) is to defend the axioms of truth-conditional semantics against a charge arising from the fact that they *apparently* do not meet the standards appropriate for genuine explanations of meaning.

Theorists of meaning face a sore dilemma. If, on the one hand, they contend that their axioms purporting to 'give the meanings' of words are explanations of these words, they render these axioms subject to the canons of explanation and are certain to draw down on many of them harsh negative verdicts. If, on the other hand, they concede that these axioms are not proper explanations of words, then they threaten to undermine such basic claims as that truth-tables give the proper explanations of certain sentence-connectives and that the validity of inferences is a matter solely of the *meanings* of the constituent sentences, and at the same

[28] M. A. E. Dummett, 'What is a Theory of Meaning?' in *Mind and Language*, ed. S. Guttenplan (Clarendon Press, Oxford, 1975), pp. 106ff.

[29] Dummett, *Frege: Philosophy of Language*, pp. 73ff., 94ff., and *The Interpretation of Frege's Philosophy* (Duckworth, London, 1981), pp. 186ff.

time they open themselves to a demand to explain what 'giving the meaning' of expressions really is and why this activity has any importance (since explanations of meaning already seem omnicompetent). In the face of this pair of unattractive alternatives, theorists of meaning adopt the strategy of vacillating between the two, now arguing as if they embraced one option, now as if they subscribed to the other. This inconsistency is itself objectionable. And so too is the constant pressure to offend against the internal connections between meaning and explanation. Truth-conditional semantics cannot live in peace with the principle that meaning is what is explained in explanations of meaning, i.e. with the denial that there is any such thing as the meaning of an expression to be found behind or over and above what is explicit in the received practice of explaining this expression. The *raison d'être* of any theory of meaning is that there may be something hidden and awaiting discovery about what expressions mean. Truth-tables and the semantic definitions of expressions of generality are taken to be pledges that this faith is justified. It must make sense to suppose that the motley of received explanations of words hide deeper normative uniformities and that speakers, in following the canons of usage laid down in actual explanations, tacitly know and follow the true meaning-rules revealed by a proper theory of meaning for a language. Were they to forswear these convictions, theorists of meaning would find themselves at a loss for a programme. Their continued activity makes sense only if they deny meaning to be exhausted by received explanations of meaning. Yet it makes the sense that they intend only if what they theorize about is exhaustively determined by the practice of explaining expressions. The phrase 'to give the meaning of an expression' draws a thin veil over this fundamental ambivalence. If pressed to explain its meaning, they find nothing coherent to say.

Theories of meaning commonly manifest specific misconceptions about the relation of meaning and explanation. An important one is a general disdain for explanations of words and phrases offered by competent speakers and accepted as correct and complete by them. Damned in this offhand manner are *all* ostensive definitions, *all* explanations by reference to a set of paradigms and a similarity-rider, *all* clarification by contrastive paraphrase, *all* contextual paraphrase, etc. The survivors of this purge are in turn subjected to a further inquisition. Speakers' attempts to formulate necessary and sufficient conditions for applying expressions are alleged to carry no presumption of correctness and have no special authority. They are based on prescientific intuitions or impressions of what words mean, and they must be tested against the actual practice of using the defined expressions as if they were hypotheses rather than norms. By this standard they are argued to be found wanting since truth-conditional theorists are wholly oblivious to the variety and complexity of the methods of projection from a rule (explanation of meaning) to its application. According to their conception the whole practice of explaining words amounts to an array of predictions about how words are used by the speakers of a language, and the participants themselves have no privileged position for assessing the match or mismatch between these predictions and their observable behaviour. The importance of speakers' explanations is completely discounted. To the observation that the adjective 'red' is (correctly) explained by an ostensive definition or that the particle 'and' is not explained by a truth-table, the theorist of meaning replies 'So what?'.

The consequence of this contemptuous retort is to cut off the branch upon which the theorist is precariously perched, viz. to sever the internal connections between understanding an expression and an explanation of *what* one understands by it, between being able to use an expression correctly and being able to explain what one uses it to say, between knowing what an expression means and being able to say what it means. By prising meaning apart from explanations of words, a theorist subverts his claim that *meaning* is the subject-matter of his theorizing. His radical and wholesale condemnation of the received practice of explanation amounts to conclusive proof that his theory is not a theory of meaning or understanding. And his penchant for treating homophonic translations as the ultimate self-explanatory basis of the mastery of a language reinforces the suspicion that his theory has no genuine subject-matter at all. His aspersions on accepted explanations of meaning are not in the least comparable to a scientist's neglect of common-sense judgments and primitive superstitions. They are rather comparable to the suggestion that a competent chess-player might be able to play chess, but not be competent to explain how the pieces are to be moved (as if an axiomatized calculus of chess might provide a 'real' explanation of what a chess-player knows only tacitly or unconsciously, but is unable to say). And his conviction that it is possible to discover and formulate the real meanings of expressions by appeal to the technical concept of a truth-condition makes the mistake of divorcing the concept of meaning from the practice of explaining the word 'meaning'. The concept of meaning (our concept of meaning) is exhausted by accepted explanations of 'meaning', and this shows that there is, as it were, no logical space for a theory of meaning to occupy.

6 Understanding

Much of the attraction of truth-conditional semantics stems from the suggestion that it alone provides an explanation for the possibility of understanding the open-ended set of utterances issued and comprehended by fluent speakers of a language. It offers a theory of understanding. Any such theory involves important presuppositions about the nature of understanding. In particular, the central thesis that the meaning of a type-sentence is derived from its structure and the meanings of its constituents bears on this issue of understanding new sentences only if understanding a sentence is a mental act which is the upshot of a process of derivation. This is indeed the preferred model. To understand a sentence is to *grasp* its truth-conditions (as determined by its structure and its constituents) or to *associate* it with the appropriate set of truth-conditions. For the moment we waive all scruples about whether understanding is an act or process, how type-sentences are related to understanding utterances, whether meanings are invariants of type-sentences, whether sentences are true, and what truth-*conditions* may be. We focus instead on the crucial claim that understanding a sentence is grasping its truth-conditions.

It is important to note that this thesis has immediate corollaries in respect of understanding words. To understand a singular referring expression is to know what object it designates; to understand a one-place predicate is to know what property it stands for; etc. This might consist in being able to state an appropriate analysis of the understood expression, but in the most basic cases it will be simply a matter of *associating* the word with the proper entity. Hence the homophonic axioms of a truth-conditional semantics encapsulate the understanding of the primitive expressions. To know, e.g., *what* 'red' stands for (viz. the colour red) is to understand the word 'red'. In the last analysis understanding boils down to *correlating* words with entities. This venerable conception informs the selection of the form of statement chosen to serve as axioms in truth-conditional semantics. There is a root-and-branch commitment to the tenability of the Augustinian picture of language.

This makes clear a fundamental flaw in truth-conditional semantics. In the case of words, there is no problem in imagining procedures that might well be called 'correlating a proper name with an object' or 'correlating an adjective with a property', e.g., a person might do so by sticking a label on a manuscript or by producing a colour-chart. The difficulty is to relate such acts with this person's *understanding* words.[30] The manifestations of his understanding extend over time, whereas acts of correlating words with things are fully accomplished at a specific moment. The crucial question is how the presence (or absence) of the appropriate correlations are exhibited *in the practice of speaking a language*.[31] Unless to pin a label on an object or to coordinate colour-words with colour-samples is to correlate a word with an entity, the notion of correlation becomes altogether opaque. But if such acts do count as making the proper correlations, then it is compatible with a person's correlating a word with the correct entity that he should subsequently misapply it in every case and still be credited with understanding it! This *reductio* might be countered by the requirement that the person be required to *continue* to correlate the word with the proper entity. But this would achieve nothing, since he could on demand always produce, e.g., the correct colour-chart but then proceed always to apply it in an unorthodox way (e.g. according to the pattern

rather than the pattern). To correlate a word with a thing is to

perform an act; but the connection between performing one act and performing another (e.g. applying a word to describe an object) or between being in a state and applying a word correctly is at best contingent, quite unlike the *internal* connection between understanding an expression and using it correctly. Incoherence results from the attempt to analyse understanding in terms of correlating words with entities, unless, of course, 'to correlate a word with a thing' is simply introduced as a (misleading!) technical expression replacing 'to understand'.

In the case of sentences matters stand even worse. The same objection would appear to hold. But in addition it is altogether unclear what is to count as an instance of 'grasping the truth-conditions of a sentence' or 'associating a sentence with its truth-conditions'! There is no analogue whatever for labelling an object or giving an ostensive definition of a predicate in the case of a sentence. The only recourse seems to be to T-sentences: to grasp the truth-conditions of the sentence 'The Pyrenees separate France from Spain' is to know that 'The Pyrenees separate France from Spain' is true if and only if the Pyrenees separate France from Spain. But it is obviously neither necessary nor sufficient for someone's having

[30] This problem is not a form of scepticism about what a speaker associates with a word or about the persistence of an association. Hence it is left untouched by the postulation of senses whose function is to glue words to the entities to which they refer.

[31] Wittgenstein, *Philosophical Investigations*, §51.

this knowledge that he formulate this T-sentence. Indeed, it is alleged to be a central problem for a theory of meaning to explain exactly what this knowledge consists in or how it is manifested in speaking.[32] But without clear criteria for grasping the truth-conditions of a sentence there seems no possible merit in the philosophical *analysis* of the concept of understanding a sentence in terms of the expression 'grasping its truth-conditions'. It would be wilful descent into obscurity.

The defence that there is here simply a lacuna to be filled is itself over-optimistic. Reasons can be adduced to show that nothing whatever could satisfy us as an explanation of the criteria for grasping the truth-conditions of a sentence.

First, the analysis of understanding a sentence as grasping its truth-conditions (or associating the proper truth-conditions with it) represents understanding as an act or state. Indeed, *grasping* a set of truth-conditions is considered to be an *action* performed at a particular moment (especially on hearing a sentence uttered), comparable to seizing a cudgel or apprehending a criminal; and associating a sentence with its truth-conditions must be either an act or a more or less continuous state (of mind). But these representations of understanding a sentence are misrepresentations, analogous to the misconception of understanding a word as correlating it with some entity. For the manifestations of understanding are *internally* related to understanding a sentence, whereas they can be only externally related to a putative state or act of grasping the truth-conditions of a sentence as conceived in semantic theories.

Secondly, there is a danger of factoring truth-conditions out of the analysis of understanding if the criteria for grasping the truth-conditions of a sentence are simply taken to be the everyday criteria for understanding words and utterances. It is indeed true that giving appropriate explanations of words or paraphrases of sentences, reacting appropriately to an utterance, uttering a sentence in suitable circumstances, correcting mistakes in others' utterances, describing how to test whether a statement is correct, etc., constitute criteria of understanding expressions, but the notion of a truth-condition plays no role in formulating any of these criteria. Consequently, if these criteria constitute a complete account of the criteria for grasping the truth-conditions of a sentence, then the concept of a truth-condition is a completely idle wheel in the analysis of understanding. Like the concept of correlating a word with a thing (i.e. of

---

[32] Cf. M. A. E. Dummett, 'What is a Theory of Meaning? (II)' in *Truth and Meaning*, ed. G. Evans and J. McDowell (Clarendon Press, Oxford, 1976), pp. 70ff.

analysing word-meaning in terms of designation), it would simply drop out of a complete account of the concept of understanding a sentence.

These two points alone seem decisive. But there is even a further general theoretical objection to the enterprise of analysing understanding sentences as a matter of grasping their truth-conditions. If meanings are what is understood in understanding sentences, then the central doctrine of truth-conditional semantics that the meaning of a sentence takes primacy over the meanings of the constituent expressions seems to carry the corollary that understanding sentences is prior to understanding the constituent expressions. Yet the *raison d'être* of these semantic theories is the task of explaining how understanding sentences is derivative from understanding words (and grammatical constructions). This tension is not resolved by the claim that the meanings of sentences have priority in the order of explanation (constructing semantic theories) though the meanings of words have priority in the order of understanding.[33] That thesis not only manifests a basic misconception about understanding (below, pp. 347–56), but also drives an enormous wedge between meaning and understanding. For how is it compatible with identifying meanings as the objects of understanding to affirm that the understanding of a sentence is parasitic on understanding its constituent words and its structure while also asserting that the meanings of the words in this sentence are parasitic on the identification of its meaning with its truth-conditions? Although truth-conditions of sentences provide the *points d'appui* for a theory of meaning, the putative act of grasping the truth-conditions of a sentence is to be analysed into more primitive acts of associating words with entities. The account of meaning and the analysis of understanding pull in opposite directions. And this puts in an uncomfortable position any theory of *meaning* whose avowed purpose is to explain the possibility of understanding sentences. Squaring the circle looks like an easier task.

Truth-conditional semantics contributes less than nothing to the clarification and understanding of the concepts of understanding words, sentences, utterances, and languages. It cultivates and propagates fundamental misunderstandings.

7 In pursuit of the phantoms of hope

These several criticisms add up to a devastating indictment. Each and every one of the fundamental theses of all versions of truth-conditional

---

[33] Dummett, *Frege: Philosophy of Language*, pp. 4f.

semantics rests on basic errors and confusions. Nothing substantial survives unscathed. The whole enterprise of truth-conditional semantics must surely look ridiculous.

Alas! this (rational!) reaction is not to be expected. No more than the general repudiation of the fashion for high-heeled shoes as a result of the (justified) criticism that such footwear is a menace to public health. The difficulty is not to elaborate criticisms which make truth-conditional semantics out to be absurd, but rather to make these criticisms *tell*. (An analogy: Wittgenstein cannot be credited with any originality in denying that the meaning of a name is its bearer, but he introduced this familiar observation into a context of argument in which it suddenly *impressed* many philosophers.) The pronouncements of truth-conditional semantics are supported by the momentum of the mainstream of modern philosophy and linguistics; they are sanctioned by great authorities. Moreover, their apparent falsity, their aura of incredibility, is paradoxically taken to be a pledge of their truth. For unless they did embody important insights, nobody would ever have arrived at the idea of proposing them as serious theories! The plain alternative to their being obviously false is their being *very* profound. According to this view, the worse the theory seems, the deeper it must be. Our criticisms, if accepted, then serve as reinforcements to what is under attack.

Such perversity is not readily moved by rational refutation. But perhaps its strength can be gradually sapped. We shall turn attention to two misconceptions that lend support to truth-conditional semantics. The first is the widespread idea that systems of rules have hidden depths which can be illuminated by constructing explanatory theories. This notion is conspicuous in the celebrated semantic conception of logical validity (the foundation of modern logic) and the conception of grammaticality offered by transformational generative grammarians (a dominant school within modern linguistics). The second support is an inverterate inclination to blur the boundary between conceptual and empirical enquiry. This is manifest in the preoccupation of philosophers and linguists with the question of how sentences are understood, since the answer to this question is conceived to be simultaneously a clarification of the concept of understanding (or meaning) and an elucidation of the mental (or physiological) mechanisms of understanding. If these myths are properly exposed, perhaps the way will be cleared towards *listening to* and even *accepting* the many important criticisms of the notion that the meaning of a sentence is its truth-conditions.

CHAPTER 7

Rules: Preliminary Clarifications

1 Clouds of confusion

The realization that a language is, in some sense, a matter of rules, that linguistic activities are normative or rule-governed, is no novelty. Individually, all language-users have occasion to *correct* themselves, and to correct, or at least to notice, *mistakes* in the speech of others. Malapropisms, spoonerisms, ambiguities and equivocations are the stock-in-trade of entertainers, a source of amusement to wide audiences. Minor grammatical errors and comic infelicities are a stuff from which dramatists standardly create light relief, usually at the expense of pretentious or boorish characters. The intelligibility of such jokes and witticisms, their widespread accessibility to audiences, depends on an immediate recognition of deviation from linguistic norms of various kinds. The normativity of language is equally evident in pedagogical activities of parents and teachers, who instruct children in the correct use of their language, explain to them norms of word usage, correct their mistakes and rectify their misunderstandings. At a slightly more sophisticated level, learning a foreign language at school may involve memorizing explicit statements of hundreds of rules. Finally, the study of grammar has, for two millennia, typically been conceived to be concerned with elaborating and systematizing rules of a language.

The novelty involved in twentieth century theorizing about languages and meaning does not lie in noticing these platitudes, which are indeed either overlooked or distorted, but rather in the role given to rules and in the conception of a rule which is involved in an explicit, articulated account of the nature of a language, whether that account takes the form of a theory or merely of a comprehensive description. It is a striking and distinctive feature of modern philosophical discussions of language that the concept of a linguistic rule is subtly transformed and shifted into the centre of a complex web of interconnected concepts in terms of which a language is described and analysed. If the conception of a rule, the picture of rule-governed activity, the notion of explanation of normative behaviour are awry, the resultant descriptions, prescriptions, theses, and theories are bound to be likewise awry. In this chapter we shall begin to examine ideas about normativity which bear upon much modern speculation about the nature of languages. We shall find that the roots of the mythology which informs contemporary linguistics and philosophical theories of meaning lie in fundamental misconceptions about the nature of rules, rule-following and normative explanation.

Even superficial scrutiny of the salient writings of philosophers, linguists, and logicians reveals some very strange suppositions about the nature of rules and the ways in which they are involved in human thought, behaviour, and speech. A few examples will demonstrate this.

(1) Frege, in harmony with a well-established tradition, conceived of logic as a *normative science*. Logic, unlike psychology, is not concerned with determining how we actually think, but rather with determining how we *ought* to think. The laws of logic lay down how we ought to think *if we are to preserve truth* in reasoning from true premises. They are rules which, if correctly adhered to, guarantee correct reasoning. These rules, however, are not free creations of human beings, which could be other than they are. They are, in some sense, *necessary* rules: 'they are boundary stones set in an eternal foundation, which our thought can overflow, but never displace'.[1] We do not have to follow them, but if we do not, our reasoning will be fallacious. They are akin to technical norms in the domain of nature. Given the existence of causal laws, and given certain facts, then, if you want to cool the room you *must* open the window. So too, Frege thought, given the nature of logical entities (such as propositions, concepts, truth-values, and logical relations), if you want to guarantee the preservation of truth in inference, you *must* reason thus-and-so. Rules of logic thus conceived are reflections or consequences of logical essences. A superphysics of logical objects provides the foundations and justification for the adamantine laws of logic.

Parallel to this Platonism about laws of logic is Frege's Platonism about concepts and abstract objects: 'what is known as the history of concepts is really a history either of our knowledge of concepts or of the meanings of words. Often it is only after immense intellectual effort, which may have continued over centuries, that humanity at last succeeds in achieving

---

[1] G. Frege, *The Basic Laws of Arithmetic*, vol. 1, tr. and ed. M. Furth (University of California Press, Berkeley and Los Angeles, 1964), p. xvi.

knowledge of a concept in its pure form, in stripping off the irrelevant accretions which veil it from the eyes of the mind.'[2] Consequently, when Frege gave a schema for defining numerals, viz. 'the Number which belongs to the concept *F* [i.e. the number of *F*s (Kings of England, books in the bible, hours of the day, or whatever)] is the extension of the concept "equinumerous with the concept *F*" ',[3] he conceived of himself as having *discovered* what kind of object an expression of the form 'the number of *F*s' really stands for. Hence when he defined a specific numeral such as '0', e.g. '0 is the Number which belongs to the concept "not identical with itself" ',[4] he thought of himself as discovering what the familiar and much used expression 'nought' or '0' really stands for. Yet here too there is a mystery that should give us pause. For we all use the words 'nought', 'one', 'two', etc. without any knowledge of Frege's definitions. We explain their use to children, but not by citing these arcane definitions. And we think of ourselves as understanding these words despite our ignorance of his definitions. Are we wrong? Do his definitions give the rules for the use of these words? And if they do, how are these rules (hitherto unknown to us and not readily understood) related to our use of the words? Do we actually follow these rules, or merely conform unwittingly to them? And if the latter, in what sense do his definitions tell us anything about what *we* mean by number-words? Like Plato's Forms, Frege's definitions leave us with a mystery about the relationships between our mastery of a linguistic practice, our understanding of the meanings of the words we use, and the 'rules' laid down by his definitions.[5]

(2) The *Tractatus* adumbrated a radical conception of a language as a calculus of meaning rules. All meaningful sentences (or sentence-radicals) are held to be analysable into truth-functional combinations (possibly of infinite length) of elementary sentences. Elementary sentences are composed of unanalysable names in grammatical coordination. The meanings of these names are the objects they stand for. The sense of an elementary sentence is a function of the meanings of its constituent expressions (and their mode of combination), and knowledge of meanings and forms suffices for the understanding of any sentence without fresh explanation. Yet here too mysteries immediately spring to view. The discovery of what

---

[2] G. Frege, *The Foundations of Arithmetic*, 2nd edn (Blackwell, Oxford, 1953), p. vii.

[3] Ibid., § 68.

[4] Ibid., § 74.

[5] This phenomenon has parallels elsewhere in philosophy, e.g. in the claim that colour-words really signify wave lengths of electromagnetic radiation, or that 'hot' and 'cold' signify mean kinetic energy.

the rules of logical syntax actually are must wait 'until we have actually achieved the ultimate analysis of the phenomena in question. This, as we all know, has not yet been achieved'.[6] Do we then follow these hidden rules *without knowing them*? Our understanding of new sentences is supposed to be explained by reference to our knowledge of the meanings of their elementary, unanalysable, constituent names. But since philosophy has not yet succeeded in completing any analysis, since the author of the *Tractatus* could not produce a single example of a simple name or an elementary proposition, can we really be said to know the meaning of any simple names (to know with what meanings they are correlated) or the logico-syntactical rules according to which they are combined? And in what way can this strangely unknown knowledge explain our capacity to understand new sentences? If the rules of the calculus of a language are buried so deep, how can they inform our current linguistic activities or our current pedagogical practices?

(3) Contemporary theorists of meaning explain valid inference patterns by reference to rules of logical semantics. Davidson,[7] for example, explains the validity of the inference from 'A shuts the door with a bang' to 'A shuts the door' by reference to quantification over events. The *reason* the inference is valid is that the *real* logical form of the premise is 'There is an event x such that x is a shutting of the door & x is by A & x occurs with a bang', from which the conclusion follows by conjunction elimination. This kind of analysis is held to 'elicit in a perspicuous and general form the understanding of logical grammar we all have that constitutes (part of) our grasp of our native tongue'.[8] But this too is puzzling. Why should the legitimacy of an inference a five-year-old has mastered turn on the in-tricacies of a novel extension of the predicate calculus? And if there are languages which lack devices for nominalizing verbs, is the inference not valid? Or are the 'grounds' of its validity beyond the comprehension of speakers of that language? Is it held that *our* inferences from 'A did φ at t, in s, in a G-manner' to 'A did φ' owe their validity to the rules of the predicate calculus? Do we ever invoke principles of quantification theory to justify or explain the legitimacy of such inferences?

No less strange is the suggestion that the rules determining the sense of a sentence containing multiple expressions of generality (e.g. 'Everyone

---

[6] L. Wittgenstein, *'Some Remarks on Logical Form'*, *Proceedings of the Aristotelian Society*, supplementary volume IX (1929), p. 171.

[7] D. Davidson, 'The Logical Form of Action Sentences', in *The Logic of Decision and Action*, ed. N. Rescher (Univ. of Pittsburgh Press, Pittsburgh, 1967).

[8] Davidson, 'Reply to comments', in ibid., p. 115.

loves somebody') involve an essential reference to a step-by-step constructional history of the sentence. 'Once we know the constructional
history of a sentence involving multiple generality, we can from . . . simple
rules determine the truth-conditions of that sentence, provided only that
we already know the truth-conditions of every sentence containing proper
names in the places where the signs of generality stand.'[9] But this is
decidedly bizarre. For even disregarding qualms about truth-conditions,
can it seriously be considered that such humdrum affairs as 'Has anyone
called all the boys?' or 'Everyone has been told by somebody to go for a
swim' *have* 'constructional histories'? Do we 'construct' such sentences by
first constructing singular sentences and then deleting proper names which
are subsequently replaced by expressions of generality? And does our
understanding of such sentences somehow recapitulate the application of
such curious rules?[10]

(4) Theoretical linguists, following Chomsky, conceive of their investigations into grammar as a peculiar branch of cognitive psychology. The
grammar of a language is 'the set of rules and principles that determine the
normal use of language', an apparently innocuous remark. It ceases to be
innocuous when Chomsky proceeds to tell us that these rules and principles
which determine what counts as a grammatical expression are not the
humdrum affairs proferred by ordinary speakers, or even the more
sophisticated rules of traditional grammarians. They are unknown to all
speakers of a language, indeed it would be *miraculous*[11] if a speaker could
become conscious of them. They are, however, 'cognized' – which is the
same as being known, only totally and irretrievably unconscious! This
system of rules, e.g. the grammar of English, *grows* or *develops* in the mind

[9] M. A. E. Dummett, *Frege: Philosophy of Language*, (Duckworth, London, 1973), p. 11.

[10] It is true that most people would not construe the sentence 'Everybody envies somebody' to license the inference to 'There is somebody whom everybody envies'. But is this to be
explained, as Dummett suggests, by the fact that 'Everybody envies somebody' 'was not
constructed by combining the sign of generality "somebody" with the predicate "Everybody
envies ξ" but by combining the sign of generality "everybody" and the predicate "ξ envies
somebody"'? It is altogether extraordinary that philosophers, under the mesmerizing spell of
a novel form of representation, viz. the predicate calculus, should feel impelled to construct
such mythologies of constructional processes (presumably occurring in the subconscious
mind!) and applications of arcane rules in order to *explain* the obvious. It is, of course, true
that *out of context* such a sentence is ambiguous; it is also true that one can *represent* each of
its possible meanings by reference to its relation to one or other of the artificial forms
'Everybody envies ξ' or 'ξ envies somebody'. But that one can so represent them shows
nothing at all about our grounds for taking such a sentence, *in a context*, one way rather than
another, let alone about 'processes' of construction!

[11] N. Chomsky, *Rules and Representations* (Blackwell, Oxford, 1980), p. 70.

in a way that is 'predetermined by the biologically given organization of the mind',[12] much as 'the organs of the body develop in their predetermined way'.[13] Indeed, language itself *is* a 'mental organ',[14] whose character is genetically determined. A speaker's 'cognizance' of the grammar of his language is only possible because all human beings innately possess a universal grammar which is 'physically represented in the genetic code and the adult brain'.[15] This universal grammar is a function that maps experience on to 'steady state grammar',[16] i.e. the grammar of a natural language cognized by a speaker and discovered by MIT linguists. Lest all this not suffice to baffle the attentive reader, one further sample may be adduced. While the sentence 'Who did they say that A had seen?' is grammatical, the sentence 'Who did they hear the news that A had seen?' is not. The explanation for this, *mirabile dictu*, is that the interrogative sentence is formed[17] by a series of transformations on the deep structure involving a rule 'Move α', where α is an arbitrary phrase category. When 'who' is 'moved', *it leaves behind a trace*, which 'though the mind does not know it at this point in mental computation, will ultimately have no phonetic realization',[18] and it is this *trace* which precludes the deviant sentence. This pseudo-scientific patter is known as 'trace theory'. *Quis explicabit ipsas explicationes?*

These glimpses of some of the things which modern writers have said about rules of logic and language are, out of context and without detailed elaboration, less than wholly fair. Surrounded by waves of theory they look altogether more impressive. Later on we shall examine some of the

[12] Ibid., p. 72.
[13] N. Chomsky, *Reflections on Language* (Fontana, London, 1976), p. 76.
[14] Ibid., p. 92.
[15] Chomsky, *Rules and Representations*, pp. 82f.
[16] Ibid., p. 187.
[17] An extraordinary mythology informs the thought of grammarian and philosopher alike here. Because we *can* specify rules for transforming, e.g., declarative sentences into interrogatives (or the deep structures we have *invented* to correspond to them) it is therefore inferred that we actually *derive* one from the other, that the one is *formed from* the other. That we do not actually derive the interrogative sentences we use in questioning from anything at all, let alone from corresponding declaratives or deep-structure diagrams is too mundane a detail to be noticed by the linguistic scientists. Doubtless they will claim that the derivation is done unconsciously! Clearly they confuse what *can be* derived according to a calculus or system of rules with what is or is not derived by a person using signs. That an interrogative is derivable from a declarative in no way shows that I derived it therefrom. After all, declaratives are no less 'derived' from interrogatives than vice versa, i.e. one can specify rules for such transformations too.
[18] Ibid., p. 160.

salient theses more thoroughly. But we have already made clear a host of commitments that are not obvious or uncontroversial, whose sense needs to be unravelled prior to any decision about truth, and whose conceptual articulations should be questioned. For according to these views, rules are capable of existing unbeknownst to those who follow them. We can, it seems, *discover* that we have been following hidden rules. Speech, on this conception, is governed by rules quite irrespective of speakers' ability to cite the rules they are following or of the fact that they do not explain what they mean by reference to the semantic rules that 'assign' meaning to what they say. Indeed the rules of language may, it seems, be too complicated for most speakers to understand. Or, the only correct formulations of these rules may invoke concepts unintelligible to the average speaker; yet he follows these rules for all that.

These commitments call out for careful investigation. And a host of more specific qualms needs airing. What are 'necessary rules'? Are the laws of logic necessary? And if so, whence their necessity? Does it make sense to justify familiar patterns of inference by reference to structures that are typically unthought of, and may even be inaccessible to most speakers? Can 'constructional histories' of which no one is aware explain the validity of inferences which everyone recognizes? Can rules be, or be like, *organs*? What does it mean for rules to be 'represented' in the mind at levels of unconsciousness 'beyond the reach of introspection or will'? And how could a genetic code, a DNA molecule, 'represent' or be a 'realizaton of' a rule of grammar? Is this any more intelligible than the idea that a configuration of stars 'represents' or is a 'realization of' my intention to go to London? Finally, does it make sense to speak of rules of grammar, as linguists and meaning theorists do, as being an *explanatory theory*? If so, are the rules of chess or tiddlywinks also explanatory theories? And if not, why not? And if they are, do they explain anything that stands in need of explanation, and is the preferred form of explanation really intelligible at all?

Many more questions lurk in the wings, but these puzzles occupying centre stage should suffice to keep us busy. And if they originate, as we shall argue, in grotesque misunderstandings of rules and of rule-governed phenomena, their resolution or dissolution should make detailed scrutiny of the rest redundant. In order to shed light on this murky scene we must first adumbrate some perfectly general features of rules. No doubt the concept of a rule does not have sharp boundaries; what one writer refers to as 'a rule' another may specify differently. Nevertheless central cases are clear enough. While borderline disagreements are legitimate, the extensive

misuse of the concept of a rule by theorists of language does not concern
the periphery of the concept, as it were, but its very core. This claim is, of
course, contentious. If one is navigating stormy seas, one should plot one's
route. In this chapter we shall outline the salient features of the concept of
a rule, clear instances of using or invoking rules, and common ways of
talking about rules and following rules. This we hope will provide the
wherewithal to demonstrate that current philosophical and linguistic
speculations on language sail headlong on to the rocks through thorough-
going misidentification of the normative features they so recklessly steer
by.

2   Rules and their formulations

The term 'rule' belongs to a large class of expressions ramifying in many
directions. We can characterize the centre of this 'semantic field' by
reference to five related groupings of each of which we give a representative sample: (1) law, statute, regulation; (2) practice, code, convention; (3)
standard, canon, model, paradigm; (4) maxim, principle, precept, recipe;
and (5) prescription, direction, directive, instruction. Though the boundaries are not sharp, and the groupings imprecise, this list reveals distinctive
focal points around which diverse normative concepts cluster, viz. (1)
formal rules, voluntarily created according to rule-governed stipulations,
and (2) informal rules, which exist in the practices of a social group and
which are not created by norm-creating acts. Such concepts as in group (3)
focus on the *evaluative* role of rules; those in (4) highlight the guiding role
of 'impersonal rules', i.e. rules not addressed to anyone in particular but
'available' to anyone who wishes to adopt them. The final group emphasizes rules *issued* by individual authorities, often *to* individual subjects.

Around these central normative concepts are clustered others, such as
the notions of custom, routine, regularity. The verb 'to rule' is related to a
large family incorporating 'to guide', 'to direct', to instruct', 'to prescribe',
'to govern', 'to influence', 'to determine', as well as a host of more political
concepts such as 'to wield authority', 'to exercise sway', etc. The passive
'to be ruled by' is importantly related not only to notions of subjection to
personal authority, but also to ideas appertaining to subjective control,
viz. 'to restrain oneself', 'to curb oneself', 'to moderate' and many other
concepts associated with self-control and guidance.

Brief reflection on these groups of concepts suffices for the extraction of
a number of fairly obvious but important points.

(1) The existence of rules typically involves regularities of conduct. But, of course, not all regularities are normative. And, on the other hand, rules can exist without ever being followed, since there may be laws on the statute book which are not enforced, or laws the operative facts of which are not instantiated. Still, the connection with regularity of conduct is clear. It is no coincidence that we speak of non-normative routines, customs, and habits as things done '*as a rule*'.

(2) Rules guide or direct action; or better, *we* guide or direct our actions *by reference to* rules. Rules may direct action mandatorily, as when they stipulate that something must or must not be done. Or they may guide action 'permissively', as when they confer an explicit permission, or stipulate a form of behaviour (e.g. uttering certain words, going through certain conventional procedures) which will have specific desired normative consequences (e.g. making a promise, becoming married, conferring rights, and imposing obligations). Or they may guide action indirectly, by laying down what is to count *as* a so-and-so (e.g. a goal in football, a contract in law, a valid inference in logic). The normative guidance of a rule is not a form of causality. Even mandatory rules do not causally necessitate action. Of course, if one wishes to effect certain normative consequences, one *must* follow the rule compliance with which *normatively* (not causally) produces them (e.g. getting married, making a will). Again, it is no coincidence that we speak of a straight-edge as a *ruler*, viz. an object that *guides* the hand in drawing lines.

(3) Rules are, or provide, *standards* of conduct. They are norms against which conduct is *assessed* or 'measured' for correctness or incorrectness. Rules of law are standards of legal behaviour, rules of grammar are canons of correct speech. Just as rules guide behaviour, so too they have an evaluative dimension. They are measures of deviance and conformity. Here too, it is no coincidence that we speak of a metre *rule*, viz. a measure for the evaluation of the length of objects.

(4) Rules may originate in very different ways. They may or may not emanate from an authority. If they do that authority may itself have been created by rules (a legislative body) or it may not. If they are not so created, the rules may exist in so far as they are generally accepted as rules in a social group, followed, alluded to in criticism, and invoked in justification – as are normative customs, practices, and conventions. Or, like maxims, principles, and precepts, their existence may not depend upon *general* acceptance but upon individual use, citation, and guidance.

(5) Rules typically possess a dual kind of generality. They are standardly general with regard to the multiplicity of occasions for their application

and with regard to their subjects. This does not, of course, mean that one person cannot, by himself, adopt a rule, but only that if he can, then the same rule can also be adopted by someone else.

Given the diversity of types of rule, the forms of rule-creation, and the modes of existence of rules, one naturally hesitates to generalize. Rules of language and rules of logic are, in many ways, unlike paradigmatic rules of law, social behaviour, or morality. But even this brief survey should suffice to plant some initial seeds of doubt concerning the possibility of rules which exist *and* guide conduct, rendering it correct or incorrect, *independently of human consciousness or volition*. We shall cultivate these seeds as we progress.

Normative activities are typically taught and explained by citing the rules which govern them. We *formulate* rules. Many kinds of sentence may be used as rule-formulations. Restricting ourselves for a moment to mandatory rules alone, note that a rule-formulation may be a deontic sentence incorporating a deontic auxiliary verb ('ought', 'must'), or a dominative (to use Bentham's term) incorporating the term 'shall'; it may be phrased frequentatively ('The President presents his Cabinet to the Assembly within a week of his election'), or couched in the imperative. It is noteworthy that sentences used for rule-formulations can typically be used for other purposes too. Deontic sentences can be used to make normative statements,[19] i.e. to state that a rule exists or is in force, or to issue directives, and the dominative or frequentative forms have obvious non-normative uses. That a sentence *is* used to formulate a rule is thus typically not a feature merely of its form.

It would be needlessly restrictive to assume that the formulation of a rule must always take the form of a *sentence*. A diagram or blueprint may function as part of a rule-formulation and may be used in the same way as a rule-formulation, guiding action and providing a standard by reference to which action is evaluated as right or wrong. So too a conversion chart (of weights and measures, or of currency exchange rates), a signpost or a traffic light fulfil rule-like functions. For *we treat* these objects as providing norms guiding our behaviour, we give normative justifications and explanations of our action by reference to them, and we evaluate action as correct or incorrect by appeal to them. Note that a norm-like instruction may be given by a mere gesture. It is further plausible to recognize as rule-formulations paradigmatic exemplifications given as normative ex-

---

[19] For this terminology, see G. H. von Wright, *Norm and Action* (Routledge & Kegan Paul, London, 1963), p. 105.

planations, e.g. 'No, one does not do it like *that*, but like *this*' (exemplifying the action). So too when it comes to giving rules for the use of words, e.g. definitions or explanations of word-meaning, we must recognize as normative not only explicit or formal definitions, but also definitions by exemplification (' "Thumping the table" means doing *this*'), by a series of examples that are to be taken in a certain way (with a trajectory, as it were) as in explanations of family-resemblance concepts, by canonical paradigms as in explanations of 'metre' or 'yard', or by arbitrary samples, as in ostensive definitions of colour-words. In many such cases the rule-formulation involves non-linguistic 'concrete' objects which are *given* a normative role in determining what counts as a correct use of an expression thus defined.[20]

These reflections on rule-formulations may prompt further questions about the relations between rules and language. Is a rule itself a linguistic (or symbolic) object, a sentence or a concrete object used as a paradigm? Or is a rule the *meaning* of a linguistic expression? What is the ontological relation between a rule and its formulation? Are rules language-dependent for their existence? Can there be rules that have never been formulated by those who follow them? Can there exist rules that have never been formulated by anyone?

We certainly speak of writing down rules, phrasing them perspicuously, rephrasing them more concisely, translating them into French, etc. This suggests that rules are linguistic entities. Yet it is very misleading to *identify* rules with their formulations. We write down, rephrase, translate propositions, statements and judgments, but it would be a mistake to identify these with the sentences that express them. If a rule-formulation is in fact in the form of a sentence, it must be an English, French, etc., sentence. But the rule formulated need not be English or French. The rule-formulation specifies the rule *in* a given language, but this does not make the rule a linguistic expression. There may be many different formulations of the same rule, but not of the same rule-formulation. We do not, in general, tailor our normative language to the form of sentences, i.e. we conform to, follow, break, violate, enact, abrogate, etc. *rules*, but not sentences.

Are rules, then, the *meanings* of rule-formulations? This too is wrong. Philosophers typically associate sentence-meaning with type-sentences. But whether a particular sentence-token formulates a rule (as opposed,

[20] For detailed elaboration of these points, see G. P. Baker and P. M. S. Hacker, *Wittgenstein: Understanding and Meaning* (Blackwell, Oxford, 1980), pp. 69ff., 168ff., 284ff.

say, to making a normative statement) depends on the circumstances of its use. Are rules then akin to statements or judgments made by the use of token-sentences? After all, one can have different formulations of one and the same rule, just as one can have different formulations of one and the same judgment or proposition. There is indeed a kinship, but not an identity. Rules are not true or false (although it may be true or false that a certain rule obtains), whereas statements and judgments may be. Unlike the abstract, timeless, objects of logic (statements, judgments, propositions), but like commands, rules are typically temporal entities that come into existence and pass away. For rules may be enacted or stipulated *at* a specific time by an authority. Or, unlike commands, they may be adopted gradually by members of a social group *over* a period of time. They may be in force in certain places and social groups and not in others. And they may be abrogated or annulled at specific times, or fall slowly into desuetude. In these and many other respects rules are unlike the apparently sempiternal objects of logic.

That rules are not linguistic entities does not prejudge the issue of whether, and in what ways, rules are language-dependent for their existence. It is obvious that some rules at least are so dependent, e.g. rules created by specific enactment. This includes statute law, formalized rules of associations or games, rules laid down by rule-creating authorities, and also explicitly stipulated meaning-rules. In these cases the mode of dependence is generative, i.e. first, the complex intention behind the enacted rule is itself language-dependent, and secondly, the rules are created by means involving the use of language. It does not follow, however, that this is the only form of dependence of rules upon language, even in the case of such intentionally created rules.

Customary rules, rules of social morality, social mores, common law, rules of etiquette and rules of grammar are not enacted nor produced by other acts conventionally recognized as norm-creating. Admittedly, *we* typically codify them and our codification often changes the normative situation inasmuch as we may use the codification as a canon; but such rules can obtain without being codified. Is their existence language-independent? We might approach this question obliquely. Can animals that lack a language have rules, follow or violate rules? Certainly animals display regular behavioural patterns, including regular *reactions* to regular behaviour. Moreover, certain kinds of deviation from regular behavioural patterns typically meet with distinctive aggressive reaction (e.g. in cases of failing to conform to the pecking order). Such behavioural interplay appears to be a rule-like phenomenon. What grounds might we have for refusing to take the additional step of attributing genuine normative behaviour to non-language-using creatures? It is that, in the absence of a capacity to formulate a rule or recognize a rule-formulation, a creature lacks other capacities distinctive of rule-following; it cannot *justify* its behaviour by reference to a rule, cannot *consult* a rule in guiding its behaviour in doubtful cases, cannot *correct* its behaviour by *referring* to the rule, and cannot *criticize* its own or others' behaviour by alluding to the rule. Although a rule is distinct from its formulation, if no formulation is possible, a creature cannot use a rule as a guide to conduct or evaluate conduct as correct or incorrect by reference to a rule.[21] Correspondingly, normative explanations of non-language-using creatures' behaviour is out of place, for normativity gets no grip in the absence of the use of symbols.

It might seem, from these remarks, that following a rule is a capacity or cluster of capacities. This would be quite wrong. Following a rule presupposes possession of distinctive capacities, but is not identical with them. It is an aspect of certain acts that they are performed with the *intention* of conforming to, or being in accord with, appropriate rules. And if the intention is satisfied, then the agent has followed the rules. But, of course, an agent may perform the same overt act, yet not be following a rule. He may merely conform (perhaps unwittingly) with the rule, e.g. his act may be precisely what a given rule (of law, perhaps) requires of him in these circumstances, even though he does not know it. Yet it would be wrong to think that whether an agent is following a rule or not must turn on what he does prior to acting as the rule requires (e.g. whether he consulted a rule) or on what crosses his mind while acting (e.g. whether a formulation of the rule occurred to him). Even if God were to look into my mind (or my brain), He could not see there whether I was following a rule, since whatever He may find there by way of my thoughts or formulations of a rule (or their mythical neurological 'realizations'), it is perfectly consistent with my *not* following a rule. And conversely, finding no such mental or neural item is compatible with my actually following a rule. For whether I am following a rule may turn on what I do and say *subsequently*, e.g. on how I justify my behaviour if pressed, how I explain what I did to someone who does not understand my action, or how I would do so if asked.

It might be objected that, since speaking a language is at least in certain respects a rule-governed affair, it must be possible to master a normative practice prior to being able to formulate rules in a language. For children

---

[21] So too numbers are distinct from numerals, but in the absence of numerals there is no mathematics.

learn to use language before they can formulate *in* language any rules at all, including the rules of the language they learn. To this one may reply that language use *begins* (with children) as imitative, reactive and habitual behaviour. *Pace* Chomsky, the roots of the mastery of language lie in *training*.[22] The normativity of the language the child is acquiring lies with the adult who trains (and the linguistic community to which he belongs), not with the child who learns. Of course the transition, both genotypical and phenotypical, from habitual, repetitive, imitative use of signs to rule-governed use of symbols is not a sharp one; the genotypical transition very likely took tens of millennia, the phenotypical one takes two or three years.

Although more argument is called for, and more detailed probing of normative concepts is necessary to clarify what is involved in rule-following, it is at least *prima facie* plausible to see rules as being language-dependent for their existence. Only a language-user or language-learner can follow (and hence violate) rules, although, of course a dog can be trained to conform meticulously with certain sorts of rules. For only a language-user can *use* rules as guides to conduct, *cite* rules as justifications of conduct, act in accord with (or, indeed, in violation of) a rule *for the reason that* such-and-such is the rule, etc. Where rule-formulations incorporate 'concrete symbols' such as samples, those concrete objects have a normative role only in so far as they are viewed from a normative perspective. To view them as normative involves not merely *reacting* to them, but seeing them as *standard-setting*, as providing grounds for evaluation, reasons for criticism and correction, and guidance for behaviour. These capacities are the prerogative of language-users (as are the capacities for having long-term intentions or expectations, a sense of the past, a conscience, etc.).

3   Normative phenomena

The social world we inhabit is made up of normative phenomena. Its very fabric is woven from rules and rule-dependent matter. Law, social and political institutions, morals and mores, economic transactions and relations, languages, logic and mathematics are run through with rules. Much human behaviour, at work or at play, in public and in private, is normative. It is therefore hardly surprising that one characteristic form of

---

[22] Although it is important to note that even trained, regular behaviour is plastic, and not unadaptable. This is so even with the higher mammals, *a fortiori* with humans.

explanation of human behaviour is normative explanation – a form which itself subsumes diverse kinds of explanation with common or linked features.

Normative behaviour, viewed externally, in ignorance of the norms which *inform* it, may seem altogether unintelligible. A story is told of a Chinese mandarin passing through the foreign legations' compound in Peking. Seeing two of the European staff playing an energetic game of tennis, he stopped to watch. Bemused, he turned to a player and said, 'If it is, for some obscure reason, necessary to hit this little ball back and forth thus, would it not be possible to get the servants to do it?'. An alien observing a Roman transferring ownership in a slave by casting a piece of copper into a balance while gripping the slave and pronouncing an appropriate formula may well think that some bizarre form of magic is afoot.[23] Having one's body smeared with oil, one's head weighed down with 10 lb. of metal, one's hand filled with a metallic ball and rod, all to the roars of acclaim of thousands, is altogether unintelligible to someone ignorant of the history, conventions and meaning of coronation ceremonies. But one need not invoke such relatively arcane practices to realize that much of our daily behaviour, including our speech, is bizarre and unintelligible save when seen from a normative point of view.

Explanation of normative phenomena may take many forms, depending upon what feature is perplexing. In general, explanation of a normative act consists in rendering the act intelligible by clarifying its *meaning*, elucidating its *goal* and the *reasons* for performing it. Why did A write his name on that piece of paper? – Because he was signing a cheque. Why was he signing a cheque? – In order to buy an insurance policy. Why did he wish to buy an insurance policy? – Because he recently became a parent and therefore had reason to make provision for his family. And so on. A normative explanation may identify an act in normative terms (identify writing one's name *as* a signing of a cheque). It may explain the normative (conventional) consequences of the act (payment for an insurance policy). It may characterize an act as conformity to a mandatory norm, or as the exercise of a normative power having normative consequences. In general, normative explanations render acts intelligible not by subsumption under causal laws, but by elucidations of their normative meaning, and the goals

---

[23] Indeed, it is amusing that Scandinavian legal realists such as Hagerström and Olivecrona thought that the *mancipatio* ceremony was only intelligible on the assumption that its participants had a host of bizarre magical beliefs. It is curious that they did not think of themselves, when signing a cheque, getting married, voting in an election, as similarly having magical beliefs!

and purposes that may be pursued, given the possibility of the act having such-and-such a meaning.

A normative explanation, therefore, explains a normative act, a normative situation, or a normative consequence by reference to some relevant rule or aspect of a rule. The manner in which the rule is invoked in, or involved in, the explanation will vary from case to case according to the nature of the question. Since such explanations are not causal (i.e. do not serve as explanations in virtue of subsuming an individual case under a general causal law), we do not seek these explanations by experimental observations and inductions. If we want to know what rules inform certain activities and give them meaning, we typically *ask the participants*. Their specifications of what rules they are following or are trying to follow typically have an authoritative status. An agent's sincere assertion that he was making a promise, kicking a goal, buying a ticket, checking his opponent's king, voting for the amendment to the motion, and so on, or that he was trying to effect these acts, are not *hypotheses*. And such an agent's explanation of what makes his utterance a promise, his kick a goal, his handing over money a purchase, etc. are not theories which he concocts on the basis of past observations. They are rather explanations of the rules which he is following or trying to follow.[24]

Where we are puzzled about the normative nature of an act, when we do not understand what it is that is being done, our bafflement may be resolved by means of an explanation of the normative significance of the act, an explanation which a participant in the practice is typically well-qualified to give.[25] This explanation, which presents the act, its antecedents and consequences, in the light of the rules under which it falls, is

[24] His explanations are not, of course, immune to error. He may himself have misconstrued the rule – but not *everyone* who plays the game can have done so. He may have unwittingly violated some rule which ensures that his purposes are frustrated (he may be offside). He may not have secured uptake in some form or other (his 'partner' may refuse his promise). These, and many other, slips are possible. But their identification as slips, infelicities, failures presupposes the possibility of an identification of the rules and of the relevant behaviour by some participant in the practice, not as a theoretical conjecture, but as a piece of practical knowledge.

[25] Typically, but not uniformly; for the more institutionalized a practice the more likely that its typical participants glimpse only a fragment of a complex whole, since the whole involves the interlocking of activities of a multitude of different people. This is strikingly obvious in the case of the law. Hence there is room there for authoritative expertise. So too in the case of complex institutionalized methods of measuring: few of the multitude who engage in weighing and measuring know much about the determination of standard units by institutes of weights and measures. Similar considerations apply to the institution and use of money.

not a piece of social scientific theory. Unlike scientific theorizing, its explanatory force is not measured by its predictive power. Indeed, the explanation often does not explain what is done when such-and-such circumstances occur, but rather what is *to be done*. Rules are sometimes violated, but non-conformity to a rule (unlike an exception to an hypothesis) may frequently confirm its existence rather than disconfirm it, since violation of rules, if detected by participants in a practice, typically calls forth critical reactions of various kinds. Identification of the rules guiding an activity renders the activity *intelligible*, but it may not make it predictable. It will make the normative (non-causal) consequences of certain acts 'predictable', but not on inductive or causal grounds. It may make subsequent acts genuinely predictable, but only by reference to considerations relevant to practical reasoning within the framework of the norms of the given practice. For, of course, when an act has been correctly identified in appropriate normative terms as, e.g., an act of conveyance, castling in chess, the making of a promise, there may still be much left to explain, namely why the person sold the slave, why he castled at this juncture in the game, what the point of making this promise was. It is noteworthy that the kinds of question that do arise here are teleological. And the forms of explanation involve citing *reasons*. These will typically specify grounds for action, goals and purposes pursued, values aimed at. In many cases the reason or part of the reason for an action whose rationale may be in question is that a certain *rule* requires it.

Normative behaviour is *informed* by rules, shaped by or given meaning by the rules that it falls under. It is the rules that make the behaviour what it is. We may term this feature the *definitory* aspect of rules. It is, however, only one aspect. Rules *guide*, *justify* and *explain* behaviour. These three features are pregnant with possibilities of misunderstanding.

How do rules guide behaviour? A rule is a standard, canon or norm of conduct that is to be followed, or a paradigm or model to be copied or emulated, not a set of rails down which one is forced. When one follows a rule (as opposed to incidentally conforming to it), the rule does not *make* one do anything (how could an object like a rule do such a thing?), but rather one makes oneself do what the rule requires. That the rule stipulates thus-and-so will typically be part of the practical reasoning involved in the justification of one's act. Rules guide us, tell us, indeed determine, what *ought to be done*. We ourselves determine what *is* done. Rules can fulfil their guiding function in many different ways. One may consult a rule prior to following it, as when one looks up the income tax laws before filling in a tax return. A rule may visibly enter into an activity, as when one employs a table of exchange rates when purchasing foreign currency or a colour-chart when ordering a particular shade of paint needed for decoration. A rule-formulation may cross one's mind before one acts, or in the course of acting. In all such cases, and other related ones, a rule fulfils a guiding function. But it is crucial to note that these cases do not exhaust the forms of guidance by rules that are criteria for behaviour to be normative. For one may not, in this sense, *use* a rule (or rule-formulation) in the course of following a rule. One may rather invoke the rule in justification. This too is an aspect of being guided by a rule.

We frequently cite a rule, a paradigmatic sample used as a rule, or an array of operative facts stipulated by a rule as conditions for a required action when we claim that we have been complying with the rule, and when we justify what we have done as being in compliance with the rule or as *counting* as satisfying a normative description. For our behaviour to be normative or rule-guided, it is no more necessary that a rule or rule-formulation 'enter into' the behaviour or reflections explicitly preceding or accompanying it than it is necessary for behaviour to be intentional that it be preceded by an act of decision. A false (typically causal) picture of voluntary and intentional action distorts our conception of human action in general, and a false picture of being guided by rules may similarly distort our conception of normative action in particular.

We invoke a rule *ex post actu* in criticizing conduct for deviating from what is required and in rebutting such criticisms. The rule (or its formulation) functions in our practices as a standard determining correct or incorrect applications of it. We use citations of rules and invoke appropriate descriptions of acts as falling under those rules in determining whether a given act is an instance of following a rule. Rules fulfil a justificative role as providing reasons or partial reasons for action, an evaluative role as providing standards of correctness or incorrectness, and a determinative role in deciding the applicability or inapplicability of normative characterizations.

Of course, most normative behaviour is not a matter of consulting rule-formulations in the course of deliberation. Nor is it typically given explicit justification by citing rules, since challenges, demands for justification and explanation are relatively rare. The behaviour of participants in a game of chess is normative through and through, yet the rules will neither explicitly 'enter into' their actions nor typically be cited in justification (the less chatter and redundant explanations in the course of the game the better). But, of course, they are in a position to offer such justifications and explanations. Typically rules are involved in our daily conduct in virtue of being incorporated in the characteristic normative descriptions of our behaviour (as, e.g., buying and selling, promising and keeping promises, voting and being elected, making wills and inheriting legacies, or getting married or divorced) and in the explanations which we give or would give of such descriptions. Typically we view our conduct in appropriate ways *under the aspect of normativity*. We do not *interpret* it thus, we see it so. Our application of normative predicates to the behaviour we view thus does not typically rest on any *inference*. When a chess player makes an appropriate move, I do not *interpret* it as a move (as if it might have been just a muscular 'tic' causing him to move his queen two squares), I take it as one. When someone says 'What is the time?', I take him as having asked me the time, not as having made a noise which now needs interpreting (viz. maybe it was Chinese, or just a meaningless sound). Yet though our use of normative language in identifying typical human conduct does not generally rest on an inference from non-normative behaviour and the existence of a rule under which it is subsumed, nevertheless our *explanations* of the meanings of the normative terminology we thus use (e.g. 'promise', 'check', 'buy', 'sell', 'vote', 'elect', 'marry', 'will', 'property') will typically involve reference to rules.

Rules also enter into our daily activities in at least three other important ways. The first is in teaching and explaining. We cite rules and explain what counts as conforming with them when we teach rule-governed activities. This is obvious in the case of teaching games, law, languages, mathematics, etc. The second is an extension of the first, since parents and pedagogues apart, we are not frequently called upon to teach, but we do constantly engage in discussion, description and evaluation of actual and possible normative behaviour. We frequently explain or argue over what is to be done, why it is unwise to act thus-and-so, whether doing thus will count as this or that, and so on. Thirdly, many of us have occasion to *make* rules, both formal and informal, when playing games with children, or when 'laying down the law', as parents or pedagogues, as committee chairmen, or as managers.

Doubtless additional refinement will reveal a host of further features. Our purpose has not been exhaustive itemization, but an assemblage of reminders of what we naturally conceive of as rules, following rules, being guided by rules, and evaluating or criticizing actions by reference to rules. We have indicated some of the ways in which normative concepts are involved in describing, explaining and justifying behaviour. Our pen sketch should suffice to make clear the fact that the existence of rules is firmly connected with conduct viewed from a normative perspective, and that following rules is firmly connected with intentional behaviour and with the possibility of giving explicit normative explanations and justifications.

4 The existence of rules and the determination of their consequences

In speaking of rules at all, we are, in a sense, speaking of fictions, as in speaking of propositions. Whether these convenient fictions will bedazzle us, leading us into muddle and confusion, or not depends upon our propensity to philosophical illusions. Many a logical theory has come to grief on metaphysical rocks through misconstrual of harmless turns of phrase about propositions.[26] Similar dangers attend investigations into normative phenomena.

We typically codify rules, giving them systematic formulation in authoritative canons. Clearly, for certain purposes codification has great utility. It contributes to a greater uniformity in practice, facilitates resolution of disputes, and may help in rationalizing the rules themselves, e.g. in ironing out potential conflicts of rules or merely in highlighting the potentialities of conflict. We speak of rules as if they were kinds of entities. We attribute a host of different properties to them. Rules may be good or wicked, efficient or cumbersome, they may have names designating their originator, they may be members of sets or systems of logically interrelated rules, and they may be simple or complex, ingenious or stupid. Some rules are conceived of as being created, capable of being changed, and liable to abrogation. Some such rules we think of as being created, but not voluntarily so, such as customs. And some rules *appear* not to be created at all, and not to be open to abrogation, such as the laws of logic.

We thus conceive of rules as *existing*, and of some rules as capable of ceasing to exist. The criteria for there being rules determining a given activity vary from case to case. Broadly speaking, rules of social morality, mores, etiquette, rules of games, and arguably rules of language, exist in so far as they are generally invoked by members of a social group, directly or indirectly, in guiding, justifying, explaining, identifying and teaching the behaviour to which they are relevant. Legal rules exist in so far as the legal system exists of which they are members in virtue of their satisfying criteria of recognition used by law-applying organs. Similar considerations apply to rules that belong to institutionalized systems of rules with recognized means of adjudication, creation and abrogation. Rules of logic (or arith-

---

[26] Cf. A. N. Prior, *Objects of Thought* (Oxford University Press, Oxford, 1971), chs. 1f.

metic) are typically conceived as sempiternal, immune to change and secure from human interference. This Platonist picture is potentially deceptive, trembling on the brink of metaphysical nonsense. The seeming sempiternality of the laws of logic is rooted not in the superphysics of Platonic objects, nor in metaphysical mysteries of the adamantine laws of thought, but in the fact that they are partly definitive of what we call 'thinking', 'inferring', and 'reasoning'. They are immovable, as it were, because we do not move them.

We noted that a rule is not identical with its formulation. A rule is not a sentence, nor does it possess properties which token formulations of it possess. But inasmuch as we feel free to speak of rules *existing*, we naturally feel inclined to wonder what kinds of things they are. It is, of course, tempting to say that rules are abstract entities, like propositions, yet unlike propositions in typically being temporal objects. This is true, but gravely misleading. When certain complex patterns of behaviour obtain then we are justified in talking of a rule as existing. It is a convenient *façon de parler*, an ontological fiction. What it conceals is that the sole reality of which we speak consists of interlocking patterns of actual and potential justification and explanation, actions and reactions, uses of rule-formulations in guiding conduct or in evaluating it. What it misleadingly suggests is that rules are kinds of objects, which exist or can exist independently of what we do with them (by invoking, using, their formulations), and which perhaps can, independently of us, determine what we do. The roots of mythology here are deep. We shall later unearth some of the nastier specimens embedded in the quagmires of modern linguistic theories.

We certainly speak of a rule's determining consequences and of something's following from a rule. We picture a rule as a necessitating force; given this rule, we say, such-and-such must be done. If a certain rule requires Bs to φ in circumstance C, and if you are a B in C, if follows that you ought to φ. Or, slightly differently, if the chess king is in such-and-such a position, and the opponent's rook moves thus-and-so, it follows that the king is in check. And again, given that p, and that p implies q, it follows that q. The rules of law, of chess, or of logic make it so!

But how can a rule determine a consequence? The picture of a normative force is clear enough, but what is the application of the picture? We must not let ourselves be any the more deceived by it than we are by the picture involved in the turn of phrase 'I have the word on the tip of my tongue'. Determining a consequence here is not a causal notion at all, but a logical or conceptual one. When we talk of rules as having or determining consequences, or of certain things as following from or being determined by a rule, we are referring to internal relations. In conceiving of a form of words as *expressing a rule*, we *ipso facto* conceive of some other form of words as a specification of what *counts* as complying with the rule thus expressed. Hence we conceive of a given rule and acts which follow it as internally related. This is part of, or an aspect of, the very concept of a rule. A rule, we might say in metaphorical language echoing the *Tractatus*, must contain a picture of what counts as compliance with it, otherwise how could it guide us, how would we know from the mere rule, what it is that we must do to follow it? This metaphor captures the internal relation between a rule and the acts of rule-following in compliance with it, and between grasping or understanding a rule and knowing what to do in compliance with it. In grasping a rule, understanding the meaning of a rule-formulation, one grasps a 'method of projection' from the rule to the specification of what counts as compliance with it. Indeed, only thus *can* a rule constitute a standard or canon, provide a guide to conduct.

It is evident that the 'picture' of a rule as an abstract entity (like a proposition) generates puzzles if we do not attend sufficiently to the way it is applied, to the circumstances of use of terms such as 'rule', 'guidance', 'determined by rules', etc. How can an abstract object, we may wonder, determine what is to be done in conformity with it? How can such an entity, by itself, determine what counts as complying with it? To take a famous example from Wittgenstein, how can the rule of a series, e.g. '+2', *determine* that 1000 is followed by 1002? If a nominalist insists, in his anti-Platonist fervour, that all that really exists here are signs, rule-formulations and specifications of consequences, we may indignantly retort that that just aggravates our bafflement. For how could a mere sign determine that something follows from a rule? Platonism about rules and its nominalist antithesis breed insoluble puzzles and confusions. For the Platonist entertains fancies about normative fields of force, and the nominalist typically construes rule-following as a matter of altogether mysterious dispositions, as if the reason one complies with the instruction to add 2 by writing 1002 after 1000 were that 'one finds it natural', or that members of a community 'have a disposition' to do so.[27] Conceived Platonistically it must be a mystery that anything can follow from, or be determined by, a rule – a mystery typically painted in the lurid colours of the superphysics of logical objects. Conceived nominalistically, it does

---

[27] For this bizarre view, see C. Peacocke, 'Following a Rule: the Basic Themes', in *Wittgenstein: to Follow a Rule*, ed. S. Holtzman and C. Leich (Routledge & Kegan Paul, London, 1981), pp. 91ff.

indeed follow that we could count anything as conforming to a given rule, given enough interpretative licence. And habits and dispositions seem the only respectable items to invoke to prevent such absurdity, even though this move evacuates rules of their essential normativity, and renders natural dispositions unnaturally normative.

Correctly viewed, the concept of a rule and the concept of what acts comply with it are not independent. We do not first grasp, understand, a rule, and then cast around to see whether we can understand what follows from it, or what counts as compliance with it. It is true that only creatures in possession of common imitative propensities can learn to follow rules. But that a certain consequence follows from a rule, is *correct*, is not a matter of our 'natural dispositions', but of our normative creations. We act in certain patterns, which we view normatively. We justify, explain and guide our actions by reference to patterns. In so doing we formulate rules, and use rule-formulations together with their method of projection on to actions in teaching, explaining, justifying, correcting or criticizing action. A rule is no more independent of its consequences (of what follows from it, of what it requires or necessitates) than is an expectation independent of what fulfils it, i.e. of what we *call* 'satisfying the expectation that so-and-so'. If we conceive of a rule as containing a picture of what counts as compliance with it, we must remember that this metaphor must be unpacked. For a rule to 'contain' such a picture simply is *for us* to treat a rule (by using a formulation of it and a variety of normative expressions internally related to its formulation) in a certain way, as a measure of correctness, a guide to conduct, and an explanation or justification of behaviour.

Rules are not mysterious Platonic receptacles containing their applications, independently of human volition. There cannot be more in a rule than we put in it, and what we 'put in it' is revealed by our normative practices. A partial prophylaxis against the Platonist receptacle picture is not to think of the rule as identical with a rule-formulation, but rather as the *manner of using* a rule-formulation. If there is a rule requiring one to follow a signpost at a given point, then, of course, the rule is not identical with the signpost (the plank of wood) or with its Platonic shadow; but what the rule is, what it 'contains', is wholly determined by the way we use the signpost in guidance, justification, criticism, explanation and normative description.

The idea of a rule determining its applications independently of us seems to have at least two sources. First, that we use a rule as a norm of correctness, and hence are prone to be misled by the partial truth that a rule determines correctness independently of us (as we might think that the Law delivers the verdict independently of judges, since the judge's verdict may be quashed, and he too may be condemned by the Law). Secondly, we misleadingly think of a rule as akin to a mathematical function, and we compound confusion by having a muddled conception of a function.[28] So we conceive of a rule as determining what follows from it (and what conforms with it) in much the same way as we think of a function as determining its value for any possible argument within its domain. But a similar fallacy operates in both cases. Pseudo-entities such as rules or functions can determine nothing of their own accord; only we can determine such things by using symbols (function names or rule-formulations), tables, samples or patterns in certain regular and normative ways. We stipulate a value for every argument of a function, or a method of calculation for it. We fix what is to *count* as following a given rule, and hence what it is to conform to it. Hence a rule can contain no more than we collectively decide, in our normative practices, to put into it.

These tentative remarks about rules, their formulation and existence-conditions, and their roles in normative behaviour and its explanation are mere sketches of a complex network of normative concepts. They do, however, provide a sufficiently detailed backcloth, of a rough-and-ready kind, against which to display the comedy of modern theories of language and their struggles with the concept of linguistic rules. Indeed, they should enable us now to have the confidence to challenge some of the fundamental commitments of such theories. Can rules of any kind exist unbeknownst to those who follow them? Can we *discover* that for centuries we have been following rules that were hidden from us? Can an activity be rule-governed even though those who engage in it cite none of the rules allegedly informing it and do not justify or explain their behaviour by reference to them? Is it possible for anyone to follow a rule which he cannot understand? Is there any room for *theories* about rules and rule-governed behaviour?

---

[28] Indeed, if we think of a function as a rule or law of correlation of mathematical entities, the circularity is patent.

CHAPTER 8

The Mythology of Rules

1 Methodological confusions

Modern theoretical linguists and philosophical theorists of meaning conduct their investigations under the aegis of a variety of dubious methodological commitments. (i) Such theorists distinguish between synchronic and diachronic investigations into languages, and typically take themselves to be exclusively concerned with the former. (ii) Their investigations are thought to have an essential psychological, cognitive, dimension. They claim to be studying what it is that a speaker *knows* when he knows a language, and this theory is supposed to *explain* how it is possible for a speaker to *understand* his language. (iii) Though trying to construct explanations of a speaker's mastery of a language, they do not concern themselves primarily with the exercise of this skill, i.e. with actual linguistic or logical performances (warts and all), but with *competence*. Moreover, (iv) it is not the competence of any particular (or average) person that is under investigation, but the competence of an 'Ideal Speaker-Hearer'. These four ideas, articulated more explicitly by linguists than philosophers, provide an essential underpinning to the theorists' investigations. We shall explain what they are, why they are viewed as indispensable, and suggest that they are, if not altogether incoherent, at best very misleading.

Synchronic linguistics

The originator of the distinction between synchronic and diachronic linguistics was Saussure. The linguist, he insisted, may study the history of the development of a given language or languages, or he may study a particular language as it exists at a given time. On his view, the latter, synchronic investigation studies not speech (*la parole*), but the system of language (*la langue*) from which it flows. This system is conceived, fairly crudely, on the bi-planar model of correlations of sound-images with concepts. It is a 'self-contained whole',[1] a 'well-defined object' which 'can be localized in the limited segment of the speech-circuit where an auditory image becomes associated with a concept'.[2] Although it is 'the social side of speech', and exists 'only by virtue of a sort of contract signed by members of a community', nevertheless 'Linguistic signs, though basically psychological, are not abstractions; associations which bear the stamp of collective approval – and which added together constitute language – are realities that have their seat in the brain'.[3] The system of language, thus conceived, can and should be studied independently of its historical evolution.

There is much confusion here. Linguistic signs are *not* psychological objects. They do not have meanings (are not meaningful) in virtue of being psychologically associated with other entities, viz. concepts; and concepts are not psychological objects. A language is not 'localized' in a segment of a mythical speech-circuit, and it does not exist by virtue of any sort of social contract. And it is absurd to insist both that a language is a social institution *and* that it is a reality having its seat in the brain (unless that simply means that one needs a brain to be able to speak a language). But despite these wild confusions, there is a kernel of sense in Saussure's remark.

Numerous historical facts about a language are irrelevant to what the expressions of the language now mean. It is not necessary for understanding of a language to know by what complex changes its grammar and vocabulary evolved. That the French '*pas*' (= step) and '*pas*' (= not) have the same origin is irrelevant to correctly explaining their current uses, which are quite distinct, and one need not know this interesting fact as a condition for knowing the meanings of the two words. Similarly, a description of contemporary English need not, in general, hark back to the evolution of English over ten centuries. Historical data concerning the development of a language are only relevant to the description of a language in so far as they enter into correct explanations of the current meanings and combinatorial forms of expressions in the langue.

This is not a point over which to quarrel. But Saussure stated his case by means of a pair of potentially misleading metaphors. He compared his synchronic perspective on a language to a botanist's cross-cut of a stem of a plant (as opposed to a longitudinal cut). The danger of the analogy between a spatial slice of a spatial object and the proper object of the

---

[1] F. de Saussure, *Course in General Linguistics*, tr. W. Baskin (Fontana, London, 1974).
[2] Ibid., p. 14; for Saussure's conception of a speech-circuit, see above p. 18.
[3] Ibid., p. 15.

science of non-historical linguistics is the suggestion that the latter should ideally study something that might be thought of as 'an instantaneous cross-cut' of a natural language. But there is no such thing, and a grammar (or dictionary) of a natural language is at best misleadingly represented as a 'temporal slice' of the language. In so far as grammar and lexicography are conceived to be what a speaker has to know in order to speak and understand a language correctly, they both have an unavoidable historical dimension. Even more confusingly, Saussure suggested that 'the most fruitful' analogy is between the functioning of a language and a positional state of a game of chess.[4] For a given position in chess is intelligible independently of the route whereby it emerged. Someone who has observed the game holds no advantage over someone who has just come to inspect it. So too, Saussure claimed, 'speaking operates only on a language-state and the changes that intervene between states have no place in either state.'[5] Again the analogy limps. One understands a chess-position in so far as one has some idea of what move to make next, some notion of what strategies are available in pursuit of the goal of checkmating one's adversary. One understands a language in so far as one can speak it, explain words and sentences of it, and respond intelligently to its use. But these speech-acts and related activities have no analogue in Saussure's picture, since subsequent moves in the game are thought of as analogous to later historical stages of the language. What corresponds to subsequent stages in language are not sequential states of a game, but generic changes in the evolution of the game, e.g. chess as played by the Vikings in contrast with chess as we now play it.

No matter, it might be said, if the analogies are lame.[6] The salient issue is that Saussure correctly saw that the history of a language is in one sense irrelevant to its current description. This is so; yet he did not *correctly* see this simple fact, but rather distorted and misrepresented it. For he assimilated this limited truth to an altogether misleading psychologization of the subject-matter of linguistics and a thorough-going methodological muddle. He emphasized that *the* salient feature of 'the facts of language is that their succession in time does not exist in so far as the speaker is concerned'.[7] But this is quite wrong, in at least two respects. First, the

---

[4] Ibid., pp. 88f.

[5] Ibid., p. 89.

[6] The best analogy for Saussurean purposes is between synchronic/diachronic investigations and phenetic (or numerical)/phyletic taxonomy; but, notoriously, phenetic taxonomy is methodologically unsound.

[7] Ibid., p. 81.

normal life-span of a human being will allow one to live through significant linguistic change, of which one will typically be aware. One can indeed talk freely as a youngster with one's grandfather and as an old man with one's grandson. Can it really be said that the synchronic viewpoint 'is the true and only reality to the community of speakers'?[8] Secondly, just because Saussure assigned a methodological primacy to speech, he neglected the fact that we live in a literate culture, a fact which gives our mastery of our language an unavoidable diachronic dimension (see below).

Having misrepresented the extent to which and manner in which the evolution of a language is irrelevant to its current mastery, Saussure proclaimed that the linguist purporting to study *la langue* must totally disregard diachrony. But his reason for this methodological principle was the claim that the linguist can 'enter the mind of speakers only by completely suppressing the past'.[9] The method of synchrony 'consists of gathering evidence from speakers; to know to just what extent a thing is a reality, it is necessary and sufficient to determine to what extent it exists in the minds of speakers'.[10] But it is only because he misguidedly thought that one can correctly characterize a language as a system of mentally correlated acoustic images and concepts that Saussure believed that the linguist *needs* to 'enter the mind of speakers', rather than examine the active and reactive behaviour of speakers of a language, their uses of language, and the explanations they give of expressions they use or encounter.

Despite these confusions Saussure retained a solid core of good sense in his characterization of a 'language state' which a non-historical linguist should study: 'In practice a language state is not a point, but rather a certain span of time during which the sum of the modifications that have supervened is minimal. The span may cover ten years, a generation, a century or even more. . . . studying a language state means in practice disregarding changes of little importance'.[11] This is indeed better sense, but it involves no dramatic new truths heralding a new science, only old truisms familiar to grammarians for many centuries. Moreover combining this truism with Saussure's psychologism produces incoherence, for systems of mentally correlated acoustic images and concepts are not 'states' that span generations or centuries.

[8] Ibid., p. 90.
[9] Ibid., p. 81.
[10] Ibid., p. 90.
[11] Ibid., p. 101.

Modern linguists following in Saussure's footsteps tread even less warily. First, it is argued: 'If we apply strictly the distinction of the diachronic and the synchronic, we will say that the notion of one language (e.g. English) existing over the centuries . . . is fallacious. What we have underlying the language-behaviour of people living at different periods are distinct language-systems'.[12] Secondly, since it is noted that temporal variations in standard English, for example, may be far smaller than regional (spatial) variations, 'what we are accustomed to think of as 'languages', for example English, French or Japanese, are not languages in the sense defined . . . what we call English may be considered to be a family of languages having as many members as there are fluent speakers of what is agreed upon as English.'[13] English, it seems, is not to be thought of as the language of Shakespeare and Dryden, Johnson and Gibbon, Dickens and Trollope, or as the language spoken, with variations, throughout the British Isles and most of its ex-colonies. Rather are there as many English languages as the product of speakers of what is 'pre-theoretically' called 'English' and the number of time-slices the synchronic theorist chooses to take. This distorts the subject-matter of linguistics before the investigation has even commenced. For it is a complete abuse of the concept of a language. It stems in part from the Saussurean psychologization of *la langue* as a system of psychological correlations underlying *la parole*, and in part from a consequent distortion of the modest idea of non-historical investigations into languages. The extent of the distortion becomes even more evident when one encounters the standard modern linguists' claim that a language is an infinite collection of sentences. This infinity of sentences is not the totality of English sentences that have been, are being, or (optimistically?) will be spoken. It is rather a synchronically conceived infinity, for it is 'the collection of sentences that a fluent person would be able to produce or comprehend had he the time [*sic*!], energy and motivation'.[14] But this infinite collection is not what the linguist studies. The language ·

make[s] available [to a speaker] an infinity of sentences from which the speaker can select appropriate and novel ones to use as the need arises . . .

A synchronic description of a natural language seeks to determine what a fluent speaker knows about the structure of his language that enables him to use and understand any sentence drawn from the INFINITE set of sentences of his

[12] J. Lyons, *Semantics* (Cambridge University Press, Cambridge, 1977), vol. 1, p. 243.

[13] D. Terence Langendoen, *The Study of Syntax: the Generative-Transformational Approach to the Study of American English* (Holt, Rinehart and Winston, Inc., NY, 1969), p. 2. Cf. Lyons, *Semantics*, p. 243.

[14] Langendoen, *The Study of Syntax*, p. 1.

language, and since, at any time he has only encountered a FINITE set of sentences, it follows that the speaker's knowledge of his language takes the form of rules ...[15]

Putting aside one's immediate qualms about speakers rummaging about in the infinite collection of sentences of their 'momentary' languages and selecting one, note that the *rules* are the favoured object for description in the linguist's synchronic study of a language. Giving a synchronic account or characterization of a language consists, it seems, in a specification of the various kinds of rules allegedly governing it.

One can, indeed, investigate a system of rules at a given time. If one wishes to know the current rules of cricket, one can obtain an authoritative statement of them from the MCC. So too, if one wishes to know the current state of the law of contract, one will find the rules spelt out in the latest edition of the appropriate legal textbook. In such cases the rule-governed activities are institutionalized, and there typically exist authoritative codifications used by appointed adjudicators to enforce normative conformity. The MCC laws specify the rules of cricket as it is currently *to be* played by officially recognized teams, and these codified rules are enforced by umpires. Such rules are published, and they are cited or referred to by participants in the relevant practice. They do not 'exist' in the minds or brains of the participants, any more than *what* a person knows exists in his mind or brain. We may speak of rules existing, meaning thereby that *there are* rules regulating such-and-such activities, as is evident in the behaviour and discourse of those who engage in, talk, or write about the activities. But we may not go on to ask *where* the rules exist, save in the sense that in England such-and-such a game is played according to such-and-such rules, whereas in the USA much the same game is played according to slightly different rules. In the only sense in which rules have a locus, their locus is wherever their jurisdiction extends, or wherever the activity they regulate occurs. And in many cases it simply makes no sense to ask *where* certain rules 'exist'.

Speaking a language is, in certain respects, a rule-governed activity. But it is not an institutionalized one.[16] It typically lacks an authoritative body

---

[15] J. J. Katz and J. A. Fodor, 'The Structure of a Semantic Theory', *Language*, 39 (1963), p. 171.

[16] Although in literate cultures some aspects of it may be, e.g. in post-Johnsonian England orthography and lexicography are, although the mode of institutionalization is altogether different from that of institutionalized games. Of course, there are numerous deeper differences which need not concern us now, e.g. a language, unlike typical games, is not a goal-setting system of rules, for nothing (certainly not truth) stands to language as winning stands to competitive games.

to pronounce upon its rules. Even when it has one, e.g. the Académie française, the legislative sway of its authority is very limited. The normativity of language-using behaviour is embedded in, informs, this behaviour. It is visible in the actions and reactions of speakers, in their use of rules in correcting, explaining and teaching, and in their overt appeal to rules in justifying their usage or criticizing others' misuses. But few, if any, speakers command a view of the whole. Our ordinary conception of a language such as English or French involves an abstraction from the speech and norms of speech of countless people over many generations. No speaker is master of the whole vocabulary. Most speakers make grammatical mistakes more or less frequently, some of which they may recognize when corrected, and others of which they may not. When we vulgar speak, quite correctly, of *the* English language, we are talking of a practice involving multifarious interactions of members of a more or less heterogeneous linguistic community over many generations. And if the linguist complains that our concept of language is not 'well-defined', that we cannot say when Anglo-Saxon became English, or whether pidgin is or is not a form of English, we may admit that this is so. But our concept of a language is none the worse for that, for if the *need* to draw sharp boundary lines arises, then we will determine criteria for doing so from considerations relevant to the need. The concept of number, that paradigm of *a priori*, crystalline concepts, is none the worse for not being sharply defined (for not including quaternions before they were introduced). A linguistic community is, as it were, a social repository of a rich array of instruments of human thought and behaviour. An individual speaker's mastery of the use of these instruments is typically partial and imperfect. The study of a language is an investigation into a 'social whole' that exists in the practices of a community, not a psychological object that exists between the ears of a speaker.

None of this precludes giving a non-historical description of a language as it is to be spoken at a given time (although it does mean that one's description will constitute a paradigm, regional and class deviations from which may be more or less common). But it is important to note that a description of the state of a language and a correct characterization of the skills of a competent speaker will have temporal dimensions which one would not find in a description of the rules of a game.

(i) It is a conceptual truth (not a happy accident) that someone who knows, has learnt, English can not only understand current speech, but centuries of English speech. Our knowledge of English is no *less* evident in our ability to read and understand Raleigh's *History of the World* than in our ability to read and understand the *News of the World*; our mastery of the language manifests itself no less in our being moved by a performance of *Hamlet* than in our being amused by a performance of *Rosenkrantz and Guildenstern Are Dead*. So does the 'infinite collection' of sentences an educated speaker 'would be able to comprehend', which constitute a synchronic segment of the (his?) English language in 1982 *include* much of English literature and letters since, say, 1450? If it does, it is a curious form of synchronicity. If it does not, it excludes much of what an educated English speaker is likely to encounter (and comprehend).[17]

(ii) Current usage in a language may remain in contact with its past in a way in which games typically do not. Past linguistic performance may sometimes mould and influence current practice and development of a language. Thus, e.g., Cicero's prose became a model or paradigm for generations of Latin speakers and writers a millennium later, and not merely a model of elegance or wit, but a paradigm of grammaticality and correct usage. Current games, of cricket for example, are, in this respect, insulated from their history. The performances of a Hutton or Compton do not mould what we count as a *correct* performance today, though they may determine the records current batsmen try to break. A language, in this respect, is more akin to the common law than to statute law.

(iii) A language, at any moment in its history, drags behind it clouds of etymology, shaping current meanings, largely through the influence of the most proficient and educated speakers who are aware of its past. Similarly, the historical associations of words, phrases, idioms, metaphors and quoted sentences still pump life-blood into current discourse. Much of our speech and writing contains intentional echoes and shadows of past uses and usages, direct quotations and indirect allusions. Eliminate these because of a distorted conception of a synchronic description of a language, and the account will leave innumerable chunks of our common discourse only half illuminated. Include them, and what remains of the radical conception of synchrony?

(iv) We noted that in modern literate societies dictionaries come to assume an authoritative status in the matter of word-meaning (and orthography), as the *OED* does in Britain. Despite modern lexicographers' frequent ritual handwashings to disclaim any normative authority, it is a fact of English life, and one to be applauded, that their work has such

---

[17] Note that the phenomenon in question is *not* confined to literate societies. The poetry and sacred literature of pre-literate societies are passed down over many centuries by word of mouth, as the Homeric poems were.

authority. A significant segment of the population uses the dictionary as a norm, a guide to correct usage. Since differences in word-meaning are culled from literary works, and since explanation of word-meaning is facilitated by examples, dictionaries compiled 'on historical principles' ensure that the linguistic wealth of a culture reposed in its literature is a vital force in the recognized norms of current usage. In lexicography a large part of past history is present.

These points do not invalidate an enterprise of a non-historical description of the state of a given language, but merely bring it into sharper focus than the muddled Saussurean and neo-Saussurean characterization of synchronic linguistics. A linguist can, in various ways, describe English as it is to be spoken at present. He might, rather futilely, tabulate the multifarious rules cited by standard average speakers in explanations, justification, criticisms and corrections. Or, much more fruitfully, he might, like the traditional grammarian, describe the normative regularities of modern English. Such a description would not always specify rules uniformly employed by all, or even most, English speakers. The grammarian's 'rules' are generally synopses of the linguistic rules used by speakers, which he formulates on the basis of noticing normative regularities that can be subsumed under more general rules than speakers commonly invoke (e.g. classifying verbs and nouns, and systematically arranging declensions and conjugations). But it is also important to note that given the pedagogic role of the grammarian in literate cultures, his products, like those of the lexicographer, assume a normative status. Grammar books are used in teaching a language, consulted in correcting mistakes, and used as canons for correct speech and writing. To the extent that this occurs the grammarian's observed normative regularities, formulated as *possible* rules, may *become* actual rules. But to the extent that it does *not* occur (e.g. in the case of the putative rules of the transformational-generative grammarian), the grammarian's descriptions have no normative significance. Rules possess no form of 'existence' over and above the uses speakers might make of humdrum rule-formulations, explanations of word-meanings, paradigmatic examples of correct use, and so forth. The principle that there is no action at a distance in grammar applies to 'synchrony' no less than to 'diachrony'. This principle is violated by the bizarre supposition that rules of a language must be 'represented in the mind' of every speaker, buried deep beyond the reach of consciousness and awaiting *discovery* by the linguist. It is this that is typically supposed when linguists and meaning-theorists attribute to language-users *tacit knowledge* of grammar or of a theory of meaning for a natural language.

Knowing a language

The conception of *knowledge* invoked by linguists and theorists of meaning is deeply confused. This is visible in the following quotations:

(1) [A] theory of meaning is a theory of understanding: that is, what a theory of meaning has to give an account of is what it is that someone knows when he knows the language, that, is, when he knows the meanings of the expressions and sentences of the language.[18]

(2) [L]et us assume that it makes sense to say, as we normally do that each person knows his or her language, that you and I know English for example, that this knowledge is in part shared among us and represented somehow in our minds, ultimately in our brains, in structures that we can hope to characterize abstractly, and in principle quite concretely, in terms of physical mechanisms.[19]

(3) To know a language, I am assuming, is to be in a certain mental state, which persists as a relatively steady component of transitory mental states. What kind of mental state? I assume further that to be in such a mental state is to have a certain mental structure consisting of a system of rules and principles that generate and relate mental representations of various types.[20]

There is, in these remarks, an apparent unawareness of the relative anomalousness of the phrase 'knowing a language' and a tendency to treat it as akin to 'knowing physics' (i.e. possessing theoretical information, knowledge of doctrine and theory) coupled with a gross misconstrual of the latter as a *mental state*.

Learning a language is not akin to learning a corpus of fact and theory. Nor, incidentally, is it to learn to correlate signs and meanings.[21] For

---

[18] M. A. E. Dummett, 'What is a Theory of Meaning?' in *Mind and Language*, ed. S. Guttenplan (Clarendon Press, Oxford, 1975).

[19] N. Chomsky, *Rules and Representations* (Blackwell, Oxford, 1980), p. 5.

[20] Ibid., p. 48.

[21] It is an extraordinary fact that linguists cleave to the idea that language or grammar consists, *inter alia*, of *pairing* sounds or signs with *meanings*, as if meanings were items that could be paired with anything. The following two passages exemplify this folly:

It is generally assumed by linguists that the function of a grammar is to link meaning with sound. Given a [well-formed] sequence of speech sounds . . . the hearer is able to process it in such a way that with the aid of circumstantial, contextual and general knowledge he arrives at the meaning . . . Conversely, a speaker, starting with a meaning he intends to formulate in his language for some purpose, is able to process this meaning in such a way that with the aid of circumstantial, contextual, and general

although learning a second language is often partly a matter of learning to correlate signs with *signs,* meanings are not kinds of entities that signs could be correlated with. We learn to use a word. But learning the use of a word is not a matter of correlating the word with a use either, any more than in learning to use money, one correlates coins with values (here the value, there the coin!).

A child who cannot yet speak, who does not know English, is not suffering from lack of *theoretical* knowledge (e.g. a theory for making processed meanings) or from lack of factual information (which meaning a given word is correlated with) although, of course, it does not know the meanings of English words. It is not ignorant of English, as it is ignorant of English history. It is rather unable to speak and understand English. English or French are not objects of knowledge in the way that biology or physics are; to know English is to be able to . . ., not to be well-informed about . . . I can, unwisely, disbelieve well-confirmed theories in physics, or wisely, disbelieve phrenology, but I cannot disbelieve English. I can be incredulous about, and lack faith in, astrology, but not about, or in, English. I can misguidedly suppose alchemy to be true, but not English. What I know when I know physics, chemistry, history, etc. is a body of fact and theory that is well-established, and well-confirmed by supporting evidence. What I know when I know English is not well-confirmed, since it is not a doctrine standing in need of confirmation, and is not supported by

---

knowledge, he arrives at a sound sequence which represents the intended meaning physically. (R. Bartsch and T. Vennemann, *Semantic Structures* (Athenäum Verlag, Frankfurt, 1972), p. 3)

Can meanings really be processed like sausages? And can one 'start with a meaning' and intend to formulate *it* (which one?) in language? Is this not like starting with a length (not a length *of* anything, but just a length) and then, after processing it, arriving at a measurement (feet or metres) which will represent it? Or, again, like starting with a value (not of any object, just a value) and then expressing it in a currency that will represent it!

When an adult learns a new language, he approaches it with certain preconceptions . . . Although the sentences of the language will be unfamiliar to him, he can expect that they will be related *to things that are quite familiar to him, namely meanings . . .*

Before he starts, he knows that no matter what language he is involved with, *he will be called upon to learn individual lexical items, that is, to pair isolated meanings with instructions as to how to pronounce the sequences of sounds that represent them.* (G. Lakoff, *Irregularity in Syntax* (Holt, Rinehart and Winston, Inc., NY, 1970), p. 1; our italics)

On such foundations is the kingdom of linguistics erected!

evidence.[22] But it is no coincidence that linguists and philosophers are prone to conceive of what I know when I know a language as a *theory of the language* (below).

Knowing one's mind is a matter of having and being able to avow a set of determinate wants and intentions; knowing one's wines is a matter of possessing taste and expertise in evaluating wines; knowing modern music well is a matter of familiarity with and capacity to appreciate for appropriate reasons features of contemporary music; and knowing a language is a matter of possession of a wide array of skills associated with speaking and understanding, of being able to use and respond cogently to the use of that language. It is wholly unclear what is meant by 'an account' of what it is that someone knows when he knows English, and even more unclear what 'an account' of knowing the meanings of expressions is supposed to be. If someone can speak a language then he can do a myriad of things with it; he can make assertions, issue statements, express beliefs, opine, reply to questions, refute accusations, concede, agree, ask questions, express doubts, and so on and so forth through an indefinitely long array of acts and activities accessible to language-users. And because he can do these things he may also be able to do countless other things, to build bridges or motor cars, to plan a military strategy or an economic policy, to study law or medicine, to get elected to parliament or to vote in an election, and so on through the endless array of characteristic activities of language-using creatures who have and make a history. To give 'an account' of what someone can do when he can speak a language (what he 'knows' when he 'knows a language') is either trivial or impossible. When someone 'knows the meanings of expressions of a language', he can say what they mean, i.e. answer questions of the form 'What does "X" mean?', just as someone who knows the time can say what time it is. He can use expressions correctly, explain them cogently, and react coherently to their use by others. Any further philosophical account of 'what someone knows when he knows the meanings of expressions' either descends to specific detail of no *necessary* philosophical interest,[23] or ascends on the wings of misguided theory into the clouds of truth-conditional semantics.

We do, indeed, say that we know our own language, and that is not something that needs to be *assumed*. But we certainly do not normally say that this knowledge is 'represented somehow in our minds', and if we do

---

[22] And although, if I know English I know the meaning of English words, i.e. I can, *inter alia*, explain the meanings of many words, my knowledge that, e.g., 'bachelor' means unmarried man, is not required to rest on evidence.

[23] Although sometimes of considerable cultural and historical interest.

need to assume *this*, we had better render it intelligible first. For what is it for an item of knowledge, a piece of information or theory, to be 'represented in my mind'? Is my knowledge that Hastings was fought in 1066 represented in my mind? Or my knowledge of the rules of cricket? Or the principles of economic theory? Is it represented in English sentences or in pictures? And how would my behaviour differ if it were not 'represented'?

Even more opaque is the idea that the knowledge might be represented *in my brain*. What is this supposed to *mean*? Is there even a single example of a neurological representation of an item of knowledge that anyone can point to? What, one might wonder, would a respectable array of neurons be doing in a business like representation? Items of knowledge are represented in symbols, and there are no symbols in brains, nor do brains employ symbols. No doubt the primitive idea underlying this absurd conception is derived from a jejune misunderstanding of computer programming. For it seems to have been forgotten that *we* represent, or rather *encode* information in the computer 'language' (which is not a language), but the computer does not *represent* anything.

Worse still is the belief that to know something is to be in a certain mental state. This is a grave misunderstanding.[24] States have genuine duration. One can spot-check whether they are still going on. They can typically be observed, continuously or intermittently. Mental states run a course; they may flare up or abate. They are subject to degrees of intensity. They can be interrupted and resumed, as when one's anxiety is briefly quietened by a talk with a sympathetic friend, only to be reawakened later. Moods such as cheerfulness or depression are mental states, as are emotional states such as excitement, terror, and anger. One may be in a state of ecstasy, or of intense concentration, but such states do not continue through loss of consciousness. One may be excited when one goes to sleep on Christmas eve, and excited when one wakes up, but one is not excited when asleep (although one may sleep less well for having been excited). Knowing is not a mental state at all, neither knowing physics, biology or arithmetic, nor knowing English or German. One does not know continuously for forty-five minutes, although one may know (*simpliciter*) German for twenty years or more. One's knowledge cannot be interrupted, only

---

[24] It stems in part from a misconception of a state as what corresponds to the grammarian's idea of a static verb. This disregards difficulties in the grammarian's classificatory principles, fails to correspond to our ordinary notion of a state and assimilates concepts that are categorially distinct. Cf. G. P. Baker and P. M. S. Hacker, *Wittgenstein: Understanding and Meaning* (Blackwell, Oxford, 1980), pp. 595ff.

forgotten and later recollected or relearnt. To forget physics, no less than to forget Latin, is not to cease to be in a certain state. And one does not cease to know something when one falls asleep. If I do not remember any Greek I have not thereby ceased to be in a state, although, faced with a Greek examination this fact may put me into a dreadful state. For one's knowledge of a language to be rusty is not for a state to be of low intensity, but for one's mastery of an array of techniques to be deficient through lack of practice. Finally, it compounds confusion to speak of mental states as having a 'structure consisting of a system of rules and principles'. What could it mean for a mood such as cheerfulness or an emotional state such as terror to have a *structure*, let alone for the structure to *consist of rules*? One may speak of brains having a structure, since they consist of cells in an organized array. One may speak of concepts as having a structure, since they stand in logical relations, themselves reflections of rules for the uses of expressions. But could anything count as a mental state having a structure of rules?

The acme of absurdity is reached in the declaration that not only is knowing a language a mental state, but that 'the language capacity' can be regarded 'virtually as we would a physical organ, and [we] can investigate the principles of its organization, functioning and development in the individual and the species'.[25] For if knowing a language were a mental state, it could not be a capacity, just as being cheerful today is not a capacity (though it may manifest a dispositional trait) and being intelligent is not a state (though it may be manifest in certain states). Furthermore, neither first-order capacities nor second-order capacities (capacities to acquire capacities) can be regarded as organs. My legs give me the capacity to run, but I cannot stand on the capacity, only on my legs. My capacity to acquire the capacity to φ can be studied by scrutiny of my efforts to learn to φ, but it is no more an organ, or analogous to an organ, than is my capacity to learn to sprint or hurdle. This muddle leads the rash linguist by quick leaps into a vortex of nonsense. Having compared a capacity to an organ, he then suggests that one can regard the 'growth of language' (presumably meaning the development of the ability to speak a language) as analogous to the development of a bodily organ.[26] But it is as difficult to regard one's increasing mastery of a language thus as it is to regard an athlete's increasing capacity to run fast as analogous to the growth of a third leg! The final self-inflicted blow comes with the declaration that *language is a*

[25] Chomsky, *Rules and Representations*, p. 185.
[26] N. Chomsky, *Reflections on Language* (Fontana, London, 1976), p. 11.

mental organ (whose character is guaranteed by genetic mechanisms).[27]
Ex uno disce omnes.

Grammatical competence

Parallel to Saussure's distinction between *la langue* and *la parole*,
Chomsky and his followers distinguish between *competence* and *performance*. As Saussure insisted that linguists' subject matter is *la langue*, so
Chomsky insists that competence ('the speaker-hearer's knowledge of his
language') and not performance ('the actual use of language in concrete
situations')[28] is the prime concern of the modern scientific grammarian. At
first blush, the distinction appears to be between an ability and its exercise
(and one might wonder what a linguist is doing studying abilities as
opposed to languages, and how one can investigate an ability without
concerning oneself with its exercise). But impressions are deceptive, since
Chomsky hastens to declare that

> By 'grammatical competence' I mean that cognitive state that encompasses all those
> aspects of form and meaning and their relations, including underlying structures
> that enter into that relation, which are properly assigned to the specific sub-system
> of the human mind that relates representations of form and meaning.[29]

Competence, then, is not an ability, but something categorially quite
distinct, namely a mental or 'cognitive' state, from which overt performance flows. What the linguist wishes to study is not actual speech and the
normative behaviour associated with it, but an hypothetical reservoir from
which it flows.

> A record of natural speech will show numerous false starts, deviations from rules,
> changes of plan in mid-course, and so on. The problem for the linguist . . . is to
> determine from the data of performance the underlying system of rules that has
> been mastered by the speaker-hearer and that he puts to use in actual
> performance.[30]

Competence, occasionally conceived as a mental organ, is held to *determine* performance (albeit with hiccups *en route*) as a causal mechanism
determines the visible motion of a machine.

[27] Ibid., p. 92.
[28] N. Chomsky, *Aspects of the Theory of Syntax* (MIT Press, Cambridge, Mass., 1965),
p. 4.
[29] Chomsky, *Rules and Representations*, p. 59.
[30] Chomsky, *Aspects of the Theory of Syntax*, p. 4.

This is absurd! 'Linguistic competence', 'knowledge of a language', 'the language faculty', if they mean anything at all, can mean no more than the ability to speak and understand a language and/or perhaps the ability to learn one. (Although it is by no means clear that these are correctly thought of as *one* ability, or a uniform set of standardly interrelated abilities, any more than that there is an economic ability or faculty). But the relation between an ability and its exercise is *not causal*. The inference from a performance (e.g. your reading a page of English aloud) to an ability (your being able to read English) is not an inference from effect to cause. My car's power to do 100 m.p.h. is not the cause of its excessive speeding, though my foot's being pressed on the accelerator is; my ability to multiply is not the cause of my working out my shopping bill correctly, though my suspicion that I have been overcharged may be my reason. Successful performance is often compatible with inability (beginner's luck or a fluke), and ability is compatible with non-performance (I may not want to do the act in question) or with occasional failure ('You could have done it').

Of course, the linguist insists that 'competence' or 'the language faculty' is a state, and states certainly can be causes (the icy state of the road may cause a car to skid). But the postulated state is altogether bogus, since the typical forms of cognition are not states; knowing, being well-informed, or having mastered a system of rules, are misconstrued when represented as *states* of mind, and grotesquely misconstrued when represented as unconscious states of mind.[31] If we are speaking of a *faculty*, of *competence*, or of *knowing*, then we cannot be speaking of a state, and only in the Looking Glass World can saying make it so. Further confusion is generated by identifying the bogus cognitive state with the putative *object* of the postulated unconscious cognition, viz. the alleged grammar. For the 'language faculty' is held to be *constituted* of a system of 'computational' rules and representations.[32] So a faculty, which is not really a faculty but a cognitive state (which is not really cognitive, nor actually a state), turns out to be a system of hypothesized rules. Since rules *can* be said to have a structure (because logical relations obtain between rules, their parts and their applications), the linguist attributes the structure of his hypothesized rules to the mythical cognitive state, to the language faculty and, finally, to the

---

[31] If I know that today is Saturday, is that knowledge conscious or unconscious? Is it conscious only when I say or write that today is Saturday, and unconscious the rest of the time? Or is it conscious for twenty-four hours, including when I am asleep? And is my knowledge that the number of the verb in English corresponds with the subject of the sentence not the object conscious knowledge or unconscious?

[32] Chomsky, *Rules and Representations*, p. 55.

brain. This muddle does explain one feature of his story, namely his inclination to view linguistic performance as flowing *causally* from competence. For if the language faculty is a set of rules, then since rules determine their applications, surely the language faculty determines the linguistic performance! But, of course, it does not. For rules determine (logically) what *is to count* as correct applications of them, i.e. we *use* rules (though not 'hidden' ones) together with a method of projection to fix *what is to be called* 'following this rule'. But the rules do not causally determine what we actually do, rather do they normatively determine whether what we do is correct or not. A neural or mental state on the other hand could *only causally* determine a consequence, not normatively or logically. It could not determine whether what is done is right, nor could it suffice to render behaviour an instance of rule-following at all.

The linguist fails to grasp the categorial distinction between a state and an ability (power or potentiality). Consequently he misconstrues the conceptual relationship between an ability and its manifestations. These confusions are then multiplied by his failure correctly to apprehend the relation of rule-governed activities to the rules that govern them.

Idealization in linguistics

The linguist's story culminates in the claim that what he studies is not *actual* speakers' competence at all. For the 'competence' that is to be investigated turns out to be neither the capacity nor the alleged 'cognitive state' of an ordinary speaker of (say) English, but rather of 'an Ideal Speaker-Hearer'.

Linguistic theory is concerned primarily with an ideal speaker-listener in a completely homogeneous speech community, who knows its language perfectly and is unaffected by such grammatically irrelevant conditions as memory limitations, distractions, shifts of attention and interest, and errors (random or characteristic) in applying his knowledge of the language in actual performance...

[O]nly under [this] idealization . . . is performance a direct reflection of competence.[33]

Chomsky adorns his 'idealizations' by borrowing suitable clothing from physics. The idealization here involved is allegedly that employed so successfully by physicists pursuing their enquiries into inanimate nature 'in the Galilean style'.[34] Indeed, linguists constantly insist that the study of

[33] Chomsky, *Aspects of the Theory of Syntax*, p. 4.
[34] Chomsky, *Rules and Representations*, pp. 9ff.

language is methodologically no different, in principle, from the study of physics,[35] which basks in the sun of intellectual respectability. These borrowed garments, we shall see, are of no avail. One cannot obtain respectability by borrowing a bikini to wear at an official banquet, and comparing idealization in normative investigations with idealization in nomological ones merely serves to underline the incongruity.

The introduction of an ideal speaker should strike one as very odd. One might wish to investigate the rules of cricket, and one might do so by asking players, umpires or MCC officials. Or one might wish to investigate cricketers' ability to play the game, and one might do so by observing their performances, training, physique, and reflexes. But why would anyone wish to investigate the competence of an Ideal Batsman-Bowler? And why should an Ideal Speaker-Hearer be 'studied' by a linguist?

The linguistic data to be 'explained' are allegedly the actual uses of language of actual speakers (although in fact they tend to be the linguist's uses[36] or his identification of a handful of grammatical or significant sentences). From these, it seems, the theoretical linguist tries to reconstruct the system of rules of language the speaker 'cognizes'. Being an aspiring scientist, he can hardly emulate the traditional descriptive grammarian, let alone conceive of asking ordinary speakers what linguistic rules they follow,[37] of examining what grammar books are used in schools to improve children's mastery of their native tongue or to teach them a foreign language, or of observing how parents teach English to their children. For were this all that is to be done, what room would be left for Galilean styles and idealized models, for insights into the structure of the mind or clues for geneticists hunting for snarks in forests of DNA helices?

---

[35] Chomsky, *Reflections on Language*, pp. 184f.

[36] To represent this as a technique of 'elicitation', to refer to it as conducted by means of the method of 'introspection' (cf. Langendoen, *The Study of Syntax*, p. 3) is ludicrous. It is as if one were to describe one's knowledge that 'ludikrous' is misspelt as obtained by the introspective technique of eliciting the spelling 'ludicrous'. To add that this technique is a 'scientific methodology' is ridiculous.

[37] The 'technique of elicitation' is not conceived as eliciting any rules at all, but only 'linguistic intuitions', i.e. judgments of correctness or incorrectness, grammaticality or ungrammaticality which are the 'raw data' for the theorist (after all, if it were not the raw data, his job might be over before it has begun!). So if someone says that the sentence 'The children wants to play' is ungrammatical because the correct way to say that is 'The children want to play', or because the verb 'wants' is singular, whereas the noun 'children' is plural, and a plural noun takes a plural verb, that is not good enough. These normative explanations are insufficiently theoretical for the modern linguist, and they do not bear the stamp of advanced science on their faces.

Even assuming that speakers cognize (unconsciously know) grammatical rules, is it assumed that they have *perfect* knowledge of the rules of the language they speak? If it is claimed that they do not, that only the Ideal Speaker-Hearer has such perfect knowledge, what relevance have the actual linguistic performances of ordinary speakers to the knowledge of this mythical creature? If it is claimed that actual performance is typically defective, what licenses the assumption that the competence underlying the performance is ideal?

The source of the muddle lies in a dim apprehension of a simple truth. A language is a *normative* practice, a practice of using signs according to rules. It is also a *social* practice. It exists in the activities of language users in a community, surviving the demise of individual speakers, as cricket survives the passing of individual players and the law the deaths of citizens and legal officials alike. Few speakers, if any, will have mastered the whole vocabulary of English. Many speakers have an imperfect command of rules of the language and unwittingly make frequent mistakes. The (dubious) 'totality' of rules and definitions of English is not extractable from the mind or the performance of any single speaker;[38] but only from the linguistic practices of a speech community, including justifications, explanations, criticisms and linguistic instruction. But the theoretical linguist wishes to be engaged in a form of psychology, not sociology; and he wants to be pursuing a normative science, not a mere description of actual speech but of *the* rules of a language. The only way to reconcile these goals is by transposing the norms of language from the market-place to the mind, postulating an ideal Speaker-Hearer to ensure that the grammar that the linguist will ultimately pull out of the hat (or skull) will be *the* grammar of the language, and not merely Tom's, Dick's or Harry's rather fragmentary knowledge thereof. But, of course, the Ideal Speaker-Hearer does not stand to Tom, Dick or Harry as a point-mass in a vacuum moving at constant velocity unaffected by any other body stands to ordinary medium-size dry goods.

Linguists' favoured analogy between idealized models in physics and their so-called 'idealizations' in linguistics is noteworthy. It stems from a catastrophic failure to distinguish nomological investigations from normative ones. Idealization in physics (e.g. treating light as consisting of dimensionless rays moving in straight lines, or treating levers as absolutely rigid bodies) is an essential aspect of constructing mathematical models of

[38] Let alone from his brain. Millennial developments in science-fiction neurology are not going to advance the compilation of an English grammar nor aid the editors of the OED.

actual physical phenomena, models which then require *interpretation* by reference to what is actually observable, and modification by reference to known factors explaining deviation from the model. But the sense in which a 'ray of light' in optics (e.g. in Snell's Law) or a 'perfectly rigid lever' (in classical mechanics) are ideal is wholly different from anything that might be meant by an 'Ideal Speaker' of English. For the 'ideality' of the latter is normative. The Ideal Speaker is one who complies[39] with 'all the rules', whose utterances are models of grammaticality, as the acts of a 'perfectly moral agent' are models of virtuous conduct. These are not theoretical constructions making possible the mathematicization of theories, but normative ideals. The Ideal Speaker is the degenerate offspring of a Kantian Holy Will, not of a Galilean model.

It is perfectly possible to contend that a grammar specifies a set of possible rules for a language with which the speech of an Ideal Speaker conforms.[40] Possible, but empty! For *pari passu* a legal textbook describes the law in terms of what the Ideal Citizen-Judge does, and a logic textbook describes logic in terms of the manner in which the Ideal-Inferrer infers ... For here too one may (vacuously) say that 'only under this idealization is performance a direct reflection of competence'. Moreover, a description of the law of the land or of the rules of a system of logic is *not* something inferred, as cause from effect, from the undifferentiated behaviour (legal or illegal; valid inferences and howlers alike) of citizens, judges, or reasoning humanity. Normative investigations are not the physics of the human sciences.

2   The psychological mythology of rules

Theorists of meaning hesitantly, and theoretical linguists exuberantly, propound a rich psychological mythology of rules. We have touched on this previously. Now we shall subject these myths to critical scrutiny, focusing on linguists, since they tend to be more candid about the matter.

[39] It is noteworthy that Chomsky's Ideal Speaker-Hearer is in fact, as R. Harris has pointed out (*The Language Myth* (Duckworth, London, 1981), p. 33) a 'communicational cripple' whose ideality is far from ideal. For his mastery of language is limited to what the theoretical grammarian can display in terms of 'semantic representations' corresponding to phonetic symbols, and that would not get a child scatheless through a day, let alone a Shakespeare through a play. A comparable Ideal Chess Master would have learnt the rules of chess but never watched or played a single game.

[40] Or indeed *follows*, if the Ideal Speaker has read the Ideal Grammar, and uses it in explanations, criticisms and justifications!

According to some theoretical linguists a child's learning its native language is a mystery which can only be explained by bold and startling hypotheses about *innate* knowledge of rules. The argument to establish this astounding conclusion is disarming in its naivety. The growing child is exposed to a very limited sample of utterances, many of which are fragmentary, and some of which are ungrammatical. From this exposure, the child must learn or 'acquire' rules of grammar. This is construed to mean that on the basis of such finite data, it has the 'inductive problem' of determining the grammar, the system of rules, underlying the utterances it has heard.

Since the language is infinite, it makes no sense to speak of it as 'given' except insofar as some finite characterization – a function in intension – is given. The inductive problem is to determine this function in intension, the grammar, given some finite amount of data. That is the problem both for the language-learner and for the linguist.[41]

But since no function is determinable from a part of its value-range, the discovery of the grammar (i.e. 'acquiring knowledge of the language') cannot be a purely inductive operation. The three-year-old child is 'frustrated by the limitations of available evidence and faced by far too many possible explanatory theories, mutually inconsistent but adequate to the data. Or – as unhappy a state – it can devise no reasonable theory'.[42] The image of the child, between its nappy changes, being frustrated by limitations of evidence for constructing explanatory theories is striking to say the least. But the linguist, struggling to get airborne on the wings of theory, may respond by posing the problem differently. No computer, he claims, could be so designed that if it had fed into it a similarly limited and imperfect string of utterances, it could, on that basis, calculate the grammar (the function in intension) which governs those utterances. Or again, to use the 'neutral language' of psychological theory, no 'organism' exposed to such linguistic stimuli could, by means of mere associative (inductive) mechanisms, generate the resultant output characteristic of human speakers. So the 'black box' whose hidden (abstract) structure must be inferred from the data of input and output, must be 'programmed' in advance with an intricate system of rules.

It seems to follow that, if the child *is* to devise a theory of grammar that will enable it to speak, it must already posses a Universal Grammar. This,

---

[41] Chomsky, *Rules and Representations*, p. 84.
[42] Chomsky, *Reflections on Language*, pp. 10f.

it appears, will consist of a set of *genetically determined* rules and principles: 'Universal grammar is part of the genotype specifying one aspect of
the initial state of the human mind and brain . . . the language faculty
assumes the character of a particular grammar under the triggering and
shaping effect of experience'.[43] This fantasy is further adorned with some
cheap baubles borrowed from physics and mathematics:

the mind passes through a sequence of states under the boundary conditions set by
experience, achieving finally a 'steady state' at a relatively fixed age, a state that then
changes only in marginal ways. The basic property of this initial state is that given
experience, it develops to the steady state. Correspondingly, the initial state of the
mind might be regarded as a function characteristic of the species, that maps
experience into the steady state. Universal grammar is a partial characterization of
this function, of this initial state.[44]

As a result of this, the depth-grammar of its language 'grows' in the child's
mind, which comes to be in a 'steady state' of 'cognizing' the rules of its
language which are buried at depths 'inaccessible to the conscious mind'. It
is a noteworthy consequence of this fantasy that

As for the fact that the rules of language are 'public rules', this is, indeed, a
contingent fact. It is a fact of nature that the cognitive structures developed by
people in similar circumstances, within cognitive capacity, are similar, by virtue of
their similar innate constitution. Thus we share rules of language with others as we
share an organization of visual space with them.[45]

Despite the rules being inaccessible to his consciousness, the child 'can
quite effortlessly make use of [this] intricate structure of specific rules and
guiding principles to convey his thoughts and feelings to others',[46] al-

---

[43] Chomsky, *Rules and Representations*, p. 82; this bizarre view seems to be the received
wisdom amongst theoretical linguists, e.g.: 'The empirical hypothesis of a universal base
component and a universal semantic component – if they can be maintained together with
well-motivated constraints on the form of grammar – could help explain such phenomena as
a child's ability to learn his native language. If it could be assumed that the child had in
advance a built-in mechanism that defined the set of possible deep structures with which he
had to associate the abstract representations that he perceived of the speech-sounds that
reached his ears, then the child's job of formulating a theory to match surface structures with
deep structures might be conceived as being within the realm of the possible.' (Lakoff,
Irregularity in Syntax, p. 109) To which we can only mutter 'Sancta Simplicitas', and avert
our eyes.

[44] Chomsky, *Rules and Representations*, pp. 187f.

[45] Chomsky, *Reflections on Language*, p. 71.

[46] Ibid., p. 4.

though how it does this is still a mystery to linguistic scientists. Finally, since the child takes its parents' utterances to be intentional speech, it attributes knowledge of a language to other people. It does this because, fortunately, it 'possesses an unconscious theory of humans in accordance with which [it] attribute[s] knowledge of language to other humans'.[47]

Philosophers do not sink so deeply into the quagmires of such pseudo-scientific fiction. But this seems partly to be explained by their reticence when it comes to explaining in detail what relation their envisaged axiomatic theories have to an ordinary speaker's mastery of his native tongue, or even to a descriptive grammar of the kind employed at a language school. This much, however, is clear. The philosopher, like the theoretical linguist, typically attributes to a speaker of a language, including a child, tacit knowledge of a vastly complex theory of meaning. According to his story too, possession of this knowledge is supposed to *explain* how it is possible for a person to understand the sentences he hears and utters (see below, chapter 9). And he too contends that speakers of a language *use* the rules of the putative theory of meaning in constructing sentences and in understanding them. These commitments alone suffice to put such a theorist of meaning in the dock.

The psychological myth of language acquisition is a grotesque distortion of familiar truths. A child is not a 'passive ear' exposed to a succession of mysterious noises, in response to which it, in due course, emits a series of noises.[48] Nor is it a quasi-computer into which linguistic data are fed, in the expectation that it will process the data and deliver a grammar. It is, unsurprisingly, a child, living in a family, exposed not merely to noises, but to parents and siblings who teach it, encourage it, train it to imitate, to use words, to ask for objects and to bring them, to identify objects and colours, tastes, smells, sounds and shapes. Its parents, brothers and sisters play games with it, sing songs and nursery rhymes with it, correct its stumbling

[47] Ibid., p. 143.
[48] But apparently linguists really do think of children as ears attached to brains in a vitreous suspension, the mind being located at some indeterminate non-spatial point: 'Consider the remarkable feat that each normal child performs in learning his native language. Having been exposed to a small number of utterances, the child begins to compose his own new utterances . . . it appears as if the child has constructed a theory of what a correct utterance is, and he attempts to use that theory to communicate intelligently . . .

'It can safely be assumed that a child, *confronted by the strange continuous sound signals emanating from his parents*, does not start from scratch, choosing random subject matter to theorize about . . . If this were so a child would be just as likely to come up with a theory of physical acoustics as with a theory of how natural languages work . . .' (Lakoff, *Irregularities in Syntax*, pp. 2f.; our italics)

repetitions and imitations, and tell it stories accompanied by pictures, explanations and exemplifications. The computer analogy grossly distorts the character of the child's experience, suggesting that it consists in being fed *information*, rather than in playing games, singing and listening to fairy tales. The analogy thereby has an homogenizing effect on the characterization of what the child is exposed to.[49] It makes it appear as if what the child encounters in the world were no more than programmable information on computer tape. Consequently, it obscures not only the wide range of the child's goals and purposes and its modes of interaction with others, but also the form of life into which it is born and which moulds its thought and action. The linguist's tale is patent nonsense, delivered by the ill-conceived services of the computer analogy, and bred from a miscegenous crossing of bastardized rationalism with Skinnerian behaviourism.

Chomsky achieved his initial fame through his criticism of Skinner's account of language acquisition. In this study he erected a pair of bogus alternatives: either language is learnt as a stimulus-response theory demands, or it is not really learnt at all, but is in some sense innate[50] (e.g. the child must have innate knowledge of a universal grammar). But (i) the linguistic and behavioural experience of the child is grossly misdescribed, and (ii) what the child is held to learn is grossly misconstrued. Chomsky's notorious review of Skinner in 1959 makes clear that these seeds of his later confusions were sown early:

The child who learns a language has in some sense *constructed the grammar for himself* on the basis of his observation of sentences and non-sentences (i.e. corrections by the verbal community). Study of the actual observed ability of a speaker to distinguish sentences from non-sentences, detect ambiguities, etc. *apparently forces us to the conclusion* that this grammar is of an extremely complex abstract character, and that the young child has succeeded in carrying out what, from the formal point of view, at least, seems to be a remarkable type of *theory construction*.

---

[49]   Cf. H. A. Nielsen, 'How a language exists: a question to Chomsky's theory', *Philosophical Investigations*, 5 (1982), pp. 60f.

[50]   It is a curious phenomenon to observe Chomsky labouring so hard to breathe life into the dead embers of the doctrine of innate ideas. For that venerable theory, particularly in its seventeenth century rationalist forms, rested on a multitude of misunderstandings and incoherences. To resuscitate it would merely bring to life old confusions, for the doctrine did not in fact render intelligible either the nature of necessary truth or the source of our knowledge of necessity. It did not make clear the nature or origin of whatever structural or *a priori* concepts we may possess. And it typically failed to distinguish first- from second-order abilities (i.e. the ability to φ from the ability to acquire the ability to φ).

Furthermore, this task is accomplished in an astonishingly short time, to a large extent independently of intelligence, and in a comparable way by all children. Any theory of learning must cope with these *facts*.

It is not easy to accept the view that a child is capable of constructing *an extremely complex mechanism for generating* a set of sentences, some of which he has heard, or that an adult can instantaneously determine whether (and if so, how) a particular item is generated by this mechanism, which has many of the properties of an abstract deductive theory. Yet this appears to be a *fair description* of the performance of the speaker, listener, and learner.[51]

Yet what the child learns is manifestly *not* a theoretical grammar, but how to speak (grammatically, correctly); how to ask for a drink, tell Mummy about the bird in the tree, call Daddy, object to dinner, insist on dressing itself without help, scold its teddy bear, play peek-a-boo, etc. Its initial uses of language are responses to *training*. The normativity of its early forays in the use of language lies in parental reactions and corrections. Only later, when its use of language has achieved a minimal standard, can the child learn to correct itself, ask what certain words and sentences mean, or explain what it means by saying such-and-such. The child no more constructs a grammatical theory for itself in the course of learning to speak than it constructs for itself the predicate calculus with identity in learning to make elementary inferences. The observed ability of a speaker 'to distinguish sentences from non-sentences' no more forces us to the conclusion that the rules of grammar he has mastered are 'of an extremely complex abstract character' than the observed ability of an eight-year-old to add, subtract, multiply and divide forces us to the conclusion[52] that he has constructed for himself the alleged set-theoretic foundations of arithmetic as propounded by *The Basic Laws of Arithmetic* or *Principia Mathematica*.

It is astonishing that elementary language-learning should even seem a *mystery*, as opposed to being *wonderful*. But it is even more astonishing to suppose that it is rendered *less mysterious* by the supposition that the child tacitly knows ('cognizes') a universal grammar which is part of its genetic endowment, and which it uses to map experience on to a 'steady state grammar', which it then employs in speaking and understanding ('decoding') its native tongue. That would indeed be to explain the obvious by reference to the miraculous.

[51] N. Chomsky, 'A Review of B. F. Skinner's *Verbal Behaviour*', *Language*, 35 (1959), pp. 57f. (our italics).

[52] *Pace* Piaget!

Not only are these suppositions not *facts* which any learning theory must explain, they are not even intelligible. If the child had to inherit a universal-grammar-carrying gene in order to construct the grammatical theory of English, which it then must use in speaking English, in what language are these grammars couched? Is universal grammar written in Esperanto or in letters of DNA? Is it intelligible to talk of constructing theories, when the alleged theorist can, as yet, speak no language? Is it intelligible to attribute even tacit knowledge of a theory to a creature who manifestly cannot understand a single sentence of any theory, let alone know that it expresses a truth? And how would the three-year-old amass the empirical data on the basis of which it is supposed to construct a theory of its native language? Must we conceive of it as ordering sequences of phonemes under various headings such as 'Probably a subjunctive-conditional', 'Possibly interrogative', 'Maybe a mixed mood with an indicative antecedent and imperative consequent'? And even if it had done this, how would it *test* its theories? What empirical evidence is there for the child's rejecting falsified hypotheses about grammar (on the basis of tests) or for its devising experiments? To accept these '*facts*' is to embrace absurd fictions.[53]

The 'ability to detect ambiguity' allegedly forces us to attribute knowledge of a grammatical theory to children or adults. Two examples are notorious: (i) 'Visiting aunts can be boring'. Of this two modern linguists claim 'in order to assign an unambiguous semantic interpretation to the sentence, we need access to information contained in its deep structure'.[54] (ii) 'They are flying planes'. Of this it is said that the question of how we discern its various 'readings' can only *conceivably* be answered by reference to a grammar that is a function from the word 'sentence' on to bracketed word-strings which constitute the sentences of English, which grammar 'is the very system of (internal (what else?)) formulae that English speaker/hearers use to represent the sentences of their language'.[55] But this is altogether extraordinary! If I ask 'Where are Tom and Dick?' and am told 'They are flying planes', I do not need any system of internal

---

[53] It is no coincidence that one of Chomsky's followers, J. A. Fodor, reached the conclusion that in order to master a language one must already have one, viz. the *language of thought*. This charming picture would have had to be invented had it not come forth from Fodor's fertile imagination.

[54] J. P. B. Allen and P. van Buren, *Chomsky: Selected Readings* (Oxford University Press, Oxford, 1971), p. 103.

[55] J. A. Fodor, 'Propositional Attitudes', in *Readings in Philosophy of Psychology*, ed. N. Block, vol. 2 (Methuen, London, 1981), p. 59.

formulae or mental representations to know that the answer means that Tom and Dick (the well-known aces of 25th Squadron) are flying their Harriers (or, in a different context, that Tom and Dick those well-known model-plane builders are currently flying their latest models in the park). Similarly, if I am walking through the aeronautics museum and the guide points at some full-scale model planes, saying 'These are only reconstructed planes, but those over there, they are flying planes', I do not need any deep structures to enable me to understand. *Pari passu*, if 'Visiting aunts can be boring' is a response to 'That old bag, Aunt Doris, is visiting us tomorrow', or a response to 'What a bore, I have to visit my Aunt Doris tomorrow', it wears its meaning on its face, not in its 'depth-grammar', let alone in any 'mental representations' thereof.

Not only does an ordinary speaker not need to have recourse ('deep in his unconscious mind') to hidden rules of transformational-generative grammar, but he could not do so if he needed to. For the alleged rules are not, as Chomsky suggests, just contingently public, they are not public at all. Indeed, there are two senses in which they are not public. First, there is no institution of use of these rules. They are not cited or referred to in explanations, criticisms, justifications, or corrections. (Many of them, when formulated in the jargon of modern linguistics, are unintelligible to ordinary speakers of a language.) They have no actual normative role in the public linguistic transactions of a community. Secondly, in so far as they refer to mental representations of anything at all, in so far as they involve instructions to manipulate 'internal tokens'[56] to conform to the syntax of 'mentalese', these rules are private in a more radical sense, namely they concern items inaccessible to other people (since, after all, I cannot have your 'representations' or 'internal tokens' any more than I can have your headaches, and you cannot even tell me about them).[57]

All this seems to show is that, as Chomsky insists, the rules of language of different speakers, at best, only accidentally coincide (presumably this is what he means by 'contingently public'). It does not show that the speaker does not, or cannot, have recourse to the rules buried in his unconscious mind or brain. But first, we can make no sense of rules which have no actual or even potential overt *use*, no normative *role* in anyone's intentional behaviour. Secondly, these putative rules are *not* in fact 'privately accessible' to the ordinary speaker. They are so private that he needs an

---

[56] Cf. Hartry H. Field 'Mental Representation', *passim* in *Readings in the Philosophy of Psychology*, vol. 2.

[57] And if it is said that nevertheless mine must be 'just the same' as yours, since we both speak English, the reply is 'What is the criterion of sameness here?'.

expert to tell him that he has them. But then they cannot have even a private normative role and so are not rules at all. Thirdly, there is no such thing as rules which are concerned with a 'syntax' of 'mental representations'. For there could, in principle, be no criterion for their correct application.[58] So even if there were here something 'accessible to consciousness', there is simply no question of there being a rule, a standard for correctly employing a sign or symbol – *a fortiori* if the objects in question are *not* accessible to consciousness. To search for such rules is to ape the proverbial blind man who looks in a pitch-black room for a black hat which is not really there.

3   The mechanical mythology of rules

Linguists are prone to spin out another, apparently complementary, tale. Puzzled, perhaps, at *how* rules that are 'far beyond the reach of will or consciousness'[59] can have any normative force or have any relation to actual behaviour, they declare that their postulated rules have a 'physical realization' in the brain:

> Studying the use and understanding of language, we reach certain conclusions about the cognitive structure (grammar) that is being put to use, thus setting a certain problem for the neurologist, whose task it is to discover the mechanisms involved in linguistic competence and performance. Noting that the mechanisms appear to function in the absence of relevant experience and quite uniformly for individuals of vastly differing experience we draw the natural conclusion that they are not learned, but are part of the system that makes learning possible. This conclusion sets a further task for human biology, which will attempt to find the genetic mechanisms that guarantee that the mental organ, language, will have the required character.[60]

The picture of the MIT linguist standing on the bridge of the Ship of Science passing orders down to his crew of neurologists and biologists has a certain comic charm. But very little relation to reality.

Linguists are, however, not alone in telling these tales. Some philosophers have concocted similar pseudo-scientific fictions. One,[61] having

---

[58] Cf. L. Wittgenstein, *Philosophical Investigations*, §§243ff.

[59] Chomsky, *Reflections on Language*, p. 4.

[60] Ibid., p. 91.

[61] G. Evans, 'Semantic Theory and Tacit Knowledge', in *Wittgenstein: To Follow a Rule*, ed. S. Holtzman and C. Leich (Routledge & Kegan Paul, London, 1981).

invented a notional primitive language, proposes two different sets of rules (theories of meaning) for it, one set being 'structure reflecting', the other not. On his view, speakers of this mini-language must have tacit knowledge of one 'theory' (grammar) or of the other. To have tacit knowledge, he claims, is to have a *disposition* to judge of a given sentence that it has certain (appropriate) truth-conditions, derivable from one or the other of the two proposed theories of meaning. Tacit knowledge of a theory of meaning is held to involve the claim that there is *a state* of a person which, given appropriate stimuli (presumably hearing the utterance of a sentence) provides a causal explanation of certain episodes. A naive reader might suppose that the episodes explained are reactions to the heard sentences (e.g. shutting the door when hearing the request 'Please shut the door' or the assertion 'It is rather draughty in here'). But that would be too gross. The episodes to be explained are *understanding* (conceived as an event preceding the actions in response to the utterance) or, what on these views comes to the same thing, acts of *assigning truth-conditions* to the heard sentence or its constituent sentence-radical. Given the two alternative theories or 'models',

The decisive way to decide which model is correct is by providing a causal, presumably neurophysiologically based, explanation of comprehension. With such an explanation in hand, *we can simply see* whether or not there is an appeal to a common state or structure in the *explanation* of the subject's comprehension of each of the sentences . . .[62]

It is interesting to note that the rules of the grammar or theory of meaning are explicitly denied to have *any* normative role in guiding speakers whose linguistic behaviour and 'comprehension' are held to be explained by reference to tacit knowledge of the grammar or theory.

Tacit knowledge of the syntactic and semantic rules of the language are not states of the same kind as the states we identify in our ordinary use of the terms 'belief' and 'knowledge'. Possession of tacit knowledge is exclusively manifested in speaking and understanding a language; the *information* is not even potentially at the service of any other project of the agent, nor can it interact with any other beliefs . . . Such concepts as we use in specifying it are not concepts we need to suppose the subject to possess, for the state is inferentially insulated from the rest of the subject's thoughts and beliefs. There is thus no question of regarding the *information* being brought by the subject to bear upon speech and interpretation . . .[63]

[62] Ibid., p. 127, our italics.
[63] Ibid., p. 134, our italics.

We may well wonder why, if the *knowledge* the speaker tacitly has, or the *information* he possesses, is as insulated and inaccessible as suggested, it is deemed knowledge at all. We may equally wonder how such unknown knowledge can explain anything concerning a language-user's speech or understanding. One suggested answer[64] is that the explanatory force lies in the fact that the 'neurological realization' of the grammatical rules or of the theory of meaning causally influences behaviour. The coherence of this supposition will be examined, but note that unless understanding or assigning truth-conditions to sentences are conceived of, improbably, as forms of behaviour or causal antecedents of behaviour, this will not get us much forward.

We might start by questioning what it is for a rule to be 'represented' in somebody's brain or to have a 'neural realization'. One can *formulate* a rule in English or French, *translate it* into German or Italian. One might call such formulations 'representations of a rule', but then one certainly cannot formulate rules in neural synapses. For the medium of formulation must be symbolic, hence must be signs used by goal-directed creatures with certain purposes and in accord with certain conventions. One can represent a rule by a concrete symbol, like a signpost or a pattern to be followed or copied. But since neural synapses are not readily accessible nor observable, no one has ever represented a rule thus. For to represent a rule is to use an array of signs or symbols in a certain way and with a certain significance. We do use, and thereby render meaningful, noises and inscriptions. But not neurons!

It seems that what is meant is a *mechanism* that will ensure conformity to the rule. For example, if Smith is an apple-sorter who is instructed when sorting apples to follow a rule – Apples of size x are to be put in the Best Apples box, apples of size y in the Standard Apples box – we might replace Smith by a machine. The apple-sorting machine might consist of a perforated incline, constantly vibrating, down which apples roll, falling through appropriate holes into appropriate boxes. This will ensure the same results as Smith's tiresome sorting. Is the perforated surface a 'representation' of the rule? Is an electronic lock which opens only by inserting an appropriately imprinted card a 'representation' of the rule: 'Only card-holders may enter'? Is the rack or locking plate on a clock a 'representation' of the rule, once followed by an appointed monk at each monastery 'Strike once at one o'clock, strike twice at two o'clock, etc'?

The suggestion is odd and disturbing. But let us, for a moment, accept it.

---

[64] Cf. J. A. Fodor, *The Language of Thought* (Crowell, New York, 1975).

Should we now say that the apple-sorting machine, the lock, the clock or a pocket calculator in whose mechanisms there are such 'representations' of rules are *following rules at all*? Surely not. For to follow a rule is to *use it* as a guide to conduct (not to be causally necessitated to do something). It is to consult it in evaluating as correct or incorrect those operations which *ought* to conform to it. It is to justify conduct, if challenged, by reference to it, to identify conduct as appropriately normative and to explain or be willing to explain one's normative identifications and descriptions by reference to the rule. But none of these acts, activities, reasons or justifications are involved in the mechanisms which we build to relieve us of tedious normative tasks. If an agent can be said to be following a rule, the agent must also possess the capacity *not* to follow the rule. Similarly, where it makes sense to talk of following a rule, it typically makes sense to talk of not following the correct rule through misidentification of the rule, or of not following the rule correctly through misapplication of the rule. This in turn may stem from misinterpretation of the rule, or from misidentification of operative facts.

Does this matter? The theorist might contend that it is a minor, but warranted extension of our normal use of the term 'rule'. If our ordinary use of 'rule' does not incorporate these phenomena, so much the worse for it. When Newton introduced such terms as 'mass', he was not bound by ordinary use, and no more should a linguistic scientist be. This response is, however, unacceptable, for it falsifies the facts. Though the linguist may introduce technical or novel terminology for his special purposes, what he is doing here is not a minor extension of 'rule' and related terms, but an incoherent one, akin to 'extending' the term 'circle' to encompass squares or 'black' to encompass white. A mechanism is *causally* related to consequences of its operation, not normatively – A rule to φ in circumstance C, or to expand a series by adding 2, *makes* φing in C, or writing '1002, 1004, 1006 . . .' follow from it, only in the sense that we determine these as what we call 'compliance' with those rules. No causal connection is in question here. A rule, like a proposition or statement, is an object of understanding. A feature of understanding a rule is that to understand it is to know what *counts* as compliance with it. There is an internal relation between a rule and acts which conform to the rule, just as there is between an expectation and its fulfilment or an order and compliance with it. This internal relation is not a Platonic mystery, an inexplicable relation between an abstract entity and acts of certain kinds. Nor is that mysterious picture demythologized by interposing a causally efficacious *mechanism* (a 'realization' of the rule) between the rule and the acts that comply with it. Rather, it is forged by the relation between the rule-formulation and the act-descriptions. It is a conceptual truth that the rule requiring A to φ in C is complied with just by A φing in C, just as it is a conceptual truth that the expectation that p is satisfied just by p and not any other state of affairs. For the rule requiring A to φ in C *is* the rule that is complied with by A φing in C. So too the rule to add 2 *is* the rule that is complied with (*inter alia*) by writing '1002' after '1000'.

But there are no such internal relations between a mechanism, which is a so-called 'realization' of a rule, and the results of its operation. For the mechanism is *not* internally related to the relevant consequences of its operation. The description of an alleged bit of neural circuitry (to keep up scientific appearances we might call it a^*_{234}) which is thought to cause appropriate linguistic behaviour does not stand in a grammatical relation to the description of the behaviour. So the *mechanism* which supposedly causes one to follow a rule cannot usurp the role of the rule in fixing what *counts* as compliance, nor can the so-called 'realization' of the rule usurp the role of a rule-formulation.

Matters are even worse when it comes to the distinction between conforming to a rule and following the rule. A causal mechanism of the kind envisaged is wholly incongruous with our *concept* of following a rule and out of place in descriptions or explanations of rule-following. The reason for this lies in the very meaning of 'following a rule', in what it is to follow a rule, and in the criteria we employ to determine whether or not a rule is being followed. In general, only if a person justifies, explains and identifies his conduct (directly or obliquely) by reference to an appropriate rule (or would do so if challenged) is his behaviour even a *candidate* for normative conduct. So even if it made any sense to say that a^*_{234} causes A to utter a grammatical sentence, it does *not* follow that A's behaviour was, in any sense, a case of following a rule. For if A does not conceive of what he did as normative (in this sense), does not guide his conduct normatively, and does not explain or justify what he did by reference to a rule and would not do so if challenged, then its mode of causation cannot render his conduct normative. For the causal role of a^*_{234} is compatible with A's utterance being unintentional or inadvertent. Though he uttered 'p', maybe he *meant* to utter 'q'. Perhaps he intended to produce an ungrammatical sentence (as a joke maybe) yet wrongly enunciated a well-formed one. Perhaps he was talking in his sleep or merely repeating what he heard without understanding. The aetiology of his behaviour cannot, in principle, provide grounds for the claim that his behaviour is normative.

At this point we might start to worry why it should matter to the theorist whether a^*_{234} is a 'neural representation of a rule' or not. After all the rule it allegedly represents carries no normative force whatever, it is 'buried beyond the reach of consciousness' and 'is not even potentially at the service' of the agent. Indeed, given, *ex hypothesi*, that a^*_{234} has the causal consequences in question, what makes a^*_{234} a neural 'realization' of a *rule*? And what difference would it make if it were not? After all, the same consequences would still ensue.

But now reflect on what makes a given performance a case of *correct* or *incorrect* behaviour. We do not surrender to *whatever* the mechanical 'representation' of a rule delivers. If the apple-sorting machine starts dropping grade A apples in grade B baskets, it is not working correctly (perhaps the perforated plate has expanded). If my pocket calculator delivers the answer 1 to the calculation $(1.362 \times 10^{13}) \times (4.729 \times 10^{-7})$, it is wrong (perhaps it needs a new battery). But we can only make sense of these truisms if we grasp that the theorists' mechanical story makes no sense. For the causal explanation they invoke can only explain why the machine produced p^* (as opposed to p), not why p^* is wrong. And if two malfunctioning components cancel each other out, so that the machine (correctly) cranks out p, the mechanical story cannot explain why p *is* the correct answer.

Leaving machines aside, it should be surprising, on this story, that any English speaker can produce at will as many ungrammatical sentences as the theorist wishes. We are no more causally constrained to speak grammatically than we are causally constrained to play chess correctly. Constraints, indeed, abound; but not by means of neural representations. It should be equally surprising that we can understand a considerable amount of ungrammatical English or that we can read and understand a great deal of archaic English, the sentences of which deviate significantly in vocabulary and structure from our daily chatter.

At this point we might back-track and begin to wonder what these paramechanical myths are supposed to explain. The representations of the rules of grammar and their neurological realizations are supposed to provide a causal explanation in 'the Galilean style' – of *what*?[65] Take the

---

[65] We have already noted that modern linguistics is in the business of explaining the 'mysterious' capacity of children to learn their native tongue. Here is another profound mystery: 'Someone . . . who does not know a word of Hungarian can be completely sure that the Hungarian verb meaning *to hate* takes animate subjects and that the Hungarian verb meaning *to believe* takes animate subjects and abstract objects. *This is a very deep fact about language which the lexical base hypothesis could explain.*' (Lakoff, *Irregularity in Syntax*, p. 111; final italics ours)

following homely scene: You come into the room on a chilly evening, leaving the door ajar. I say 'Shut the door, please'. What questions need answering? Why did I ask you to shut the door? The answer is straightforward – to reduce the cold draught. Why did I say 'Shut the door, please'? – Because I wanted you to shut the door. Why did I use the words 'Shut the door, please'? This is a curious question *in this context*. What alternative is envisaged? Why did I not say 'Would you be so kind as to close the door'? Or why did I not say 'Fermez la porte, s'il vous plaît'? Or is it that the grammarian worries over the question why I did not say 'Door the please shut'? And is that a serious question? All one could say, with patience rapidly running out, is 'Look – "door" means this ↑; "shut" means doing *thus*; "shut the door" means going like *this*. And if one is polite, one says "please" when making a request, as I was, that someone should shut the door.' What else is calling out for explanation? Is there anything at all which the mechanical myth *could* explain?[66]

4 The Platonic mythology of rules

Throughout its long history philosophical reflection on thought and language has manifested a marked tendency to oscillate between poles, alternative grand strategies, contrasting pictures. Where one generation opts for a form of idealism, or intuitionism, or monism another will gravitate towards realism, or naturalism, or dualism. The pictures reappear in very different colours in different epochs, and often are not easily recognized.[67] Caught by the tides of language, philosophers typically find themselves swept in one or other direction, each equally unsatisfactory. To navigate between the rocks and whirlpools has proved no easy task, and the sea-lanes are littered with wrecks. One such venerable pair of poles consists of psychologism and Platonism.

In the late nineteenth century Frege conceived of his Platonist doctrines as the only coherent alternative to the widespread psychologism of the

---

[66] To forestall misunderstanding, it should be stressed that nothing in our polemic precludes scientific investigations into what parts of the brain are causally related to linguistic abilities, e.g. which areas of the cortex are indispensable for the capacity to form coherent sentences, or for mastery of vocabulary. Our arguments are concerned with the conceptual nature of normative phenomena, and the case we have been pressing is that neurological structures cannot have a normative role.

[67] e.g. Central State Materialism, which purports to be anti-Cartesian is actually only anti-idealist, displaying a profound affinity to Cartesian dualism; it merely replaces a mind–body dualism with a brain–body dualism.

day. He conceived of concepts not as the invented products of human activities but as discoverable sempiternal entities that we correlate with certain linguistic expressions. He contended that numbers are abstract logical objects for which numerals stand. And he thought of rules, in particular of the laws of logic, as Platonic objects that govern normative relationships. These doctrines have, on the whole, fallen from favour in modern writings. But more subtle forms of Platonism about rules of logic and language commonly lurk in the background of contemporary calculus conceptions of language. For whether or not the rules of the calculus of language (of the theory of meaning for a natural language) are thought of as abstract, non-mental, entities, they are typically conceived as churning out consequences (e.g. derived rules, sentence-meanings, and truth-conditions of sentences) quite independently of us. The *mechanism* of rules is conceived as operating of its own accord, as if the rules were pieces of aethereal machinery. Indeed, the axioms and rules of a theory of meaning must, allegedly, suffice to *generate* the *infinite* totality of meanings of sentences of English, even though that infinity is inaccessible and un-surveyable to finite creatures such as us. Though not commonly conceived as a form of Platonism, and though espoused by philosophers who openly repudiate older versions of Platonism, the underlying picture sufficiently resembles typical Platonist conceptions of mathematics according to which the theorems of number theory flow ineluctably from the axioms, definitions and inference rules, to justify being so denominated. A further feature of modern conceptions is that rules are thought of as determining their own application, and our applications of rules as merely conforming or failing to conform with what the rules, of their own accord as it were, require.

Modern linguistics has been deeply committed to wild, if not Bacchanalian, forms of psychologism, of which we have sampled heady draughts. Recently one of Chomsky's followers, suddenly alerted to one or two minor defects of his teacher's psychologism, has boldly hurled himself from the rocks into the whirlpools with the cry 'Back to Frege!':

This book argues, on the basis of grammatical fact [sic!] and the methodological considerations appropriate to linguistics, that a Platonist interpretation of linguistic theories is preferable to either a nominalist or conceptualist interpretation.[68]

The facts about language learning, speech, and our emotional responses to them are compatible with a Platonist conception of language, ... the apparent incompatibility

---

[68] J. J. Katz, *Language and Other Abstract Objects* (Blackwell, Oxford, 1981), p. 16.

is due to a confusion between a language and knowledge of the language. The language is a timeless, unchangeable, objective structure; knowledge of a language is temporal, subject to change, and subjective. Someone becomes a speaker of a language by virtue of acquiring a set of tacit beliefs or principles that stand in the relation 'knowledge of' to a member of a set of such linguistic structures.[69]

The Psychological conception of grammars and linguistic theory has to be replaced with a conception of them as theories of the sentences of a language taking the sentence as abstract objects like numbers. Only a Platonist conception can succeed where psychological conceptions fail, that is, only a Platonist conception offers a theory of language consistent with and capable of explaining the existence of absolute necessary truths in natural languages.[70]

The noise of the splash, as the author disappears into the vortices of naive Platonism, reverberates through the subsequent pages. This is not the place for a detailed examination of the ills of serious forms of Platonism, let alone of those of the more jejune varieties. Our primary concern is much narrower, namely the Platonist conception of rules, be they of logic, mathematics or language (including rules determining concepts). Our treatment will be schematic.

Platonism correctly insists against psychologism that concepts are not mental entities. A concept is neither an 'idea', like an after-image, nor a 'mental representation' (whatever that might be). To have a concept is not like having a headache. Two people may possess one and the same concept, but not, or not in the same sense, one and the same headache. Furthermore, the Platonist insists, the laws of logic are normative, not nomological; they specify how we ought to think if we are to preserve truth throughout inferences, not how human beings happen to think. For we can and do violate the (logical) laws of thought, infer incorrectly, and argue incoherently. But there is no such thing as 'violating' the psychological laws of thought. Logic and mathematics are not branches of psychology; the entities they study are not private and mind-dependent, and the truths they propound are objective.

Taken as platitudes, these claims are defensible, but taken as reportage from the *Transcendental Times*, they are as pernicious as the psychologistic confusions they displace. Platonism defends platitudes as if they were profundities involving far-reaching 'ontological commitments', and does so by mystery-mongering. It paints a picture, while claiming to offer an explanation, and provides no method for applying that picture in

[69] Ibid.
[70] Ibid., p. 6.

any way that will render it explanatory. Thus, while insisting that different people may possess the same concept or apprehend the same proposition, Platonism provides no explanation of how this is possible. Patter about intuition or 'standing in the relation of knowing' to abstract entities are merely questions masquerading as answers. Frege, at least, was candid about this.

'Grasping a thought [i.e. a proposition] is a mental process! Yes, indeed, but it is a process which takes place on the very confines of the mental and which for that reason cannot be completely understood from a purely psychological standpoint. For in grasping the [thought] something comes into view whose nature is no longer mental in the proper sense, namely the thought; and this process is perhaps the most mysterious of all. But just because it is mental in character we do not need to concern ourselves with it in logic. It is enough for us that we can grasp thoughts and recognize them to be true; how this takes place is a question in its own right.[71]

In effect, what Frege did was to purchase a bogus form of objectivity for concepts, propositions and numbers at the intolerable cost of generating a mystery about understanding.

Similar strains and stresses are visible in the typical Platonist story about the laws of logic. While correctly insisting against psychologicians that these laws are normative, Frege found their normative force logically inexplicable:

The question why and with what right we acknowledge a law of logic to be true, logic can answer only by reducing it to another law of logic. Where that is not possible, logic can give no answer.[72]

Consequently, while he conceived of the laws of logic as the ultimate and uniquely valid laws of truth, he could give no account of their uniqueness. Since he did not envisage competing systems of logic (alternative logics), he provided no method for settling whether a given system is 'correct'. If there are beings who have not had the fortune to 'apprehend' the true laws of thought, their thinking might overflow the eternal boundary stones of the laws of logic. They might think non-logically, e.g. they might believe that an object is *not* identical with itself, or that if it is true that q, and that if p then q, then it is true that p.[73] Of course, their thinking would strike us as a

---

[71] G. Frege, *Posthumous Writings*, ed. H. Hermes *et al.* (Blackwell, Oxford, 1979), p. 145.

[72] G. Frege, *The Basic Laws of Arithmetic*, vol. 1, tr. and ed. M. Furth (University of California Press, Berkeley and Los Angeles, 1964), p. xvi.

[73] And presumably they might believe that $25^2 = 624$!

'hitherto unknown type of madness', madness in not according with the *correct* laws of logic. But it would, on this conception, *be* thinking for all that.[74]

The conjunction of the Platonist's conception of objectivity of concepts and propositions and his picture of the normative laws of thought generates a wide range of insoluble puzzles. What is the relation between these curious abstracta and our uses of language? Can we use words without knowing what concepts they stand for? Might we all be mistaken about what concept a word designates? Did people *understand* such words as 'if . . . then . . .', 'and', 'number' prior to Frege's discovery (or was it invention?) of the 'real' rules for their use? If so, did their understanding outstrip their capacity to explain what it was that they understood, so that they knew what these words mean, but could not say? If not, did they use these words throughout their lives without knowing the rules for their use, without understanding them? Or is it that they had an 'implicit' knowledge of their meanings, so that Plato implicitly knew Frege's definition of the concept *number* and his set-theoretic account of the natural numbers, only could not say so? Similar puzzles attend Platonism about laws of logic. Did generations who moulded their reasoning into the forms of syllogistic really follow the principles of the predicate calculus? Did Frege discover laws of thought that intelligent men already implicitly knew and actually *followed*? No less baffling is the supposition that there *exist* rules, unknown to us all, which can be *discovered*. For how could there be rules which have never been formulated, which are never used to guide action, consulted to determine correctness or incorrectness, or invoked in justification or explanation? None of these questions is profound, but all of them are nonsensical expressions of profound confusions.

These questions (and many others) become urgent when we examine the ideas underlying contemporary ruminations about theories of meaning. For by construing a language as a calculus of rules and definitions (axioms), conceiving of sentence-meaning as a matter of truth-conditions, and of truth-conditions of sentences as derived from the axioms and rules independently of any human normative practices, the meaning-theorist assigns to his rules an autonomous existence. The rules, of their own accord, as it were, generate sentence-meanings. Like aethereal machinery

---

[74] The idea that the laws of logic are partially *definitive* of thinking, inferring, reasoning, that there is no such thing as systematic non-logical *thinking*, but only babbling (although, of course, we make many mistakes in reasoning), that logic is antecedent to truth, is wholly alien to Platonism. The Platonist has a picture of the laws of logic as the superphysics of abstract objects. This, of course, is not a theory, it is the mythology which informs his theories.

they crank out truth-conditions irrespective of the practices of language-users or of their modes of explanation and justification, criticism and correction. Indeed, the 'totality' of sentences of English and their meanings are 'stored up' or 'contained' in the axioms and rules of the putative theory of meaning, much as the 'totality' of the theorems of mathematics might be conceived to be stored up in a few axioms and definitions of number theory in advance of mathematicians' constructing proofs.

This picture has been animated by modern developments in formal logic. The invention of quantification theory was typically conceived as the discovery of the real machinery determining the validity of inferences. It revealed the true logical forms of propositions, and explained for the first time the logical relations in which they stand. Given that no one had antecedently dreamt of such function-theoretic forms, let alone used them in inference, it seemed that they must owe their correctness to the nature of concepts and propositions, or to the *hidden* nature of thought, or both. Philosophers, intoxicated with the new mathematical gadgetry, were typically torn between Platonism and psychologism – torn, because they seemed to *need* both. On the one hand, they required a Platonist conception as a *picture* to validate the correctness of the novel logical analyses of, e.g., inferences involving multiple generality, propositions concerning belief and other propositional attitudes, and adverbial inferences. On the other hand, they needed a psychologistic picture to *connect* the newly discovered logical forms of thought and inference with our actual thinkings and inferrings.

Although the young Wittgenstein repudiated Frege's Platonism about logical objects, numbers, concepts and laws of logic, he faced a similar dilemma. A very powerful form of psychologism was required in order to explain our grasp of inferential relations, which, according to the *Tractatus*, rested on 'implicit knowledge' of the ultimate analysis of names and propositions.[75] This was duly swept under the carpet as being of no concern to philosophy. On the other hand, there was an explicit commitment to the Platonist conception of rules as generating consequences independently of us.

The conception of deep-structural analysis in the *Tractatus* had a wide impact through the Vienna Circle. It still informs much of modern philosophy of language and theoretical linguistics. The same bizarre combination of Platonism about rules generating their consequences and

---

[75] Cf. A. J. P. Kenny, 'Wittgenstein's Early Philosophy of Mind', in *Perspectives on the Philosophy of Wittgenstein*, ed. I. Block (Blackwell, Oxford, 1981).

psychologism about understanding, inferring, knowing a language is evident. It stands forth clearly in one of the mainsprings of confusion that move the psycholinguists, namely the idea that 'language is infinite' hence, 'it makes no sense to speak of it as "given", except insofar as some finite characterization – a function in intension – is given'.[76] This so-called 'function in intension', it will be remembered, *is* the grammar of the language, the rules and lexicon. Given these, then the infinite sentences of the language *are* given, stored up in the calculus, irrespective of whether we mere humans can survey them. Nothing so strikingly manifests linguists' adherence to this metaphysical picture than their insistence that English contains sentences which are more than a million words long.[77] Although no one has ever used such a sentence, and although no mere mortal could understand one,[78] nevertheless among the totality of English sentences there are (very likely infinitely many) such sentences. Similarly the linguists insist that there are (exist) English sentences containing dozens of nested relative clauses, even though no English speaker could understand them. These claims rest on the supposition that the rules of grammar and the lexicon, of their own accord, confer meaning on these bizarre objects, even though we, speakers of the language, cannot grasp their meanings through purely 'medical limitations' (as Russell once put it).

When Wittgenstein returned to philosophical work in the 1930s, he subjected the doctrines of the *Tractatus* to critical scrutiny. Though he now adopted a conventionalist conception of logical necessity, he clearly revealed the Platonist shades lurking in the picture of logical consequence adumbrated in his first book. There can be no hidden, unknown, *conventions*. Rules are not pieces of aethereal machinery grinding out derived rules independently of us. And the nature of the *application* of rules is not something that can be left to 'take care of itself'. Reflections upon these subjects are the central themes of Wittgenstein's *Philosophical Investigations* and *Remarks upon the Foundations of Mathematics*, but they have been little understood. Most philosophers have found the questions he posed well-nigh incomprehensible and the answers he suggested wholly paradoxical. The dominant conception of rules of logic and language, of their consequences and applications is quite different.

---

[76] Chomsky, *Rules and Representations*, p. 84.

[77] Chomsky, *Syntactic Structures*, p. 23.

[78] Unless the alleged sentence is of the childish type – "Twas a dark and stormy night and the sailor said to the captain, "Captain, tell us a tale", and the captain began as follows, " 'Twas a dark and stormy night and the sailor said to the captain..." ' and so on. But this is a *joke*, and it does not consist of a sentence millions of words long!

Modern philosophical logic, built upon the foundations of function-theoretic formal logic, fostered a mythology of rules and conventions. These rules, which the hard labour of philosophers brings to light for the first time, determine consequences quite independently of us and our actual cognition. The rules of the predicate calculus determine the validity of inferences involving multiple generality; and a novel extension of the predicate calculus reveals why adverbial inference is actually valid, thus showing us the true logical form of our thought for the first time. Modal logics, epstemic logics, tense logics, deontic logics, all sprouted exuberantly, producing cornucopiae of hitherto unknown rules. Conceived as new *inventions*, as novel calculi which might have an intrinsic interest (like chess) or a philosophical interest (as new forms of representation), these systems of rules are harmless, and may even have a use. But they were, and are, typically conceived as discoveries, revelations of truths and hidden mysteries. Thus conceived they involve a pernicious and incoherent conception of rules and of rule-following, of the use of rules and of what it is for something to follow from a rule.

5   The mythology of scientific method

That linguistics is a natural science, employing the methods of the well-established natural sciences, is an article of faith of the mainstream of modern theorists of language.[79] It conducts its investigations, so it is claimed, in the 'Galilean style', hoping (and claiming!)

> to move beyond superficiality by a readiness to undertake perhaps far-reaching idealization and to construct abstract models that are accorded more significance than the ordinary world of sensation, and correspondingly, by readiness to tolerate unexplained phenomena or even as yet unexplained counter-evidence to theoretical constructions that have achieved a certain degree of explanatory depth in some limited domain . . .[80]

The toleration of counter-evidence and unexplained phenomena is evident enough, the explanatory depth, even in a limited domain, is open to question. We shall not examine further the putative credentials *seriatim* (e.g. 'explanations' of the ambiguity of 'They are flying planes', or of why

---

[79] It is 'on a par with other branches of empirical science'; cf. Chomsky, *Reflections on Language*, p. 185.

[80] Chomsky, *Rules and Representations*.

nonsense is nonsense). Such a strategy, even if successful, would only
encourage the linguist to try harder in the hope that next time he might
succeed in achieving explanatory depth. Rather shall we adopt the indirect
approach, suggesting not merely that the results hitherto achieved are
worthless, but that future results, if pursued in this pseudo-scientific
manner, are bound to be equally worthless, since the enterprise is misconceived. To show this we need to do little more than bring together various
threads in the previous discussions.

Explanation in the physical sciences typically consists in subsumption
under a theory-sanctioned causal law. Such a law may explain the puzzling
phenomenon (e.g. the orbit of Mars) by showing it to be subsumable under
a generalization covering all phenomena of a given type (e.g. Kepler's three
laws of planetary motion). In a developed science, relatively particular
laws (e.g. Kepler's) may be shown to be special cases of much wider
generalizations embedded in complex theories themselves involving
substantial degrees of idealization and abstract model-building (e.g.
Newtonian mechanics). A different form of explanation may involve
ascent in a hierarchy of theoretically related entities, where the puzzling
phenomenon (e.g. the solubility of gold in aqua regia) is explained in terms
of regularities of interaction of entities higher up in the hierarchy
elaborated by the theory (e.g. molecules, atoms, ions). What typically
lends a theory its persuasiveness is neither its predictive power alone nor its
simplicity (the Copernican solar-centric theory was neither predictively
more successful nor simpler than the developed Ptolemaic theory), but
rather its explanatory force (in Kepler's case, the fact that his theory
yielded general planetary laws of motion, and more generally, that it made
a substantial step towards unifying the Geometry of the Skies with terrestrial physics).

The crucial question to be faced is whether law, morals and etiquette,
games, logic and mathematics and (the case that concerns us) language are
an appropriate subject-matter for theory-building and theoretical explanation *of the form involved in physics*. Certainly rules and the normative
phenomena associated with them give rise to a multitude of questions,
puzzles and difficulties. Observing unfamiliar normative behaviour immediately generates questions that seek for an interpretation of the behaviour. The observer strives to understand the *meaning* of what he sees
and hears. Two people are patting a little ball across a net. Why? What is
the point and purpose of the activity? What are the rules governing it? And
the answers will consist in an explanation of the rules of tennis, and, if
necessary, of the point of playing games. Similar patterns of explanation

will accompany questions about alien rituals (e.g. coronations), legal transactions (*mancipatio*), etiquette, and so on. And typically the explanation is obtained by asking the *participants*. The questions that arise when one is confronted by alien speech are similar, though not identical. One strives for explanations of meaning, so that one many understand what is said. And if one wishes to master the language oneself one will try to discover the meanings of individual words, not by correlating alien words with familiar meanings, but by correlating them with familiar words in one's own language. And, of course, one will have to master rules of word-combination. Again, typically, the native speakers are one's guides and authorities, and the ready route to understanding consists neither in correlating phonemes with semantic representations[81] nor in determining methods of generating truth-conditions from axioms and formation-rules, but in participating in the activities of the natives and in particular learning from their explanations, corrections and criticisms.[82] The endeavour is not to construct an axiomatized theory of meaning for the language, let alone a 'depth-grammar', but to learn to speak and understand it. And for that no theory-building in Galilean style is either necessary or possible.

Of course, there are many other questions about rules and rule-governed activities that commonly arise. One may not understand the import of a rule, even though it is written down before one, and then one typically has recourse to experts, as when a child asks its parent to explain the rules written on the back of its Monopoly box or an adult consults an accountant or solicitor over an opaque law. One may understand a rule-formation, but be unsure how the rule is to be applied in 'hard cases'. Here too one may consult experts who are familiar with precedents. In the absence of precedents the decision (by oneself or, in law, by an authority) unavoidably involves judicial legislation. Such creative adjudication, however, is not arbitrary, but guided by principles and interpretative canons. It is not, however, guided by theories in the 'Galilean style', in which, on the basis of data, one infers the nature of an independently existing abstract entity (as it were, a normative electron) which contains its own application

---

[81] Short of insanity, the one thing the anthropologist would not do is avert his eyes from the natives' activities, remain wholly uninvolved, and take three years' worth of tape-recordings of arbitrary utterances. On the basis of this data he should (according to Chomsky), if only he had the wit of a child, be able to construct an unconscious theory of the native language!

[82] Of course, this is not always possible. Ancient Egyptian was deciphered without any access to behaviour save writing, but only through the good fortune of finding the Rosetta Stone. Without such luck one may indeed be helpless, as is the case with Etruscan.

to the hard case in advance of our applying it. Many other kinds of problems arise with respect to norms and normative phenomena (e.g. resolution of conflicts of norms, relations between different normative systems (municipal and international law)), but in no case is there room for theory construction of the kind envisaged by the theoretical linguist.

This should give us pause. Normative phenomena are legion, but while language is no doubt distinctive, is it *so* different? One of the most striking features about modern theoretical linguists is the drastic shortage of material in need of any explanation whatever. The types of normative problems just adumbrated do not occur in the studies of a theoretical linguist. He is not in the position of confronting a dead, unknown, language, such as Etruscan, nor even in the position of the anthropologist confronting the language of an alien people. He is concerned with English, he knows what such-and-such words mean, he understands sentences of the language, knows how to use words and sentences, and knows what people are typically doing when they use a given sentence in a given context. Are there really any genuine *problems* for the theoretical linguist to explain, as opposed to materials for the descriptive linguist to itemize and anatomize? Ambiguity, in context, is far less common than theorists typically pretend,[83] and disambiguation is a simple operation requiring no descent into the seven circles of modern linguistic theory.

It is, of course true, that the so-called 'surface grammar' of different sentences may look very similar, yet the sentences may have very different uses. The constituent expressions may look as if they are of a kind in one context, yet may enter into altogether different combinations in different sentences. These phenomena, responsible, no doubt, for a multitude of philosophical (and other) confusions, are noteworthy, but not recently discovered. Nor do they require us to create mythologies about depth-grammar in order to clarify them. Nothing is concealed, and no crypto-science is necessary to reveal hidden depths. The 'workings of language' do not need to be laid bare by *theories*; they are already open to view.

Linguists typically conceive of the grammatical rules they construct as part of an explanatory theory. This theory, however, does not extend as far as linguistic performance. That, it seems, is a mystery:

Once the system of language and other cognitive structures are developed by the mind, the person has a certain range of choices available as to how to use these systems . . . Now, however, we face some real mysteries, namely, those relating to the theory of human action. The rules that a person 'accepts' do not tell him what to say . . .

The study of the development of cognitive structures . . . poses problems to be solved, but not, it seems, impenetrable mysteries. The study of the capacity to use these structures and the exercise of this capacity, however, still seems to elude our understanding.[84]

Is this to be taken seriously? Is it suggested that it is a *mystery* why people say 'Shut the door, please' when they want someone to shut the door, or 'What time is it?' when they want to know what time it is? Surely the linguist must have great difficulty in coping with everyday life if he can never understand the 'mystery' of why people say the things they say? This is ludicrous. We constantly explain why people say what they say by reference to their goals, purposes, reasons, and motives, within the context of familiar customs and conventions. These explanations are among the most familiar forms of explanation there are, and they are perspicuous, well understood, and commonly correct. Without their availability we would be truly lost in the human world, as lost as the linguist in his illusory mysteries.

A fundamental error of theoretical linguists is their conception of linguistic rules, whether semantic or syntactic, as elements of a theory, or, worse, as postulated theoretical entities with an explanatory force within the context of a theory modelled on physics. The child, that well-known amateur linguist, has to construct the grammar of the language to which he is exposed by invoking his innate universal grammar and testing various hypotheses on the limited data available to him. Thus he comes to possess the grammar of his native tongue and is able to understand his language. The linguist goes through a similar operation rather more slowly, although curiously *he actually speaks and understands the language.* His goal, he claims, is to construct a theory of a speaker's competence:

a generative grammar attempts to specify what the speaker actually knows ['far beyond the level of actual or even potential consciousness'] not what he may report about his knowledge. Similarly, a theory of visual perception would attempt to account for what a person actually sees and the mechanisms that determine this rather than his statements about what he sees . . .[85]

This grammar is conceived to be a theory, akin to a scientific theory about a natural, non-normative, phenomenon. It is, strictly speaking, a

[84] Chomsky, *Reflections on Language*, p. 77.
[85] Chomsky, *Aspects of the Theory of Syntax*, p. 8.

psychological theory (according to Chomsky) about the inner constitution of a speaker's competence, the structure of his language faculty, the nature of his mind. With the comparison of a grammar to a theory of visual perception, Chomsky squarely hits the nail on his thumb. For this comparison highlights the fundamental confusion involved in assimilating normative explanation to hypothetico-deductive explanation in empirical science. The further contention that the grammarian's theory is to be tested for 'descriptive adequacy' by reference to the 'linguistic intuitions' of the native speaker, whether or not he may be immediately aware of this,[86] merely pours oil on the fires of absurdity.

A natural scientist, faced with a phenomenon which, for one reason or another is puzzling, constructs a theory which he hopes will explain the phenomenon, account for why things happen in such-and-such ways, or why objects of this kind have properties of this type, etc. Having constructed the theory, the scientist will subject it to experimental tests. Given a specification of initial conditions, and given no interfering factors, he hopes to be able to derive from the theory a true characterization of what occurs in the test or experiment. Nothing remotely like this obtains when the linguist confronts normative phenomena *which he fully understands* (viz. English speech). For thoroughly *bad* reasons, he thinks that linguistic performance is too mysterious to explain, and for equally bad reasons, he insists that his task is to explain only ideal performance by an Ideal Speaker-Hearer, not empirical performance by human beings. Strictly speaking, he insists, he is trying to explain competence. But as we have seen, it is far from evident that there is anything here to explain, or at least, anything for a *linguist* to explain.

Shifting his ground somewhat, the linguist will contend that he is constructing a grammatical theory (just like a theory in physics) from which he hopes to be able to derive only grammatical sentences of the given language. Then, using as his test the intuitions of a native speaker, he will have proved that the native speaker's *cognized* grammar, which is represented in his mind and realized in his brain, is of the nature specified in this theory. Surely, this is just the sort of activity respectable scientists engage in!

The answer is, surely not! The strategy is deeply flawed, for reasons already rehearsed. (i) There is no action at a distance in grammar,[87] i.e.

[86] Ibid., p. 24.
[87] L. Wittgenstein, *Philosophical Grammar*, ed. Rush Rhees (Blackwell, Oxford, 1974), p. 81, *The Blue and Brown Books* (Blackwell, Oxford, 1969), p. 14.

rules cannot guide conduct independently of the human beings whose conduct is in question. They are not invisible rails down which we unconsciously glide, but norms which we use to guide ourselves. There is no normative behaviour as long as the norms await discovery. 'Rules' that are far beyond the level of even potential consciousness can have no normative function at all. Hence to look for such hidden rules, as a scientist looks for hypothetical entities, is as senseless as looking for unowned sense data on the Costa del Sol. (ii) Consequently, no system of rules could be a theory about anything. An anthropologist might conjecture, on the basis of observation of natives, that the rules of the game they play on a board are such-and-such. But while the conjecture that they play according to such-and-such rules may, loosely, be called 'a theory', the rules according to which they *do* play are not a theory of anything. The rules of chess are not a theory about chess, nor about how chess-players move their pieces. For the rules specify what is to *be* done, not what *is* done, and many a chess-player doubtless cheats.[88] (iii) Hence, furthermore, the way to 'discover' the rules of a normative practice is to *ask* the practitioners. For if their activities are rule-governed, then they must *use* the rules, consult them, guide their actions by them, and explain what they are doing, and why it is right, by reference to them. For conduct to be normative, the agents must view their own behaviour under the aspect of normativity, describe their own actions in terms which they themselves explain by reference to particular rules, and criticize and correct their own and other's behaviour in terms of these rules.[89] (iv) Were we to invent a set of rules the applications of which coincided with the normative activities of rule-followers, or even with what they merely *say* would be *correct*, it in no way follows that they are following the set of rules we concocted. Even if it were a fact that one can do arithmetic in the set-theoretic notation of Frege's logical calculus, this would not show that everyone who had calculated and computed prior to 1893 had unknowingly been following the rules and axioms of *The Basic Laws of Arithmetic*. It merely shows that one can map one system of rules on to another. The traditional grammarian elaborated possible rules, typically extrapolated from the critical normative practices of speakers. These possible rules rapidly acquired a genuine normative role in a European literate culture, being used in formal school instruction, consulted for

[88] But not, of course, an Ideal Chess Player, whose performance will, under ideal conditions, truly reflect his competence! The rationale for this manoeuvre is now perspicuous.

[89] All of which is, of course, compatible with occasional error or slip both in practice and explanation.

guidance, and referred to in criticism. But at no stage of this development
were they theories. *A fortiori* the 'rules' of transformational generative
grammar are neither theories nor rules. (v) The relationship between the
grammarian's invented grammar (theory!) and its application is not akin
to the relation between a scientific theory and an observation predicted
from it. Nor is the assent of a native speaker to the 'predicted' grammaticalness of a sequence of words akin to the confirmation of an hypothesis.
To derive a prediction from a scientific theory, one requires not merely a
specification of the theory, or an appropriate part of it (e.g. a functional
law specifying systematic nomological relations between variable
magnitudes), but also a specification of factual (so-called 'initial') conditions. But the linguist's 'grammatical theory' is a *calculus of rules*. Its
application produces *theorems*, not hypotheses, and it neither has nor
could have (until it becomes a theory of performance) any room for factual
initial conditions. To this it will, of course, be replied that the grammatical
theory *predicts* that a given sequence is grammatical, and this is confirmed
or confuted (just as in physics!) by experience, viz. the grammatical
intuitions of the speaker. But this is quite wrong. The grammar *entails* that
a sequence is, according to its rules, licit or grammatical. That an average
English speaker accepts that word sequence as decent English[90] *is in no
way* predicted by the grammatical theory (any more than the theorems of
geometry are predictions). And the fact that he does so, *in no way* confirms
that he 'cognizes', 'tacitly knows' or 'has a mental representation of' the
linguist's grammatical concoction.

The theoretical linguist claims that he deals with deep questions about
the nature of the mind. His investigations, he contends, go deeper than
those of the psychologist. He outstrips the philosopher in conceptual
clarification. He will provide a research programme for biologists and
neurophysiologists. His successful methods will be the basis for other new
sciences, such as developing a 'universal grammar of faces'[91] which will
'explain' our ability to recognize faces, and a 'universal grammar' of
scientific theories[92] to explain our 'science forming capacity', and even an

[90] A great mystery surrounds the linguist's patter about native speakers' grammatical
intuitions. Are these meant to be 'intuitions' (whatever they are?) that a sequence is *grammatical*?
And according to *whose* conception of grammar? The speaker's or the linguist's? Or are they
intuitions of 'acceptability'? But then acceptability by whom? In the barrack-room or the
officers' mess? Acceptable for what purpose? For speech or for writing? In an examination at
university or in a drunken conversation in a pub? etc.
[91] Chomsky, *Rules and Representations*, p. 248.
[92] Ibid., p. 251.

aesthetic grammar which will explain the 'humanly accessible' systems of music, literature, etc. This is *folie de grandeur*. The pretensions are as great as those of astrology, and the achievements altogether comparable. After decades full of this sound and fury, can one honestly say that the tale signifies anything?

CHAPTER 9

The Generative Theory of Understanding

1 Plus ça change . . .

There are certain venerable philosophical phantasms which mesmerize the mind. They reappear from generation to generation, occasionally in fresh guise, but still recognizable as variations upon ancient figments. We are drawn to them as a moth to a candle, and only rigorous philosophical criticism can save us from illusion. What we shall call the 'generative theory of understanding' is one such ancient conception decked out in modern dress. This theory, propounded by both linguists and philosophers in different forms, some more ambitious, some less, purports to provide the only possible answer to a seemingly deep question: how is it possible for us to understand sentences we have never heard before. For we can do so; we can understand a myriad of novel sentences without having been taught what they mean. This fact, and not the starry sky above nor the moral law within, strikes awe in the heart of the contemporary psycholinguist and philosophical theorist of meaning. The general form of their answers to this question typically involves the claim that the meaning of a sentence is composed of the meanings of its constituents, or that the meanings of its constituents consist in their contribution to the meaning (truth-conditions (?)) of any sentence in which they may occur. We understand sentences, it is held, because we *derive* the meaning of a sentence from the meaning of its constituents and from the combinatorial rules which conjointly determine it. The meaning of a sentence flows from the axioms and rules of a theory of meaning, and we understand a language in virtue of our 'tacit knowledge' of such a theory.

This picture replaces an older one of marked similarity. The limits of possible thought and their relation to experience were prominent issues in post-Cartesian philosophy. In this tradition, experience is typically conceived in terms of passive receptivity on the one hand and a more or less active mind on the other. The mind receives an array of sensory data, variously called 'impressions', 'ideas', or 'perceptions'. It then organizes these items into a coherent experience of an objective realm. Thinking was commonly conceived to be a transaction with *ideas*. According to empiricists, these are derived from perceptions, and are, in some sense, copies of original impressions. Rationalists thought of the mind as capable of contributing ideas of its own that are neither copies of nor caused by impressions received in perceptual experience. All ideas, it was generally agreed, are either simple or complex, and any complex idea was conceived as analysable into combinations of simple ideas. Simple ideas, the 'given', are the basic building blocks of thought. The limits of thought were then, it seemed, determined by the available fund of simples and the forms of combination which the mind can impose on its ideas. The mind was conceived as a sort of kaleidoscope, although the number and reliability of its constituent mirrors, as it were, was a controversial question.

There is more wrong with this picture (sketched here with great oversimplification) than is worth trying to unravel now. Even the fundamental conceptions of what is 'given' and what is 'contributed' by the mind are a distorting presupposition. So too was the conception of judgment as a composition or synthesis of antecedently given ideas into a complex. Given the dominant conception of an *external* relation between thought and language, it is hardly surprising that grammatical forms were held to provide only relatively tentative guidelines in the painting of this picture of the limits of thought.

With the development of the new function-theoretic logic by Frege and then by Russell and Whitehead, the venerable picture of the Kaleidoscopic Mind was painted in fresh and startling colours. The new logic displaced subject/predicate logic by a richer, more flexible array of forms derived from function theory. Instead of identifying the fundamental form of combination characterizing the proposition with the attachment of a predicate to a subject by means of a copula, the new logic identified it with the assignment of a value to a function for an argument. But names of different functions of any given level may take one, two, three, or any stipulated number of argument-expressions, hence could represent concepts (unary functions) and relations of any degree of polyadicity. And from the hierarchy of functions were introduced into logic higher-level functions, taking lower-level functions as arguments and mapping them on to truth-values or propositions. With the aid of this new machinery crucial areas of inference and reasoning were illuminated and reduced to structures in which logical relations are given a formally perspicuous representation. It was not, therefore, implausible to think of the new calculus as *revealing*, for the first time, the true forms of thought.

If so, it was plausible to conceive of the new logical calculus as an *improvement* over natural language for specialized purposes of displaying deductive relationships. And so, indeed, did Frege argue, conceiving of natural languages as having the function-theoretic forms of his calculus, only in an *imperfect* and rough-and-ready fashion. But another strategy also emerged, namely the claim that the underlying, *hidden* forms of languages *were* the forms of the logical calculus. Any language, when correctly analysed, *must* turn out to have a depth-structure *identical* with that of (some version of) the new logic. So, indeed, did the young Wittgenstein argue in the *Tractatus*, taking the further radical step of insisting that there must be an *internal* relation between thought and language. He wrote excitedly in his notebook in 1916: 'Now it is becoming clear why I thought that thinking and language were the same. For thinking is a kind of language. For a thought too is, of course, a logical picture of the proposition, and therefore it just is a kind of proposition.'[1] Logical form, accurately reflected in a perspicuous notation, is a condition of the possibility of representation. Every representation, be it a picture, model, diagram, sentence of language, *or a thought* must, according to the picture theory of the *Tractatus*, have something in common with what it represents. This is logical form;[2] i.e. the elements of what represents must have the same combinatorial possibilities as the elements of what is represented. The picture must be logically isomorphic with the pictured.

Hence, it might be argued, the logical syntax of the new function-theoretic calculus must hold the key to the possible forms of combination in thought of whatever is *given*. But what is conceived to be 'given'? The answer, running parallel to the classical answer of 'simple ideas', was: the interpretation of the primitive non-logical vocabulary. Since language is (was taken to be!) analysable, and reality is decomposable ('in thought'), then the primitive indefinables of language will correspond to simple entities in reality, and the logical forms of the depth-grammar of any possible language will coincide with the range of possible reality and thought alike. Given the syntax, the semantical interpretation of the primitive non-logical constants, and the truth-functional analysis of the syncategorematic combinatorial devices, the meanings of all licit forms of

---

[1] L. Wittgenstein, *Notebooks 1914–16*, 2nd edn. (Blackwell, Oxford, 1969), p. 82.
[2] Wittgenstein, *Tractatus*, 2.18.

combination might well appear to be predetermined once and for all (give or take a few local difficulties).

Armed with some version of this picture and the mechanics of the predicate calculus, philosophers found themselves in possession of a powerful solution to a problem that had not yet occurred to them. In the 1910s and 1920s different philosophers raised what appeared to them, and to our contemporaries, to be one of the deepest questions about language. It was formulated in the *Tractatus* (1921) thus:

> 4.02   . . . we understand the sense of a propositional sign without its having been explained to us.
>
>   . . .
>
> 4.026   The meanings of simple signs (words) must be explained to us if we are to understand them.
>
>   With propositions, however, we make ourselves understood.
>
> 4.027   It belongs to the essence of a proposition that it should be able to communicate a *new* sense to us.
>
> 4.03   A proposition must use old expressions to communicate a new sense.[3]

An important feature of the picture theory of the proposition was that it seemed to explain how it is possible for us to understand sentences we have never heard before and which have never been explained to us. It apparently renders perspicuous our ability to grasp a new sense.[4]

A different formulation of the same issue was given by Frege in 1923, quite independently of Wittgenstein's picture theory.[5]

It is astonishing what language can do. With a few syllables it can express an incalculable number of thoughts, so that even a thought grasped by a human being

---

[3] These remarks date back thematically to the 'Notes on Logic' written in 1913 (see *Notebooks 1914–16*, Appendix I).

[4] Yet given that the account apparently assumed knowledge of unknown structures, viz. elementary propositions (which still awaited discovery) and familiarity with unknown objects, viz. simples (which still awaited final analysis) it could well be claimed that the explanation is more apparent than real.

[5] Independently of the picture theory, certainly; but was it independent of Wittgenstein? Frege's remarks date back to his essay 'Logic in Mathematics' (see G. Frege, *Posthumous Writings* (Blackwell, Oxford, 1979), pp. 225, 243, and to a letter to Philip Jourdain both written (apparently) early in 1914 (see G. Frege, *Philosophical and Mathematical Correspondence* (Blackwell, Oxford, 1980) p. 79). Frege and Wittgenstein had conversations in 1913, but whether the idea originated with one or the other, or in discussion, it is impossible to say.

for the very first time can be put into a form of words which will be understood by someone to whom the thought is entirely new. This would be impossible, were we not able to distinguish parts in the thought corresponding to the parts of a sentence, so that the structure of the sentence serves as an image of the structure of the thought.[6]

The thought (proposition) is here conceived as composed of elements or thought building-blocks (*Gedankenbausteine*) which correspond to the words of a sentence. Our capacity to understand new sentences, to grasp new thoughts, is conceived to be explicable by reference to our knowledge of word meanings and combinatorial forms, in virtue of which we can 'arrive at' (or 'derive', 'compute' (?)) the meanings of sentences which we have not encountered before.[7]

It is evident that the question, which came to be characterized as the 'creativity of language', was in the air at the time. For much the same problem, and a similar solution to it, is to be found in Schlick's *Allgemeine Erkenntnislehre* (1918) couched in the jargon of nineteenth century logic:

We do not need to learn separately which fact is designated by a particular judgment; we can tell this from the judgment itself. A cognitive judgment is a *new* combination made up exclusively of *old* concepts. The latter occur in innumerable other judgments, some of which (e.g. the definitions of these concepts) must have been known to us already . . .

Only the primitive concepts and judgments . . . depend on conventions and have to be learned as arbitrary signs. . . . Language, for its part, operates in a fashion similar to the cognitive process . . . The most highly developed language is the one that is able to express the entire wealth of thought with a minimum number of different forms . . .[8]

---

[6] G. Frege, 'Compound Thoughts', tr. R. H. Stoothoff, *Mind*, LXXII (1963), p. 1.

[7] It is noteworthy that this *Gedankenbausteine* picture sits most uneasily upon Frege's general conception of logic, thought and inference. It presupposes that thoughts have a unique analysis, while Frege's application of function theory to logic required that thoughts be capable of irreducible alternative analyses. It involves strict isomorphism between sentence and thought, which is inconsistent with the core of Frege's theories. And the synthetic, compositional conception of thoughts as built up out of antecedently given building blocks fits ill the analytical conception of thoughts as decomposing in irreducibly different ways into function and argument. Indeed Frege had originally propounded his new function/argument analysis in logic precisely to get away from the sterile synthetic conception of judgment. The analytic *decomposition* of judgments into function and argument was, in his view, more flexible and versatile, revealing richer logical forms and novel modes of concept-formation. The *Gedankenbausteine* picture in Frege's late writings is therefore a regression to an explicitly repudiated style of thought in logic. For detailed defence of this criticism, see G. P. Baker and P. M. S. Hacker, *Frege: Logical Excavations* (Blackwell, Oxford, 1984), pp. 381ff.

[8] M. Schlick, *General Theory of Knowledge*, tr. A. E. Blumberg (Springer, New York, 1974), p. 67.

This striking passage was written before Schlick had read Wittgenstein's *Tractatus*. Indeed, it makes obvious one respect in which Schlick found the *Tractatus* so inspiring. For the picture theory of the proposition must have seemed to him a lucid and profound resolution to questions for whose solution he himself had been groping.

Frege's brief remark on the 'creativity of language' lay buried in the little read pages of *Beiträge zur Philosophie des deutschen Idealismus*, III (1923), but the *Tractatus* had great influence on the Vienna Circle, and, through its members' diaspora, upon philosophy in America and elsewhere. However, the initial excitement died away in the 1940s and 1950s, the heyday of 'ordinary language philosophy'. Wittgenstein himself was busily undermining his first philosophy, and no more was heard from him about either a compositional or a generative conception of understanding. But in the 1960s and 1970s the seed sown by the *Tractatus* quickened, first among linguists and later among philosophers. Once the seed had germinated, it grew rapidly to sizeable proportions. But whether what grew was a Tree of Knowledge or a tangle of weeds and nettles remains to be seen.

2   The plants that grew

One main team of gardeners is theoretical linguists following more or less faithfully in the footsteps of Chomsky. They go so far as to rest the rationale of their whole 'science' on the need to answer this crucial question: 'Empirical linguistics takes the most general problem of the study of language to be that of accounting for the fluent speaker's ability to produce freely and understand readily all utterances of his language, including wholly novel ones.'[9] But one may suspect that, far from the linguists' theories being called forth to resolve this question, the question was called forth by the existence of a theory and a battery of techniques (especially the operations sanctioned in Chomsky's transformational generative grammar).

Philosophers who follow Dummett and Davidson in seeking a theory of meaning at least *seem* to place themselves in the same position:

The fact that anyone who has a mastery of any given language is able to understand an infinity of sentences of that language, an infinity which is, of course, principally

[9] J. Fodor and J. J. Katz, 'What's Wrong with the Philosophy of Language?', in *Philosophy and Linguistics*, ed. C. Lyas (Macmillan and St Martin's Press, London, 1971), p. 281. The prominence given to this 'problem' in this quotation is not idiosyncratic. The claim enjoys a general consensus among modern linguists.

composed of sentences which he has never heard before . . . can hardly be explained otherwise than by supposing that each speaker has an implicit grasp of a number of general principles governing the use in sentences of words of the language . . . [A]n explicit statement of those principles an implicit grasp of which constitutes the mastery of the language would be, precisely, a complete theory of meaning for the language.[10]

Careful examination of the writings of philosophers reveals at least an *apparent* spectrum of views on the matter of the point and purpose of a philosophical theory of meaning. While there is general agreement amongst them that the 'infinity' or 'creativity' of a language needs to be explained, one can discern, at one end of the spectrum, a minimalist position whose commitment to providing *an explanation* of understanding is slender, and at the other end of the spectrum a full-blown commitment similar to the linguists' psychologism. Between these extremes are various tentative ventures, which are difficult to characterize because of their studied vagueness or reticence over the relationship between the theory of meaning envisaged and a speaker's mastery of a language.

A theory of meaning for a natural language is conceived to be an *empirical* theory, and 'its ambition is to account for the workings of a natural language'.[11] Its task is to give the meaning of every meaningful expression:

An acceptable theory should . . . account for the meaning (or conditions of truth) of every sentence by analyzing it as composed, in truth-relevant ways, of elements drawn from a finite stock . . . [T]he theory [should] provide a method for deciding, given an arbitrary sentence, what its meaning is. (By satisfying these two conditions a theory may be said to show that the language it describes is *learnable* and *scrutable*).[12]

One might wonder about the point of such a theory. For even if it were to tell us what a host of English sentences mean, this would be news from nowhere. That it does so by means of deduction from an axiomatized theory may strike us as weird, but *chacun à son goût*. If it is indeed possible to construct a formal system mapping word-meanings and sentence-

[10] M. A. E. Dummett, 'Can Analytical Philosophy be Systematic and Ought it to be?', in *Truth and Other Enigmas* (Duckworth, London, 1978), p. 451.
[11] We have met this phrase in previous chapters. This time, however, it is from D. Davidson, 'Truth and Meaning', *Synthese*, 17 (1967), p. 311.
[12] D. Davidson, 'Semantics for Natural Languages', in *Linguaggi nella Società e nella Tecnica*, ed. B. Visentini (Edizioni di Comunità, Milan, 1970), p. 178.

structures on to sentence-meanings, that is of no greater philosophical interest than the possibility of mapping Mozart's Piano Concertos on to graphs of sound waves is of aesthetic interest. For this possibility to be of any philosophical moment it must signify something about our mastery and understanding of language.[13]

The addition is readily made by the minimalist theory. 'Empirical power in such a theory', Davidson contends,[14] 'depends on success in recovering the structure of a very complicated ability – the ability to speak and understand a language'. What 'recovering' amounts to is opaque; so too is patter about 'the structure of an ability'. Our qualms may, however, be allayed by a further remark: 'we are entitled to consider in advance of empirical study what we shall count as knowing a language, how we shall describe the skill or ability of a person who has learned to speak a language.'[15] From which it seems that in some sense a theory of meaning is a 'characterization' of the ability to speak a language. But in what sense?

An ability is typically characterized by specification of its exercise, by elaboration of what it is that the possessor of the ability can do.[16] A person understands a sentence, it is argued, if he can systematically associate with it an appropriate set of truth-conditions. He understands a language if he can associate with any sentence of the language an appropriate set of truth-conditions. (We shall keep our doubts in abeyance while developing the argument.) But the sentences of a language do not form a surveyable totality. It would therefore be impossible to characterize knowledge of a language by stating, for each sentence, in what an understanding of it consisted. This is conceived to be precisely parallel to the thought that one cannot characterize the ability to multiply numbers by listing correct answers to all possible multiplications which a person who can multiply can calculate. The intelligibility of speaking of a denumerable set, it is held, depends upon the possibility of generating a set of designations of its elements from a finite set by finitely many finitary operations. Hence characterizing knowledge of a language requires a recursive characterization of the understanding of sentences of the language in terms of the meanings of sentence-constituents. A systematic theory of meaning will

---

[13] Of course, it might also be of interest for design of computers!

[14] Davidson, 'Truth and Meaning', p. 311.

[15] D. Davidson, 'Theories of Meaning and Learnable Languages', *Proceedings of the 1964 International Congress for Logic, Methodology and Philosophy of Science in Jerusalem* (North-Holland, Amsterdam, 1965), p. 387.

[16] The following account is indebted to an unpublished paper which Professor Dummett presented to a seminar we gave at Oxford University in June 1979.

deliver, in a systematic manner, a means of 'specifying the sense' of an arbitrary sentence (or sentence-radical) of the language by characterization of its truth-conditions as derived from the axioms of the theory (the 'lexicon'), the formation-rules and recursion formulae. This will constitute a 'theoretical representation of a practical ability.'[17] It is alleged that it is an *a priori* truth that only thus *can* one give a comprehensive and proper characterization of what it is that someone who has mastered a language can do.

Though fundamentally mistaken, as we shall show, the minimalist enterprise is comparatively modest. Its objective is merely a 'truly scientific' characterization of a practical ability, viz. the mastery of a language, a clarification of what understanding 'consists in', rather than an explanation of the mechanics of understanding. But even a philosopher who pursues something akin to the minimalist enterprise tends to move by a few quick steps to something much more ambitious, namely to an explanation of 'how understanding is possible'. This explanation is typically given in terms of the rule-governed *operation* of the meaning-calculus delivered by the 'tacitly known' theory of meaning. Even Davidson, normally so reticent about understanding and the psychological hinterland of his theory, reveals his commitments from time to time: 'speakers of a language can effectively determine the meaning or meanings of an arbitrary expression (if it has a meaning) and . . . it is the central task of a theory of meaning to show how this is possible'.[18] His theory is connected

with the possibility of learning a language. When we regard the meaning of each sentence as a function of a finite number of features of the sentence, we have an insight not only into what there is to be learned; we also understand how an infinite aptitude can be encompassed by finite accomplishments.[19]

To be sure, this is merely a small tip of a well-submerged iceberg. For on pain of theoretical vacuity and pointlessness, there must be much more than is revealed in Davidson's artfully reticent papers.

One's suspicions that this enterprise must slide along the spectrum towards a full-blown explanatory theory of understanding are strengthened

---

[17] M. A. E. Dummett, 'What is a Theory of Meaning? (II)' in *Truth and Meaning*, ed. G. Evans and J. McDowell (Clarendon Press, Oxford, 1976), p. 69.

[18] Davidson, 'Truth and Meaning', p. 320; note also his supposition that a theory of meaning will yield insight 'into the design of the machinery of our linguistic accomplishments' (ibid., p. 311). By their metaphors shall ye know them!

[19] Davidson, 'Theories of Meaning and Learnable Languages', p. 387.

by brief scrutiny of Dummett's writings. For though he insists that all a theory of meaning purports to do is to give a 'theoretical representation of a practical ability', he writes:

A theory of meaning will . . . represent the practical ability possessed by a speaker as consisting *in his grasp of* a set of propositions; since the speaker *derives his understanding* of a sentence from the meanings of its component words, these propositions will most naturally form a deductively connected system. The knowledge of these propositions that is attributed to a speaker . . . [is] . . . implicit knowledge.[20]

The enterprise no longer looks *merely* descriptive; an impression easily strengthened by other citations. For he insists that it is 'an *undoubted fact* that a *process of derivation* of some kind is involved in the understanding of a sentence',[21] and a theory of meaning will both clarify how this derivation is possible, and what the formal nature of the processes involved in understanding are.

The full-blown explanatory enterprise lies at the heart of the new science of theoretical linguistics. For, in accord with a tradition inaugurated by Saussure, Chomsky and the majority of his followers conceive of linguistics as a branch of psychology. The grammar which the linguist constructs is not merely a predictive device for hypothesizing the native speaker's 'linguistic intuitions', but it is also held to be something the 'speaker-hearer' implicitly knows. '[G]rammar is a system of rules and principles that determine the formal and semantic properties of sentences. The grammar is put to use, interacting with other mechanisms of the mind, in speaking and understanding language.'[22] As we have seen in the previous chapter, Chomsky's 'theory of understanding' is rich, elaborate and fantastical beyond anything to be found in the pages of philosophical theorists of meaning. Although, as we know, the child's knowledge of grammar is a matter of 'mental processes that are far beyond the level of actual or even potential consciousness',[23] nevertheless a scientific investigation reveals that the child's mind is richly furnished with rules of grammar, e.g. 'the child's mind (specifically, its component LT(HL))[24]

[20] Dummett, 'What is a Theory of Meaning? (II)', p. 70, our italics.
[21] Dummett, 'What is a Theory of Meaning?' p. 112, our italics (cf. p. 109, and 'What is a Theory of Meaning? (II)', p. 69).
[22] N. Chomsky, *Reflections on Language* (Fontana, London, 1976), p. 28.
[23] N. Chomsky, *Aspects of a Theory of Syntax* (MIT Press, Cambridge, Mass., 1965), p. 8.
[24] This is the scientific way of writing 'Learning Theory of Human Languages'; this theory is, of course, known to the child (implicitly!).

contains the instruction: Construct a structure-dependent rule, ignoring all structure-independent rules',[25] and lo and behold! the infant obeys this instruction and constructs as part of its grammar a structure-dependent rule for converting declaratives into interrogatives. The grammarian is at work trying to discover the system of rules, syntactic, semantic and pragmatic, which we all allegedly know (tacitly), and constantly use when we speak, think or understand the speech of another person. For it is held that we 'derive' our understanding of a sentence by 'computing' its meaning:

What a speaker does when he understands or produces an utterance must include at least the implicit analysing of its syntactic structure. It is this ability that a theory of syntax seeks to explicate . . . A semantic theory takes the solution to the general problem of production and understanding a step further. It seeks to account for the speaker's ability to assign interpretations to sentences on the basis of his knowledge of the meanings of their parts . . .[26]

The full-blown enterprise incorporates the minimalist one in a qualified sense. It would be wrong to suggest that any theorist pursuing a theory of understanding which postulates tacit knowledge of a theory of meaning *must* also claim that the theory of meaning itself constitutes a 'theoretical representation of a practical ability' or a 'recovery of the structure of a very complicated ability'. He might deny the very intelligibility of this claim. But a theory of meaning which will deliver the possibility of specifying 'in a systematic manner' the meaning of any sentence of the language is a common instrument in the achievement of the divergent objectives.

For the time being we shall focus exclusively upon the full-blown enterprise. We do so for three reasons. First, it is this above all which purports to answer the question of how we can understand sentences which we have never heard before. Secondly, it is intellectually more ambitious, linking understanding with mental processes, and flaunting explanatory pretensions in psychology. Thirdly, it (and not the minimalist enterprise) is *the* primary point of contact between contemporary philosophy of language and theoretical linguistics; hence a critical investigation may pay double dividends. We shall return to consider the minimalist position only at the end of our primary investigation.

Even within the camp of theorists engaged in the full-blown explanatory enterprise, the differences between linguists and philosophers are not trivial. Even the disagreements within each group are not insignificant. Yet

[25] Chomsky, *Reflections on Language*, pp. 32f.
[26] Fodor and Katz, 'What's Wrong with Philosophy of Language?', p. 282.

the overall similarities are striking. A composite Galtonian picture of the enterprise may be unjust in detail to specific theorists, but it serves to illustrate the general nature of their endeavour. For our concern is not to question the details of these grand theories, but their fundamental pre-suppositions, what they have in common and what is never called into question because it seems self-evident.

3 The elements

The various programmes for full-blown theories of language have in common the idea that the units or elements upon which formation- and transformation-rules work are typically words or 'lexical items' and that our understanding of sentences is 'constructed' or 'derived' from our grasp of word-meanings. Many myths lie hidden behind this seemingly in-nocuous supposition, and we shall expose a small selection. We shall disregard phonological and morphological considerations as being of less obvious philosophical concern than semantic ones. We shall also pass over substantial difficulties[27] that arise for the rule-obsessed generative grammarian with semi-productive formations that are irregular and not sharply circumscribed (e.g. adding '-ness' to an adjective, which applies happily to 'white', 'black', 'blue', but unhappily to, say, 'purple' and not at all to 'magenta' or 'eau-de-nil'). We shall begin with words, taking the term in a down to earth manner. It will be helpful to start with an outline of the strategy pursued by one group of linguists, although it should be noticed that our criticisms raise points which have to be answered by any enter-prise that purports to 'derive' or 'construct' sentence-meanings from the meanings of constituent words and their form of combination.

Words are 'the atoms of the syntactic system',[28] for the fundamental idea is 'that the process by which a speaker interprets each of the infinitely many sentences is a compositional process in which the meaning of any syntactically compound constituent of a sentence is obtained as a function of the meaning of the parts of the constituent.'[29] These syntactically elementary constituents of a sentence are, in the grammarians' jargon, 'assigned a semantic representation'. This is done by a 'dictionary' (not a book, but a 'theoretical construct' consisting of all the rules assigning meanings to words in the language). According to advocates of so-called

[27] P. H. Matthews, *Generative Grammar and Linguistic Competence* (Allen & Unwin, London, 1979), pp. 27ff.
[28] J. J. Katz, *The Philosophy of Language* (Harper & Row, New York, 1966), p. 153.
[29] Ibid., p. 152.

'componential analysis' the meaning of a lexical item 'is not an un-differentiated whole. Rather, it is analysable into atomic conceptual elements.'[30] Meanings of words 'are not indivisible entities but, rather, are composed of concepts in certain relations to one another, the job of the dictionary [being] to represent the conceptual structure of the meanings of words'.[31] The semanticist's analysis of the lexical items is explicitly compared to the chemist's analysis of chemical compounds, and the former's diagrammatic representations of his analyses are held to be precisely parallel to the latter's chemical notation. This naive composition and the accompanying bizarre ontology do little to encourage confidence in the sanity of the proceedings, but we shall disregard this dangerous and objectionable style of thought. The fundamental idea is independent of the ontology, and it is the former which we aim to evaluate. The analysis of a word's meaning represents it by 'semantic markers'. Thus to the word 'bachelor' there will correspond four different entries to budget for semantic ambiguity which 'has its source in the homonymy of words':[32]

 (i) (Physical Object), (Living), (Human), (Male), (Adult), (Never Married).
 (ii) (Physical Object), (Living), (Human), (Young), (Knight), (Serving under the standard of another).
 (iii) (Physical Object), (Living), (Human), (Having the academic degree for the completion of the first four years of college).
 (iv) (Physical Object), (Living), (Animal), (Male), (Seal), (Without a mate at breeding time).

The semantic markers are not words or even linguistic expressions, although the grammarian 'represents' them thus. Rather, 'they are to be regarded as constructs of a linguistic theory, just as terms such as "force" are regarded as labels for constructs in natural science'.[33]

Philosophers often subscribe to a more schematic method of assignment of meaning to constituent non-logical expressions in a language. There

[30] J. J. Katz and P. M. Postal, *An Integrated Theory of Linguistic Descriptions* (MIT Press, Cambridge, Mass., 1964), p. 14.

[31] Katz, *The Philosophy of Language*, p. 154.

[32] Ibid., p. 153.

[33] Ibid., p. 156. Numerous objections to this way of playing the game may cross the mind of any reader. Items (ii)–(iv) are not 'analyses' of the meaning of 'bachelor' at all, but of 'bachelor of art', 'bachelor-knight', and 'bachelor-seal'. Otherwise these latter three expressions would be, in context, pleonastic, which they are not; they would be necessary only for disambiguation, but they are not. We shall disregard such qualms about detail in order to focus on more general objections.

appears to be a general presumption that the non-logical vocabulary of a language can be divided into two grand classes, viz. definables and indefinables. The definable terms are to be defined or analysed into their characteristic marks (or *Merkmale*) or by some other formal definition of a more complex kind, as in definitions of an ancestral relation. In all such cases, since the meaning of a word is held to consist of its contribution to determining the truth-conditions of any sentence in which it may occur, its meaning is held to be specifiable by stipulating conditions necessary and sufficient for its application. However, when it comes to the meaning of 'indefinables' the theorists are remarkably silent. Some assume that homophonic T-sentences *are* explanations of meaning that link language to reality. Others perhaps assume that an ostensive definition is the primary means of explaining indefinables, and thus it is this device which links language to reality. And some apparently presume that indefinables *cannot* be explained at all, but rather a grasp of their meaning consists in an ineffable recognitional capacity.

It is perhaps no coincidence that the grammarian's Boolean analyses are tailored to the operations of a digital computer, and that the philosopher's story is so well adapted to the forms of the predicate calculus. Be that as it may, these regimented programmes must face two kinds of difficulties which have been little discussed, if at all, by these theorists.

(i) A huge variety of words of many different types do not lend themselves to explanation along the lines required by these theorists. A few examples of such kinds of expression are as follows:

(a) *Summa genera* such as 'substance', 'property', 'relation', and 'concept' are obviously problematic, not being readily analysable by Boolean semantic markers, nor by enumeration of characteristic marks or other formal definition.

(b) Family-resemblance terms whose extension is not united under a unitary concept in virtue of shared characteristics stand equally in need of different treatment. In Wittgenstein's view numerous terms are of this kind, including such philosophically important ones as 'proposition', 'language', 'number', and 'understand'.

(c) Psychological 'indefinables' must be problematic. For the only way (apart from behaviourism) that seems available to the theorist is to fall back on a form of private ostensive definition. Some will doubtless do so, but they must first demonstrate the intelligibility and coherence of this procedure as a method of explaining the meanings of terms of a public language.

(d) Indefinables whose meaning is explained by reference to public samples, whether canonical, as in the case of the standard metre (or yard, etc.) or standard, as in the case of shades of colours, materials at a drapers, etc. (where books of samples are used). Whether these theories make room for such terms is debatable. The grammarian's mental lexicon clearly does not, since the mind can contain no standard metre rods or samples of colour or cloth. If the philosopher's theory allows room for such terms, he owes his audience an account of how these forms of explanation fit into an axiomatic calculus.

Many other kinds of neglected expressions are no less problematic. Expletives, greetings, vocatives, prepositions, modal auxiliaries, and hosts of other parts of speech whose uses are familiar and readily explicable, are neither explained nor obviously explicable in the stipulated forms.

(ii) A quite different objection would challenge the supposition that there are clear principles of individuation for word-meanings. It is supposed that meanings or 'interpretations' are 'assigned to' or 'paired with' words, and that every significant use of a word in a sentence involves that word being paired with one meaning or another. But is this not a piece of mythology that stems from viewing language as a formal calculus which is given an interpretation? For quite apart from objections to the bi-planarity of the conception, there are no absolute, definite, principles for counting how many meanings a word has. Take the verb 'to play' and observe but a small segment of its ordinary, richly diverse use:

He plays cricket.
He plays the ball straight down the wicket.
He plays Mercutio.
He plays the violin.
He plays the second violin sonata.
He plays Mozart.
He plays the fool.
He plays fair (or foul).
He plays himself in.
He is played out.
He is playing up.
He plays them off against each other.
He plays with women.
He is playing into her hands.
He plays his cards well.
He plays on words.

England will play its part.
The light plays upon the water.

What meaning is 'associated' or 'paired' with the verb 'to play'? Or is it ambiguous? If so, *how many* meanings does it have?

It might be thought that the example is exceptional, perhaps because 'play up', 'play down', etc. are to be treated as distinct and semantically indivisible (like prepositions separated from verbs with separable prefixes in German) or because 'to play' is a family-resemblance term. But the phenomenon is ubiquitous. The word 'air' is surely not a family-resemblance term. But are there any agreed non-arbitrary ways of counting how many meanings it has? For one may air one's blankets before the fire, but one's opinions before the company; however, one would be ill-advised to air the room in the evening, for the night air is damp. One may rejoice to return to one's native air, delight to take the air in the afternoon, find, once out in the open air, that the air is sweet in the fields. Since there is a light air from the south, one may go sailing, and crowding on canvas, sail with gentle airs for a few miles. But the gentle airs with which one sails are not the airs one puts on. Those who do not put on airs may have a warm air, although their chatter may be a lot of hot air. The air we breathe may be cool, and if we are on Everest, thin. Yet if a ghost melts away into thin air, it may be at sea-level for all that, not thousands of feet up in mid-air. Although we may appear to be building castles in the air, since all this has an air of paradox, the points we are making have been in the air for some time, though not often heard on the air.

Obviously, an actual dictionary must use some *ad hoc* principles for determining the number of entries for an expression. But no lexicographer would claim special status for his principles, and different dictionaries will employ different principles. The generative grammarian's hypothesized mental lexicon, however, can hardly allow such flexible, pragmatic, principles in an enterprise that claims *explanatory* force. For while an ordinary lexicographer merely attempts to explain the uses of a word, typically by invoking hosts of illustrative examples, the language *theorist* attempts to explain both understanding and derivation of sentence-meaning from the composition of lexical items whose meanings must be laid down in advance of composition.[34] The mind, be it noted, is here conceived as a very powerful computer!

[34] It might be argued that since the hypothesis is underdetermined by the data, the theorist must simply choose the best hypothesis. But it is altogether absurd to suppose that 'the mind' has a set of principles for the individuation of numbers of meanings words have, as opposed to the lexicographer deciding on *ad hoc* principles relative to his purposes.

The two general kinds of difficulty suggest that the task of 'discovering' the entries in the theoretical lexicon, or of stipulating the axioms of the theory of meaning, may prove harder than is commonly envisaged. But this may simply spur the theorist on to yet greater ingenuity and more strenuous efforts in his theory-constructing enterprise. He might try to budget for family-resemblance terms by analysis into differentially weighted disjunctions of characteristic marks, the satisfaction of some weighted majority of which would license application of the expression. He might devise a hard and fast criterion for determining numbers of dictionary entries for a given expression. He might postulate 'neural representations' of samples, on the argument that only the further development of his theory will show whether his postulate makes sense.

All this, however, is of no avail. For the deep objection is not that the task is Herculean, but it is Sisyphean, because altogether misconceived. For even if the theorist can come up with appropriately complex explanations, what would their normative status be? We explain family-resemblance words by a string of examples plus a similarity rider, not by complex formulae involving weighted averages of semantic values, whatever they might be. We typically explain 'indefinables', such as colour predicates or predicates of perceptual qualities in general, by ostensive definitions by reference to paradigmatic samples. We typically explain prepositions by contextual paraphrase. We explain some expressions by *contrastive* paraphrase; others by exemplification. These are not indirect gestures towards the 'real' meaning of such terms, but genuine and correct explanations in their own right.[35] The language theorist will, of course, acknowledge that we do not, in our ordinary explanatory practices, deliver explanations of word-meaning in the regimented form of axioms or semantic markers specifying necessary and sufficient conditions. But this, in his view, merely shows that an ordinary speaker does not have explicit knowledge of a theory of meaning which the linguist aims to reconstruct. The *correct* theoretical explanations will have the stipulated forms, for only thus can language be represented as a calculus which delivers the meanings of sentences as consequences of axioms.

However, these axioms or dictionary entries are supposed to represent a speaker's tacit knowledge. For, as noted, the speaker is said to *utilize* his knowledge of the 'dictionary' to obtain the meanings of compound expres-

---

[35] For more detailed elaboration of these points, see G. P. Baker and P. M. S. Hacker, *Wittgenstein: Understanding and Meaning* (Blackwell, Oxford, 1980), pp. 69ff.

sions. The theorist presents the axioms of his theory as meaning-rules,[26] or as semantic markers. Each lexical item has its meaning itemized by a unique rule (or, in the case of ambiguity, each meaning of a homophone is uniquely stipulated). But now notice a further discrepancy with our ordinary conception of explanation. We not only give explanations in forms not acknowledged as legitimate for the calculus of language, but we recognize as legitimate different explanations of one and the same un- ambiguous expression. The term 'circle' can be explained as 'the shape of a penny piece'; or it can be explained ostensively by pointing at a circular object and saying 'A circle is *this* ↑ shape'; or it can be explained by exemplification: 'Look, this ↻ (drawing in the sand) is a circle'. And a geometer might explain it as 'the locus of points equidistant from a given point'.[37] Wholly disregarding other uses of 'circle' (e.g. 'The Vienna Circle', 'the endless circle of parties', 'in such social circles', etc.), which of these explanations of the meaning of 'circle' is the native speaker alleged to know? If a person is asked what 'circle' means, and points at a plate, saying 'The shape of that ↑ is a circle', does this reveal his knowledge of the 'dictionary entry' or 'axiom' for 'circle' or not? Or is it that he uses some *other* unique and regimented form of definition, which he implicitly knows, and on which basis he gives such 'unsatisfactory' overt explanations? If the former, then the tales of axioms and lexicons are redundant. For what the speaker knows when he knows the meaning of a given word is just what he explains when he explains its meaning (whether by ostension, formal definition, exemplification, examples, paraphrase, constrastive paraphrase, or whatever) and what he acknowledges as a correct explanation when he encounters one. But if the theorist insists, as he doubtless will, that the speaker's typical explanations are incorrect, at best only ersatz versions of the correct theoretical axioms or semantic markers, then he wilfully opens a vast gulf between our ordinary explanatory practices and the 'explanations' of the theory.

The theorist will indeed do so, in the name of scientific progress. Theory-construction in linguistics is no more constrained, in his view, by our common-or-garden explanations of meaning than theory-construction in physics is constrained by common-or-garden explanations of motion,

---

[36] The theorist might deny that his axioms are rules. But by that very token he must, self-defeatingly, deny that they 'give', or explain, the meanings of words. For explanations of word-meanings are normative, they specify the correct way of using an expression, deviation from which, in a given context, is a mistake.

[37] It might indeed be argued that, far from the geometer's definition being the 'correct' one, it defines a somewhat different concept of circle from the common-or-garden one.

Surely only in material mode; in formal mode they are descriptive.

334   *The Generative Theory of Understanding*

force or acceleration. The correct form and uniqueness of a semantic axiom or a conglomeration of semantic markets are dictated by its role in a powerful explanatory theory. The actual explanations given by a speaker are mere inductive evidence for his tacit knowledge of the 'dictionary entry'.

However, borrowing the jargon of advanced science does not make speculative linguistics into superphysics. Inductive evidence presupposes non-inductive identifications and subsequent correlations. If the linguist invokes a putative analogy with 'theoretical entities' such as electrons, whose existence is allegedly 'postulated' by physicists, we should remind him that one can weigh them, measure their velocity or electric charge, and manufacture or annihilate them. But the analogy is not merely weak, it is altogether misplaced. For the theorists' 'dictionary entries' or 'axioms' are in effect hidden rules conceived to operate at a distance. They are 'tacitly known' or 'cognized'. Even though buried at inaccessible depths of unconsciousness, they are used whenever we speak or understand what is spoken. But this is to fall victim to a mythology of rules. Rules cannot 'act at a distance'; there is no such thing as a rule determining behaviour unbeknownst to anyone who might cite it, consult it, and invoke it in explanation, criticism or justification. To think that rules await *discovery* by linguistic theorists is to confuse the appropriate forms of explanation of normative phenomena with forms of explanation appropriate only to the physical sciences. If explanations of word-meaning are rules for the correct use of words, at any rate these explanations cannot, on pain of incoherence, be represented as objects, awaiting discovery, which have no overt use in public linguistic transactions. Nor can they be unintelligible to those who are alleged to use them (as would be, e.g., Frege's explanations of the meanings of number words), for then they *could not* use them. A rule is not a predictive device, and whether a speaker does or does not guide his linguistic behaviour by reference to a given rule is not decided by a prediction that he will behave in such-and-such a manner.

Consequently, to the extent that the theorist tries to meet objections of one of the two general kinds adumbrated above by constructing more and more elaborate hypotheses about wonderful and hitherto unknown rules, his ingenuity is misplaced and his efforts misguided.

4   Combinations of elements: phrases and sentences

The abstract lexicon or the axioms of the theory of meaning represent the meanings of words. The meanings of combinations of words must be displayed as derived from the meanings of the words combined. But not any combination of words has a meaning. And given that many, perhaps most, words have multiple entries, theorists are inclined to seek out general principles whereby we select an appropriate entry for a given combination of words.

> This selection of senses and exclusion of others is reconstructed in the semantic component by the device . . . [of a] . . . selection restriction. Selection restrictions express necessary and sufficient conditions for the readings in which they occur to combine with other readings to form derived readings.[38]

These selection restrictions can be formulated as Boolean functions of semantic markers, e.g. the restriction on 'honest' for its reading 'characteristically unwilling to appropriate for himself what rightfully belongs to another, avoids lies, deception, etc.' is the Boolean function $\langle(\text{Human})\ \&\ \overline{(\text{Infant})}\rangle$ where the bar over the semantic marker indicates *exclusion* in the reading in question; for its archaic reading 'chaste', the selection restriction in written $\langle(\text{Human})\ \&\ (\text{Female})\rangle$. Projection rules are then held to stipulate the manner of amalgamating readings of individual words to give readings for phrases and sentences.

> The projection rules of the semantic component for a language characterize the meaning of all syntactically well-formed constituents of two or more words on the basis of what the dictionary specifies about these words. Thus, these rules provide a reconstruction of the process by which a speaker utilizes his knowledge of the dictionary to obtain the meanings of any syntactically compound constituent.[39]

This 'theory' not only explains the 'process' of understanding, it is also allegedly rich in predictive power:

> We can now show how a semantic component of English can predict . . . facts about the semantic anomaly of sentences such as 'The grain of sand is good' . . . etc. and the non-anomalousness of sentences such as 'The razor blade is good' . . . etc. Sentences of the former type have subject nouns whose reading contains no occurrence of an evaluation semantic marker and thus, in their semantic interpretation, these sentences receive no readings because the readings of their subjects do not satisfy the selection restriction in the reading for 'good'.[40]

---

[38] Katz, *The Philosophy of Language*, pp. 159f.
[39] Ibid., pp. 161f.
[40] Ibid., p. 297.

Variations upon this form of 'componential analysis' were common among linguists in the 1960s and 1970s. Other types of analyses, however, proliferated. And controversy raged over whether transformations do or do not change meaning, and whether the 'model' of linguistic description should be 'syntactically based' or 'semantically based'. None of this need concern us, since our qualms arise at a more elementary level than these internecine feuds.

It is clear enough that if one is embarked upon the construction of any theory of meaning which will enable the derivation of the meaning of any sentence from the meanings of its constituents and mode of combination, one must take steps to exclude nonsense or semantic anomaly. But it is unclear what falls under this heading, and theorists disagree radically among themselves about how to draw the bounds of sense. What counts as nonsense can be variously characterized. One might call a type-sentence nonsensical only if it has no intelligible use in any conceivable circumstance; or only if the established practice of explaining meanings gives it no standard use. Alternatively one might call an utterance nonsensical if it is unintelligible to competent speakers, even if other utterances of the same type-sentence in different circumstances would be intelligible. Likewise, the criteria for judging an expression to be nonsensical can be differently stipulated or described. One might require that competent speakers assent to the metalinguistic statement ' "*p*" is nonsense'; or that utterances of the problematic sentence standardly evoke responses of incomprehension; or that a particular utterance is unintelligible to a competent speaker. Theorists of meaning seem oblivious to these differences. They evidently consider that the sense/nonsense distinction marks circumstance-invariant features of type-sentences, and they show no awareness that different standards, appropriate to different intelligible purposes, might yield discrepant results. They hanker after general principles which will draw a once-for-all dichotomy between type-sentences, and they assume that a sentence which makes sense will *invariably* be intelligible to a competent speaker.

To the extent that compositional theories of meaning are committed to these presuppositions, they are rooted in nonsense and confusion. There are no tolerably general principles which lay down necessary and sufficient conditions for combinations of words to make sense. It is notorious that attempts to construct general theories of categories tend towards the absurd conclusion that there are as many categories as there are words,[41]

[41] Cf. W. and M. Kneale, *The Development of Logic* (Clarendon Press, Oxford, 1962), p. 671.

and in any case competent speakers do not invoke any such rules in justifying their discrimination of sense from nonsense. The idea that a sentence *invariably* makes sense or *invariably* fails to make sense is chimerical, and defending this dogma by categorizing intuitively ill-formed sentences as necessarily false leads from one absurdity into another. These are serious difficulties for compositionalism. For it would be preposterous to retreat to the position that *any* combination of individually significant words makes sense.

The context-dependence of sense and nonsense was argued in Chapter 6. A pair of further illustrations will drive the point home. To understand the quip 'the worst passions of the human mind are called into action by the pulverists and the lumpists', one needs to know that Sydney Smith is recounting an argument between those who favoured sweetening their tea with powdered sugar and those who favoured lump sugar.[42] Out of context, the following might pass for nonsense:

Victory has got a half-Nelson on Liberty from behind. Liberty is giving away about half a ton, and also carrying weight in the shape of a dying President and a brace of cherubs. (One of the cherubs is doing a cartwheel on the dying President's head, while the other, scarcely less considerate, attempts to pull his trousers off . . .[43]

But in its context this is immediately understood to be a wickedly witty description of a nineteenth century memorial statue (to a Brazilian president in Rio de Janeiro). The circumstances surrounding an utterance often make the crucial difference between grasping what is meant and not being able to conceive what on earth is conveyed.

A stronger objection to compositionalism must also be sustained. Such a theory of meaning must presumably classify as nonsense any combination of words which would *standardly* be unintelligible. Such a combination as 'dead rainbow' would assuredly be excluded by selection restrictions (or other combinatorial rules). But suppose a little boy sees diffraction rings on a film of oil floating on a puddle after a rainstorm, and exclaims 'Here is a dead rainbow'. Is his remark to be judged unintelligible because the phrase is nonsensical? Or should the theorist conclude that contrary to our prior convictions, the phrase really made good sense all along? Both horns of this dilemma are unattractive. But it is only forced upon us by the absurd

---

[42] Hesketh Pearson, *The Smith of Smiths* (Folio Society, London, 1977) p. 98.

[43] Peter Fleming, *Brazilian Adventure*, quoted in J. J. Norwich, *Christmas Crackers* (Allen Lane, London, 1980), p. 76.

presupposition that semantic rules uniformly determine the legitimacy of combinations of words in advance of their actual production and thereby fix their meaning in combination with 'projection rules'.

This conception, while purporting above all to explain the nature and possibility of linguistic creativity, in fact grossly distorts and misrepresents it. For parallel to the empiricist's picture of the Kaleidoscopic Mind, so too the grammarian's tale reduces creativity in the use of language to the realization of a range of combinatorial possibilities which are pre-determined and delimited in advance by a set of tacitly known rules. This not only involves a misguided mythology of rules, it debases creative use of language by arguing that it is a mechanical application of a calculus of meaning-rules, which, as it were, contains in advance the possibility of that novel use. Linguistic creativity, whether by poet, scientist or child, lies in exploiting combinations of expressions not readily foreseen or laid down as correct by rules of the language. (Could the rules foresee the possibilities to which the speakers were blind?) It is rooted in our genuinely creative capacity for seeing analogies, moulding language to new contexts, and imposing new patterns upon the phenomena we experience.

If a compositional theory grants sense to any combination of words which *might* conceivably be used to say something intelligible, much of what passes for nonsense must be reckoned among expressions which really make sense, and it will be difficult definitely to identify any outright nonsense at all. If, on the other hand, nonsensical expressions are admitted sometimes to make intelligible statements, the theory must abandon the thesis that what a speaker says must be calculated from the sense of the sentence uttered. Compositional theories of meaning are stranded in no man's land, caught in a deadly crossfire.

Their only apparent refuge is to embrace the less unpalatable alterna-tive. They may advocate conceptual anarchy, denying the legitimacy of any discrimination of sense from nonsense. Or, more plausibly, they may argue that there are no selection restrictions proper to semantics; only *syntactically* ill-formed expressions are nonsensical, while combinations commonly excluded as nonsense are rather necessarily false. According to this view, such sentences as 'Green ideas sleep furiously', 'This geranium is honest', or 'Here is a dead rainbow' are anomalous only in the same way as are 'This mat is both round and square' or 'Two is prime and two is not prime'.

This position lacks any sound supporting argument. One attempted defence is patently circular, since it falls back on compositionalism itself. Confronted by the phrase 'honest geranium', one linguist reasons:

after all, I know what properties an entity must possess in order to be properly described by such a phrase – namely that it must be a flower of the genus pelargonium which is fair and upright in speech and act. Now it might be objected that no one has ever encountered such an entity in the real world; but that is a *pragmatic* fact [*sic!*] about the way things happen to be in the world right now.[44]

But what justifies the claim that he knows what it would be for a geranium to be honest, apart from the fact that he knows what 'honest' and 'geranium' mean in other contexts? Could he even *imagine* encountering an honest geranium? At this point recourse to a second argument may seem attractive. The theorist may invoke fairy tales, in which inanimate objects talk, feel pain, fall in love, where geraniums may tell lies and ideas might be green. Surely, he may say, we *can* imagine these episodes and we do understand these stories. They may be false, but they cannot be nonsense, for then we should not understand them. Invoking imagination, however, is misguided, since part of the criterion for whether one *can* imagine such-and-such is precisely that specification of the object of imagination makes sense. Our powers of imagination give us no independent handle upon what makes sense, and the frontiers of the logically impossible, the conceptually absurd, and the nonsensical cannot be pushed back by daily exercises to stretch one's powers of imagination. To invoke our understanding of fairy tales begs the question in so far as clarification of what counts as so understanding fairy tales is problematic. One might rather argue[45] that such applications of concepts are *essentially* secondary, as is evident if we try to envisage the application of 'honest' *only* to flowers.

Neither of the two arguments to show that what passes for nonsense should be reclassified as 'necessarily false' is compelling. Compositionalism backs itself into a dilemma about distinguishing sense from nonsense. The only escape from the impasse is to think out afresh the relation between meaning and understanding.

5   Understanding and tacit knowledge

Hitherto our discussion has focused upon difficulties which must be confronted in constructing any theory of meaning which will display sentence-meanings as derived from the meanings of constituent words and

[44] A. Radford, 'The Origins of Katzian Semantics', unpublished preface to a collection of articles entitled 'Katzian Semantics', in the Taylorian Library, Oxford University, p. 29.

[45] Wittgenstein, *Philosophical Investigations*, § 282.

their mode of combination. Though we concentrated on linguists' compositional theories, many of our objections constitute difficulties that have to be surmounted by non-compositional theories too, e.g. theories that conceive of word-meanings as contributions to determination of truth-conditions. It may well be that most, perhaps all, of the difficulties we have raised will be viewed as challenges to be overcome, as a spur to greater ingenuity and theoretical inventiveness. So to respond only makes sense to the extent that the full-blown explanatory generative theory of understanding (1) can coherently make use of the envisaged theory of meaning in giving an explanation of understanding, and (2) that it is intelligible to explain, in the requisite sense, *how* we understand sentences. Now we shall examine the first issue.

The construction of a theory of meaning is held to involve a theory of understanding in so far as it is supposed that a speaker of a language has *tacit knowledge* of the theory of meaning. The theory of meaning is meant to replicate the theory tacitly known or 'cognized' by a speaker. Hence understanding is explained as involving an analysis of sentence-constituents, a coordination of their contributions to the meaning of the sentence in which they occur, an analysis of the structure of the sentence (surface and 'logical' or 'deep' structure) and thence the derivation of the meaning of the sentence. This notion of tacit knowledge[46] has never been properly explained. Indeed, in some cases, e.g. Evans's (above, p. 295), it is virtually obvious that there could not *possibly* be any good grounds for talking here of knowledge at all. It is true that the notion has been

---

[46] Even Dummett, when engaged upon the minimalist enterprise, invokes language appropriate only to the full-blown one: 'A theory of meaning of this kind is not intended as a psychological hypothesis. Its function is solely to present an analysis of the complex skill which constitutes mastery of a language, to display, in terms of what he may be said to know, just what it is that someone who possesses that mastery is able to do; it is not concerned to describe any inner psychological mechanisms which may account for his having those abilities. If a Martian could learn to speak a human language, or a robot be devised to behave in just the ways that are essential to a language-speaker, an implicit knowledge of the correct theory of meaning for the language could be attributed to the Martian or the robot with as much right as to a human speaker, even though their internal mechanisms were entirely different.' ('What is a Theory of Meaning? (II)', p. 70)

If the minimalist task of the theory of meaning is merely to give a proper analysis of the speaker's ability, to display what it is that he *can do*, why is implicit knowledge of the theory of meaning which constitutes the theoretical representation of the practical ability attributed to the speaker? What is the criterion for possession of such implicit knowledge and what distinguishes it from total ignorance? Is there any more reason to attribute implicit knowledge of the grammar of our language to this robot than there is reason to attribute implicit knowledge of mathematics to a pocket calculator?

variously employed throughout the history of philosophy. Plato's suggestion in the *Meno* that the slave was *recollecting a priori* truths of geometry
inasmuch as he had not *learnt* them might be thought to exemplify one
form of allegedly tacit knowledge. The Leibnizian account of 'virtually
innate knowledge' is perhaps another, slightly different, variety. Few,
apart from theoretical linguists, would wish to revive these long dis-
credited conceptions. But something that might be termed 'tacit knowledge' can be of a quite different nature. For example, Ryle's distinction
between knowing how and knowing that might be thought to intimate
tacit knowledge of whatever *practical* principles are, in some sense, followed in exercise of an ability. Quite differently, a psychoanalyst's patient,
who, under analysis, comes to realize that his motives were related to a
childhood trauma might also be said to possess tacit, but not explicit,
knowledge of his motives. Again, a pianist who can play and recognize
Bach trills and Chopin trills might be said to have tacit knowledge that the
former begin above the printed note and the latter on the printed note. For
although when asked, he does not give this answer, when told the answer,
he immediately recognizes it as correct. These are all *different* kinds of
case, some unquestionably misguided and all of them unilluminatingly
described as cases of tacit as opposed to explicit knowledge.

When the theorist of language attributes to every speaker of a language
tacit knowledge of a theory he must, in the first instance, clarify what this
means. First, what are the grounds for attributing to a speaker such tacit
knowledge? That our speech *can* (perhaps) be mapped on to a complex
calculus no more shows that we have been operating one than the mere
possibility of mapping Zulu war dances on to chess shows that Zulu
warriors are chess-players. The questions of what distinguishes tacit
knowledge from explicit knowledge on the one hand, and of what
distinguishes tacit knowledge from ignorance on the other, must be
answered coherently. For it is far from obvious that theorists use of the
term 'tacit knowledge' is intelligible. Like Locke's notion of tacit consent,
tacit knowledge may be no more than a device for tacitly burying problems
raised by the theory itself. If we are to ascribe tacit knowledge of a theory
of meaning to a person there must be something that will reveal the
difference between tacitly knowing the theory and total ignorance of it,
something other than the mere fact of the speaker's correct discourse. If his
correct discourse is *all* that shows his tacit knowledge and incorrect
discourse is *all* that shows ignorance, then the hypothesis that he can
produce and understand sentences *because of* such tacit knowledge is both
untestable and vacuous.

Secondly, grammarians and philosophers construct different theories of language. They are all designed, more or less, to match the linguistic 'output' of speakers (actual or ideal), to 'explain their linguistic intuitions' or to 'predict' their judgments of grammaticalness or meaningfulness. But, presumably, any sequence of behaviour can be mapped on to more than one 'rule' or system of 'rules'. So even if it made sense to attribute tacit knowledge of rules of a grammar to a speaker, how would we select between various possible rules? Traditional grammarians, with peda- gogical purposes, might select different rules in writing a grammar book according to ease of surveyability by learners. Logicians, with their interest in formalizing canons of inference, will concoct rules according to ease and perspicuity of representing valid inference (and, of course, there are *many* possibilities here). But such purpose-relative principles of choice in *laying down* rules are not open to our theorists, who are bent on 'discovering' rules. For they are concerned with revealing *the* hidden rules which a speaker *knows*, rules the knowledge of which *explains* the speaker's ability to speak and understand.

Thirdly, the earlier arguments have demonstrated that the very notion of hidden rules exercising their sway at a distance, and discoverable only by scientific investigation, is unintelligible. At the phenomenological level of understanding it is obvious that we do *not* calculate, compute or derive the meaning of a sentence from the meanings of its constituents and their mode of combination, *a fortiori* not according to the rules of some hitherto unheard of grammar. Indeed, even *after* we have, with the aid of linguists and philosophers, rendered some (?) of this treasured knowledge *explicit*, we still do not engage in any calculations or computations, save in excep- tional circumstances such as 'deciphering' a sentence involving multiple embedded relative clauses – and then we invoke more mundane grammars anyway (and perhaps the aid of paper and pencil).

To this it will be replied that the whole point of introducing the notion of *tacit* knowledge was precisely because of these very phenomenological features. Although we do not engage in such calculations consciously or explicitly, we engage in them unconsciously and implicitly, and very, very quickly. After all, computers perform derivations in a flash, and, surely, the brain is just a very complex biological computer! This manoeuvre involves a false conception of understanding as a mental act, activity or process, a conception which runs like a canker through all such generative theories. We shall return to this. It also commits the homunculus fallacy[47]

---

[47] A. J. P. Kenny, 'The Homunculus Fallacy', in *Interpretations of Life and Mind*, ed. M. Grene (Routledge & Kegan Paul, London, 1971).

in a flagrant manner. We shall pass over this absurdity with the simple remarks that what the brain does and what a person does are two different things, that brains do not *understand* anything, and that if brains performed 'derivations', they would have to communicate the results of the derivation to the persons whose brains they are. This would require that both brain and person speak a common language. But the brain neither speaks nor understands any language. It would also require that the person understand the brain's communication, for which, *ex hypothesi*, he would need a further brain to calculate its meaning from the meanings of its constituent symbols and their mode of combination.

Could our qualms about tacit knowledge not be put to rest by a terminological adjustment? Chomsky, confronted by objections to his misuse of the term 'know', introduces as a 'technical term' the expression 'cognize':

Let us say that if a speaker knows the language L, then he *cognizes* L. Furthermore he cognizes the linguistic facts that he knows (in any uncontroversial sense of 'know') and he cognizes the principles and rules of his internalized grammar, both those that might be brought to awareness and those that are forever hidden from consciousness.[48]

Indeed, it turns out that one cognizes principles of universal grammar, e.g. that transformations apply in cyclic ordering and obey SSC, that initial phrase markers and surface structures contribute to semantic interpretation, and that transformations are structure-dependent. In short, there is more cognized in Chomsky's philosophy than is dreamt of in heaven and earth. Is the matter a mere terminological disagreement? Chomsky suggests as much:

It is unclear that more than terminology is at stake here. [One] might choose to abandon the terms 'knowledge' and even 'knowledge of language' (if some find that offensive), while noting that there is little warrant in ordinary usage for these decisions. If so, he will speak of acquiring, cognizing and competence, instead of learning, knowing and knowledge.

As long as we are clear about what we are doing, either approach seems to me quite all right. 'Provided we agree about the thing, it is needless to dispute about the terms' (Hume).[49]

---

[48] Chomsky, *Reflections on Language*, pp. 164f., cf. *Rules and Representations* (Blackwell, London, 1980), pp. 69f.

[49] Ibid., p. 166.

Indeed, no one need suggest that we abandon the term 'knowing English'. It is unproblematic, and we all know how to use it. One may indeed know *a* language more or less well. The Bard's mastery of English was unique, and in addition he knew a little Latin, and less Greek. But did he know language? This phrase is *not* one we are all familiar with, and it requires explanation.

When a person knows something he can typically tell one what he knows or display what he knows (and not merely *that* he knows) when asked, or at least recognize what he knows when it is specified (if he found it difficult to articulate). But, of course, none of this applies to knowing principles of Chomsky's theoretical linguistics or of truth-conditional theories of meaning. These objects of putative knowledge an ordinary speaker cannot rehearse on demand; he cannot immediately recognize a theorist's rehearsal as a correct articulation of what he was attempting unsuccessfully to express. So what is meant by saying that he 'tacitly knows' these theoretical mysteries? Invoking Hume's confusions in support of modern muddles hardly shifts the onus of proof. Unless the disputed terms *are* clarified, we do not even know what 'thing' it is about which we are supposed to agree.

At least some cases of using the phrase 'tacit knowledge' can be clarified by elaborating the criteria for tacitly knowing (say, Chopin trills) as opposed to explicitly knowing or being ignorant. But what exactly differentiates cognizing from knowing? Chomsky insists that:

I don't think that 'cognize' is very far from 'know' where the latter term is moderately clear, but this seems to me a relatively minor issue, similar to the question whether the terms 'force' and 'mass' in physics depart from their conventional sense (as they obviously do).[50]

But physicists have the decency to give very precise definitions of the terms 'force' and 'mass', and their divergence from the non-technical use of these words is by no means a relatively minor, but an absolutely crucial (if perspicuous) issue. The use of 'cognize' (or 'tacitly know') is only 'explained' to the extent that it is said to be just like 'know', except that one who only cognizes cannot tell one what he cognizes, cannot display the object of his cognizing, does not recognize what he cognizes when told, never (apparently) forgets what he cognizes (but never remembers it either), has never learnt it and could not teach it, and so on. In short,

---

[50] Chomsky, *Rules and Representations*, p. 70.

cognizing is just like knowing, except that it is totally different in all respects. This is a travesty of the term 'know', of the introduction of technical terms in science, and of respectable reasoning.

If there is any point in using language at all it is that a word is taken to stand for a particular fact or idea and not for other facts or ideas. I might claim to be able to fly ... Lo, I say, I am flying. But you are not propelling yourself about while suspended in the air, someone may point out. Ah no, I reply, that is no longer considered the proper concern of people who can fly. In fact, it is frowned upon. Nowadays, a flyer never leaves the ground and wouldn't know how. I see, says my baffled interlocutor, so when you say you can *fly* you are using the word in a purely private sense. I see I have made myself clear, I say. Then, says this chap in some relief, you cannot actually *fly* after all? On the contrary, I say, I have just told you I can.[51]

This redefinition of the word 'fly' is no more intelligible than Chomsky's explanation of 'cognize'. Until we are told what it is to cognize but not know something, until we are given criteria for saying of someone that he cognizes something, and until it is explained to us how one can 'utilize' what one cognizes (but does not know) in understanding and speaking a language, we need pay no more attention to claims about cognizing theories of meaning or grammars than to the anatomy of borogoves.

6   Understanding new sentences

It has seemed to many theorists that the most powerful argument in favour of representing 'the workings of language' in the form of a calculus is precisely that it apparently *can* explain how it is possible for us to understand sentences we have never heard before. This 'creative' capacity of human beings is commonly thought to be at the root of much that is essentially and uniquely characteristic of our species. Does not the *explanatory power* of the very idea of a systematic theory of meaning of the kind in question justify it in the face of any criticism, including the arguments thus far rehearsed? Chomsky evidently believed that repudiation of his theories would require one to embrace behaviourism. One might doubt whether Chomsky's ghostly machine in the mind is the only alternative to Skinner's clockwork. But even if one did reject this crude dichotomy, one might think that any theory, or at least the *programme* for such a theory, which held out the hope of explaining our ability to

[51] T. Stoppard, *Travesties* (Faber, London, 1975), pp. 38f.

understand new sentences, was to be preferred to any account which left so fundamental a feature of human nature shrouded in mystery. Accordingly one will be prone to view objections as provisional difficulties, the cost of desirable, bold hypothesizing, to be paid for later when the theory is further developed. This response is quite mistaken. There is, we suggest, no mystery here, *a fortiori* no need for theories to render something comprehensible. Rather, 'we interpret the enigma created by our mis-understanding as the enigma of an incomprehensible process'.[52] What is needed is more careful scrutiny of the *concept of understanding* (not theories about phenomena or processes which, we think, *must* occur since otherwise we would not be able to understand). Then the question 'How is it possible to understand new sentences?' will lose its aura, and its muddled presuppositions will be brought to light.

What is the apparent problem? Let us rehearse it yet again, in the favoured manner. We are, as language learners, exposed to a limited range of sentences. Somehow, on the basis of this exposure, we acquire the ability to understand infinitely many sentences. We can, in this way, do things we have never learnt, employ sentences we have never heard before and respond coherently to novel sentences. As Chomsky remarks, 'It is immediately obvious that the data available to the child is quite limited – the number of seconds in his lifetime is trivially small as compared with the range of sentences that he can immediately understand . . .'[53] The infinite range of our understanding must be explained. The only way to do so appears to be by reference to a theoretical grammar ('a function in intension') or theory of meaning for a language which is 'tacitly known' or 'cognized' by a speaker. This knowledge or cognition can explain the processes involved in understanding.

Before jumping to the customary conclusion, we should re-examine the seemingly profound question 'How is it possible for us to understand new sentences?'. It is by no means perspicuous. Is it a philosophical question? With its Kantian echo it seems to be one. Or is it an empirical one, to be answered by linguists, who themselves insist that they are empirical scientists? Does it differ from the question 'How do we understand new sentences?', and does that question make sense? We shall examine three central issues: (1) the concept of understanding; (2) the kind of possibility

in question; and (3) the relevance of the novelty of the object of understanding.

The question 'How is it possible to understand new sentences?' *appears*
to be akin to any question that asks for the methods for the performance of
an act or activity. It looks like the perfectly clear question 'How is it
possible to start a motor car without an ignition key?'. It is clear that
theorists of language typically conceive of it thus. Hence they answer it on
the pattern of answers to questions of how one *does* something. In
particular, they explain that understanding is possible in virtue of tacit
knowledge of a grammatical theory or theory of meaning. For, as we have
seen, it is held that 'a process of derivation of some kind is involved in the
understanding of a sentence'.[54] The speaker's understanding of a sentence
is held to involve an instantaneous determination of its generation by the
rules of the theory ('an adult can instantaneously determine whether (and
if so, how) a particular item is generated by this mechanism').[55] Or, if
understanding a sentence is conceived not as an act or activity but as a
state, then the question about its possibility is conceived as a question
about the mental *processes* or activities that bring about this state: 'What a
speaker does when he understands or produces an utterance must include
at least the implicit analysing of its syntactic structure . . . [and the
assigning of] interpretations to sentences on the basis of his knowledge of
the meanings of their parts.'[56]

But understanding is neither an experience one undergoes nor an act one
performs, although there are commonly many experiences which accompany understanding an utterance. No inner act or activity is either necessary or sufficient for understanding, for performance of any such mental
acts or activities is compatible with gross misunderstanding or failure of
understanding. Indeed, we would not deny a person's understanding a
given utterance, where this is manifest in his behaviour and speech, on the
grounds of the absence of some correlative mental act, activity, or process.
A fortiori unconscious inner processes, even if there were any evidence for
such implicit analysings, derivings or assignings, neither constitute nor are
either necessary or sufficient for understanding.

Not only is understanding not an act, activity, or process one engages in,
and of which one might ask 'How does one do it?', it is not a state of mind
brought about by an antecedent act, activity or process of the mind. The

[54] M. A. E. Dummett, 'What is a Theory of Meaning?', in *Mind and Language*, ed.
S. Guttenplan (Clarendon Press, Oxford, 1975), p. 112.
[55] N. Chomsky, 'Review of Skinner's *Verbal Behaviour*', *Language*, 35 (1959), pp. 57f.
[56] Fodor and Katz, 'What's wrong with the Philosophy of Language?', p. 282.

reason for this is *not* that mental acts or activities are *never* engaged in prior to, and as a route to understanding something (as in recapitulating the steps in a proof in the endeavour to understand a theorem), it is rather that understanding is not a state of mind at all.[57] There is no such thing as being in *a state of understanding* a sentence, an utterance or a language. One may understand something *from* a certain time (the time at which one learnt it or read it with understanding) *for* a certain time (as long as one passes 'tests' of understanding, i.e. satisfies criteria of understanding). But though I may have understood, been able to speak, French from the age of fourteen to my mid-thirties (by which time it had become so rusty as to be useless), it would be absurd to say that I understood it *continuously* for twenty years, and no less absurd to say that I understood it intermittently. Understanding is subject to degrees in many cases, since I may understand a lecture, an hypothesis, a statement, more or less well, but not more or less *intensely*. If my concentration is interrupted I may not understand what I am concentrating on, but given that I understand it, my understanding cannot be interrupted. When I fall asleep my excitement at having understood a difficult problem abates, but my understanding does not cease. One may indeed suddenly cease to understand a problem, and one may equally suddenly regain one's understanding of it (the solution may have a *Gestalt*-like quality). But this is *not* like the abating of a pain under the impact of an analgesic, and its subsequent resumption when the drug wears off. Rather is it like suddenly forgetting and subsequently recollecting. I may indeed forget what something (e.g. a statement of a theorem) means, and then I no longer understand it. But forgetting something previously understood is not a fall from a state of intellectual grace. (Yet note that although I may have understood what someone said when he said it, it would be wrong to say that when, half an hour later, I have forgotten what he said, I no longer understand what he said.)[58]

This negative analysis is by no means fruitless. By reference to it the intellectual landscape may take on new aspects. Note, for example, the striking fact that theorists who present a generative account of understanding sentences typically focus upon understanding sentences uttered by someone else. This tendency is not accidental. For understanding what one hears or reads lends itself to the favoured picture of understanding as an act, activity, or process, or as a state produced by such antecedent acts,

---

[57] For a brief characterization of states, see above, p. 279f.
[58] For a more detailed account of understanding, see G. P. Baker and P. M. S. Hacker, *Wittgenstein: Understanding and Meaning*, (Blackwell, Oxford, 1980), pp. 595ff.

activities, or processes. One hears a sequence of noises, it seems, and recognizes them as words whose meanings one knows. 'As quick as a flash' one derives the meaning of the sentence from the known meanings of the words and their mode of combination by using the principles of the tacitly known grammar or theory of meaning of the language. Then, having carried out this instantaneous calculation, further aided perhaps by a theory of force or principles of pragmatics, one understands what one heard. Just how misguided this picture is becomes evident if, bearing in mind that understanding is not an act, activity or state, we view the matter from the perspective of a normal speaker who understands the sentences he himself utters and knows what he is saying by using them. The hearer understands a sentence, the theorist is inclined to say, when he has heard it and carried out the appropriate derivation. But when does a speaker understand a sentence he utters, according to this account? *Before* he utters it? But how is it possible for him to understand what he says before he says it? Indeed, what *is* there to understand before the sentence is spoken? Is it that he speaks it to himself quickly before he speaks it aloud? But that idea merely generates an infinite regress, for the question of when he understands the sentence he silently says to himself now arises. If only *after* he says it to himself, does he then say it to himself without under-standing it, as it were, to see what sense it will make? This is absurd. But if *before* he says it to himself, then how is *that* possible? Antecedent silent soliloquy is an empty move. Does it then follow that a speaker does *not* understand what he says aloud until after he has said it, that he must wait to hear what he says before he can know what he means? This too is absurd. Here the favoured *picture* of understanding clashes violently with its application. Of course a speaker typically understands what he says. But his understanding is not something that occurs before, simultaneously with, or after his utterance, any more than being able to play chess occurs before or after moving a chess-piece in a game.

Understanding is *akin* to an ability,[59] rather than to a state, act, or activity. It is an aspect of our concept of understanding that a person who understands an utterance *can* typically do certain things, e.g. explain what it means, respond to it appropriately, paraphrase it. His understanding manifests itself in the *exercises* of such abilities. And it is the overt exercises of these abilities that constitute the grounds upon which we legitimately ascribe understanding to him. Such behavioural manifestations constitute

---

[59] Although it would be misleading to say that it *is* an ability, cf. Baker and Hacker, *Wittgenstein: Understanding and Meaning*, pp. 617ff.

the *criteria* justifying the ascription of understanding to a person. They do not entail understanding, since a criterion may obtain, yet be defeated in the circumstances. Yet the behavioural manifestations of understanding are not inductive evidence of understanding either, since that would suppose that we had a concept of understanding enabling us to identify cases of understanding independently of behaviour, which we could then inductively correlate with the behaviour.[60]

Understanding is *not* identical with the behaviour manifesting it, nor is it an inner state or process from which that behaviour flows. Its kinship with an ability is here evident. The power or ability of a car to go at 70 m.p.h. is not identical with its going at 70 m.p.h., but nor is it an inner state or activity of the car. An ability is no more identical with what might be called[61] its *vehicle* or the *structure of its vehicle* than it is with its manifestations or exercise. One cannot find the car's horsepower under its bonnet, or a person's understanding in his brain.

Consequently, the question of how it is possible for a person to understand new sentences boils down to the question of how it is possible for a person to be able to do those things which manifest understanding, namely react to, use and explain the meanings of new sentences. This question is still far from clear, but it is clear that it cannot be correctly understood as a question about the means or methods of performance of a special mental act or activity, viz. understanding. Of an ability one cannot ask 'How does one *do* it?'. *A fortiori* it makes no sense to ask how it is possible to do it. There are no methods of understanding, any more than there are methods, ways or means of being able to do something. There are methods of learning how to do something, ways of bringing it about that someone is able to do something or other, i.e. methods for the acquisition of an ability, but no methods of 'doing' the ability.

Since abilities are not 'done', and since understanding a sentence or utterance bears a conceptual kinship to an ability, it is not surprising that the question 'How is it possible to understand a new sentence?' should occasion a sense of mystery. For interpreted in one way, it gravitates towards categorial confusion. One does not understand a sentence any *how*.[62] Of course, there are circumstances in which the question 'How can

---

[60] Bear in mind that the first-person utterance 'I understand' is not typically a judgment resting on evidence nor is it an identification of a mental act, activity or state.

[61] Cf. A. J. P. Kenny, *Will, Freedom and Power* (Blackwell, Oxford, 1975), p. 10.

[62] Although there is, of course, a perfectly straightforward use for 'How do you understand this sentence?', namely 'How do you take it, what do you understand by it?'

you understand?' is in order. If a speech is given amidst hubbub, one might ask someone how he can understand what is being said in the uproar. The answer might be that he lipreads; but lipreading is not a method of understanding the meanings of sentences but one way (like hearing) of discerning what a speaker is saying. The question here concerns circumstantial possibility, namely given that most people cannot understand utterances in such a noise (since they cannot hear the words spoken), how it is that this person is not prevented by these circumstances from understanding, how is it that he can tell us what is said, explain it, paraphrase it, etc. This kind of question is not at issue in the case of a speaker's understanding sentences or utterances in his native tongue in optimal circumstances. A different kind of case arises when someone is seen to exercise a complex ability which has not apparently been learnt and yet is obviously not innate. Thus a hearer might explain that he can understand a lecture in Spanish, even though he has never learnt Spanish, because he knows Italian and Portuguese, and can guess most of what is being said on that basis. This explains the possession of an unlearnt ability as a consequence of possession of other learnt abilities (as one might explain one's ability to play squash (after a fashion) by reference to one's having already mastered tennis and badminton). But neither learning Italian and Portuguese nor knowing Italian and Portuguese are means or methods of understanding a Spanish lecture, even though this person's understanding it can be explained by reference to his mastery of Italian and Portuguese. Again, this kind of question is not at issue when one asks how it is possible for one to understand sentences of one's mother tongue.

Given that understanding is akin to an ability, the question as to its possibility seems to amount to the question of how it is possible for a person to do those things that are manifestations of understanding. How should this be interpreted? We can rule out any question of methods of doing those things (how to shut the door in compliance with an order to shut it). Is it then a question about empirical causes and psychological or neurological underpinnings of our linguistic ability? We can construe it in various ways. It may be taken as a question about the structure of the *vehicle* of our linguistic ability; or about the mode of acquisition of the ability; or about the prerequisites for the possession of the ability.

Explanations of powers and abilities are characteristically given, in the advanced sciences, by specification of the physical structure of the bearer of the ability (e.g. the magnetic attraction of a magnet or corrosive power of an acid are explained by reference to, although not reduced to, molecular structures). If one wishes to speak of the vehicle of an ability, one might be inclined, with some qualification and risk of confusion,[63] to claim that the vehicle of a person's understanding is his brain. Neurophysiology may, one day, give a description of the neural structure of the cerebral cortex which will contribute to our understanding of the physiological foundations of our linguistic and cognitive skills. Of such possible explanations three points should be noted. First, such explanations are empirical and contingent. They will, therefore, not reveal any *internal relations* between understanding and language which it is the business of philosophy to investigate. Nor will they reveal any structural properties of languages which it is the business of grammarians to study. Secondly, there is no *a priori* guarantee that significant or extensive explanations will be forthcoming. There may simply not be any sharp and determinate correlations between cerebral organization and the highly diffuse and complex abilities and dispositions and their indefinite and multiple forms of exercise which manifest understanding sentences and utterances. Thirdly, such an explanation would not be normative, i.e. it would not display linguistic behaviour as a case of rule-guided conduct. One could not see from the cerebral structure that is (according to the supposed theory) essential for linguistic mastery in all its diversity which rules are being followed, or discern what counts as correct compliance with them. Normative phenomena are public and social, not private and neural.

If the question of how it is possible to understand new sentences is concerned with cognitive prerequisites of understanding, we might construe it as a psychological question. For it might be a question about the mode of acquisition of linguistic skills, or some facet of mastery of a language. To that extent it would aim to elicit the psychological or pedagogical prerequisites for their possession. Taken thus the question is far too crude for any answer. Duly refined, and broken down into numerous manageable questions, it would perhaps be interesting and fruitful. But be that as it may, it is a matter for empirical investigations in experimental psychology. These issues, however, are wholly undeveloped and bedevilled by misguided theories concocted by linguists and philosophers which stand between the psychologist (learning theorist) and careful observation of the phenomena. The question so construed is also philosophically irrelevant.

Finally, we may take the question analytically. For it can be construed as a question about what a person must know in order to understand new sentences. The general form of the answer to *this* is neither mysterious nor

---

[63] It is unclear, for example, why the person himself is not the vehicle of his understanding.

startling: one must know whatever is requisite to satisfy the criteria for understanding new sentences, i.e. know whatever is necessary for the performance of those acts or for those reactions and responses the ability to perform which is constitutive of understanding. For how else can it be shown that one *must* know something in order to understand a given new sentence? One can only show this by demonstrating that the manifestation of understanding is internally related to possession of such knowledge. Hence, altogether unsurprisingly, one normally has to know what the constituent words of the given sentence mean, since in explaining what the sentence means one typically also explains what its constituents mean in that context. But, equally unsurprisingly, one does not have to know any depth-grammar or 'logical form', since manifestation of understanding of a new sentence is wholly independent of manifestation of knowledge of theoretical linguistics or philosophy of language.

Three things now become evident. First, the novelty of the sentences one understands is a red herring. It seemed relevant insofar as it was an objection to crude behaviourist theories of understanding that they could not make sense of the fact that we can understand new sentences. But stimulus–response theories cannot 'explain' understanding previously heard sentences any better. The novelty of a sentence is immaterial. For the grounds for attributing to a person an understanding of some sentence are not different when it is a new sentence from what they are when it is familiar. Indeed, we commonly do not know, when we judge that someone understands it, whether it is novel or familiar to him.

Secondly, the question of the *number* of sentences we can understand is profoundly misleading. Contrasting the 'trivially small' number of seconds of the child's life with the vast number of sentences he can understand encourages confusion. How very clever of the child to learn so much in so little time! We think that in some sense the child 'already' understands an infinity of sentences now, even though he has only heard a very small range of sentences.[64] If he *can* understand, we are inclined to argue, then in some sense he *does* understand already. But if he already understands, we confusedly think, then the infinity of sentences must be, as it were, stored up in the child's mind, if not in the form of encoded sentences, then in the form of a grammar, a lexicon, and a decoding device. These myths stem from treating the illegitimate question 'How many sentences can the child understand?' as if it were parallel to 'How many

---

[64] As Zeno might have thought that the toddler has traversed an infinite space, on the ground that his few steps contain an infinity of spaces!

sentences has the child uttered?'.[65] But it is not. Understanding shares the open-endedness characteristic of abilities. It is of the nature of many abilities that in acquiring them one becomes able to do many things not hitherto done. Many human skills are plastic. Learning to draw or to paint, to throw pots on a wheel, to act or mime, and so on, all involve an open-endedness which is misrepresented if it is held to be especially mysterious or baffling. It would be absurd to be amazed at the vast number of possible pictures the artist can paint, the huge number of possible pots the potter can throw, the endless number of potential roles the actor can act. For not only is the plasticity of the skill *not* mysterious, the idea of counting the number of possible pictures that one could paint, and comparing it with the 'trivially small' number of seconds of one's life is silly. What would really be mysterious is a person's only being able to understand (and speak with understanding) 7,568 sentences, *and not a single one more*. That would be baffling!

Thirdly, there is no unique thing that a person must know in order to satisfy the criteria for understanding some arbitrary sentence. He must, indeed, use it correctly, react to it appropriately and explain it cogently. If he does these, then other things being equal, we attribute understanding to him. But there is no general mechanism for 'derivation' of the meaning of the sentence from its constituents which is pertinent to the criteria of understanding. There is not, in general, a privileged form of explanation of what a sentence means which requires the use of any *special* knowledge in order that a person should justifiably be said to understand a sentence. In particular, knowledge of a theory of meaning for a language or of a transformational-generative grammar does not have to be displayed in explaining what a sentence means in order to satisfy criteria of understanding. And conversely, Chomsky's knowledge of his grammar and his use of it in explaining a line in Shakespeare, say, is perfectly compatible with his grossly misunderstanding this line.

Our ability to understand sentences is not an ability to make lightning-quick calculations in which we derive the meaning of a sentence from the meanings of its constituents and their mode of combination. We typically grasp or 'take in' the meaning of a sentence or utterance as a whole, and not by means of any computational techniques. It is quite false to suggest that we hear nothing but noises or read nothing but marks on paper, which

---

[65] Cf. *Wittgenstein*'s *Lecturers on the Foundations of Mathematics, Cambridge, 1939*, ed. Cora Diamond (Harvester Press, Sussex, 1976), pp. 31ff., for a parallel discussion of the question of how many numerals one has learnt to write down.

dead signs we have to recognize and process, endowing them with an appropriate meaning, and then computing the meaning of the whole from the meanings of the parts. This is of a piece with the suggestion that what we see are just colours and shapes (not chairs and tables, trees and buildings) which we then have to process and 'interpret' to yield our 'picture' of the objective world. This ancient myth of the 'given' and of what the mind, contributing structure from its own resources, makes of it is not rendered respectable by being dressed up in late twentieth century garb. It makes sense to ask me how I know that when you said 'Give me a drink' you wanted a gin and tonic, but not to ask how I knew that you wanted a drink. This is parallel to the fact that it makes sense to ask how I know that a seventeenth century Dutch still-life of flowers in a vase represents the fleetingness and vanity of life, but not to ask how I know that it is a still-life of flowers in a vase.[66]

In this respect understanding sentences is not unlike understanding genre paintings. Indeed, a language theorist may be equally impressed by our ability to understand an 'infinite' number of paintings (putting historical paintings aside). He may even insist that the possibility of this understanding must be explained in generative terms. The analogy is perhaps worth pursuing, for it may help relieve the manifold pressures that push one into embracing complex grammatical theories or philosophical theories of meaning as essential underpinnings for an explanation of understanding. In the case of sentence and painting alike the whole is not the mere sum of its parts, but of its parts and their mode of combination. Similarly, in both cases the meaning of a part depends on its juxtaposition with other parts, and with features of the whole which are neither parts nor relationships of parts (e.g. chiaroscuro). In both cases there are rules of representation which are presupposed, and also more complex theories of representation which may be known (e.g. rules of fixed point perspective) but which need not be known for the understanding of the painting. Strikingly, in both cases the identification of the unit of significance in the whole is problematic. For although one may say that the painting is composed of parts, it is impossible to say, in advance of specific purposes, what is to count as a part – a line, a patch of colour, a shape, a determinate representation (and each of these is in turn problematic). In the case of

---

[66] Of course, in both cases a psychologist may investigate what aural or visual elements are indispensable 'cues', in the sense that if they are removed or interrupted in some way, I will not be able to say what the painting is of, or what the utterance meant. It does not, however, follow that such 'cues' are my *grounds* for 'recognition'. There is here typically no question of recognition, no inference, *a fortiori* no ground of judgment.

paintings, as with language, the conventions of representation must be learnt. The most important analogy lies at the level of understanding. We take in a painting *as a whole*. We do not understand it as, e.g., a painting of a mountain landscape in a rainstorm with cattle drinking at a brook, by calculating or constructing this correct 'interpretation' from our grasp of (the meaning of) the parts and their mode of combination. Of course, we can anatomize the painting, identify the cattle, brook, falling rain, etc., even identify the various brush strokes and impasto that create the image of a lowing cow. But it does not follow that our understanding of the whole rests on, has as its *grounds* the antecedent anatomization of the picture and the derivation of the meaning of the whole from the meanings of its parts. Nor, indeed, does it mean that we can anatomize a painting into elementary constituents identifiable as such-and-such representations independently of the picture as a whole. There is no specially problematic question or deep mystery about our capacity to recognize a painting of something that we have never seen (e.g. a knight killing a dragon) as opposed to a painting of something familiar (e.g. a vase of flowers). In neither case do we need to know any complex *theory* of pictorial representation. (Of course, there is ample room for psychological and physiological investigation into perception and recognition.)

There is no deep question of how it is possible for us to understand sentences we have never heard before, only deep confusions about the concept of understanding, which we then mistake for mysteries about the phenomena of understanding. Consequently, the alleged capacity to answer this question is no vindication of the idea of a theory of meaning for a language, or of a theory of grammar tacitly known by every speaker. The seeds sown by the *Tractatus* and Frege have indeed germinated. The plants that have grown from them infest the intellectual landscape. But despite their size, they are barren.

7   Residual business: the minimalist enterprise

We turn finally to the minimalist enterprise pursued by some philosophers. They construct 'theories of meaning for a natural language', but hasten to add that these theories are not, or not directly, of any psychological moment. They do not explain (although they might be invoked in explaining) how language is learnt or how linguistic skills evolve. Their analytic role has been variously characterized. On one view a theory of meaning is a conceptual clarification of what a language is. This being achieved, the results can be handed over to a psychologist who can investigate, if he wishes, the 'mechanisms' whereby 'linguistic input is processed' to yield understanding.[67] According to a different conception,[68] a theory of meaning specifies an array of axioms and theorems together with principles such that, *if* someone knew them, he *would* be able to speak the language. This is alleged to provide a clarification of 'what is involved' in speaking and understanding a language, even though it is not contended that actual speakers really know any such theory.[69] A third variation on this apparently modest theme is the suggestion that a theory of meaning is 'a theoretical representation of a practical ability'. It represents or characterizes, in a *systematic* manner, what it is that a person who has mastered a language, acquired the practical ability of which understanding a language consists, can do.

If our criticisms of the very project of constructing a theory of meaning are correct, if the necessary distinction between sense and force is incoherent, if the various ideas of the truth-conditions of a sentence are all muddled, if the representation of a language as a calculus of meaning-rules is a misrepresentation, then this way of explaining what the mastery of a language consists in is foreclosed. We shall, however, suspend our disbelief and examine the feasibility of one of these projects afresh.

We shall not dwell on the first proposal. It is no less absurd to suppose that an elaborate axiomatized theory provides a conceptual clarification of what a language is than to maintain that the logical calculus of *Principia Mathematica* first revealed to us the true meanings of our familiar number-words. Even if the theorist *could* deliver a complete T-theory for English, that would not show that English is a calculus of T-sentences, any more than a Mercator projection shows that the Earth is flat. Proficient speakers of English use names of languages such as 'English', 'French', 'Chinese' perfectly correctly, but they do not mean, by these names, to signify axiomatized theories (still awaiting construction!) for the derivation of sentence-meanings from a set of axioms (or specifications of word-

---

[67] This in effect hands the philosopher's dirty linen over to the cognitive psychologist. When the latter engages in pseudo-science of the kind previously discussed, and is criticized for so doing, the theorist of meaning will typically turn, with deceptively innocent tones, and insist that the psychologist is an empirical scientist whose theory-building endeavours lie beyond the purview of conceptual analysis and criticism.

[68] D. Davidson, 'Reply to Foster', in *Truth and Meaning,* ed. G. Evans and J. McDowell, (Clarendon Press, Oxford, 1976), pp. 33f.

[69] Cf. M. A. E. Dummett, 'Objections to Chomsky', *London Review of Books,* 1–14 October, 1981.

meanings). Rather, we use 'a language' to designate a complex normative practice governed by motleys of rules familiar to and acknowledged by competent speakers. There is, of course, more to be said about this first proposal. This will be done when the third variant is subjected to critical scrutiny.

We shall pass over the second suggestion almost equally quickly. It is typically propounded as an empirical thesis about languages. Thus construed, it is objectionable. In the first place, knowing the axioms and being able to derive the theorems of a theory of meaning for a natural language would not, in any sense, qualify one as a speaker, any more than knowing the rules of cricket would render one a qualified batsman or bowler. Mastery of a language is a skill, and it is not a skill which manifests itself in performing derivations of T-sentences. Mere knowledge of such a theory would leave one, in Harris's phrase, a communicational cripple (and this would *not* be because one had mastered the semantics of a language, but was shaky on the pragmatics). On the contrary, if we were concerned to clarify what is 'involved' in speaking English, we might more plausibly mention dictionaries and school grammars. After all, it is by using these that foreigners come to be able to speak English. If it is claimed that this enabling 'knowledge' is insufficiently systematic, inasmuch as it does not display the derivability of sentence-meanings from axioms and formation-rules, the reply is surely that the knowledge that suffices for speaking English does not have to incorporate anything 'systematic' in *this* sense as a necessary component. In order to know what utterances mean, one does not have to know how to derive their meanings from anything at all. The requirement that the knowledge which would suffice to enable its possessor to speak a language take the form of a systematic calculus stems from the fallacy that only thus can one 'explain' the possibility of the 'infinity' of sentences of a language. Finally, it is altogether opaque why specification of a body of knowledge *allegedly* sufficient to enable one to speak a language (though evidently not necessary, since it is not contended that anyone does know the theory) should be held to provide an illuminating account of 'what is involved' in understanding a language.

The thesis can, however, be taken not as an empirical claim, but as an analysis of the concept of understanding a language. If understanding a language is conceived as being able to assign to any arbitrary sentence of the language its truth-conditions, and if a theory of meaning is an axiomatic theory which assigns to every well-formed sentence its truth-conditions, then trivially knowledge of the theory of meaning suffices for understanding the language. On this construal, the second suggestion collapses into the third. It must, however, be stressed that the theory cannot both be an *empirical* claim as to what knowledge suffices for understanding a given language and *also* an *a priori* claim about what understanding a language consists in.

We shall focus on the third view, namely that a theory of meaning for a natural language is a 'theoretical representation of a practical ability'. According to this conception a theory of meaning 'present[s] an analysis of the complex skill which constitutes mastery of a language ... what it is that someone who possesses that mastery is able to do'.[70] It is argued that understanding is a 'practical ability' and that abilities are characterized by specification of what it is that they are abilities to do. It is, of course, recognized that among the things a speaker of a language can do is to perform a myriad of speech-acts. These are given a 'theoretical representation' by means of the theory of force. '[A]gainst such a background ... it makes sense to say that to know the meaning of a sentence is to know the condition for its truth'.[71] Waiving objections to the intelligibility of such a theory of force, we focus here on whether understanding a language is a 'practical ability' intelligibly 'represented' by means of a theory of meaning, in particular whether this ability is correctly characterized in terms of an axiomatic theory for derivation of truth-conditions of sentences from stipulated axioms.

The philosopher's primary move is to contend that to understand a sentence is to assign (or to be able to assign (?)) to the sentence a set of truth-conditions. But there is no such thing as understanding a single sentence of a language and no other (although one might know the meaning of a single Chinese sentence). To understand a sentence is to understand a language. A language is, it is held, an infinite set of sentences. Understanding a language is a remarkable capacity precisely *because* it involves the ability to comprehend an infinity of sentences. But now, it is argued, we cannot characterize the mastery of a (given) language by a complete enumeration correlating each of its 'infinity' of sentences with its truth-conditions, even though so pairing sentences with truth-conditions

---

[70] Dummett, 'What is a Theory of Meaning? (II)', p. 70; as noted above (p. 325) Dummett's account is marred by constant intrusion of remarks about implicit knowledge, implicit derivations of theorems from axioms, coupled with insistence that the account involves no psychological hypotheses, even though this knowledge is said to *issue* in a general ability to speak (Ibid., p. 71), that implicit grasp of general principles *issues* in recognitional capacities to determine syntactic well-formedness, that the speaker *derives* the meanings of sentences from implicit knowledge of axioms. We shall disregard this muddle.

[71] Ibid., p. 73.

would be, *sub specie aeternitatis*, a correct characterization of what understanding this language is. Rather, as mere finite mortals, we must formulate general laws from which, for an arbitrary well-formed sentence, we can systematically calculate its truth-conditions. Mastery of a language will be characterized correctly as an ability to derive the logical consequences of such laws, viz. the meanings of sentences of the language. Or, on the assumption that derivations take care of themselves, it will be characterized as 'knowledge' of these general laws, or of the 'function in intension' which generates an infinite set of correlations of sentences with their truth-conditions.

Knowing a language (mastery of a language) is identified not merely with knowledge of the axioms of an axiomatized theory, but rather with this together with knowledge of general rules capable of iterated application. Assigning truth-conditions to an arbitrary sentence is thought to parallel stating the answer to an arbitrary multiplication problem. In the latter case, a recursion formula such as $(a + 1) \times b = a \times b + b$, together with the axiom $0 \times 1 = 0$, determines what integer is paired with any pair of integers as their product. Hence mastery of multiplication is identified with knowledge of this recursion formula (and the axiom). Similarly, knowledge of a language is conceived as knowledge of axioms and recursion formulae which correlate every well-formed sentence with its truth-conditions. Accordingly, a theory of meaning for a language will provide a theoretical representation of a practical ability (a characterization of what understanding a language consists in), just as recursion formulae in arithmetic constitute a theoretical representation of a practical ability (knowing arithmetic).

The number of prestidigitations in this brief account is very great. To see how the conjuring trick is effected, we shall have to examine it closely, as it were in slow motion. Prior to detailed scrutiny, however, two crucial points about its general contours must be stressed.

First, this reasoning provides no support whatever for a generative theory of understanding or a compositional theory of meaning. Rather, it *presupposes* some such theory. Unless the meaning of an arbitrary sentence could in principle be calculated systematically from its constituents and its structure, there would be no such thing as a recursive specification of the truth-conditions of the infinity of sentences in a language, and hence the analogy between understanding a language and the ability to multiply would collapse at a vital point. Without some independent argument, we have no assurance that it is even intelligible to speak of such a theoretical representation of the ability to speak English,

French or Chinese. The minimalist enterprise rests on a determination to cast natural languages into the forms of formal calculi, and hence it makes sense only if languages satisfy this Procrustean demand. But, as we have shown by a plethora of arguments, they do not.

Secondly, although *knowledge* of axioms and recursion formulae is invoked in explaining the notion of a theoretical representation of a practical ability, it plays no essential role in the reasoning. This is important. It justifies the claim that this characterization of understanding a language is rightly classified as a minimalist account. This theoretical knowledge plays no part in any explanation of *how* somebody under-stands a sentence (the subject-matter of the full-blown explanatory enter-prise) but rather concerns only the circumscription of what he understands and a clarification of what his understanding a language 'consists in'. Furthermore, the subsidiary role of knowledge circumvents a problem. It seems that characterizing an ability in terms of knowledge of theoretical principles is altogether different from characterizing it in terms of specify-ing what constitutes its exercise (i.e. what it is an ability to do). But this issue can be by-passed if the exercises of the ability can be characterized directly in terms of the principles themselves. This is held to be the case with the recursion formula for multiplication, and by analogy, with the principles of a theory of meaning. The formula itself is alleged to generate the correct answer to every possible multiplication problem. But it is the giving of *these answers* which constitutes the totality of the *exercises of the ability* to multiply. Hence the recursion formula itself seemingly circum-scribes precisely and fully what somebody who has mastered multiplica-tion can *do*, and it does so independently of any characterization of this ability in terms of theoretical knowledge (even if, under certain idealizing suppositions, that might also be illuminating). The pairing of each sentence of a language with its truth-conditions is supposed to flow from a theory of meaning in the same direct way, making no essential detour via the concept of theoretical knowledge. And it is *these pairings* which are alleged to be the essential components in an analysis of the totality of the *exercises of the ability* to speak a language. 'Tacit knowledge', in this context, is considered to be a picturesque wrapping for such a theory of meaning. What a person who can multiply can do is just *whatever* some-body who knew the recursion formula would do (assuming that he always applied it correctly and drew out its consequences, however remote). *Pari passu*, what a person who has mastered English can do is whatever the Ideal Speaker-Hearer who knew the entire theory of meaning for English would do.

The strategy of the minimalist enterprise is clear enough. But it is unclear whether the reasoning is sound at the tactical level, and hence too whether anything intelligible is achieved. Doubts turn on three issues: the opacity of the notion of '*characterizing* an ability', the interpretation of the phrase '*a full* characterization of a practical ability', and the appropriateness of the analogy between the ability to speak a language and the ability to multiply integers. We shall examine each of these matters in turn.

The minimalist enterprise starts from the insight that it is integral to the concept of any particular ability that it be possible to explain what counts as the manifestations of this ability. If a human agent is ascribed the ability to ride a bicycle, draw caricatures, purchase a loaf of bread, or speak English, then it must be clear what acts of his are exercises of such an ability. This can always be done by exploiting the schema: if A has the ability to φ, then A's φing is an exercise of this ability. But, of course, in many cases more illuminating accounts can be given for particular purposes. We are often interested in inculcating abilities in pupils, and hence we look for ways to analyse 'complex' abilities such as playing tennis, or composing music into 'component' abilities which can be taught and practised in relative isolation from each other (e.g. playing forehands, playing backhands, volleying, serving, and scoring). There is, however, no warrant for maintaining that every human ability must admit of some such analysis into component abilities, and there is equally no presumption that any ability has a unique purpose-independent decomposition into other abilities. If either of these ideas is attached to the alleged conceptual requirement that it be possible to 'characterize' any ability in terms of what it is an ability to *do*, then this requirement is illegitimate (indeed, incoherent).

The minimalist might abjure this requirement but none the less claim that understanding a language can be decomposed into component abilities the major one of which is the ability to assign to each well-formed sentence its truth-conditions. This of course has not yet been accomplished; we see the 'analysis' through a glass but darkly, not face to face. The crucial question is not the grounds for this faith, but the intelligibility of what is taken on trust. As a putative analysis of a complex ability, this one makes sense only if 'assigning to a sentence its truth-conditions' is an understood expression designating a human act or activity. This is not so. The phrase is opaque, a bit of theoretical jargon standing in need of explanation. What counts as somebody's engaging in this act? Is it a private mental act known only through introspection? Or can one observe another's performing this act? And how could any act completed at a particular moment be coordinated with the manifestations of someone's understanding a sentence, since these may be spread out over an indefinitely long period? There is pressure here to treat assigning correct truth-conditions to sentences as itself an ability manifested in speaking fluently, but then 'assigning to each sentence its truth-conditions' no longer characterizes an ability in terms of actions which manifest this ability! The putative analysis of mastery of a language is confused and incomprehensible.

This negative verdict is reinforced by bringing to light muddles about the notion of *completeness* in characterizing practical abilities. It is obvious that an explanation of what it is to have a particular ability may be criticized because it implies an inadequate account of what constitutes the exercises of this ability. It would be a joke to say that the ability to cook well consists in the ability to make a soufflé, or that the ability to play the piano is the ability to play C-major arpeggios in contrary motion. Such clarifications of abilities are clearly incomplete. This is not because they fail to meet some absolute standard of completeness. Rather, it is because they adumbrate an analysis of a complex ability, but leave out important component abilities coordinate with the ones listed. If, e.g., in clarifying what is involved in being able to play the piano, one mentions the ability to play arpeggios, it would be misleading to omit mention of the abilities to play scales and trills since these are general abilities at the same level of specificity (unless the explanation were addressed to somebody who understood that the list of component abilities was open). Whether the characterization of an ability is complete or incomplete turns on whether it leaves out component abilities which *should* be listed, and this depends on the *purposes* for which it is offered. This distinction parallels the distinction between exact and inexact descriptions, for a description is properly called inexact only relative to the purposes which it is meant to serve.[72]

The concept of the completeness of the characterization of an ability is distorted by imagining that what pass for complete characterizations should be measured more rigorously against an absolute ideal of completeness. As if there might be at every level of specificity a listing of acts manifesting an ability which left out *no* act constituting an exercise of that ability. But this ideal is chimerical (like the parallel 'ideals' of a perfectly exact description and of an explanation of meaning assigning a completely determinate sense to a word). There is typically no such thing as specifying *everything* that a person can do who has a particular ability, and many

[72] Wittgenstein, *Philosophical Investigations*, § 88.

explanations of abilities by giving examples of component abilities (or examples of their exercises) are, and are treated as, correct and complete. One does explain what it is that persons who can cook can do without listing all the possible dishes which they can produce or all the possible activities (buttering cake tins, whipping egg-whites, etc.) which they can engage in. Moreover, if these were condemned as incomplete explanations, there would be no such thing as a complete explanation of the phrase 'able to cook' because there is no possibility of listing without omission every dish that might be cooked or every action performed in cooking. But if there is no such thing as a complete explanation, then there is also no such thing as an incomplete one. If the 'full characterization' of an ability demands an explanation complete by this bogus standard, then the very idea of giving full characterization of *most* practical abilities is ridiculous.

Mastery of a language, like many other human abilities, is both diffuse and open-ended. It is diffuse (or perhaps complex) in that no single act or activity constitutes the exercise of this ability as jumping eight metres constitutes the exercise of the ability to jump eight metres. Rather it has many facets or aspects. A competent speaker can do innumerable (but 'infinitely many'?) things: make statements and assertions, give descriptions or instructions, ask and answer questions, issue and obey orders, crack jokes and tell stories, wonder, beg, entreat, pray, and so on and so forth. It thus resembles the ability to play the piano. A competent pianist can play scales, trills, and arpeggios, sight-read, perform a crescendo or diminuendo, execute a phrase staccato or legato, etc. Moreover, mastery of a language (and each of its component abilities) is open-ended. There is no fixed list of compositions which a competent pianist can play (nor any closed totality of phrases) and no fixed list of tunes which a competent whistler can whistle. Similarly it would be absurd to attempt to exhaust by enumeration all of the jokes that a competent speaker could laugh at or tell, all of the instructions that he could issue, all of the questions that he could ask, etc., let alone all of the sentences that he could use or respond to. Does it follow that there must be, in the case of every open-ended ability, some formula which recursively characterizes its possible exercises?

To this it might be replied that the abilities to play the piano, to whistle or compose music differ from a linguistic ability precisely because music, unlike a language, is not (in general) representational. Understanding music, it might be argued, is, *pace* Wittgenstein, totally unlike understanding English: we may, for the sake of argument, grant the objection. Nevertheless, it achieves nothing. Let us take as our examples of parallel open-ended abilities such abilities the exercise of which *does* result in the production of objects that *are* representative, namely drawing, painting, sculpting and modelling, with the proviso that we restrict our attention to genre paintings, etc. and exclude historical representations. Let us correlate with these artistic abilities the complementary abilities to understand drawings, paintings, sculptures, models as being of whatever objects they represent. The 'possible drawings' which someone who is able to draw can draw do not form a finite surveyable set (or an infinite one). No more so do the 'possible drawings' which someone who can understand drawings can understand. Does it not follow that to characterize what it is that someone who can draw, or someone who can understand drawings, can do requires a recursive characterization of the generation of drawings in terms of their constituent (lines (?), shadings (?), etc.) or of their 'meanings' from the 'meanings' of their constituents?

Such open-ended abilities are readily characterized, if need be, by examples of their exercises and a similarity rider. Someone who can understand or recognize drawings or paintings can tell you what a Hobbema landscape represents, what a Van der Velde seascape is a painting of, what a Steinberg cartoon wittily portrays or what an Escher etching ambiguously and contradictorily represents, and so on. Such characterizations of the relevant abilities are not defective or inadequate. They do not leave us ignorant of what it is that painters, sculptors, musicians can do, nor of what it is that viewers and hearers who understand what they produce can understand.[73]

The open-endedness of the ability to understand a language is held to be captured in the claim that a language is an *infinite* totality of sentences. But this thesis is trebly misleading. First, the only clear model of a set with an infinite number of members is a set specified by citing a formula which recursively generates its members (e.g. the definition of the natural numbers as the set whose members are generated from the number 0 by iterations of the operation of adding one (the successor operation)). Hence, the *intelligibility* of treating mastery of English as represented by an *infinite* set of pairings of sentences with their truth-conditions *presupposes* that there is available a recursive mechanism for generating these pairings. But that begs the central question. The need for a theory of

---

[73] One should not, however, exaggerate. Understanding paintings or engravings, just like understanding sentences, is a matter of degree. One may understand that Dürer's 'Melancholia I' represents a winged figure deeply sunk in thought, surrounded by geometric and craft instruments and accompanied by a putto, without understanding the inconographical significance of the engraving. But equally one might understand Hamlet's 'Get thee to a nunnery' speech without grasping its cruel innuendo.

meaning turns out to be a product of a dubious description of what a language is. Secondly, the alleged 'infinity' of English blurs a crucial distinction. The argument for holding English to consist of infinitely many type-sentences is simply that, given any listing of well-formed meaningful sentences, we could always add one more which is not already on the list. But this does not establish that the meaningful sentences of English form a totality whose members can be correlated one-to-one with the natural numbers. That requires a *law* for generating an English sentence from each natural number and vice versa (parallel to the operation of multiplication by two which correlates the integers one-to-one with the even integers). In absence of such a law, the possibility of adding yet one more well-formed English sentence to *any* list of grammatical English sentences shows merely that there is no such thing as the totality (or number) of well-formed sentences of English (just as, though for different reasons, there is no totality of small integers or deeds that a person has performed in his lifetime). Thirdly, even if a mathematician and a linguist together produced a law which effectively correlated each natural number with a grammatical English sentence and vice versa, it would not follow that there is even a possibility of constructing a law which pairs each English sentence with its sense (truth-conditions). That presupposes that the distinction between sense and nonsense applies to each type-sentence independently of the circumstances in which it is uttered (cf. above, pp. 218–28). Once this error is rectified, the idea of characterizing understanding in terms of an infinite set of type-acts (of pairing sentences with their senses) becomes ludicrous; for then somebody might *ex hypothesi* manifest his understanding of a *nonsensical* utterance by making sense of it!

Hitherto we have concentrated on the motivation for the minimalist's making a comparison between mastery of language and knowing how to multiply. This rests on deep confusions. But so too does the analogy itself. It presupposes that a meaningful sentence of English resembles a multiplication problem. But where is the analogy? A sentence is not a problem calling for a solution. Of course, one can pose the problem of what a sentence means (how it is to be understood); *then* giving an explanation of what it means is an answer to this question as well as a criterion for understanding the sentence. Yet uttering a sentence is not to ask what it means, and understanding what is said is not typically manifested in explaining what has been said by another, but rather in responding appropriately to it, either in speech or in non-verbal behaviour. Only if a sentence is misconceived as *encoding* a message is there scope for construing understanding speech on the model of solving multiplication problems.

The other half of the analogy is equally strained. What is the counterpart of producing the correct answer to a multiplication sum? Presumably it must be 'assigning truth-conditions to a sentence'? But, as already noted, this phrase is opaque. It does not designate any act, mental or overt, for which there are any known criteria, and it is doubtful whether any *act* could constitute an explication of understanding a sentence (since this is an *ability*). Understanding a sentence comprises a variety of abilities, e.g. the abilities to use it correctly in appropriate circumstances, evaluate the correctness or appropriateness of what is expressed by its use in different contexts, respond appropriately to its use by others, paraphrase it, and explain it in different ways if misunderstandings arise. Many theorists would claim that understanding a sentence is a matter of knowing its meaning and then they might compare knowing what a sentence means with knowing the answer to a multiplication problem. But this argument achieves nothing. For 'knowing the meaning of a sentence', like 'knowing the time', 'knowing the way the wind blows', 'knowing the value of Dürer prints', 'knowing the correct way to behave', designates not an act, but an ability to answer a question. Knowing the meaning of a sentence is knowing what the sentence means, just as knowing the time is knowing what time it is, and knowing the way the wind blows is knowing which way it blows, etc. And to know *such* things is *to be able to answer* the questions, here stated in *oratio obliqua*. If 'assigning a sentence its truth-conditions' is to explain what it is to know the meaning of a sentence, then it too must designate an ability, not an act. This, however, destroys the analogy with the case of multiplication, where mastery of multiplication is manifested by the *acts* of producing answers to sums. The analogy would not be restored by substituting 'knowing the correct answer' for 'producing the correct answer', for that would undermine the idea that the recursion formula for multiplication characterizes what the competent arithmetician can *do* (since knowing the correct answer is not an act, but an ability too). There is no such thing as an act of assigning truth-conditions to a sentence which stands to mastery of a language as giving an answer to a multiplication problem stands to mastery of elementary arithmetic. The analogy is altogether lame.

The endlessly variegated exercises of the mastery of a language are not characterizable by a 'theory of meaning for a natural language'. Lack of such a theory does not imply inability to characterize what it is to understand a language, nor does it suggest that we know, but cannot say, what such an understanding is, let alone that we do not even know what it is to understand a language, even though we all understand our native tongue. There is here a resemblance between 'understands' and other (by no means homogeneous) cognitive verbs like 'knows', 'believes', or 'remembers'. Remembering, like understanding, does not connote an act or activity, even though one can try to remember, as one can try to understand, succeed in remembering, as one can succeed in understanding, suddenly remember, as one can suddenly understand. The relation between 'remember' and 'can remember' is as slippery as that between 'understand' and 'can understand'. One may fail to remember, as one may fail to understand, misremember as one may misunderstand. Remembering, like understanding, is akin to an ability. For a person who can remember something or other can do numerous things which someone who has forgotten it cannot. He can give correct answers to questions, correct other people's erroneous claims, make true statements on the matter, engage in various activities such as depicting, modelling, re-enacting, or mimicking what it is that he remembers. Nevertheless, it would be wholly misguided to search for an answer to the question 'What does remembering *consist in?*' There is no act or activity, either physical and overt (e.g. behaving as if such-and-such were true) or mental and covert (e.g. having a vivacious or familiar image) which is or constitutes the remembering. So too the question 'What does understanding a language *consist in?*' is confused. To produce a theory of meaning for a natural language in answer to it is to match a nonsensical reply to a nonsensical question.

The minimalist enterprise does not succeed in establishing a theory of meaning according to which the meanings of sentences are generated out of their constituents and their structures. Rather, it begs the question of whether there is any such thing, and it ignores arguments that show the idea of such a theory to be incoherent. Like the full-blown endeavour, it founders on fundamental misunderstandings about human understanding.

CHAPTER 10

Turning Full Circle

1 Kernels of truth?

We have presented a sweeping indictment of modern theories of meaning. Under the guise of rigorous theorizing, philosophers propound as fundamental truths nonsensical answers to nonsensical questions. Theoretical linguists too incur the same harsh verdict despite their pretensions to develop an empirical science of language. Our investigations have turned up many absurdities, and further excavations have revealed deeper levels of nonsense beneath the surface strata. It may seem as if our purpose were to show that theories of meaning consisted of nonsense atop nonsense atop nonsense . . . – that they were nonsense all the way down.

Against this extreme claim many men of goodwill and sound understanding will protest. 'Surely,' they will insist, 'there must be *something* in all of this work. Confusions, inconsistencies, absurdities, unclarities and exaggerations there may be, but these do not warrant a *total* rejection of the entire content of every theory of meaning. It must be conceded that there is *some* connection between sentence-forms and speech-acts performed by utterances, *some* relation between meaning and truth, and *some* link between syntactical rules and understanding sentences. Hence truth-conditional semantics must be acknowledged to rest on unshakeable foundations, even if the superstructure is unstable. Moreover, directing philosophical attention to questions about language is not *altogether* misguided. For it must be granted that this has yielded much illumination: e.g. it has clarified the nature of valid inference and of logical laws, and it has facilitated the clarification of many psychological concepts. Though the products of the investigation of language may fall short of what enthusiasts claim, they are far from negligible. Would it not be absurd to contend that modern theories of meaning add not one jot or tittle to our understanding?'

This objection has great persuasive power. One has a strong inclination to accept it at once. How could so many well-intentioned and intelligent persons have accomplished nothing at all? Who can reasonably put himself in complete opposition to the wisdom of his age? Only the arrogant (or the insane) would fail to accept a truce on these minimal terms.

But perhaps this inclination to make peace should be resisted for the moment while the strength of the objection is more carefully weighed. The argument must be that modern *theories of meaning* have some redeeming features, i.e. that something can be salvaged *from them*. For were it admitted that only those statements which were antecedent to any theory-building could be defended, it would also be acknowledged that the theories themselves had achieved *nothing* of value. A counter-argument is easily developed along these lines: the platitudes cited as the foundations for truth-conditional semantics are typically misrepresented when cast in this role, and when properly understood they owe nothing to any theory of meaning.

Consider for example, the connection between sentence-forms and speech-acts. Educated speakers of English do single out a class of sentences termed 'interrogative sentences' or 'questions', and another called 'imperatives'. It is platitudinous that interrogative sentences are standardly used to ask questions and that imperatives are typically used to issue orders or to make requests. But such truisms relating syntactic forms of sentences to speech-acts are altogether independent of the thesis that every identification of a speech-act rests on an *inference* from the form of an uttered sentence to the specification of the speech-act performed. It is far from platitudinous to claim that every intelligible language must provide *means of recognizing* what use a speaker makes of an arbitrary sentence. But such psychological theses are the stuff of theories of force in philosophy and in theoretical linguistics, and these claims are wrongly taken to be the proper 'scientific explanations' of the prescientific rough-and-ready generalization that sentence-forms are standardly connected with speech-acts. What is distinctive of theories of meaning are not truisms, and the genuine truisms owe nothing at all to these theories.

Similar conclusions hold in respect of other cited platitudes. Consider, e.g., the alleged connection between meaning and truth. If meaning is a feature of sentences and truth a property of statements, and if the notion of a truth-condition is not intelligible, then any possibility of a simple connection is precluded. A claim that substituting one word for another with a different meaning will typically alter the truth-conditions of a sentence will boil down to the truism that what is asserted in uttering a sentence will typically depend on what words are uttered, hence that changing words may alter what is said (e.g. transforming a true statement into a false one). A parallel argument connects the syntactic structure of a sentence with what is said in uttering it. But these truisms are quite independent of any thesis distinctive of truth-conditional semantics.

Such counter-arguments suggest that nothing can be salvaged from modern theories of meaning. We shall strengthen this case by a synopsis of our earlier criticisms. But first, lest this conclusion be rejected out of hand, we note that the same verdict must be returned in respect of many theories that have exercised the ingenuity and excited the passions of philosophers. For centuries debate raged about universals, as realists and nominalists touted their rival panaceas. Other generations of philosophers warred over the reality of relations and the universal applicability of subject/ predicate decomposition of judgments. Yet others laboured to attack or defend the power of pure reason alone to attain knowledge. And so on. How much can philosophers now salvage from these great controversies? It is striking that most of the arguments no longer make sense, at least as they were then formulated. Important presuppositions are now thought to be incoherent or indefensible, and many crucial concepts are held to be confused. The debates lapse, and great philosophical theories are put away on high shelves and left to gather dust. Truth-conditional semantics would enjoy the solace of having the most distinguished of companions if it were overtaken by a similar fate. No other dead philosophical theory can boast of substantially greater achievements.

2 Discredited methodology

One main ground for a wholesale condemnation of modern theories of meaning, whether in philosophy or in linguistics, is a pair of fundamental misconceptions about methodology. Both have been spelt out in the course of earlier criticisms. But their cardinal importance merits their inclusion in the recapitulation of our reasoning.

The first of these misconceptions concerns the *problems* addressed by modern theories of meaning. We have argued that the basic problems are all bogus. Theorists seek answers to a range of distinctive questions: How does one recognize the speech-act performed by a given utterance? How are explanations of word-meanings to be extended to non-declarative sentences? How is identity and difference of meaning determined? How is the meaning of a molecular sentence generated out of the meanings of its parts? How does one understand sentences never before encountered?

And so on. Each of these questions (at least as interpreted by theorists) makes no sense. Some of them arise out of conceptual confusions (e.g. about recognition and understanding). Others of them grow out of the basic presuppositions of truth-conditional semantics (e.g. that explanations of words are tailored for occurrences in declarative sentences). In the first case, the 'problems' would completely disappear once the misunderstood concepts were clarified. In the second, far from the 'theory' providing the answer to an independent problem worthy of investigation, the 'problem' is parasitic on the 'solution'; hence, were the 'theory' to be put aside, nothing would remain to be explained. Truth-conditional semantics suffers from a dire disease: it is at a loss to find any genuine problems. The theorist is equipped with some exciting machinery (e.g. the predicate calculus, or a theory of truth for a formalized language); he considers it to deserve wider application (because of the intrinsic beauty of its design); but he lacks any raw material which might be fed into it to some purpose. Casting around, he is apt to latch on to some range of pseudo-problems or else to retreat to some hopelessly vague question (e.g. 'How does language work?'). Even if the consequent 'theories' made sense, they would explain nothing whatever. Would it not be perverse to ascribe intellectual value to statements which cannot be displayed as answers to any intelligible questions?

The second misconception concerns the nature of the *explanations* offered by modern theories of meaning. We have argued that such theories embody radical confusions about the concept of an explanation. They model their explanations on the hypothetico-deductive theories of advanced physics, proclaiming the virtues of bold postulation of theoretical entities and of unification of hypotheses under covering generalizations. But this concept of explanation is inapplicable to the clarification of *normative* practices; there a different concept of explanation is applied – one in which a rule invoked to explain an agent's (or a group's) actions must itself figure explicitly in the intentions of the agent and in his *normative behaviour* (e.g. teaching others, correcting himself or others, and justifying actions). Since speaking a language is itself a normative practice (as many theorists insist), explanations of meanings must take the form of rules which are acknowledged constituents in the practice; such explanations must have normative functions (as cited standards of correctness), and they must be rules actually *followed* by speakers of the language. Consequently, any 'explanations of meaning' which involve postulating theoretical entities or discovering radically new generalizations must be excluded *a priori*. There is no such thing as a mere hypothesis which constitutes a genuine explanation of the meaning of an expression. Rules, unlike the forces that figure in explanations in physics, cannot 'act at a distance'. In truth-conditional semantics, two distinct concepts of explanation are crossed, and the offspring are 'explanations of the meanings' of particular words which are not *explanations* of *meaning* at all. Is there any greater merit to be found in statements delineating the physics of the rules implicated in speaking a language than in statements describing the normative practices of Newtonian point-masses?

This pair of methodological misconceptions deprives truth-conditional semantics of any interest. The principles of such a 'theory' serve no serious purpose. They have no place in promoting an understanding of the concepts of meaning, understanding, explaining meaning, language-mastery, symbolism, etc., and they contribute nothing to the clarification of any of the multitude of concepts grasped by competent speakers of natural languages. The point is not that there is no scope for deepened understanding of concepts employed in describing languages and intelligent speech; nor is it that there is no room for various degrees of misunderstanding or lack of understanding of expressions in circulation among competent speakers. Clarification of concepts is always possible and sometimes necessary. But a misguided methodological orientation guarantees that the meanings of expressions, which are aspects of a normative practice of using symbols, hang out of reach of any explanation generated out of a theory of meaning. In the quest for understanding, the cultivation of truth-conditional semantics is a pointless and time-consuming detour.

3   A mythology of symbolism

The second main ground for a wholesale condemnation of modern theories of meaning is a host of interlocking and proliferating conceptual confusions. Many have been exposed already. We have argued that rules are conflated with regularities, that understanding is misconceived as a mental process, that explanations of meaning are mistaken for applications of expressions, etc. We have revealed that such notions as sentence, mood, sentence-structure, truth, synonymy, context-dependence, and nonsense are grossly distorted. And we have indicated that such semi-technical expressions as 'force', 'truth-condition', 'deep structure', and 'tacit knowledge' are incoherent – the surface manifestations of vain attempts to compensate for underlying confusions. Misconceptions exhibit exponential growth like virulent bacteria. Each one produces many more until the sound tissue of internal relations among concepts gives way under the onslaught. According to our diagnosis, truth-conditional semantics is a vast network of interrelated misconceptions. If these were unravelled one by one, the biological niche occupied by this 'theory' would cease to exist.

It would be tedious and pointless to rehearse, or even to recapitulate, the web of earlier arguments demonstrating the conceptual confusions integral to truth-conditional semantics. But we might profitably indicate a number of important misconceptions not previously highlighted. Further attention to these might be a prophylactic against contamination by ones already discussed.

Theories of meaning take rise from the preconception that a human language is a *system*. This faith is deeply entrenched. So much so that theorists treat it as a brute fact that languages are systems. Nobody seems shocked by the suggestion that 'a language is definable in terms of a set of rules . . . which combine with each other to form a system – a grammar – which gives us an explicit and exhaustive description of every sentence which goes to make up a language.'[1] Nobody finds it ridiculous to elaborate 'a theory of meaning which represents mastery of a language as the knowledge . . . of deductively connected propositions'.[2] The path to these ideas is made smooth by the initial conviction that a language is a system. But the transition is none the less extraordinary. How is the term 'system' to be understood? What justifies its application to a natural language? And, more importantly, what are the implications of characterizing English as a system? We speak of systems of musical notation, systems of weights and measures, systems of transport, systems of criminal law, judicial systems, systems of education, systems of political checks and balances, electoral systems, etc. But some systems are, as it were, more systematic than others. Who would not scoff at the proposal to exhibit the network of trunk roads in Britain as the output of a calculus imposing a minimizing constraint on satisfaction of needs to travel between different points? One is predisposed to view the road system differently, as the more or less haphazard product of a host of piecemeal improvements (and natural

[1] N. Smith and D. Wilson, *Modern Linguistics: the Results of Chomsky's Revolution* (Penguin, Harmondsworth, 1979), pp. 13f.; cf. N. Chomsky, *Syntactic Structures* (Mouton, The Hague, 1957), p. 18.

[2] M. A. E. Dummett, 'What is a Theory of Meaning?', in *Mind and Language*, ed. S. Guttenplan (Clarendon Press, Oxford, 1975), p. 112, cf. 'What is a Theory of Meaning? II', in *Truth and Meaning*, ed. G. Evans and J. McDowell, (Clarendon Press, Oxford, 1976), p. 70.

disasters!) spread over two millennia. Would it not be at least as plausible to consider the English language to be a similar system? Has it not also evolved over a long period by gradual accretion and loss of vocabulary, phrases, and grammatical constructions? It is certainly open to us to look at a natural language as a loosely integrated normative practice, a *motley* of rules on a par with the common law. Once this possibility is acknowledged, our viewing English under the guise of an axiomatic calculus must be considered a matter of choice. The crucial questions then become what purposes are served by making this decision, and what intellectual costs are incurred. And these questions would lead back to a careful scrutiny of the concept of a system. This seems an urgent task to forestall the spinning of fairy-tales about natural languages.

A second array of unclarities surrounds the applications of the term 'language'. By ignoring important distinctions and disregarding certain internal relations, theorists of meaning fall into a myriad of misconceptions. One range of confusions arises out of insouciance about the distinction between a sortal noun ('a language', 'languages') and an abstract mass-noun ('language' *simpliciter*). We speak of English, French, Russian, etc. as particular languages, and we may contrast the colour-vocabulary in our language with that of another. Each language has its own grammar, and hence its syntactic structures may differ from those of other languages. Similarly, each language has a distinctive vocabulary, and this is linked with a distinctive practice of explaining the meanings of these words. Linguists and philosophers are aware of all these platitudes, but they readily lose sight of them in the desire to achieve greater generality or profundity. Linguists slip into speaking of 'language-learning ability' and 'the depth-structure of language' rather than sticking with 'English-learning ability' or 'the depth-structure of Russian'. And philosophers investigate 'the logical structure of language' (not of English or French), 'the isomorphism between language and the world', or 'how language connects with experience'. This practice is well-entrenched, yet none the less dubious. Any question about the generality of a theorist's observations is openly begged, and a specious air of profundity is produced by verbal sleight-of-hand. Parallel questions framed with abstract mass-nouns are apt to appear silly; e.g. 'What is *the* relation between law and human action?', 'How does money connect with goods and services?', 'What is the essential structure of literature?', or 'Is music-learning ability acquired or innate?'. And equally ridiculous are the results of retreating from the mass-noun 'language': who would wish to explore the logical structure of French, the possibility of isomorphism between Algonquian and the

world, or how Hopi connects with experience? Is there any cogent reason for supposing *all* languages to have the *same* 'logical structure' or to 'connect with experience' in the *same* way? Perhaps the sole foundation for philosophy of language [sic!] and theoretical linguistics is a misuse of 'language'.

Another range of confusions concerns the boundaries of languages.[3] Theorists carry on as if what belonged to a given language were a clear datum, beyond doubt or controversy. They think of a language as consisting solely of verbal symbols, *words* both spoken and written; or they characterize a language as an infinite set of meaningful *sentences*. Both syntax and semantics study only such symbols; everything else, whether gestures, samples, non-verbal voiced sounds, social conventions, etc. is relegated to the separate science of pragmatics. Mastery of a language is held to be limited to the ability to assign the correct meaning to every sentence of the language. All of these contentions manifest a distorted conception of speaking a language, and each of them propagates further confusions. Gestures, samples, tones of voice, etc. often play crucial roles in communication, and they often qualify as symbols (as theorists acknowledge in speaking of gesture-languages). Many of them are both specific to particular languages and capable of explanations parallel to explanations of the meanings of words. Is there any cogent reason for putting them beyond the pale of particular languages apart from their manifestly failing to fit into any version of a formal calculus? What purpose is served by excluding French gestures from the investigation of the French language? The consequences of this excessive narrowing of the concept of a language are clearly disastrous. One is a ridiculous separation of the question of whether an utterance makes sense from the question whether it is intelligible; e.g. there would be no ground, on this view, for calling into question my understanding of English if I say 'Her hair is this ↑ colour' while pointing at a man and producing a tone with a tuning fork. Another consequence is a distorted notion of mastery of a language. Somebody who has perfect mastery of English must be capable of carrying on conversations, making and responding to requests, asking and answering questions, etc. But these aspects of speaking English are interwoven with a vast range of other activities, and they interlock with many kinds of skill and knowledge. Intelligent speech manifests general *savoir faire* as

---

[3] One (not further discussed here) is a distortion of the principles for individuating languages that springs from philosophers' claims that a 'metalanguage' must be a distinct language from its 'object language'.

well as familiarity with social customs or practices and specific knowledge about architecture, engineering, literature, gardening, games, etc. The ability to speak English merges into such other abilities as social skills, memory, motor control, and the capacity to articulate knowledge clearly. It is a mistake to consider that mastery of a language is an ability which is sharply circumscribed and properly described independently of other abilities. In particular, it is wrong to isolate understanding from behaviour by denying that somebody's saying something unintelligible or his reacting inappropriately to an utterance are criteria for his not correctly understanding what is said. The corollary of misdrawing the boundaries of a language is a set of confusions about the concepts of understanding and of mastery of a language.

The misconception about the boundaries of a language is but one manifestation of a confused conception of symbols. Theorists tend to think that words and sentences are intrinsically symbolic, as if these were the only genuine symbols and other things (gestures, samples, diagrams) were symbols merely by analogy. The truth, however, is that classification of something as a symbol depends on how it is used. If it is to be seen within a particular community as conveying a message or expressing something, then it is a symbol (at this time for these persons). Nothing has an inalienable status as a symbol; even words, sentences, or monograms can be used for mere decoration or to compose concrete music (e.g. a word-fugue). Conversely, nothing perceptible is excluded from functioning as a symbol; it may be incorporated as an element in a code, a signal, or a sample. Something is a symbol if it is to be seen as a symbol. Consequently, it is a mistake to accord words and sentences some privileged status in the clarification of the concepts of a symbol and of communication by symbols. Theorists make other errors as well. One is to analyse sentences into depth-structures whose elements have no realizations at all. As if there could be such a thing as a symbol which is in principle not perceptible! Both this error *and* the opposite are also widespread in the discussion of the type/token distinction. A written token-word is identified as a physical object, and hence no such single token can intelligibly be said to occur in two places at the same time.[4] It must be a symbol which cannot in principle be replicated. On the other hand, we say that the same word occurs twice on a single page of a book; hence, what occurs twice cannot be a physical object, but must be an abstract pattern or design of which two separate realizations occur on the page. This type-symbol, being an abstract object,

---

[4] Spoken tokens raise other problems, equally acute.

is veiled from the senses by its tokens. As if there were such things as symbols which cannot be reproduced and symbols which cannot be perceived! These muddles are symptomatic of deep misconceptions about symbols. They would be remedied only by a thorough-going clarification of how concepts of perceptible objects (and events) are related to the concept of a symbol.

To this catalogue of confusions about very general and basic concepts must be added a distorted conception of understanding. Theorists tend to treat understanding as a form of information-processing, and this generic activity is further likened to machine-translation. Theories of meaning present 'models' or 'representations' of understanding in the form of mechanical derivations within formal calculi. This outlook produces many absurdities. One obvious consequence is that understanding a sentence is analysed as translation from one symbolism into another (perhaps into 'the language of thought'!); but this generates a vicious infinite regress. Another consequence is to demote various criteria of understanding to the status of mere inductive evidence. In particular, how someone reacts to utterances depends on factors other than his ability to 'decode' what the speaker has said, and hence it appears to have no direct bearing on his understanding; but this conclusion misrepresents the concept of understanding in an important respect. Yet another consequence is to impoverish this concept by neglecting vital internal relations with other concepts. One of these is the relation of understanding to explanations of meaning. Another is its relation to mastery of a practice and indirectly to imagination. This can be illustrated by analogy. Somebody who has mastered chess may see his opponent's pawn-move as a threat to his distant king, whereas a neophyte could not; or somebody familiar with solid shapes and the physical possibilities of their orientation might see a diagram as a triangle which has fallen on to its side, whereas a very small child or a cat could not. In such cases, mastery of certain techniques and certain powers of imagination are crucial to the 'interpretation' of what is perceived. The same conceptual links are obviously vital to understanding human speech and writing. A modest degree of imagination is required to see the remark 'It's getting rather late' as a request to leave, and a far more complex conceptual background is needed to see this paragraph as part of a criticism of truth-conditional semantics. Construing understanding on the model of derivations within a calculus screens from theorists' view many significant aspects of the concept of understanding.

Unless these exploratory remarks about the concepts of a system, language, a language, a symbol, and understanding are utterly misguided, modern theories of meaning should not be conceded to have gone off the rails somewhere down the line. Rather, they never succeeded in putting themselves on the rails at all. Or, to change the metaphor, they rest on confusions that extend to rock-bottom. Indeed, such theories are simply the products of conceptual confusions. For various reasons, we are all prone to misinterpret certain concepts that we use without any hitches in ordinary discourse. Philosophers, being peculiarly sensitive to these influences and brazen in developing their consequences, give accounts of these concepts which are at first subtly askew and which become more and more outlandish. Then complex theories are adumbrated to compensate for nonsense. Unclarities about the concepts of words, sentences, languages, understanding symbols, explanations, etc., do not issue in the clarification of these concepts through careful exploration of how problem-causing words are explained, understood, and applied. Instead, these unclarities about concepts are misinterpreted as mysteries about phenomena and hence serve as the impetus to searching for explanatory empirical theories. Confusions about the concept of understanding are projected on to the world by considering understanding to be a queer and very complex mental process whose nature must be revealed by psychological investigations. Mysteries about depth-structures, tacit knowledge, truth-conditions, logical forms, and so forth are parallel manifestations of conceptual confusions. So too is racking one's brains over the intractable question of revealing how language works. No explanatory theory can alleviate the intellectual discomforts caused by the difficulty of making perspicious how concepts interlock. Anybody satisfied by truth-conditional semantics must be twice duped and doubly confused.

4 Forms of representation

Conceptual confusions may be diagnosed as the nutrient in which modern theories of meaning prosper. But they do not alone account for the particular directions in which these theories grow. This depends on various features of the intellectual climate of the present century. Trying to catalogue these influences would be an enormous undertaking, and there would be no agreed standards for deciding when the list was complete. We have indicated *en passant* a number of influences that seem important. Among these are the status of Euclidean geometry as the model of a perspicuously articulated *a priori* science, the growth of computer technology and the investigation of 'artificial intelligence', the rise of a behaviourist psychology based on the notion of conditioned responses to stimuli, and the evolution of new forms of mathematics. But above all we have stressed the overarching importance of two influences on theories of meaning: the 'Augustinian picture of language' and Frege's invention of the predicate calculus. These jointly inspired the creation in the 1930s of the science of logical semantics, and its leading ideas have informed subsequent elaboration of theories of meaning in both philosophy and theoretical linguistics. The shape of things even now unfolding is foreshadowed in an age-old picture of the essential role of words and sentences and in a sophisticated mathematical symbolism for representing inferences among complex generalizations. Recognizing these roots is vital for understanding theories of meaning – and their allure.

We have presented this synopsis of the development of twentieth century reflections about language in various historical sketches, and we have supported it with detailed analysis of modern ideas. This account informed our original selection of the *Tractatus* as the pivotal influence on the growth of theories of meaning. For there Wittgenstein manifestly put Frege's new logic to use in vindicating a particularly stark version of the Augustinian picture of language. The *Tractatus* recapitulates in microcosm the phylogeny of truth-conditional semantics. This point is particularly worth noting since the sins of the *Tractatus* have been visited on its intellectual offspring.

In order to explore this baleful influence, we must once more highlight certain main features of the *Tractatus*. This is best accomplished by contrast. Let us recall the philosophical foundations of Frege's invention of the predicate calculus. He first proposed his concept-script and his formalization of inference for the specific purpose of checking the cogency of proofs in mathematics; his aim was explicit and limited. He took the subject-matter of logic (i.e. what he analysed into function and argument) to be propositions, judgments, or 'judgeable-contents', not declarative sentences expressing them; he followed traditional wisdom in stressing that the grammatical forms of sentences are often misleading guides to the logical forms of judgments. He emphasized and exploited the possibilities for analysing a single judgeable-content in different ways into functions and arguments of different levels. Finally, he argued that an expression contributes to what a sentence expresses only if it stands for some object or function; hence, in particular, he held logical constants to name certain functions and number-words to name certain objects. It is noteworthy that some of these ideas underwent changes and diminished in importance in the course of Frege's career. In particular, he came to view predicates of declarative sentences as themselves names for functions ('concepts'); accordingly he adopted the idea of a relatively close correspondence of the grammatical forms of sentences with the logical forms of the propositions expressed by them, and ultimately he was seduced by a vision of an isomorphism between sentences and what they express to the detriment of his doctrine about possibilities for alternative analyses of judgments. Yet the origins of Frege's invention of the predicate calculus lay in a clearly articulated set of doctrines uncontaminated by these later intrusions.

The *Tractatus* was the culmination of a drift away from these doctrines in the direction already adumbrated in Frege's own thinking. First, logic evolved into part of a general theory of symbolism; its subject-matter was no longer thought to be abstract entities (propositions or thoughts) *as opposed to* declarative sentences, but rather it came to be viewed as the investigation of what sentences express *through* considering the features of these sentences themselves. Secondly, the flexibility of function-theoretic categories facilitated the logical analysis of aspects of expressions traditionally accorded no explicit attention; e.g. the definite article could be exhibited as a second-level function mapping a concept on to an object (Frege) or as a complex quantifier (Russell). Thirdly, logical analysis of sentences into function and argument became infused with the notion of conceptual analysis prominent in classical empiricism. 'Molecules' are step-wise broken down into simpler constituents, ultimately into 'atoms'; the conviction blossomed that every significant sentence has a unique ultimate analysis, and apparently different analyses must represent different stages on this route to the final analysis. Fourthly, Russell's theory of definite descriptions entrenched a modified conception of analysis: an 'incomplete symbol' is an expression which has no (independent) meaning but which none the less contributes in a systematic way to the significance of any sentence in which it occurs. Accordingly, it became possible to analyse an expression, not by explaining what it means (stands for), but by explaining it away in favour of other expressions which do have independent meanings. Finally, the predicate calculus ceased to be regarded as an instrument employed for particular purposes, but instead was held to embrace the logical structures of all fully analysed sentences. Logical analysis reveals every judgment *really* to be built up out of objects and concepts by means of quantifiers and propositional connectives. The *Tractatus* exemplified all of these developments in a strikingly spartan form. Every proposition was claimed to be a truth-function of elementary propositions, each of which consisted entirely of expressions standing for entities. With the exception of logical connectives, category names and numerals, every expression conformed to the Augustinian picture, and the exceptional expressions were explained in terms of their contributions to the senses of the sentences in which they may occur or else placed on the index. Analysis was held to show that sentences, thoughts, and facts were isomorphic, each with the other.

Wittgenstein later came to the realization that much of the thinking in the *Tractatus* manifested a disease of the intellect. He gave careful scrutiny to the nature and sources of the underlying philosophical illusions, and he catalogued his diagnostic insights in the *Philosophical Investigations*. These are worth pondering. The fundamental error is a fascination with or captivation by a form of representation. For a variety of reasons we have strong inclinations towards depicting matters in certain ways. It seems deeply satisfying to view words as names and to present inferences in the guise of transformations within a mathematical calculus – so satisfying that we are willing to turn a blind eye to hosts of obvious and powerful objections. Tensions persist. But they are resolved in characteristic ways. One is to offer a philosophical theory as an *ideal* to which language or thought only approximates (e.g. to follow Russell in considering the *Tractatus* to outline the structure of an 'ideal language'). The other is to present the theory as an *analysis* of what it represents, as delineating the reality masked beneath misleading appearances (e.g. to hold the *Tractatus* to lay down the hidden structure of any possible language capable of expressing truths about experience). Each of these manoeuvres is confused. The first overlooks the truism that what is ideal for one purpose may be inappropriate for another, or it presupposes the absurdity that there are purpose-independent standards for what is ideal. The second falls into a related misconception, as if there were an absolute standard of what counts as an analysis (and corresponding absolute standards of simplicity and complexity). The second also exemplifies dogmatism. For no good reason it is insisted that things *must* be thus-and-so (e.g. that every sound inference must exhibit a pattern validated by the predicate calculus, or that every meaningful expression must stand for some object or function). This unshakeable faith justifies confidence that it will one day be discovered exactly how these requirements are met, even if we now have no inkling of how this might be done. The mistake here is to 'predicate of the thing what lies in the method of representing it'.[5] The primary symptom is grotesque misuse of expressions, which can be made clear by careful comparisons between philosophers' uses of crucial expressions and the down to earth

[5] Wittgenstein, *Philosophical Investigations*, §104.

uses of these expressions in everyday discourse (e.g. 'sentence', 'object', 'fact', and 'symbol'). As philosophers, 'impressed by the possibility of a comparison, we think we are perceiving a state of affairs of the highest generality. . . . We can avoid ineptness or emptiness in our assertions only by presenting . . . an object of comparison . . . as a measuring-rod, not as a preconceived idea to which reality *must* correspond'.[6] The danger is *projecting* a form of representation on to the phenomena represented.

This diagnosis of philosophical illusion contains not only a negative view about misuses of forms of representation, but also positive suggestions about their proper use in philosophy. This is important. The correlate of Wittgenstein's criticism of the *Tractatus* is not that the predicate calculus must be jettisoned, or even that we must dismiss as worthless any suggestion that the meaning of a name is the object named or that sentences are pictures of states of affairs. Rather he indicates that the very same ideas which typically mislead philosophers have potentialities to serve as illuminating objects of comparison. We may profitably compare a name to a label attached to an object, a sentence with an architect's plan, or a stretch of scientific discourse with a complex arithmetical calculation, provided that we do not exaggerate the similarities or neglect the differences. It is crucially important to bear constantly in mind the purposes for which the comparison is made, and to be clear about the purposes thwarted as well as those served by the comparison. A well-chosen model may help to make perspicuous certain matters whose significance is not appreciated just as juxtaposing a familiar piece of music with another one may throw some of its features into high relief. Philosophical illusion often arises from the fact that a comparison is illuminating: we are prone to think that any greater understanding must be the consequence of discerning some deep pattern capable of fruitful generalization, and we rush ahead into formulating explanatory theories to satisfy this craving for generality. To counteract these tendencies to error we should remember that comparisons are not primitive hypotheses, that limitations on comparisons can be as illuminating as exact correspondences, and that confusion is the price of extending comparisons beyond their intrinsic limits. More positively, we should remind ourselves of the purpose-relativity and the limitations of comparisons by deliberately exploiting *many*, not just one, in respect of any matter requiring philosophical clarification. It may be useful to compare naming something with attaching a label to a thing, but equally useful to compare a name with a definite description or a demonstrative, and using a name

---

[6] Ibid., §§104 and 131.

with summoning somebody or transfixing him with an arrow. Similarly, it may be helpful to compare an expression of generality with a second-level mathematical operation such as differentiation, but equally important to distinguish quantifiers from function-names or to differentiate among the patterns of inferences licensed by various 'universal generalizations'. Objects of comparison are not misleading in themselves. It is misuses of comparisons that are misleading and correspondingly their judicious use which promotes philosophical understanding (a synoptic view or *Übersicht* of relations among concepts). Whereas the illusions of the *Tractatus* stemmed from projecting methods of representation on to generalizations about the phenomena represented, the insights of the *Investigations* arise from careful selection of objects of comparison with the conscious purpose of spotlighting significant resemblances and differences among concepts.

Wittgenstein castigated the *Tractatus*, and many of his trenchant criticisms are now widely accepted. Most philosophers now ridicule the notion of a logically proper name, and they also repudiate the contention that every significant sentence must be a truth-function of any of its constituent sentences. Such reactions have meant that rejection of the *Tractatus* has taken place independently of any exploration of the underlying general reasons for its defects, as if all of its errors were matters of comparative detail. This in turn has facilitated the growth of more sophisticated but closely allied doctrines within truth-conditional semantics. The *Tractatus* has been reborn, allegedly purged of its initial crudities by progress in formal logic and exploiting the resources of appropriate metalanguages. The acme of formal logic is the working out of a precise semantic conception of validity for inferences in the predicate calculus. This turns on generalizations over all admissible interpretations of well-formed formulae, and that allows logicians to cut themselves free from any absolute notion of logical form and hence from the metaphysical idea that logical truths mirror a language-independent structure of the world. Logic is no longer fettered to any doctrine of analysis. What has taken the place of the thesis that every significant sentence is a truth-function of elementary sentences is a much more liberal and characteristically second-order claim. One popular version is a truth-theory for a language: a statement of the truth-conditions for any significant sentence must be derivable within an axiomatic metatheory by appeal to rules of designation for its constituents together with rules specifying how the designations of well-formed combinations of constituents depend solely on the designations of their parts. Another popular version builds in a similar metalinguistic theory about the intensions of sentences. Both officially renounce the pretension that a proper semantic analysis of language be unique because it is an article of modern faith that any number of coherent theories are compatible with any body of 'data'. Semantics and logic are linked in the doctrine that a correct theory of meaning for a language must exhibit logical truths as sentences true under all admissible interpretations of their constituent terms. Whereas the *Tractatus* considered analysis to be translation into a perspicuous notation, modern theories of meaning rest on metalinguistic generalizations about all assignments of interpretations to expressions which are compatible with judgments about the truth-values of speakers' statements.

This modern wisdom draws on the same sources of inspiration as the *Tractatus*. It is still obsessed with the predicate calculus; the 'workings of language' are held to be perspicuous in the case of the formal semantics for the predicate calculus, and the conscious aim of theorists is to extend this successful model to account for the meanings of all expressions in a language. Attachment to the Augustinian picture is equally clear, since the notion of an interpretation in formal semantics is explained as a correlation of expressions with suitable entities (which thereby correlate sentences with sets of truth-conditions). Although differently expressed, the continuity of inspiration is evident. So too is the underlying defect of the *Tractatus*: modern theories project the method of representation on to what is represented. This generates characteristic dogmatism: every sentence *must* decompose into a separate force-indicator and sentence-radical, and the truth-conditions of any sentence *must* be derivable from its constituents and its structure. Some fresh arguments (especially deductions from the possibility of understanding new sentences) and some novel conceptions (especially about data-processing and computer technology) feed this dogmatism. Furthermore, some fresh expressions are given to the dogmatism itself (especially patter about deep structures of sentences and the projection of function-theoretic categories on to the syntax of sentences). But the continuity with the dogmas of the *Tractatus* stands out.

Modern dogmatism is damned for the same general reasons as its predecessor. Its roots are conceptual confusions and infatuation with preconceived pictures. The mystery of the 'creativity of language' expresses the fundamental misapprehension of understanding as a mental process whose mechanism must be brought to light. The insistence that speaking a language is closely analogous to operating a mathematical calculus manifests a misplaced faith in hidden system. Apart from philosophical clarification aimed at bringing light into these dark corners of the modern *Zeitgeist*, the most effective therapy for modern dogmatism is to press each theory for answers to the questions 'What are the *purposes* it serves?' and 'What are the *distortions* it introduces?' These are the basic issues. Attaining a proper grasp of problematic concepts is more akin to coming to a full understanding of a genre of music than to apprehending the laws of motion of the planets. The value of an explanation cannot here be measured independently of the purpose that it is meant to fulfil, and there are excellent reasons for thinking that none will be absolutely the best (i.e. against the background of any conceivable purpose). Few are useless, but none is omnicompetent. Consequently, it would likewise be wrong to react to modern theories of meaning by repudiating *all* of their tenets or all of their apparatus as utterly misguided. The predicate calculus has a legitimate role in clarifying the forms of certain inferences, especially for mathematicians who find its function-theoretic concepts perspicuous; but it does not delineate the essence of a language. Similarly, model theory has a respectable, if limited, role as a *mathematical* investigation of formalized reasoning; but it has no intrinsic philosophical cachet, and it cannot be presumed to illuminate anything whatever about natural languages. It is a platitude that what 'Socrates is wise' expresses is true if the person designated by 'Socrates' has the property of being wise; but it is mistaken to take the predicate 'is wise' to designate a property or the sentence 'Socrates is wise' to be true, *a fortiori* to erect a theory of truth on these foundations. And so forth. The proper reaction to philosophical criticism here is to dethrone the dogmatism of modern theories of language, but not to line up all of its deliverances before a firing squad. To the extent that philosophical illusion arises from projecting forms of representation on to what is represented, the error is attractive precisely because particular comparisons may be genuinely illuminating up to a certain point and for certain purposes. The antidote is not an absurd denial that these comparisons have any utility at all, but rather a recognition of points of dissimilarity and of purposes not served. The cure is no less subtle than the disease.

5 Philosophy of language

Philosophers bent on constructing theories of meaning for natural languages have arrogated to themselves the phrase 'philosophy of language' to label the product of their activities. This is now considered to be one of the main subdivisions of philosophy, on a par with ethics, metaphysics, formal logic, epistemology, and philosophy of science. Some have made more grandiose claims on its behalf:

Because philosophy has, as its first if not its only task, the analysis of meaning, and because, the deeper such analysis goes, the more it is dependent upon a correct general account of meaning, a model for what the understanding of an expression consists in, the theory of meaning, which is the search for such a model, is the foundation of all philosophy . . .[7]

It is even maintained that this shared faith is the hallmark of modern analytic philosophy: 'the philosophy of language is seen both as that part of the subject which underlies all the rest and as that which it is currently most fruitful to investigate'.[8] Certainly the effort devoted to arguing about the general form of a theory of meaning has waxed in this last decade, while the piecemeal clarification of particular problematic concepts has waned. Philosophy of language has assumed the status of the Young Pretender.

The thesis of the centrality of philosophy of language is difficult to support even in theory, and the faith has not been cemented in place by any noteworthy works. If the critical arguments of this book are not totally awry, this failure is hardly suprising. Philosophy of language, as commonly conceived, has no coherent subject-matter, and its artefacts are uniformly nonsensical. There is no such thing as a theory of meaning for a language, and hence there is no such thing as a significant contribution to such an enterprise. Any claim by philosophy of language to the throne in philosophy is specious.

The title, however, might be transferred to other undertakings which have real content and point. One of these would be the subject earlier called 'philosophical logic'. This attempts to clarify the role of certain kinds of expressions against a background of conceptual problems or perplexities. In the past philosophers have tried to elucidate how various kinds of referring expressions function (e.g. definite descriptions, demonstratives, proper names introduced by ostensive definition, or proper names of historical figures) or what kinds of speech-acts are performed by making moral pronouncements (e.g. evaluation, commendation, prescription, or prohibition). Such enquiries are legitimate responses to particular kinds of puzzlement (e.g. the uses of proper names in works of fiction or the occurrence of definite descriptions in counterfactual conditions). Explanations of how expressions are correctly used may clear away diffi-

[7] M. A. E. Dummett, *Frege: Philosophy of Language* (Duckworth, London, 1973), p. 669.
[8] M. A. E. Dummett, 'Can Analytical Philosophy be Systematic, and Ought it to Be?', in *Truth and Other Enigmas* (Duckworth, London, 1978), p. 441.

culties, especially those that beset philosophers in search of generalizations about the employment of expressions of certain forms. Provided that the problems are genuine, there is scope for philosophical investigations to resolve or dissolve them. In so far as a large part of the philosophical technique of so doing consists of detailed descriptions of the use of various grammatical categories of expressions, this activity might be termed 'philosophy of language'. It would be one part among others of a general striving after philosophical clarity.

Another study that might inherit the title 'philosophy of language' is the clarification of concepts used in describing and analysing languages. This would embrace the investigation of the uses of such terms as 'language', 'a language', 'system', 'rule', 'sentence', 'symbol', 'meaning', 'explanation (of meaning)', 'true', and 'context'. It would also encompass such semi-technical or technical jargon as 'truth-condition', 'sentence-radical', 'context-dependent', and 'verification-transcendence'. For the present, the primary purpose of this study would no doubt be a general criticism of the misuse and misexplanation of these expressions by theorists of meaning. For, as we have argued at length, these concepts are severally distorted and the internal relations among them neglected or misrepresented. Natural languages are mistakenly treated as formal calculi, and conducting intelligent conversation likened to carrying out formal derivations. The notion of a symbol is perverted, and the relation of meaning with explanations of meaning is slighted. These misconceptions proliferate and nurture each other. Nothing less than a fresh start is needed, a total reorientation of thinking about languages based on a sound understanding of basic concepts. A critical 'philosophy of language' will emphasize that whether something is a symbol depends on how it is used, that the meaning of an expression is what is explained in explaining correctly how it is to be used, that understanding is an ability not a mental process, that the explanation of a word has the status of a rule or standard of correctness, and that whether a sentence formulates a rule depends on how it is employed. The widespread acceptance of truth-conditional semantics shows how far most theorists of meaning are removed from any grasp of these fundamental aspects of the concepts that they invoke and misuse. And it is important to correct these misunderstandings because their pernicious influence is disseminated through much of contemporary thought, from molecular biology to literary criticism. This book is intended to be a start on this task of philosophical clarification.

This critical 'philosophy of language' might be considered a prelude to fresh attempts to construct theories of meaning for natural languages. If contemporary work is indeed flawed by conceptual confusions, then might the clarification of basic concepts not permit rebuilding of the envisaged superstructures on solid foundations? If our arguments carry any weight, this hope is vain. Theories of meaning are not merely confused, but also lack any purpose. The clarification of concepts will not conjure up the need for a theory where there was previously no scope for theorizing. On the contrary, it will annihilate the *impression* that explanations are needed by removing the confusions which are misconstrued as mysteries about phenomena. Theories of meaning will appear ridiculous because they will be seen to address such bogus problems as *how* somebody *recognizes* what speech-act is performed by an utterance, *how* new sentences are *understood*, or what *determines* the grammaticality of an utterance. Truth-conditional semantics will suffer death by a thousand clarifications. It will not be ranged with Newtonian mechanics and Mendelian genetics in the museum of the history of science, but it will be relegated to the basement to moulder away in the company of phrenology and the theory of the humours, the New Way of Ideas and the Theory of Forms. Philosophical criticism should seal its fate. A viable theory of meaning for a natural language cannot rise like a Phoenix if truth-conditional semantics is properly reduced to ashes.

Index